Transpersonal
Research
Methods
for the
Social Sciences

Transpersonal Research Methods for the Social Sciences

Honoring Human Experience

William Braud
Rosemarie Anderson

SAGE Publications
International Educational and Professional Publisher
Thousand Oaks   London   New Delhi

For information:

SAGE Publications, Inc.
2455 Teller Road
Thousand Oaks, California 91320
E-mail: order@sagepub.com

SAGE Publications Ltd.
6 Bonhill Street
London EC2A 4PU
United Kingdom

SAGE Publications India Pvt. Ltd.
M-32 Market
Greater Kailash I
New Delhi 110048 India

Printed in the United States of America

Library of Congress Cataloging-in-Publication Data

Main entry under title:

Transpersonal research methods for the social sciences: Honoring
    human experience / William Braud and Rosemarie Anderson.
        p.   cm.
    Includes bibliographical references and index.
    ISBN 0-7619-1012-3 (hardcover : alk. paper)
    ISBN 0-7619-1013-1 (pbk. : alk. paper)
    1. Psychology—Research—Methodology. 2. Transpersonal
psychology—Research—Methodology. 3. Social
sciences—Research—Methodology. I. Anderson, Rosemarie. II. Braud,
William.
    BF76.5 .T73 1998
    150.19'8—ddc21   98-8870

98   99   00   01   02   03   04   8   7   6   5   4   3   2   1

Acquiring Editor:	Peter Labella
Production Editor:	Astrid Virding
Editorial Assistant:	Karen Wiley
Typesetter/Designer:	Danielle Dillahunt
Indexer:	Jan Fisher, Ph.D.
Cover Designer:	Candice Harman
Print Buyer:	Anna Chin

CONTENTS

*We dedicate this book
to our teachers and students.*

PREFACE

This book introduces transpersonal research methods to the study of the transformative or spiritual dimension of human experience. Although these new approaches can also be applied to more traditional topics of inquiry, the methods are intended primarily for studying extraordinary or ultimate human experiences, such as unitive consciousness, peak experiences, transcendence, bliss, wonder, group synergy, and extrasensory and interspecies awareness. The list is endless because ordinary experiences can have numinous dimensions as well. Researchers in transpersonal psychology (or, more generally, transpersonal studies as applied to many traditional fields); humanistic psychology; existential psychology; and applied areas such as consciousness studies, learning communities in corporate business, transpersonal medicine, and psychospiritual immunology will find these transpersonal approaches directly applicable to studying the more extraordinary dimensions of human experience. More traditional researchers may find these methods complementary to other research methods because transpersonal approaches expand the usual dimensions for studying human experience by directly employing alternative modes of awareness and intuition in the conduct of research.

This book is intended to be used along with more traditional texts in advanced undergraduate and graduate research courses in psychology and related disciplines. Most of the methods presented in this book are qualitative in nature because in-depth approaches tend to better suit the idiographic and personal nature of transpersonal experiences. Quantitative approaches are presented only briefly and usually in the context of blending them with transpersonal approaches. An overview of qualitative and quantitative research methods presently available in psychology is given in the appendixes.

This book is about ways of knowing and methods of inquiry that are especially appropriate to transpersonal topics and to human experience generally. Because of the nature of the approaches and the subject matter, it is necessary to address certain aspects of epistemology, as well as certain assumptions and practices of science itself. This book is *not* a history of transpersonal psychology, although significant aspects of the field's history and development are presented in the introduction. Nor does this book attempt to present the many findings, concepts, and theories that have arisen from transpersonal studies and scholarship—with the important exceptions of specific content needed to contextualize and elucidate particular research assumptions, approaches, and methods.

Readers are cautioned that one of the unique properties of applying transpersonal approaches to research is the potential transformation of the researcher. Because these methods ask the researcher to use intuition and apply alternative states of consciousness such as direct knowing, dream and imagery work, and meditation to the research process, pursuing these transpersonal methods potentially becomes a self-realizing act. In following these techniques and procedures, the encounter with the transcendent dimension of the topic of inquiry not only can inform but also can change the researcher, sometimes radically. Transpersonal researchers learn about the topic *and* about themselves, and, therefore, tend to engage research with a spirit of adventure, anticipation, and some trepidation. We, the authors of this book, know—we have been there. Self-realization is, after all, a risky business. Ultimately, it is the source for initiating and realizing authentic change in our world.

WILLIAM BRAUD'S STORY

At a professional conference, not long ago, the participants were asked to say a few words about themselves. When it came my turn to introduce myself, I heard myself saying that I seemed to be on four simultaneous trajectories in my life and work: from matter to spirit, from experimental to experiential, from quantitative to qualitative, and from seeking to service. This spontaneous utterance surprised me because I had not previously dwelled on such possible patterns in my work or in my path through life. Later, in considering those four dimensions more carefully, I found that they did, indeed, summarize much of where I had been and where I seemed to be heading, both professionally and personally.

In my variegated adventures as a researcher, I was fortunate to have been exposed to and to have become proficient in an extensive set of research approaches and methods. I absorbed natural science methods and viewpoints in my undergraduate physics studies. In doctoral work in experimental psychology at the University of Iowa, I was trained in the behavioral and hypothetico-deductive approaches of the Hull/Spence learning theory tradition and studied philosophy of science, epistemology, and ontology with Gustav Bergmann, a member of the Vienna circle of logical positivists. Later, through university and medical center appointments in Houston, Texas, I supplemented behavioral approaches to learning, memory, and motivation with clinical, psychophysiological, and pharmacological methods. At a private research laboratory (Mind Science Foundation, San Antonio, Texas), I worked on new research methods for exploring topics in biofeedback, physiological self-regulation, altered states of consciousness, and parapsychology; with collaborators at several health science centers, I conducted studies in the then new field of psychoneuroimmunology.

The number and diversity of the research approaches encountered at different points in my career have been serving me well—providing me with a broad range of powerful methods for exploring the natural world and the worlds of human beings. As I tried on and immersed myself in each methodology, and in its accompanying worldview or mind-set, each approach seemed to be the most significant and most efficient key to disciplined inquiry into Nature's secrets. Gradually, however, the limitations of each method became evident, and it was time to explore other, more appropriate tools. An aspect of my temperament—akin, perhaps, to some sublimated hoarding instinct—did not allow me to discard any of the previous tools. After all, these were excellent tools, well adapted to their respective purposes, and it seemed a shame to abandon any of them. So my collection of methods—my toolbox—grew progressively larger, its contents remaining handy, awaiting future opportunities to be of use.

Still another aspect of my temperament—which I whimsically call my Cajun-Taoist nature—kept me from seeing any of these diverse methods as incompatible or antithetical to one another. I saw them as complements: one providing what another lacked, each an essential yet incomplete part of the whole. For me, the methods were interlocked in an embrace, not of conflict or battle but of dance—swirling together to the tune of "both-and" rather than "either-or."

My move, in 1992, to the Institute of Transpersonal Psychology in Palo Alto, California, coincided with a decreasing interest in the certainties that the laboratory could provide about general principles and mechanisms that might underlie psychological processes and experiences and a growing interest in the experiences themselves, as they occur in everyday life—the various ways people understand and appreciate their experiences and attribute meanings and interpretations to them and the strong impacts that exceptional experiences can have on health, well-being, and development. I came to appreciate, increasingly, the value of an idiographic approach of focusing on particular instances—particular stories of unique individuals— and what in-depth studies of individual cases might reveal.

With this shift away from a nomothetic, experimental, quantitative emphasis and toward a more idiographic, experiential, qualitative empha- sis, a shift in my stance toward research also occurred. The earlier stance was characterized by a quest for a high level of certainty about my findings, concerns with fine-grained nets of causality (what "really" caused what?), and much concern about not fooling myself. This was accompanied by an attitude of excessive caution, skepticism, doubt, and mistrust—especially of people's "merely anecdotal" subjective reports. The newer stance in- volved less concern with certainty about fine-grained mechanisms or paths of causality but greater feelings of trust—trust that things were as they appeared to be and trust that people could be aware and discerning enough to be able to give valid accounts of their experiences and their impacts. I was more trusting of the abilities of research participants to discriminate more important from less important factors—to filter wheat from chaff— and to remain free from self-deceptions in presenting their accounts of what was going on in their lives and in the world. I was more trusting of my own abilities to make responsible judgments about my findings without excessive reliance on the automatic decisional tools that sophisticated designs and statistics had previously provided. I was more trusting in the abilities of my audience—the future readers of my research reports—to weigh evidence on their own subjective scales, exercise sound judgment, and reach valid conclusions about presented findings.

Contributing to these gradual changes were my own research findings, my familiarity with an increasingly greater range of the findings and writings of others, my self-expanding discussions with colleagues and students, and, perhaps most important, my own personal experiences— particularly those experiences that Rhea White calls *exceptional human experiences* (see Chapter 7) and experiences with what Paul Tillich (1963) called *matters of ultimate concern.*

ROSEMARIE ANDERSON'S STORY

Balancing my spiritual practice and workaday life as research psychologist has been a heartfelt, yet tenuous, endeavor for nearly 30 years. There has never been a time when I did not pray, meditate, and muse about the ethics of how to live well and graciously, despite my small successes in doing any of them well. I kept telling myself that it was sufficient to do ethical psychological research, promote the public good, and pray when I could. Yet eventually, it wasn't enough just to juggle, as if psychology and spirituality were free-floating pins but never genuinely relating. Now within the field of transpersonal psychology, my livelihood is less secure, there is an uneasy excitement every time I walk into class because who knows what will happen, and the field seems to conceptually free-float even more than I do on a given day—but I'm no longer juggling the impossible. I feel like a laborer in a vineyard of possibilities. And there is much to do. Long before academic psychology and spirituality can comprehend the more expansive aspects of human nature, key reconceptualizations in theories and praxis must occur, beginning with how humans know what we know—epistemology.

Although nearly 30 years have passed since my doctoral training at the University of Nebraska-Lincoln, epistemology still vies for priority among my professional endeavors. I recall my undergraduate and graduate classes as extraordinary adventures to aver and appreciate the complexity and variety of human experience, even if trained to shape rats to bar press through successive approximation and master mathematical equations determinate of drive reduction. Even now as a transpersonal psychologist—with a whimsical only-in-California style—I warmly remember and value my training and many ensuing years of experimental work. As a researcher and theorist, scarcely anything has served me as well as those rarely definitive discussions with colleagues about design and analyses, those midnight conversations with myself striving to operationalize variables, those exhilarating hours pondering printouts of multivariate analyses, and those crystalline moments when bewildering data formed inchoate yet perceptible patterns. Practice hones the intellect, the discerning mind. In these moments, I began to learn to observe and record carefully, to watch patiently for emerging patterns, and to acknowledge the range and variety of human experience, as it richly presents itself.

At the same time, I also think of myself as a recovering behaviorist. Along with the rigor and praxis, there are assumptions, procedures, and protocols that no longer serve my scientific activities. Internal states of spiritual experiences rarely lend themselves to the Procrustean bed of external observation. In my research, the rigor of explicit behavioral observation per se has given way to precise in-depth, reflective, qualitative analyses of experience. The rigor of quantifying has become the articulation of comprehensive portrayals of particularity and attributes of human experience.

Along the way, a wide variety of research methods including feminist approaches to research, textual hermeneutics, and narrative analysis, as well as personal experiences with meditation, spiritual practice, and the creative arts, have provided keys to unlocking the complexities of conceptualizing research and analyzing data. Feminist methods broke down the conventional barriers to seeing research as relational, contextual, and political. During theological training at the Graduate Theological Union (Berkeley, California), scriptural exegesis, textual hermeneutics, and narrative analysis allowed me to see sacred text, interview, and symbols in new and illuminating ways. A special acknowledgment goes to the altered state of consciousness of traveling and living in Third World countries and the University of Maryland's Asian Division, which supported my teaching career, while I otherwise roamed around. Daily meditation and practice of writing have shattered, mirrored, encouraged, and sustained intuition and reflection through a lot of dry years. Gradually, the intuitive aspects of my life clamored "out of the closet." Intuitive skills now reside at the heart of my research praxis, informing every phase of the inquiry. Any artificial separating of the creative arts from research seemed analogous to sundering the actions of one hand—or one countenance of brain activity—from the other.

OUR JOINT STORY

With the shift toward idiographic, qualitative approaches, toward an interest in more significant topics that could not be adequately addressed by the earlier methods, and toward a stance of greater researcher involvement in all phases of the research endeavor, there came—for both of us—a melting away of the boundaries between three activities that typically are kept separate and distinct: research, clinical (and other) applications, and our personal psychospiritual development. All these were now happening simultaneously, mutually informing one another, playing off of and reinforcing one another. Our own "lived world" experiences—including a variety of transpersonal experiences—were more fully informing and being incorporated into our research projects. Research suddenly became much broader, more relevant, and more exciting.

We both joined the core faculty of the Institute of Transpersonal Psychology in 1992. Although we conducted our own research and directed students' research with an open mind for innovative approaches, it soon became apparent that studying transpersonal phenomena required greater variety and breadth in sources of data, protocols for analysis, and expression. In particular, by 1993 to 1994, we were encouraging students to use alternative modes of listening as they analyzed their data, to rely on their own internal resources to complement more traditional analyses.

In 1994 and 1995, a set of unexpected circumstances led to one of the most fruitful collaborative endeavors of our careers. We began teaching Quantitative and Qualitative Research Methods together. The course became a laboratory to expand and extend traditional research methods *transpersonally*. One afternoon, wanting "to set a field of intention," we practiced what we were asking our students to do. We timed ourselves. In 8 minutes, we had articulated a comprehensive list of ways in which a conventional research method could be extended or expanded to make it much more appropriate for addressing transpersonal issues. These were epistemological extensions—ways in which we might push forward the envelope of research by collecting, interpreting, and reporting data in new ways. Knowing we were not asking our students to do what we had not done, we encouraged them to consider and explore transpersonal extensions of the various research methods treated in the course. How might we interview in new ways? How might we let our collected data enlighten us in ways other than in the familiar rational, linear manner? How might we present our findings in ways that could more effectively convey their meanings and power to the reader? Excitement grew as we witnessed how quickly and creatively new research possibilities arose in the classroom. Soon, these extensions seemed to burst out of the classrooms. They were appearing everywhere. They were in the air. The "field" was active and growing. New suggestions built on earlier ones, and a marvelous synergy developed.

Increasingly, students began building transpersonal methodological extensions into their dissertation work. We continued to encourage this in our classes, in dissertation proposal committee meetings, and in individual consultations with students who were planning their dissertations. Student-initiated extensions grew in parallel with the methodological extensions that we ourselves continued to develop both individually and together. Other colleagues in the field of transpersonal studies were proposing similar extensions. We have gathered together, in this book, some of the fruits of these "envelope-extending" exercises.

ACKNOWLEDGMENTS

We acknowledge and thank our many teachers and students. We're not going to list teachers' names from years past because we don't want to suggest that any of them is responsible for how we are presently thinking. We just want them to know that we are grateful. Through the years, we have taught and conducted research at the University of Iowa, the University of Houston, the Mind Science Foundation (San Antonio, Texas), University of Nebraska-Lincoln, Wake Forest University, University of Maryland's Asian and European Divisions, and the Institute of Transpersonal Psychology.

Special thanks and acknowledgments are extended to our generous students at the Institute of Transpersonal Psychology who have asked creepy and salvific questions, thwarted ill-founded directions, checked our obtuse grandiosity, encouraged our thinking, honed our inchoate formulations, and trusted us sufficiently to try out these new ideas in their own research. We've had a wonderful time. Thank you.

A Note From William Braud. I especially wish to acknowledge the invaluable support and contributions of my wife, Winona Schroeter, throughout all stages of my involvement with this book. Her joyful encouragement and her superb editing and copyediting skills immeasurably contributed to the final realization of those sections of the book for which I had chief responsibility.

PERMISSIONS

Grateful acknowledgment is made to the following for permission to reprint material:

Drossoula Elliott, of the Athenian Society for Science and Human Development, for use of the table entitled "Report of Group 4," from the *Report on an International Symposium on Science, Technology, and the Environment* (January 3-7, 1990), by the Global Co-Operation for a Better World, Athens, Greece. Copyright © 1990 by Global Co-Operation for a Better World. Reprinted by permission.

Institute of Noetic Sciences, for use of Table 1, from Willis W. Harman, *A Re-Examination of the Metaphysical Foundations of Modern Science* (Noetics Report CT-1), Institute of Noetic Sciences, Sausalito, CA. Copyright © 1991 by Institute of Noetic Sciences. Reprinted by permission.

Brian Josephson, for use of material from Brian Josephson and Beverly Rubik, "The Challenge of Consciousness Research," 1992, *Frontier Perspectives,* 3(1), 15-19. Copyright © 1992 by Brian Josephson and Beverly Rubik. Reprinted by permission.

David Lorimer, for use of the table entitled "Complementary Approaches to Science" (tabular format), from David Lorimer, *Towards a New Science: A Critical Appraisal of Scientific Knowledge,* paper presented at the 17th Annual Conference of the Unity of the Sciences, Los Angeles, CA, November 24-27, 1988. Copyright © 1988 by David Lorimer. Reprinted by permission.

Random House, Inc., for material from *The Selected Poetry of Rainer Maria Rilke* by Rainer Maria Rilke, translated by Stephen Mitchell. Copyright © 1982 by Stephen Mitchell. Reprinted by permission of Random House, Inc.

Maja Apolonia Rodé, for use of original artwork appearing on the cover ("Integration," "The Seed," "Inspiration"). Copyright © 1994 by Maja Apolonia Rodé. Used with permission.

Beverly Rubik, for use of material from Brian Josephson and Beverly Rubik, "The Challenge of Consciousness Research," 1992, *Frontier Perspectives, 3(1),* 15-19. Copyright © 1992 by Brian Josephson and Beverly Rubik. Reprinted by permission.

Winona Schroeter, for use of original artwork appearing as Figure 12.1. Copyright © 1997 by Winona Schroeter. Reprinted by permission.

Huston Smith, for use of the table appearing in "Chapter 10: Beyond the Modern Western Mindset," from Huston Smith, *Beyond the Post-Modern Mind*

INTRODUCTION

Rosemarie Anderson

The field of transpersonal psychology emerged amid the cultural melee of the 1960s in the United States. The challenges and exaggerations of the 1960s awakened many of us, as if we had been sleeping while awake and listlessly unaware. The Vietnam War raged in Asia. Experimenting with psychedelics was commonplace. American culture rocked with voices of conflict and derision. Fresh, even fabulous, perspectives rushed in, as if replacing a vacuum. Ancient spiritual lineages, notably those from the East, were openly discussed and explored, and young people went particularly to Asia to explore things for themselves. In the context of this vigorous sorting out and shifting of new ideas and values, the field of transpersonal psychology began in rather humble ways—friends gathered to talk in their homes, met with others while on the road lecturing, and exchanged letters with others around the world. Among the earliest innovators were Abraham H. Maslow, Anthony Sutich, James Fadiman, Robert Frager, Stanislav Grof, Sonja Margulies, Michael Murphy, and Miles Vich.

This transpersonal vanguard was "epicentered" in northern California. Everyone "in the know" at least visited San Francisco in the 1960s. It is difficult to imagine how the newly emerging field of transpersonal psychology, with limited funds and few resources other than a dedicated cast of volunteers, could have been nurtured and sustained without the zany, high-voltage atmosphere of the San Francisco Bay Area of the 1960s and 1970s. Even now, with its present international audience, the field still tends to be home-based in the Bay Area. The *Journal of Transpersonal Psychology*, the offices of the two large professional associations (the Association for Transpersonal Psychology and the International Transpersonal Association), and the five graduate schools where doctoral studies in transpersonal psychology can be actively pursued on site (California Institute of Integral Studies, Institute of Transpersonal Psychology, John F. Kennedy University, Rosebridge Graduate School of Integrative Psychology, and Saybrook Institute) are all within a 2-hour drive of each other in the greater San Francisco Bay Area. (See Centers for Transpersonal Studies at the end of this book for a current list of transpersonal graduate programs in the United States.) If the notices and flyers arriving in our faculty mailboxes are any indication, the plethora of transpersonally oriented trainings and workshops available in the Bay Area, and increasingly around the world, is astounding.

Since the late 1980s, however, many unique transpersonal associations and interest groups have been forming globally. In particular, momentum has been growing in Europe, with the founding of national associations, the European Transpersonal Association (EUROTAS), and many other more informal interest groups. EUROTAS presently links groups from 13 member nations ("European Transpersonal Association Links," 1997). Unlike their North American counterparts, many European transpersonal psychologists are often inside public institutions, teaching and working in well-known universities and medical centers. Although the American Psychological Association has declined two attempts to form a division focused on transpersonal psychology, the British Psychological Society has recently formed a new Transpersonal Section to provide a "much-needed impetus for research, as well as offering a forum in which ideas and initiatives can be exchanged and developed" (Fontana & Slack, 1996, p. 269). Educated in a broad and classical understanding of human nature and less identified with the positivistic-behavioral perspective, European psychologists seem more accommodating of a transpersonal perspective and willing to acknowledge the importance of spiritual experiences in determining and motivating individual and cultural attitudes and actions. In Australia and Japan, professionally focused transpersonal associations have also been formed (see McLean, 1997, for information on the Japanese Transpersonal Association). We might well anticipate unique and complementary forms of transpersonal psychology to develop soon, especially in Europe (e.g., Nalimov

& Drogalina, 1996) and in other countries in which classical and metaphysically friendly education has been historically prevalent.

In many indigenous communities and Asian countries, in particular, spiritual and transcendent values are already so well integrated in everyday life that one wonders if a distinct professional discipline is relevant or necessary, except where academic disciplines have adhered to a Western model. Mark Epstein (1995), for example, has persuasively argued that the application of Buddhist thought is a form of depth psychology worthy of making any psychoanalyst proud. Indeed, from its inception in the late 1960s, one of the distinguishing characteristics of transpersonal psychology has been a keen desire, even an urgency, to integrate the learnings and spiritual practices of indigenous and ancient spiritual traditions, especially forms of shamanism around the world, Buddhism, and Hinduism. In more recent years, mystical and indigenous forms of Judaism, Christianity, and Islam (especially Sufism) have also been increasingly influential in shaping the transpersonal orientation to understanding human experience.

DEFINING TRANSPERSONAL PSYCHOLOGY

As a field of research, scholarship, and application, transpersonal psychology seeks to honor human experience in its fullest and most transformative expressions. It is usually identified as the "fourth force" in psychology, with psychoanalytic, behavioristic, and humanistic psychologies as its historical predecessors. The word *transpersonal* has its etymological roots in two Latin words: *trans,* meaning beyond or through, and *personal,* meaning mask or facade—in other words, beyond or through the personally identified aspects of self. Whenever possible, transpersonal psychology seeks to delve deeply into the most profound aspects of human experience, such as mystical and unitive experiences, personal transformation, meditative awareness, experiences of wonder and ecstasy, and alternative and expansive states of consciousness. In these experiences, we appear to go beyond our usual identification with our limited biological and psychological selves. As the field has matured, a more general study of the common boundary between spirituality and psychology has expanded to include the shared affinities between "the transpersonal" and an increasingly wide spectrum of professional endeavors, including anthropology; sociology; medicine; and especially immunology, parapsychology, consciousness studies, philosophy, religion, Yoga, the creative arts, and a variety of bodywork and healing practices.

Originally, transpersonal psychology was conceived as the study of "those *ultimate* human capacities and potentialities" specifically related to the

> *empirical,* scientific study of, and responsible implementation of the findings relevant to, becoming, individual and species-wide meta-needs, ultimate values, unitive consciousness, peak experiences, B-values, ecstasy, mystical experiences, awe, being, self-actualization, essence, bliss, wonder, ultimate meaning, transcendence of self, spirit, oneness, cosmic awareness, individual and species wide synergy, maximal interpersonal encounter, sacralization of everyday life, transcendental phenomena, cosmic self-humor and playfulness, maximal sensory awareness, responsiveness and expression; and related concepts, experiences and activities. (Sutich, 1969, p. 15)

In surveying the many definitions of transpersonal psychology proposed between 1968 and 1991, Lajoie and Shapiro (1992) conclude by defining the contemporary field of transpersonal psychology as "concerned with the study of humanity's highest potential, and with the recognition, understanding, and realization of unitive, spiritual, and transcendent states of consciousness" (p. 91). Many definitions of transpersonal psychology stress the "beyond the limits of ego and personality" feature of transcendent awareness (e.g., Walsh & Vaughan, 1980, p. 16). Especially in therapeutic and health-related fields, there is particular focus on understanding the factors and dynamics that encourage or limit transpersonal experiences and the effect of these experiences on the individuation and integration of the self. Through time, transpersonal psychology (and, more generally, transpersonal studies) has become a more generously inclusive field, both assenting to the many contributions of psychoanalytic, humanistic, and behavioral inquiry within psychology and drawing on the strengths of other related disciplines as it endeavors to further understand the expansive potential of human experience. Although transpersonal psychology is obviously an interdisciplinary approach, it might be possible to consider it as part of a still larger frame of reference. As recently suggested by Charles Tart (1995), all "conventional scholarly disciplines and activities are . . . subsets of the general transpersonal perspective" that seek to understand "our fundamental unity and oneness with each other and all life" (p. 5).

Transpersonal psychology is one of these subsets focusing on the psychological features of this general transpersonal perspective.

Another common approach to understanding transpersonal psychology is to consider it a basic orientation applicable to all human endeavors and experiences. Roger Walsh and Frances Vaughan (1980) call this orientation a *perspectivist* approach. Ordinary experiences are not typically thought of as transpersonal or potentially transformative in nature. Nevertheless, to inquire about their transpersonal nature or potential changes the frame of reference for understanding these ordinary experiences. As found in all spiritual traditions, implicit in transpersonal psychology are a sense of wonderment about the commonplace, an acceptance of life as precious, and a recognition of the miraculous strata of all experiences. Considered alchemically, life's ordinary ingredients may suddenly add up to personal and cultural transformation. Whether studying extraordinary and uncommon experiences such as unitive experiences and altered states of consciousness or more ordinary experiences such as grief and joy, work and play, and love and pain, transpersonalists seek to sacralize the ordinary.

Although it is not the purpose of this book to review the many historical roots of transpersonal psychology, we note that many psychologists have laid important groundwork, most notably William James, Carl Jung, Otto Rank, Karen Horney, Erich Fromm, Viktor Frankl, Ludwig Binswanger, Medard Boss, Roberto Assagioli, Rollo May, and many others. The writings of William James and Carl Jung continue to have an enormous influence on the theory and everyday practice of many transpersonal psychologists, as do the contemporary writings of Ken Wilber. Wilber—as a theorist, rather than as a researcher—has contributed influential ideas regarding ways of knowing, stages of psychospiritual development, and the nature and development of consciousness, blending Eastern and Western insights. A single quote from William James (1909/1977) will suffice to illustrate the transpersonal currents of thought evident among these creative thinkers.

> We with our lives are like islands in the sea, or like trees in the forest. The maple and the pine may whisper to each other with their leaves, and Conanicut and Newport hear each other's foghorns. But the trees also commingle their roots in the darkness underground, and the islands also hang together through the ocean's bottom. Just so there is a continuum of cosmic consciousness, against which our individuality builds but accidental fences, and into which our several minds plunge as into a mother-sea or reservoir. Our "normal" consciousness is circumscribed for adaptation to

our external earthly environment, but the fence is weak in spots, and fitful influences from beyond leak in, showing the otherwise unverifiable common connection. (pp. 798-799)

THE BEGINNING YEARS OF
THE *JOURNAL OF TRANSPERSONAL PSYCHOLOGY*

The story of transpersonal psychology begins in the turbulent 1960s. In early January 1966, two prominent figures in humanistic psychology, Abraham H. Maslow and Anthony J. Sutich, were participating in seminars at the Esalen Institute in Big Sur, California. During one of the seminars, an unexpected occurrence—like wind-blown seeds alighting in good soil— catalyzed some of their emerging thoughts in surprising ways. As Sutich (1976a) tells the story,

> In one exchange with a number of Jesuits present the question was asked, "Has any one of you ever had a mystical or similar personal experience?" The answer was "No." Very shortly after this there was another question, "Is it an official policy on the part of the church to systematically encourage and foster the attainment of a mystical experience on the part of each lay member of your church?" The answer again was "No." (p. 5)

The humanistic psychologists in attendance were surprised: Although it is unlikely that such an exchange would occur today—because, by now, the Church, too, has changed—in 1966, amid a backdrop of experimentation and exploration, the turgidity of this quasi-official policy was arresting. In exploring the vast domains of mystical experiences, "the concept of self-actualization was no longer comprehensive enough" (Sutich, 1976a, p. 7). This singular encounter, along with other events, and the prevailing expansive atmosphere of the 1960s, provoked disquieting questions about the basic humanistic perspective.

Conversations particularly continued among friends who gathered around Anthony (Tony) Sutich, who together with Abraham Maslow had founded the *Journal of Humanistic Psychology,* the first issue appearing in 1961. Sutich had already begun to explore anew the implications of peak and mystical experiences when applied to transcendence of the self. Maslow was a well-known public figure and traveled extensively. Sutich was a busy psychotherapist and organized his private practice and professional activities at home. As a result of an accident in a baseball game at age 12 leading to progressive arthritis, Sutich was severely disabled. For years, he used his home in Palo Alto, California, as a gathering place for innovative thinking and conversation. Following the Esalen event, a kind of salon formed in Sutich's living room to discuss the forming of a new journal that recognized this emerging new "fourth force" in psychology (Miles Vich & Sonja Margulies, personal communication, October 27, 1996). By mid-1967, Sutich was actively searching for a comprehensive term to name this emerging force and engaged in the exacting work of clarifying terminology for this new endeavor. In January 1967, he wrote Maslow asking him to write the foundational definition for what they then tentatively called a *transhumanistic psychology*. Sutich (1976a) eventually wrote it himself, incorporating Maslow's suggestions.

On September 14, 1967, Abraham Maslow gave a public address at the First Unitarian Church in San Francisco, which is generally regarded as the first open and formal presentation concerning what he considered the next step, the fourth force to address transcendent experiences and values. About midway in that address, Maslow (1969) stated,

> The fully developed (and very fortunate) human being, working under the best conditions tends to be motivated by values which transcend his self. They are not selfish anymore in the old sense of that term. Beauty is not within one's skin nor is justice or order. One can hardly class these desires as selfish in the sense that my desire for food might be. My satisfaction with achieving or allowing justice is not within my own skin; it does not lie along my arteries. It is equally outside and inside: therefore, it has transcended the geographical limitations of the self. Thus one begins to talk about transhumanistic psychology. (p. 4)

By 1968, the salon at the Sutich home had become an editorial board for the new *Journal of Transpersonal Psychology*. Local editors met at Tony's home every Wednesday afternoon and into the evening to review submitted manuscripts, discuss the latest developments, and converse with guests representing a wide variety of spiritual traditions. Although actively lecturing around the country, Abraham Maslow was occasionally present. Because of his extensive travel schedule and declining health, Maslow's influence was felt mostly through his writing and lively correspondence with Sutich (excerpts from letters in Sutich, 1976a, 1976b). Miles Vich, Sonja Margulies, James Fadiman, and Thomas N. Weide were active as editors from the outset and still are. Frances Vaughan joined in the mid-1970s. Other editors around the world reviewed incoming papers and participated through correspondence. When editorial review was completed for the day, invited guests and authors, such as Daniel Goleman, Stanislav Grof, Michael Murphy, Alyce and Elmer Green, Chogyam Trungpa, Ram Dass, and many others, would drop by to visit (Miles Vich & Sonja Margulies, personal communication, October 27, 1996).

In June, 1969, the first issue of the new journal was published. Its opening article (Maslow, 1969) was Maslow's September 1967 San Francisco address titled "The Farther Reaches of Human Nature."

WHAT IS EMPIRICAL?

From the beginning of launching the new journal, Abraham Maslow and Anthony Sutich were convinced, as were others, that mainstream research in psychology (then primarily behavioristic) was too limited. To deal with the rich scope of transpersonal phenomena in a more inclusive yet systematic way, Maslow advocated keeping the articles empirical, or that at least they should have an empirical base (Sonja Margulies & Miles Vich, personal communication, October 27, 1996). A wide variety of methods in psychology and other social sciences were encouraged. Nonetheless, implicit in their early discussion was a recognition that methods more fitting to the nature of transpersonal phenomena would eventually have to be created and validated within the scientific community. As part of this discussion, an expanding definition of "what is empirical" must eventually be clarified in relation to mystical and transcendent experiences, which by their nature are usually private and unobservable by an external observer (Miles Vich & Sonja Margulies, personal communication, October 27, 1996). It was enormously encouraging to us, as authors, to realize that many of the research methods proposed in this book were core—almost archetypal—concepts among the founders of the field.

HONORING HUMAN EXPERIENCE

Honoring the full measure and depth of human experience is essential to conducting consequential transpersonal research and to scientific inquiry more generally. At minimum, honoring human experience asks the researcher to incorporate, advocate, and verify the full and expansive measure of any human experience studied, however it presents itself to awareness. Ideally, a comprehensive definition of human experience also anticipates the inclusion of appreciation, humility, and wonder as intrinsic values fundamental to scientific inquiry.

Perhaps it is impossible for us to fully appreciate the vast potential of human experience. Some of our life experiences connect us deeply with the essence of our sense of being, others seem transcendent, other experiences remain mysterious or enigmatic, and still other experiences seem to connect us with events and people far away, even outside our time and place. The metaphor of a diamond might help to explicate the varieties of experience. We might imagine that each human being encounters life as if experience were a crystal or a diamond, with each individual facet reflecting another's experience to create a yet more brilliant diamond reflecting our essential communal and interconnected nature. Our experiences, especially uncommon experiences, lead to transcendent realities beyond the limits of our egos and personalities. Reflected in these realities, we can become more integral and whole, finding our more authentic and creative selves. In finding ourselves, we learn to trust impulses toward transcendent realms beyond our limited selves.

At birth, when we first opened our eyes, the surprises and explorations began. Honoring human experience is an ordinary human exploration, practiced here in the focused context of research. It particularly requires approaching each research topic with *a beginner's mind,* an attitude that feels wonder, enjoyment, surprise, playfulness, awe, and deep appreciation. Because every scientific inquiry is an exploration into unknown territory, the sketchy maps left by previous researchers take us only short distances on the journey. If research does not feel enlivening and risky, perhaps it is best left for someone else to do. If the wonder is lost in the middle of the study, we can try resting more, and follow the procedures lovingly, as if tending a child. We need an imaginative, even outlandish, science to envision the potential of human experience and awareness, not just more tidy reports. Even the more repetitive and labor-intensive moments of research (and there are many) can be imbued with gratitude—they seed knowledge and insight, albeit painstakingly slowly. To honor human experience is to unconditionally appreciate all the dimensions ordinarily considered—including cognitive, emotional, proprioceptive, kinesthetic, spiritual, and transcendent—*and* the dimensions yet unimagined. When the inquiry proceeds further than the sketchy maps left by others, following the surprises and "chance" occurrences of the inquiry will guide the way to more gratifying insights and far-reaching conclusions and understanding.

Human experience, as understood in this book, is spacious and multi-dimensional, more like a panoramic photo than a snapshot. In transpersonal research, the landscape of a particular experience may have many layers and qualities. A penetrating and revealing portrayal is generally more desirable and complete; comprehensive meaning is often conveyed more fully through subtlety and nuance. Even time has elasticity from a transpersonal point of view. In a study of the experience of sorrow, for example, the researcher may want to gather interview data, on-site observations at wakes, depictions in fiction, and descriptions from sacred texts. The range in sources enhances the distinctiveness, fullness, and complexity of the ensuing portrayal. In a study of the experience of joy, the researcher may want to attend celebrations and record spontaneous conversations, videotape fans when their favorite team wins the play-off, gather a focus group together to share their understanding of joy, or analyze the carefully thought through, prereflective constituents that occur prior to experiencing joy itself. The diversity of data sources lends itself to rich and full portrayal. Because the researcher is seeking to describe the qualities and dynamics of the experience, commonalities and differences across time and culture might well be portrayed in the participants' own voices, allowing them to speak for themselves without necessarily resolving the tensions between different voices. Obviously, exploring and envisioning these "farther reaches of human nature" require loosening up on some of the conventional uses of experimental control, especially what has been known as internal validity. Much of the containment of control and the appeal of objectivity is unattainable, as a growing number of scientists have attested in the past decade or so. Instead of tightening controls, in this book we are proposing the rigors of full disclosure and complexity.

In transpersonal research, the Renaissance view of the artist may present a more complete model for investigating human experience than that of the 19th-century physical scientist. Evaluated candidly, the most eloquent speakers today on the human experience often seem to be poets, novelists, playwrights, filmmakers, storytellers, and theologians—and, more *rarely,* psychologists, anthropologists, sociologists, and other scientists. By copying the objectivist and positivist views of the physical scientists (who are now abandoning that model themselves) and owning radical positivism and psychological behaviorism as the epistemological imprimatur, psychologists and other human scientists have ignored and even trivialized vast realms of fascinating human experiences. A well-known existential clinical psychologist, James Bugental, puts the dilemma quite succinctly: "The objectivist view of psychology . . . regards all that is not familiar as dangerous, mythical, or nonexistent" (cited in Valle & Halling, 1989, p. ix). Even when investigating extraordinary human experiences, researchers often seem content with meaning-diminishing methodologies. Without supporting methodologies, rich topics such as the study of passion, making love, giving birth, grieving, ecstasy, quietude, and mystical experiences are too often neglected. Frequently, research methods fall flat before the fullness of being human, the extraordinary experience of being human day-to-day. Having ceded the exploration of the expansive nature of being human to others by default, we may find it time to reenchant our methods of inquiry and related epistemologies with the rigors of imagination and more fully dimensionalized concepts and theories.

THE "REENCHANTMENT OF SCIENCE"

The paradigms of science are shifting. The stage is set for change. To quote Adrienne Rich (1979), we must get beyond the "assumptions in which we are drenched" (p. 35). Along with the theories and critiques proposed by transpersonal psychologists and scientists in related fields, other developments and critiques have loosened the exclusive hold on psychological research that the experimental method has enjoyed. Some of these alternative views stem from the counterculture of the 1960s and 1970s, feminist critique and theory, existential-phenomenological theory and phenomenological methods, deconstructionism and the postmodern critique of culture, the epistemological insights of quantum and high-energy physics, parapsychological investigations, narrative methods and discourse analysis, in-depth case studies, heuristic methods, and the concerns about external and effectual validity taking place within experimental psychology. There has been a series of critiques within psychology itself, notably from Bruner (1990) in reconceptualizing cognitive psychology as folk psychology, and from recent developments in the human sciences, in general. Once thought of as unassailable epistemologies, behaviorism and some aspects of cognitive science have been besieged by still more complete and far-reaching ideas and methodologies. In wave upon wave, these critiques have enlivened scientific discourse as academic disciplines once again search for more suitable epistemologies and methods of inquiry.

The transpersonal research methods and epistemologies presented in this book provide new methods and frameworks from which to further explore "the farther reaches of human nature," as Abraham Maslow (1969) put it so well 30 years ago. In exploring the vast and multidimensional nature of human experience, our methods need to be as dynamic as the experiences studied. These transpersonal research methods incorporate intuition, direct knowing, creative expression, alternative states of consciousness, dreamwork, storytelling, meditation, imagery, emotional and bodily cues, and other internal events *as possible strategies and procedures in all phases of research inquiry.* Both the topics of research inquiry and the methods employed are potentially transpersonal or spiritual in nature. Researchers, participants, and readers may be enlivened, even transformed, by the transpersonal elements of the study. Despite the demanding and often tedious aspects of all scholarly inquiry, it is hoped that transpersonal research will be imbued with a sense of wonder and joy. Discovery for its own sake is joyous, and more seemingly serendipitous events may bring a windfall of new understanding.

Along with these transpersonal research approaches, of course, conventional qualitative and quantitative methods may also be employed, depending on how well they, or a blend of methods, suit the topic of inquiry. By presenting these transpersonal approaches to research, we hope to enliven scholarly and scientific inquiry in many fields with transpersonal approaches to investigating the nature and potential of human experience and, more generally, to support renewed imagination, creativity, and wonder/wonderment throughout all scientific inquiry and discourse.

The methods provided are intended for researchers in all professional fields in which understanding the scope of human experience is essential to the fruition of their endeavors. It is a unique pleasure and honor for both of us to offer transpersonal methods and insights at a time when the scientific community welcomes new explorations and insights in epistemology and methodology. We are grateful for the opportunity.

OVERVIEW OF THE
CONTENTS OF THE BOOK

The need for, and the concepts presented in, this book already have been situated in the contexts of our stories (Preface) and of the field of transpersonal studies (this Introduction). We present here, by way of preview, a brief description of the structure of the book as a whole.

The book is divided into four parts. Part I (Critiques and Extensions) contrasts the assumptions and practices of conventional research approaches with the complementary assumptions and practices of the extended and expanded approaches to research that are developed and advocated in this book. Part II (Expanded Methods of Disciplined Inquiry), the heart of the book, describes how the new assumptions, concepts, and practices take particular, concrete forms in five specific methods of transpersonal inquiry (integral inquiry, intuitive inquiry, transpersonal-phenomenological inquiry, organic research, and inquiry informed by an emphasis on exceptional human experience). Part III (Applying the Principles: Selected Examples) presents ways in which the major principles of the five transpersonal approaches have actually been applied in particular research projects. The applications of the new principles are organized into three major clusters: new ways of acquiring information, new ways of working with the data acquired, and new ways of expressing and communicating findings to various audiences. In Part IV (Further Extensions), we consider how the features of the new methods illuminate issues of the validity of knowledge claims and how they contribute to a model of transformative integration that blends aspects of research, practical application, and the growth and development of everyone touched by the research project. This part also treats additional implications of the new methods, ethical considerations, and future challenges.

We include three succinct, yet detailed, appendixes that we feel will be especially useful, ready resources for students and practitioners. Appendix A provides synopses of the five new transpersonal research approaches. Appendix B summarizes the major features of six related approaches to research (phenomenological, heuristic, feminist, experiential, cooperative, and participatory approaches). Appendix C provides summaries of the nature, strengths, and weaknesses of 17 more conventional qualitative and quantitative research methods. The book concludes with a listing of graduate degree-granting centers that emphasize transpersonal studies, an integrated reference listing, an index, and notes on the contributors.

PART I

CRITIQUES AND EXTENSIONS

CHAPTER 1

CONVENTIONAL AND EXPANDED VIEWS OF RESEARCH

William Braud
Rosemarie Anderson

Many of the most significant and exciting life events and extraordinary experiences—moments of clarity, illumination, and healing—have been systematically excluded from conventional research, along with the ways of recognizing and encouraging these exceptional experiences. Such unfortunate exclusions, through which we deprive ourselves of new and nourishing forms of knowledge and experience, are attributable to the narrowness of conventional conceptualizations of research and of the appropriate methods for its conduct. By privileging only certain ways and aims of knowing—and by ignoring or devaluing others—we, as researchers in the social or human sciences, are unnecessarily and unwisely limiting the content and approaches of our disciplines.

Indications that we have gone astray are feelings of dissatisfaction and disappointment among both the producers and consumers of research—feelings that something is missing, that important topics are being ignored or are not receiving the attention or honor that they deserve, and that our findings are not having sufficient impacts on the growth and expansion of our conceptualizations and theories or on our practices, ourselves, and our world. Indeed, we often experience tensions or incompatibilities between research and service (clinical, social, educational, or other forms of practice or application) or between research and our own personal experiences, growth, and development. The more significant the subject matter and the greater its relevance to vital issues and concerns, the greater are these feelings of tension and unease. In transpersonal psychology—which concerns itself with issues of consciousness, alternative states of consciousness, exceptional experiences, transegoic development, and humanity's highest potentials and possible transformation—this tension between subject matter and research is strongly felt. Both students and practitioners ask whether it is possible to research the transpersonal without violating, distorting, or trivializing what we are studying. Is it possible to live, appreciate, and honor our transpersonal aspects and our most purposeful human qualities while, at the same time, conducting systematic research into these most significant facets of our being?

We maintain that it is possible to conduct significant and satisfying research on all facets of human experience—even the most sensitive, exceptional, and sacred experiences—but only if we modify our assumptions about research and extend our research methods so that they become as creative and expansive as the subject matter we wish to investigate. The tensions and unease mentioned above need occur only if research is identified with a type of quantitative, experimental approach that models itself after the methods of a particular type of natural science. If we broaden our conceptualization of research to include complementary qualitative, nonexperimental methods, and if we acknowledge and include alternative modes of knowing and of working with and expressing our findings, this new research approach more faithfully honors complex and exceptional human experiences, and the bothersome tensions and unease dissolve and can even disappear.

ASSUMPTIONS AND PRACTICES OF
CONVENTIONAL APPROACHES TO RESEARCH

Research programs that have the respect and support of editorial boards of well-regarded professional journals, institutions of higher learning, and funding organizations usually are guided, either explicitly or tacitly, by the following assumptions and research practices:

• Research is a special human activity that provides unique access to accurate, valid knowledge and possesses unique safeguards against error that are not found in other human activities.

• Research is value-free and should, therefore, be distinguished from other human endeavors in which values and meanings play important roles—that is, endeavors such as practical applications (clinical, social, educational, and other practices and services) and work contributing to the researcher's growth, development, and possible transformation.

• The major aim of research is the discovery of general principles or universal laws that provide the possibility of explanation, prediction, and control.

• Quantitative methods are privileged over qualitative methods, and more experimental approaches are privileged over more naturalistic approaches. Qualitative and/or naturalistic methods of inquiry are recommended only as interim strategies that might provide suggestions or hints for later quantitative and/or experimental determinations.

• The preferred empirical and theoretical research approaches model themselves after those of the physical sciences of the 18th and 19th centuries.

• The only valid knowledge of the world is obtained via data derived through the senses, consensually validated by others, and extended and expressed via logically sound mathematical and linguistic formalisms.

• A researcher's ideal stance is to be as neutral, uninvolved, and distant as possible with respect to what is being studied. Because researchers' qualities are irrelevant to their objective observations, researchers may be interchanged. Virtually identical findings are expected from all researchers who repeat the research procedures, provided they are appropriately skilled and have been properly trained.

• The ideal research environment is isolated from other influences and characterized by simple sets of variables or events whose mutual interactions can be straightforwardly analyzed to determine sources and directions of causality.

Purposive and teleological considerations have no place in serious research, and the consciousness of the research personnel can have no direct influence on the phenomena being studied.

• The researcher is the expert, the authority whose observations, views, hypotheses, and interpretations are privileged over those of the research subjects.

• In reviewing the literature for relevant findings and interpretations, the researcher goes primarily or solely to research reports that have been published in the premier professional journals of the discipline during the past 5 to 10 years. Older reports, or observations appearing outside scientific literature, are not especially valued or useful.

• The researcher's main energies are devoted to the accumulation of original empirical findings and the development of models and theories that help explain those findings.

• The preferred outlets for original research findings and interpretations are peer-reviewed journal articles and professional conference presentations; the researcher communicates primarily with professional colleagues.

THE LIMITATIONS OF THESE ASSUMPTIONS AND PRACTICES

During the past three decades, we have become increasingly aware of the limitations of these assumptions and practices. They have been scrutinized, questioned, and criticized by theorists and practitioners within the human sciences (Polkinghorne, 1983; Tesch, 1990), the human services (Monette, Sullivan, & DeJong, 1990), education (Borg & Gall, 1989), health and nursing research (Morse, 1991, 1992; Parse, 1996), naturalistic inquiry (Lincoln & Guba, 1985), feminist research (Nielsen, 1990; Reinharz, 1992b), and those who have been exploring the philosophical foundations of science itself (Harman, 1991; Harman & DeQuincey, 1994; Lorimer, 1988; Skolimowski, 1994; Smith, 1976, 1992). The gist of these critiques is that although such assumptions and practices have been useful in certain areas of science for certain purposes, they are incomplete, contain unnecessary biases, are unsatisfactory for addressing complex human actions and experiences, and are inadequate even within the natural sciences themselves. More important, such assumptions and practices yield a picture of the world, and of human nature and human possibility, that is narrow, constrained, fragmented, disenchanted, and deprived of meaning and value. Such a view is more consistent with feelings of emptiness, isolation, and alienation than with feelings of richness, interconnection, creativity, freedom, and optimism.

To counter this prevailing conception of science and of research, a number of contemporary thinkers have offered complementary assumptions and practices to correct previous imbalances and provide a more complete view of science and research that can more adequately apprehend the complexity, breadth, and depth of our world and of humanity. In the

TABLE 1.1 Comparison of the Modern Western Mind-Set With its Logical Alternative

	Modern Western Mind-Set	Logical Alternative
Motivation:	Control	Participation
Epistemology:	Empiricism	Intuitive discernment
Ontology:	Naturalism	Transcendence
Resultant:	Alienation	Fulfillment

SOURCE: From "Chapter 10: Beyond the Modern Western Mindset" (p. 211), in *Beyond the Post-Modern Mind* (Updated and Revised, 3rd Quest Printing), by Huston Smith, 1992, Wheaton, IL: Quest/Theosophical Publishing House. Copyright © 1989 by Huston Smith. Reprinted by permission.

interests of conciseness and brevity, we present some of these complementary conceptualizations in the form of six tabular summaries. In these tables, the terms *modern Western mind-set, orthodox science, positivist paradigm,* and *separatist science* are used to denote the prevailing, conventional view of science and research, whereas the terms *alternative, complementary, naturalist, wholeness,* and *extended science* denote the complementary features, axioms, assumptions, and practices that are being proposed. These terms are not ours but those of the thinkers whose views we are summarizing.

TABLE 1.2 Characteristics of Orthodox Science and the Proposed Complementary Science

Orthodox	Complementary
Reductionist/analytical	Integrative/synthetic
Objective	Participatory
Outer-oriented	Inner-oriented
Sensory/separative	Mystical/intuitive
Quantitative	Qualitative
Efficient causality	Final causality
Monocausal/monolevel	Multicausal/multilevel
Replicable/nomothetic	Unique/idiographic
Skeptical doubt	Open-minded clarity
Knowledge	Wisdom
Coercive law	Self-organizing order

SOURCE: From "Complementary Approaches to Science" (tabular format), in *Towards a New Science: A Critical Appraisal of Scientific Knowledge,* by David Lorimer, 1988. Paper presented at the 17th Annual Conference of the Unity of the Sciences, Los Angeles, CA, November 24-27, 1988. Copyright © 1988 by David Lorimer. Reprinted by permission.

TABLE 1.3 Contrasting Positivist and Naturalist Axioms

Axioms About	Positivist Paradigm	Naturalist Paradigm
The nature of reality:	Reality is single, tangible, and fragmentable.	Realities are multiple, constructed, and holistic.
The relationship of knower to the known:	Knower and known are independent, a dualism.	Knower and known are interactive, inseparable.
The possibility of generalization:	Time- and context-free generalizations (nomothetic statements) are possible.	Only time- and context-bound working hypotheses (idiographic statements) are possible.
The possibility of causal linkages:	There are real causes, temporally precedent to or simultaneous with their effects.	All entities are in a state of mutual simultaneous shaping, so that it is impossible to distinguish causes from effects.
The role of values:	Inquiry is value-free.	Inquiry is value-bound.

SOURCE: From *Naturalistic Inquiry* (Table 1.1), by Yvonna Lincoln and Egon Guba, 1985, Beverly Hills, CA: Sage Publications, Inc.

Note the substantial overlap among these six views. Summaries of Smith, Lorimer, and Lincoln and Guba are shown in Tables 1.1, 1.2, and 1.3.

Whereas Lorimer (Table 1.2) views the two sciences as existing in a complementary relationship, Harman (Table 1.4) includes *separateness science* as a special, limited case within an extended *wholeness science*— much as classical Newtonian physics could be considered a special, limited case within a more general relativity physics.

Table 1.5 represents the characteristics of the prevailing scientific paradigm and of a proposed alternative scientific paradigm as viewed by the participants in an International Symposium on Science, Technology, and the Environment, held in Athens, Greece, in 1990 (Global Co-Operation for a Better World, 1990).

Two years later, in early 1992, a Second International Symposium on Science and Consciousness was held in Athens (Athenian Society for Science and Human Development and the Brahma Kumaris World Spiritual University, 1992) to develop further the ideas that had arisen at the first symposium. Some of the conclusions of this conference were later summarized and published by Josephson and Rubik (1992), both of whom had participated in the symposium deliberations (see Table 1.6). We feel this table is of special interest because of its extensive and inclusive nature and because it was prepared by individuals from within the natural science community—Brian Josephson is a physicist and Nobel laureate, and Beverly Rubik is a biophysicist.

We find it productive and satisfying to view the emphases of the left and right sides of Tables 1.1 through 1.5 as truly complementary positions. Each half of each table describes an approach that is valid and useful for some purposes but not for others. Each side of each table provides only a partial account of the whole; each side addresses what the other side omits. The assumptions and emphases of the left side of each table are especially appropriate for the study of relatively simple systems that are self-contained and isolated from dynamic interactions with other systems. These approaches are well suited to physical phenomena of the middle realm (i.e., the familiar, macroscopic realm in which Newtonian and Euclidean principles prevail) and to a range of biological, psychological, and sociological phenomena that are simple enough to resemble those of the physical middle realm. These approaches, however, become less useful and increasingly inadequate when a researcher attempts to study physical phenomena outside this middle realm (i.e., those events associated with extremely large masses, extremely high velocities, and extremely small and energetic particles to which the different—non-Newtonian and non-Euclidean—principles of relativity theory and quantum mechanics now apply); complex physical or chemical systems that are dynamically interactive and far from equilibrium; complex living systems that defy entropy and move toward increasing order; or complex psychological systems characterized by volition, purposes, awareness, self-awareness, and consciousness. For the latter, the axioms and approaches described in the right sides of the tables now become more appropriate and more adequate.

ASSUMPTIONS AND PRACTICES OF
AN EXPANDED APPROACH TO SCIENCE,
RESEARCH, AND DISCIPLINED INQUIRY

Informed by the content of Tables 1.1 through 1.6, and by our own acquaintance with the objects, methods, and findings of a variety of forms of research, we propose the following assumptions and practices as complementary guides to an expanded view of science, research, and disciplined inquiry.

TABLE 1.4 Characteristics of Separateness Science and the Proposed Wholeness Science

Separateness Science	Wholeness Science
The universe is composed, ultimately, of fundamental particles and quanta which are separate from each other except insofar as there are specifiable connections such as fields.	The universe is a single whole within which every part is connected to every other part; this wholeness includes the physical world as well as all contents of consciousness.
A scientific explanation of a phenomenon (specifying its causes) consists in relating the phenomenon to more general and fundamental relationships or scientific laws; the ultimate explanation would be in terms of motions and interactions of the fundamental particles and quanta involved.	Pragmatically useful scientific explanations enhance understandings of phenomena by relating them to other phenomena and relationships. Since things are so interconnected that a change in any one can affect all, any accounting for cause is within a specific context for a specific purpose. The search for ultimate reductionistic cause is futile; there is no cause and effect but rather the evolution of a whole system. Order is observed in the physical world, but is never free from the possibility of "downward causation" from consciousness "down" to the physical.
All scientific knowledge is ultimately based on data (quantifiable information) which is obtained through the physical senses.	Reality is contacted through physical sense data, but also through being ourselves part of the oneness—through a deep intuitive inner knowing. Awareness includes (objective) sensation as well as (subjective) intuitive, aesthetic, spiritual, noetic, and mystical aspects.
The truest information about the objective reality is obtained through the observer being as detached as possible; the "observer effect" in any observation places an upper limit on such objectivity.	Understanding comes not from being detached, objective, analytical, coldly clinical, but rather from identifying with the observed, becoming one with it; objective knowledge leads to only partial understanding.
The universe is scientifically understood to be ultimately deterministic.	The concept of a completely deterministic universe (even in a quantum mechanical statistical sense) stems from the "separateness" assumption; there is no reason to expect it to be borne out in experience.
The material universe evolved to its present state from the "Big Bang" by random physical processes and, after the advent of life, mutation and natural selection; consciousness is a product of material evolution.	There is no a priori reason to assume that scientific laws are invariant; they too may be evolving. Hence, extrapolation to the "Big Bang" may be suspect. Consciousness may have evolved with or may have been prior to the material world.

TABLE 1.4 *Continued*

Separateness Science	*Wholeness Science*
There is no scientific evidence for anything in the universe resembling "purpose," "design," or teleology. What exists has survived through natural selection.	Since we humans are part of the whole, and experience "drives" or "urges" such as survival, belongingness, achievement and self-actualization, as well as "purpose," and "values," there is no a priori justification for assuming these are not characteristics of the whole. The universe may be genuinely telic.
The wide range of commonly experienced phenomena known as "meaningful coincidences" and "anomalous or paranormal phenomena," wherein two or more events appear meaningfully connected, but there is no discernible physical connection, must ultimately be shown either to have a physical connection or to be, in fact, merely coincidence.	"Meaningful coincidences" are not to be explained, but rather apparent separateness. The question is not "How can we explain apparent telepathic communication?" but rather "Why are our minds not cluttered by all that information in other minds?"; not "How can we explain apparent psychokinetic phenomena?" but rather "Why do our minds have such limited effects in the physical world?"
Non-normal states of consciousness, dissociation, etc., are phenomena that are to be studied largely in the context of the pathological, and in terms of their effects on behavior.	The entire spectra of states of consciousness are of interest, including religious and mystical experiences and experiences of "other dimensions of reality." Such experiences have been at the heart of all cultures, including our own. They have been among the main sources of the deepest value commitments; they may be an important investigative tool, a "window" to other dimensions of reality.
The explanations of ontogenesis, morphogenesis, regeneration and related biological phenomena are to be sought in terms of coded instructions in the genes and similar mechanisms.	The ultimate explanations of ontogenesis, morphogenesis, regeneration and related biological phenomena probably will turn out to include something in consciousness analogous to "image" or idea.

SOURCE: From *A Re-examination of the Metaphysical Foundations of Modern Science* (Noetics Report CT-1, Table 1, pp. 100-101), by Willis W. Harman, 1991, Sausalito, CA: Institute of Noetic Sciences. Copyright © 1991 by Institute of Noetic Sciences. Reprinted by permission.

• Research (disciplined inquiry) is simply a modified form of a more general approach to life, and to our professional activities, in which we attentively make observations and thoughtfully draw conclusions about

TABLE 1.5 Symposium Summary of the Prevailing and Alternative Scientific Paradigms

Prevailing Paradigm	Alternative Paradigm
Monolithic; "truth" viewed as universal and singular (i.e., "one truth"); denies the validity and value of alternative world views, value systems, methodologies	Pluralistic; "truth" is acknowledged to reflect the vantage point of the observer; open to alternative ways of knowing
Mechanistic, reductionistic, rationalistic; analytical atomism regarded as the only fully creditable approach	Balances mechanistic/reductionistic, rational approaches with organismic, holistic, intuitive, experimental ones
Fragmented/fragmenting	Interconnected/unifying
Objective; observer regarded as "detached"; subject/object dichotomized; dualistic	Interactive; scientist is both an observer and a participant
Cognitive; excludes and disparages emotions, feelings, passions; claims to be neutral and value-free; "hard" is superior to "soft"	Harmonizes and integrates feminine and masculine qualities; recognizes humanity as part of the natural world; "hard" and "soft" are equally acceptable
Aristotelian; categorical; dualistic; opposites imply right/wrong; conflict; antagonistic	Multiplex; complementary; both/and dialectical thinking; dynamic; "the opposite of a deep truth is another deep truth"
Argument; certainty; clarity	Co-operative dialogue; accepts uncertainty; tolerates ambiguity, fuzziness; process-oriented
Discontinuous; linear	Continuous; cyclical; helical
Closed, authoritarian, competitive	Open, dialectical, co-operative
Absolute ("right answer")	Perspectival; relative; multipartiality
Elitist; individualistic	Egalitarian; consensual
Secretive	Open
Arcane	Participatory
Hierarchical	Democratic (entails co-operative dialogue both across disciplines and between science and society)
Arrogant	Humble
Alienated/alienating	Liberating
Morally/ethically "neutral"; socio-culturally separate; "uninvolved"	Morally/ethically committed; involved
Jargon isolates "experts" from rest of society	Language and concepts generally accessible/comprehensible

SOURCE: Global Co-Operation for a Better World (1990, pp. 25-26). From "Report of Group 4," pp. 24-28, in *Report on an International Symposium on Science, Technology, and the Environment* (January 3-7, 1990), by the Global Co-Operation for a Better World, Athens, Greece. Copyright © 1990 by Global Co-Operation for a Better World. Reprinted by permission of Drossoula Elliott of the Athenian Society for Science and Human Development, Athens, Greece.

consistencies, inconsistencies, and patterns. Ideally, we do this with mindfulness and discernment, basing our judgments on all available relevant information and weighing the sources of these judgments for their histories of accuracy and use. In formal research, we simply are more careful and more explicit about our observational and decisional processes. Although we have created formal decision rules—evidential and statistical—to help us in our research endeavors, these are not always effective safeguards against error. Ultimately, responsibilities for determining the adequacy of knowledge claims rest in the informed judgments of investigators and research consumers.

• Research is value laden. Our research methods are influenced by judgments about their soundness, trustworthiness, and use, and these involve considerations of value and worth. Methodological and theoretical criteria such as consistency, parsimony, and elegance are, themselves, not value-free. Individual, societal, and cultural values influence the types of subject matter, topics, and research questions we study and also influence how we carry out our work and how that work is supported, encouraged, communicated, and received.

• An aim of research is the discovery of general principles or universal laws that provide the possibility of explanation, prediction, and control. An equally acceptable and valid aim is the full description, understanding, and appreciation of individual cases or instances. Windelband (1894/1904) distinguished *nomothetic* (concerned with *was immer ist*—what always is) and *idiographic* (concerned with *was einmal war*—what once was) approaches to research. In our view, these two aims have equal places in research.

• Quantitative methods are not privileged over qualitative methods, nor are experiment-like methods privileged over more naturalistic approaches. Quantitative/experimental and qualitative/naturalistic methods provide different types of information about different domains of inquiry. The former is appropriate for certain research questions, aims, and subject matter, whereas the latter is appropriate for other questions, interests, and topics. The nature of the research question determines which method is chosen. The investigator's interests and temperament also influence method choice. Qualitative and quantitative methods may be used alone or in combination.

• We acknowledge the achievements of mechanistic research approaches, especially in the physical sciences and technologies. Physics itself, however, has demonstrated the limitations of its more conventional views. These limitations are highlighted by developments in the domains of relativity

TABLE 1.6 Summary of Symposium Views on Consciousness and an Extended Science

---

- The study of consciousness should be concerned not just with definitions of consciousness but with descriptions of its mode of operation. The phenomena of consciousness should be studied in the aspect of subjectively lived experience rather than exclusively in terms of objective data (as is most often the case with cognitive psychology). As a result, an extension is needed in the concept of what constitutes science, defined as knowledge or the quest for knowledge.

- The extended science is envisioned as in principle a continuum of activity ranging from science as it is currently practised to the humanities and the arts, and possibly including insights that may be gained from spiritual or religious practices. It will explicitly include consciousness in its many dimensions, including creativity; the use of symbol, myth, and metaphor; the role of the feminine; the historical perspective; and cross-cultural aspects.

- There are many artificial dualities to be overcome by the extended science. These dualities or splits owe their origins both to contemporary science and to the dominant paradigm, and include those between ourselves and nature, mind and body, mind and matter, the feminine and the masculine, the observer and the observed, science and values, inductive vs. deductive logic, and philosophy and science. In particular, science cannot be divorced from philosophy, because one always brings some philosophy to bear in one's thinking.

- We need to move from the fragmentation that reductionism produces to principles of complementarity and integration, from "either/or" to "both/and" thinking. The conventional notion of causality as local and physical needs to be broadened to take account of networks of causation, non-local interconnectedness, and correlations. The world has suffered from the conventional fragmentary approach, its integrity violated by considering only the parts and thus losing sight of the whole. Again, it must be recognised that no single language or approach can grasp the richness or elusiveness of nature; thus the new science should be open to new and multiple approaches.

- While science has conventionally been regarded as an objective endeavour leading to the truth about the nature of reality, we need to shift our thinking toward regarding its insights as being context dependent, and to recognising that all approaches to reality are relative. We need actively to address the limitations of scientific approaches, verification, and theories, and to find a place in our world view for personal knowledge gained through introspection. The importance of intuition as a contributing factor in the process by which knowledge advances needs to be fully acknowledged. Language can itself provide an effective means of exploring quasi-objectively what has previously been characterised as being purely subjective.

- The extended science will develop in its scope beyond the conventional framework to the qualitative attributes of being and feeling, and will stress the importance of both quality and quantity. The range of scientific information will expand to include the anecdotal and the more tenuous. Codification and other ways of utilising such information need to be developed. There is the recognition and the acceptance that insights of the extended science occupy a domain that falls in between ignorance and precise knowledge.

TABLE 1.6 *Continued*

- A radically different attitude needs to be cultivated in the new science. The old humility (*humus* = the earth; hence humility = close to the earth), awe, wonder, and delight in the cosmos must be restored. These are critical to regaining a reverence for nature. It is felt that the attitude that predominates in science at present is arrogance, which has fostered dogmatism and scientism. In doing science, the prerequisite attitude involves letting the phenomena speak for themselves, rather than forcibly imposing one's hypotheses on the phenomena. The importance of the scientist's attitude toward his or her work, preconceptions, and deeper motivations must be stressed. Effects, however subtle, of the experimenter on the experiment are to be anticipated and must be examined; thus self-examination on the part of the experimenter must be included as part of the scientific process so as to make the processes of description more complete.

- There is a novel role for the scientific collective in the new science. A newly emergent group creativity, seemingly involving a "group mind" that exhibits camaraderie and cooperativeness in regard to solving problems in addition to the creativity of the individual should be nurtured, recognising that the power of the harmonious group has been lost in contemporary Western society.

- Any studies on consciousness must acknowledge the inherent wholeness and unity of the body/mind, and equally avoid losing sight of the total person. The holistic point of view, contrasting with the admittedly highly successful alternative of assuming a Cartesian split and operating under largely reductionistic principles, seems essential in order to study consciousness in its full subtlety, and to explore its deep interrelationship with the realm of the physical.

- The foundations of contemporary science, and its limitations, should be taught to and understood by all scientific practitioners. While the uniqueness of both individuals and groups presents difficulties for formalising a science of consciousness, consciousness studies are to be regarded nonetheless as having equal status to the physical sciences.

- The new science, as science with both consciousness and conscience, will concern itself with the consequences of science to the individual, society, and the whole world: it is a science for the integrity of both people and planet that should be translatable into action. The potential value to life of the discipline as a whole should not be compromised by the pursuit of more limited goals. At a personal level, the new science should help people be able to comprehend themselves and their place in nature, facilitate the development of empathic processes which aid mutual understanding, and enhance the meaning of life for individuals and for society.

SOURCE: From "The Challenge of Consciousness Research," by Brian Josephson and Beverly Rubik, 1992, *Frontier Perspectives*, 3(1), 15-19. Copyright © 1992 by Brian Josephson and Beverly Rubik. Reprinted by permission.

theory, quantum mechanics, the zero-point field, dissipative structures, chaos, and complexity. We, therefore, recognize the shortcomings of the earlier physical views that several contemporary disciplines still use as templates for sound scientific thinking and practice. Expanded approaches to research (disciplined inquiry) are informed by the more recent developments in physics and also by alternative research developments from ethology, ecology, systems theory, anthropology, sociology, all areas of psychology, and the human sciences in general.

• In addition to recognizing that most of our knowledge is obtained through sense data capable of being consensually validated by others and extended and expressed via logically consistent mathematical and linguistic formalisms, we also recognize the possibility of alternative forms of knowing and of extending and expressing knowledge. We recognize the importance of tacit or personal knowledge and of knowledge obtained through intuition, direct knowing, empathic sensitivity, and what might be considered paranormal means. We recognize that alternative modes of accessing, processing, and sharing knowledge may occur in nonordinary states of consciousness and that it may be possible to develop *state-specific sciences* based on these modes and states, as envisioned by Tart (1972). Most important, we recognize the validity of working with the subjective experiences of research participants and researchers. We emphasize private, first-person experiences and experiential accounts as valid forms of knowing that complement third-person accounts of what is publicly observable. We supplement outer (*etic*) descriptions with inner (*emic*) ones, and we do not privilege the former over the latter either epistemologically or ontologically.

• The researcher is an extremely important component of any research effort. Personal characteristics of the researcher may have profound impacts on the outcomes of the research project. Characteristics such as the researcher's background, training, skills, sensitivities, biases, expectations, judgments, and temperament can affect, and potentially distort, any and all phases of a research project, including framing the research question; selecting the research method; drawing participants into the study; interacting with participants and conducting the actual research; and collecting, processing, interpreting, and communicating the data and findings. The researcher's preparation and even his or her *very being* may importantly influence the nature and outcome of a research study, and some of these factors can be quite subtle and operate through equally subtle means. A standardized, distanced, and objective researcher who remains apart from what is studied is an illusion. Investigators cannot be interchanged or substituted for one another with an expectation of virtually identical study outcomes. Because the role of the investigator is so critical in this expanded view of research, we will devote more attention to researcher characteristics in a later section of this chapter.

• Simple, artificial, unrealistic research environments or research situations may yield correspondingly simple, artificial, and misleading findings, conclusions, and theories. Topics of great meaning, and most human experiences, are usually too complex, rich, and contextualized to be amenable to simple analytical designs without distorting or even trivializing the topics or experiences. To attempt to simplify or simulate such experiences in isolated—and necessarily artificial—contexts, to determine their components and which factors influence which other factors, is always risky and often impossible to accomplish with any real success. The experiences exist as processes that are in dynamic interaction with other processes, and it is difficult or impossible to study these in the absence of their generating and supporting fields. A complementarity principle seems operative here. The researcher must give up the possibility of certainty as to exact components, and certainty as to source and direction of causality, to wholly and faithfully apprehend rich experiences. The researcher can analyze and determine components and identify sources and directions of causality but only of experiences that are simplifications and artificial analogues of the real thing. Significant human experiences arise and are sustained in contexts that are rich, but such contexts also are rich in ambiguity.

• The purposes, intentions, and goals of all research personnel (researcher, participants, and audience) contribute significantly to the design, conduct, and outcomes of research studies. Parapsychological research indicates that consciousness may have direct influences on the physical world and on other people. Direct consciousness interactions with remote systems can provide veridical knowledge about those systems and also can influence those systems in measurable ways. Direct consciousness interactions may occur among personnel in all phases of research, interact with more conventional pathways of knowing and of influence, and contribute to what happens and what is learned in a study.

• In an expanded view of research (disciplined inquiry), the researcher's status or importance is not privileged over that of the other research participants. There is a democratization of the research enterprise, with all personnel contributing inputs and able to comment on a study's interpretations and conclusions. The terms *coresearcher* and *participant* are used, rather than the term *subject,* to emphasize an egalitarian stance toward all contributors to the research project. Those who are most familiar with the experiences being studied—as a result of having had these experiences—are the true experts in any investigation of those experiences. The researcher submits raw materials, and often the interpretations of those materials, to the participants, who check them for accuracy and for agreement with their own interpretations; these *member checks* provide additional indications of the validity of the study's conclusions.

• Although emphasizing recent research reports within the discipline, the researcher does not ignore older reports or relevant observations and thoughts found outside this discipline when reviewing the literature or searching for data and conceptualizations related to the topic being studied. Persons outside a professional discipline can approach topics with *fresh eyes,* or *beginner's mind,* enabling them to see things new or old in original and creative ways impossible for members of the in-group. The latter's perceptions and ways of thinking may have become overly narrowed, structured, and rigidified through excessive exposure to, and overlearning of, limited approaches. It is not uncommon to hear psychologists remark that philosophers, novelists, poets, artists, musicians, and those familiar with enduring spiritual or wisdom traditions frequently have more profound understandings of the human psyche and are better able to communicate those understandings than professional or academic psychologists. For this reason, it is wise not to overlook the insights of persons outside the researcher's immediate and related fields. Equally, ancient thoughts continue to have contemporary relevance; there are no limitations or expiration dates for valid knowledge or wisdom.

• Much of a researcher's energy is devoted to making original empirical observations and to creating theories, models, or conceptualizations that help account for those findings. There are, however, other forms of scholarship, research, and disciplined inquiry that involve conceptualizing or integrating old findings or different areas of learning, developing and implementing practical applications of research, and disseminating research findings to others through training and teaching. A researcher's attention and energy also go toward exploring the implications and practical outcomes or fruits of a research project. Significant research contributes to the knowledge gain of the discipline but also provides purposeful experiences and beneficial opportunities for the researcher, the participants, the audience of the research reports, and society at large.

• A researcher continues to publish original research findings and interpretations in peer-reviewed journals and to present these findings and
concepts at professional conferences to share research outcomes with
colleagues and to obtain feedback from peers. In addition to these outlets,
a researcher disseminates his or her thoughts to other audiences—in the
form of semipopular books; popular articles; media presentations; and
lectures, seminars, workshops, and trainings for professionals and for the
general public. These diverse publications and presentations ensure that
the researcher's contributions do not remain restricted to only certain small
groups but rather are shared with the community at large so that as many
as possible may benefit from the research. Unlike the conventional view,
the expanded view of research and disciplined inquiry does not privilege
any form of communication or education over another; each approach is
valued and appropriate for its own purposes.

These axioms and practices are elaborated elsewhere in this book,
especially in the chapters of Part II. Several of these, however, because they
are especially salient and are common to all the approaches described in
Part II, deserve special attention here.

THE SUBJECT MATTER OF
EXPANDED RESEARCH PROGRAMS

The expanded approaches to research and disciplined inquiry that we
present in this volume are especially suited to research topics involving
human experiences that are *personal, subjective, significant,* and *relevant.*
Personal experiences are those that researchers have directly encountered
in their own lives, that they consider to be significant, and about which
they would like to learn more. These events typically have been private,
subjective, and inwardly experiential; they may or may not have had
obvious external concomitants that could have been noticed, *at the time
the experience occurred,* by external observers. These experiences are rich,
however, and provide new insights, new and effective ways of dealing with
or transcending crises or difficulties, and new appreciations of the experiencer's deeper nature and of the nature of others and of the world. They
have had profound impacts and significant, perhaps radically transformative, influences on the experiencer's life. They may allow the experiencer

to rediscover, remember, and relive aspects of being and of self that had been forgotten, ignored, or neglected. Further, the experiences' transformative effects are not restricted to the experiencer alone; they affect others as well. These impacts may be on significant others, family members, friends and acquaintances, or society at large. Actions based on or motivated by these experiences may have profound political, social, and ethical consequences. Often, they inspire creative expressions through art, music, dance, drama, poetry, or other forms of writing that have far-reaching and persisting inspirational influence. In short, we are dealing here with Big Events. Their study cries out for and deserves research methods that are as powerful and encompassing as the experiences themselves.

THE QUALITIES AND ROLE OF THE RESEARCHER

The expanded methods recognize the critical importance and pervasive role of the researcher's qualities, sensitivities, and being in all phases of a research project. They do not attempt to minimize the role of the researcher or attempt to treat investigator influences as annoyances to be hidden beneath illusory veils of objective methodological stratagems, pretending that such influences cease to be active when they are ignored. Rather, the role of the investigator is highlighted and emphasized in these transpersonal approaches.

There is a view that one of the distinctions between clinical practice and research is that in the former, the practitioner can connect closely with and become part of the experiences of the client, whereas in the latter, the researcher must remain distant, apart, aloof, and uninvolved with what is being studied. We do not subscribe to that dichotomy, preferring, instead, to dissolve the usually firm boundary between these two activities. Much can be learned by sharing and partaking of experiences with participants in a research project, and much can be accomplished through thoughtful, careful, and discerning observations in clinical practice. These are complementary *human* qualities that have their appropriate places in all activities.

We have already mentioned the researcher's involvement in the selection of the topic to be studied, how the research question is framed, and how the research methods are chosen and employed. The investigator's prior familiarity with, and understandings of, the experiences being studied contribute to any research effort. The researcher's personal qualities and predispositions influence participant selection, and the qualities of personal interaction with participants during research sessions influence the nature and depth of the information that is disclosed. Although the researcher is implicitly involved in many ways even in objective quantitative research designs, in qualitative approaches the researcher is the actual measuring instrument, and his or her qualities and sensitivities become critically important. All materials are collected, processed, interpreted, and expressed through the filters that are the researcher's personal qualities.

In grounded theory, researcher qualities are recognized in the concept of *theoretical sensitivity,* in which the investigator's prior familiarity with what is studied and his or her observational and interpretative experiences and skills help inform the theories that are being developed along with data interactions throughout the research project (Glaser, 1978). Ecophilosopher Henryk Skolimowski (1994) has outlined a philosophy of participation in which mind, consciousness, evolution, reality itself—indeed, all modes of knowing, being, and becoming—are manifestations of the myriad *sensitivities* of all entities and creatures. For humans, our epistemology is simply a description of the spectrum of our various sensitivities, and our reality is cocreated through those sensitivities. For Skolimowski, *"The universe reveals nothing to the unprepared mind.* When the mind is prepared, through its strange magic, it co-creates with the universe" (italics in original; p. 82).

This notion of preparedness is addressed by economist-philosopher E. F. Schumacher (1978, pp. 39-60), who maintains that to know, apprehend, or experience within any realm, the knower and his or her organs, faculties, and capabilities must be appropriate to and appropriately prepared for the knowledge, apprehension, or experience; that is, the knower must have *adaequatio* (adequateness) with respect to that which is to be known. At a practical level, the microscopist or X-ray technician must possess an eye that is sufficiently practiced before being able to discern fully what the lenses or the photographic plates reveal. Schumacher cites a less mundane illustration from the *Majjhima Nikaya, LXX* Buddhist text:

> One can not, I say, attain supreme knowledge all at once; only by a gradual training, a gradual action, a gradual unfolding, does one attain perfect knowledge. In what manner? A man comes, moved by confidence; having come, he joins; having joined, he listens; listening, he receives the doctrine; having received the doctrine, he remembers it; he examines the sense of the things remembered; from examining the sense, the things are approved of;

having approved, desire is born; he ponders; pondering, he eagerly trains himself; and eagerly training himself, he mentally realises the highest truth itself and, penetrating it by means of wisdom, *he sees*. (p. 47)

Reality (being) and knowing are coconstitutive. We can perceive and know only that for which our sensitivities have prepared us, and these sensitivities depend on aspects of our being. The perennial wisdom is rich in acknowledgments of this principle: "We behold that which we are" (Underhill, 1911/1969, p. 423). "Only the Real can know Reality" (Underhill, 1911/1969, p. 436). "No man can create anything greater than his own soul" (Witherspoon, 1951, p. 1013). "In the world of spiritual realities, knowledge is always a function of being; the nature of what we experience is determined by what we ourselves are" (Aldous Huxley, quoted in Heard, 1949, p. 78). "To listen *to* the soul, they must listen *with* the soul" (Gerald Heard, quoted in White, 1984, p. 57). "If we change ourselves, changing our power of apprehension, we change the universe confronting us" (Heard, quoted in White, 1984, p. 62). "Every insight into the outer world must be balanced by an equally enlarged knowledge of [our] true and full nature" (Heard, quoted in White, 1984, p. 62).

As researchers, our preparedness, *adaequatio,* sensitivities, and being are shaped by our experiences, by what we learn from others in our research and application projects, and by the changes and transformations that occur in us through our personal growth and spiritual development. What happens and what we learn and become in each of these areas feed and are fed by the others, and every person influences and is influenced by all others. Thus, continual, dynamic interplay among research, practical application, and personal development loosens and dissolves the boundaries among these three areas. The states of being that develop in one area allow particular types of knowing to occur in other areas, and sensitivities mold being and being molds sensitivities in an endless cocreative, dialogical dance.

TELEOLOGICAL AND NARRATIVE CONSIDERATIONS

Since the 1960s, cognitive psychologists such as Jerome Bruner (1986, 1990) have advocated the importance of narrative and story in creating meaning throughout the human developmental cycle. Narrative therapies have recently become popular as forms of therapeutic intervention wherein clients are encouraged through time to create stories of their lives that include the possibilities of happy endings (Bruner, 1990). Likewise in theological analysis, finding analogous patterns between one's personal life, or the life of one's community, and the stories of scripture has been central to both Jewish and Christian thought—both scholarly and popular—for a long time. Enriched by psychological insight, the use of narrative strategies for interpreting personal or community life has been advanced in recent years as an emerging field known as *narrative theology* (e.g., Goldberg, 1982; Stroup, 1981).   Stoue

Narrative is particularly relevant to the field of transpersonal studies. Our stories form the core and nuances of our personal identities. Although rooted in specific historical, psychological, or spiritual events, stories plumb the depths of the human psyche, as if searching among the many narrative possibilities for interpretation and subtleties of meaning. Responsive to context, audience, and more recent events, stories unfold differently on each telling, if only slightly. Each telling brings new elements and joins different elements together in the advancing saga of telling the important stories of one's life, or the important stories of one's community, tribe, or people.

In telling a story, the past as remembered and retold sheds light on the present and implicates the future. We tell stories situated in the present, and, as we tell them, we transport the memories of the past into the present through memory and imagination. Implicitly, the phenomenology of telling a story cycles from present (in which the story is told) to the past (in which the story took place and is retained in memory) to the present again (as it is told) in a line of narrative projectory. The narrative projectory implicates and illuminates not only the present but also the future. The sweep of the narrative seems to bring the future more luminously present and possible because narratives inevitably point forward. Fueled by the dynamic of narrative, they inherently move forward bearing insight on present and future. The unknown terrain of the future seems more knowable and also more vivid, imaginable, and likely. In this way, like threads pulling us into the possibilities of the future, we live into our stories, not in a deterministic manner, but imaginatively. This movement, the projectory of the narrative, may even create new events in awareness—possibilities and realities scarcely imagined without the stories' thrust. Of course, stories rarely turn out as we hope and imagine. Yet while passing through our awareness, the stories may have helped create a projection of consciousness we commonly know as the future.

For transpersonal researchers, stories about spiritual experiences affect personal and consensual realities to support their validity. In telling our own stories of spiritual experiences and hearing those of others, spiritual experiences seem more vivid, imaginable, and, from the view of consciousness, more likely to occur again. Put directly, the more we can imagine ourselves experiencing the ineffable, the more possible the experiences seem. In that sense, we are dreaming our way into the future. Through the telling of stories, a more fully enriched spiritual awareness seems not only possible but more probable.

SCHOPENHAUER'S QUERY

This discussion of narrative and teleology brings to mind a wonderful essay of Arthur Schopenhauer (1851/1974). In "Transcendent Speculation on the Apparent Deliberateness in the Fate of the Individual," Schopenhauer points out how when one views one's life, retrospectively, it seems that "the course of an individual's life, however confused it appears to be, is a complete whole, in harmony with itself and having a definite tendency and didactive meaning, as profoundly conceived as is the finest epic" (p. 204)—that there is an "inner compass, [a] mysterious characteristic, that brings everyone correctly on to *that* path which for him is the only suitable one; but only after he has covered it does he become aware of its uniform direction" (p. 206). He elaborates this idea:

> The external operation of circumstances had to assist one another in the course of a man's life in such a way that, at the end thereof when it had been run through, they made it appear like a well-finished and perfected work of art, although previously, when it was still in the making, it had, as in the case of every planned work of art, the appearance of being often without any plan or purpose. But whoever came along after its completion and closely considered it, would inevitably gaze in astonishment at such a course of life as the work of the most deliberate foresight, wisdom, and persistence. (p. 207)
>
> [If we acknowledge the similarity of the individual life to a dream, we should] note the difference that in the mere dream the relation is one-sided . . . only one ego actually wills and feels, whereas the rest are nothing but phantoms. In the great dream of life, on the other hand, a mutual relation occurs, since not only does the one figure in the dream of the other exactly as is necessary, but also that other figures in his dream. Thus by virtue of a

real *harmonia praestabilita,* everyone dreams only what is appropriate to him . . . and all the dreams of life are so ingeniously interwoven that everyone gets to know what is beneficial to him and at the same time does for others what is necessary. . . . It is the great dream that is dreamed by that one entity, but in such a way that all its persons dream it together. (pp. 219-220)

Such thoughts bring to mind similar notions that are latent in the *participatory universe* (Wheeler, 1974) and *anthropic principle* (Barrow & Tipler, 1986; Polkinghorne, 1987) ideas of modern physics and cosmology. According to these views, the universe must have exactly the right and delicate balance, and extremely fine tuning, of its physical constituents, physical constants, laws of operation, and (perhaps) special initial circumstances as the universe now has for it to contain and sustain sentient creatures such as human beings who can inhabit, observe, and theorize about such a universe.

These theories, as well as Schopenhauer's musings, contain the teleological flavor of persons or histories being able to coordinate or assist themselves in bringing about optimal or expected ends or goals—benignly intervening on their own behalf. They contain suggestions that future goals perhaps may be able to influence earlier events in curious time-displaced ways. Could the endings of our stories somehow determine their beginnings and intermediate courses?

WORDS

The commonly understood meaning of *research* is to investigate thoroughly. The research methods presented in this volume are being developed not only to honor the breadth and depth of human experience but also to honor the thoroughness of a research endeavor. The proposed methods are more inclusive and more intensive than conventional research methods; only through such fullness can they do justice to the rich topics toward which they are directed.

If we look more closely at the meanings of *research,* we see that the word also suggests searching again, anew, back; going about again or going around again; and circling around again. This circling around again and again provides a fine metaphor for the research enterprise: By moving around a topic, examining it carefully from many perspectives, we eventually gain a more complete understanding of what we are examining. The image of the circle suggests completeness, wholeness, regularity, order, and, indeed, disciplined inquiry itself. The image and metaphor bring to mind a statement Carl Jung (1965) made in connection with personal growth and development: "There is no linear evolution; there is only circumambulation of the self" (p. 196).

As we circle around the object of inquiry, we look at it again and again. Another word also carries the flavor of repeated looking: *respect*. When we respect someone or something, we look again (*re-spect*), we pay special attention, we honor. The resemblances of these words suggest that at some important level, *research* and *respect* are synonymous. Both imply a fullness of attention, with minimal distortion, minimal filtering, minimal projection, minimal denial, and minimal preferences or biases.

Dwelling more deeply on a few additional words can convey a great deal about the nature of several approaches to research. The conventional, positivist approach to research *describes, explains, predicts, controls.* The heuristic approach *describes, understands, appreciates.* The feminist approach *tells, listens, emancipates, empowers.* The transpersonal approach *expands, enlarges, enriches, opens, interconnects* (within and without), *integrates, unifies, awakens, transcends, transforms,* and (ultimately and hopefully) *enlightens.*

CHAPTER 2

A PREVIEW OF
NEW METHODS

Rosemarie Anderson
William Braud

In a time when the sciences are expanding and the scientific community and the wider public are more attentive to spiritual values, researchers are seeking innovative and rigorous research methods to explore both the experiential *and* transformative nature of human experience. As we explored in depth in Chapter 1, these rich domains of human experience seemingly are often missed or trivialized within the scientific discourse of 19th-century positivism and 20th-century behaviorism and cognitive science, within the broad spectrum of science in general and within psychology in particular.

Thus, the field of transpersonal psychology and related endeavors—such as wellness health care, transpersonal medicine, mind-body therapies, psychospiritual dimensions of counseling, and consciousness studies—has arisen in the past 25 years to investigate these rich psychological and transformative domains of human experience. The field of transpersonal psychology has been immersed during these years with establishing itself as an academic discipline. The prevailing concerns of transpersonal psychologists during this period have been defining the discipline, especially the transpersonal; distinguishing the uniquely transformative aspects of spiritual development and maturity from emotional and intellectual maturity; and establishing the discipline's institutions and traditions of intellectual discourse. There has just been so much to do that developing research methods uniquely relevant to exploring the transformative dimensions of human nature has not received focused attention. Transpersonal researchers and graduate students tended to borrow research methods from the positivistic paradigm, rather than create their own. This book seeks to remedy this situation by providing transpersonal research methods that uniquely complement the dynamic nature of existential and transformative human experience.

At a time when scientific paradigms are shifting, the presentation of these new transpersonal research methods is timely. The widespread interest in spiritual concerns has created a more congenial atmosphere. Within the scientific community, the needs of conventional and transpersonal researchers are converging, to the point that it is sometimes hard to keep the players straight. Transpersonal researchers are starting to sound like conventional researchers concerned with validity, reliability, baselines, and proximal stimuli, and "hard" scientists are talking about the subjectivity of observation, the interconnectedness of mind and matter, and the influences of spiritual values and practices on physical health and well-being. During the past 25 years or so, conventional scientists in many disciplines have gradually grown weary of conventional research methods and attendant epistemologies. Some of them have already moved into a postpositivist paradigm. The field of transpersonal psychology is also ready—indeed eager—to engage the scientific community with its perspectives and insights.

In this book, we and our colleagues introduce five new transpersonal research approaches. Each approach seeks to honor the diversity and expansiveness of human experiences by facilitating comprehensive descriptions, analyses, and presentations of "the farther reaches of human nature," as Abraham Maslow (1969, 1971) beautifully expressed it nearly 30 years ago. The traditional values of precision, rigor, and clarity are extended and deepened to comprehensively explore topics addressing the transformative nature of human experiences, such as imagery and healing, synchronicity and personal growth, indigenous wisdoms and healing, the psychospiritual dimensions of martial arts, creativity, intuition, and synergistic leadership. The usual ways of knowing, analyzing data, and expressing findings are expanded to include alternate forms of knowledge, novel ways of working with collected data, and creative ways of expressing these findings. Quantitative methods that measure and isolate variables are no longer privileged over the in-depth and relational methods of qualitative research. Quantitative methods are encouraged, or blended with other methods, when appropriate to the facet of experience being studied. Seeking balance between quantitative and qualitative methods is a distinguishing feature of transpersonal research. Several of these methods advocate combining and blending qualitative and quantitative methods to provide rich and comprehensive portrayals of research topics. In its own way, each of the transpersonal research methods introduced in this book encourages expansion in conventional scientific discourse and in the conduct of research, especially in the conceptualization, analysis, and expression of research findings.

PREVIEWING THE FIVE
TRANSPERSONAL RESEARCH METHODS

The five new transpersonal research methods presented in Part II are crafted to accommodate the nature of spiritual and transcendent experiences. The understanding of *empirical* is defined closer to its etymological roots to include all experience.

In Chapter 3, "Integral Inquiry: Complementary Ways of Knowing, Being, and Expression," *integral inquiry* is introduced by William Braud. Integral inquiry provides both a comprehensive overview of psychological research methods and a means to apply and blend these methods to a particular research topic. Beginning with the affirmation that human experience is multileveled and complex, research methods must be correspondingly multifaceted and pluralistic. Researchers and practitioners in applied areas are encouraged to expand and extend conventional research, clinical practice, and other applications both to learn more about ordinary human experiences and to develop means of exploring exceptional human experiences. Such methods inherently help expand the knowledge base of scholarly disciplines in new and important ways. The cornerstone of integral inquiry is the presentation of a continuum of qualitative and quantitative research methods, both conventional and avant-garde, from which researchers may choose (or blend) methods to best suit their research questions. Integral inquiry is then extended to include alternative forms of knowing (collecting data), alternative ways of working with the data (analyzing data), and alternative ways of expressing findings (presenting results). These innovative extensions include consideration of the transformative effects on the researcher, research participants, and intended audience as a result of participating in research endeavors, especially when investigating the nature of transpersonal experiences.

In Chapter 4, "Intuitive Inquiry: A Transpersonal Approach," *intuitive inquiry* is proposed by Rosemarie Anderson. Intuitive inquiry brings a heuristic, phenomenological, and feminist focus to using various modes of intuition in conducting research. Essential features of the method include compassion as instrumental to gleaning a comprehensive understanding of a research topic and the importance of particularity (especially the researcher's voice and the participant's voice) in communicating the unique and yet potentially universal nature of the experiences studied. Intuitive inquiry uses transpersonal skills, such as intuition and alternative states of consciousness, as core methods of inquiry. Research investigations are enriched and expanded by applying transpersonal skills to every level of inquiry, including choosing a compelling research topic, collecting data from a wide variety of sources, incorporating the researcher's insights, analyzing data through a variety of intuitive modalities, and interactively communicating results to the intended audience(s). A variety of innovative concepts are proposed, including sympathetic resonance and circles of sympathetic resonance as validating procedures for research findings, "trickstering" as a means to enliven research, and ritualizing intention to guide and sustain the research endeavor.

In Chapter 5, "Transpersonal Awareness in Phenomenological Inquiry: Philosophy, Reflections, and Recent Research," Ron Valle and Mary Mohs bring a transpersonal awareness to phenomenological methods of inquiry. Beginning with a discussion of the existential-phenomenological perspective that informs *phenomenological inquiry,* they provide an inspiring analysis suggesting that transcendent/transpersonal awareness is "prior to" any prereflective structure of a particular experience. This transpersonal awareness is not of the phenomenal realm of perceiver and perceived but rather of a noumenal, unitive space from which both intentional consciousness and phenomenal experience manifest in life. When the transpersonal presents itself in awareness, these experiences can be explored using empirical phenomenological research methods. A preliminary analysis of seven recent phenomenological studies of experiences with transpersonal qualities revealed 11 common themes interwoven throughout the descriptions of these experiences: transcendent awareness manifesting through the vehicle of a given experience, intense emotional or passionate states, being in the present moment, transcendence of space and time, expansion of boundaries and sense of connectedness, stillness or peace, sense of knowing, unconditional love, feeling graced, ineffability, and self-transformation.

In Chapter 6, "Organic Research: Feminine Spirituality Meets Transpersonal Research," a discussion of *organic research* is presented that has grown from a research group including Jennifer Clements, Dorothy Ettling, Dianne Jenett, and Lisa Shields. The fundamental technique of organic research is telling and listening to stories. The topic of an organic research study grows out of the researcher's own story, and the methods used in the research are expected to creatively evolve in response to influences from within the researcher's psyche and from external events that affect the work in progress. At its core is an emphasis on the transformative power of inviting, listening to, and presenting individual participants' stories about significant experiences, using the participants' voices and words as much as possible. Because the story of a study is recorded and told in the researcher's voice, organic research presupposes a moderately high level of psychospiritual development by an organic researcher. Ultimately, organic research seeks to nourish personal transformation in the researcher, coresearchers (research participants), and readers, alike.

In Chapter 7, "Becoming More Human As We Work: The Reflexive Role of Exceptional Human Experience," Rhea A. White invites researchers to record insights and exceptional experiences that so often inform or prompt scientific investigations. In keeping a record of exceptional human experiences (EHEs) during one's life (EHE autobiography) and EHEs connected with one's research (scientific EHE autobiography), the dynamic growing edge of personal and scientific exploration is not only recorded but also creatively invited. White has provisionally classed EHEs in five broad categories: mystical experiences, psychic experiences, unusual death-related experiences, encounter experiences, and exceptional normal experiences. Such experiences may occur throughout life, and many of them can provide insights to professionals. By bringing spontaneous occurrences of research-related EHEs into scientific discourse, EHEs can provide new forms of knowing and insight to research from within the scientific paradigm itself. *Insight banks* for gathering EHEs related to scientific inquiry are proposed, and an on-line means of communicating is provided.

By advocating transpersonal approaches to research and presenting unique methods, we and our colleagues hope to enliven the imagination of researchers and to stimulate innovative inquiries to uniquely accommodate the facet of human experience under investigation. These five new transpersonal research methods represent a modest but substantial beginning in creating research methods that enrich and refresh our understanding of the nature of human experience with a renewed sense of creativity and insight. As Henryk Skolimowski (1994, 1996) reminds us, we live in a vast and participatory universe; our methodologies must applaud and recognize our unique and necessary involvement. If our nature is vast, our methods must be creative, mutable, and open-ended. Consider these transpersonal research methods as starting points in discovering new ways to investigate this dynamic nature of human experience. Together with the generativity of like-minded researchers and the present shifting scientific paradigm, transpersonal research methods will continue to develop as pathways for investigating and abetting "the farther reaches of human nature."

OTHER SECTIONS OF THE BOOK

The five chapters of Part II represent, we feel, the heart of this book. Chapter 1 of Part I provided the context, and indicated the need, for these new methodological extensions. The three chapters of Part III describe particular, concrete illustrations of some of the creative ways in which features of the five new methods already have been realized in recent research projects. Part IV indicates possible directions for further elaborations of transpersonal research methods. Chapter 11 provides ways in which expanded research methods can contribute to a broader view of validity in scientific research. In Chapter 12, we consider ethical issues and the responsibilities of practitioners of these new methods. We present a simple model of important features common to research, application, and psychospiritual development—principles of mindfulness, discernment, understanding and appreciation, transformation of self, and transformation of others. For quick reference, and for assisting students and researchers in selecting the most appropriate methods for exploring their research topics, we present summaries of many old and new research approaches in three appendixes. We indicate the strengths and weaknesses of the various approaches and provide illustrative examples and references to additional resources. Finally, we give a listing of graduate degree-granting centers that emphasize transpersonal studies. References for all chapters are consolidated in a complete listing at the end of the book.

PART II

EXPANDED METHODS OF DISCIPLINED INQUIRY

CHAPTER 3

INTEGRAL INQUIRY

Complementary Ways of Knowing, Being, and Expression

William Braud

> The one consciousness which is whole and integral thus divides
> into two streams in order to provide this subjective-objective
> play of manifestation—this *Lila* of *Bhagavan*.
>
> —I. K. Taimni (1975, p. 361)

Two complementary parables from India set the stage for this chapter. The first is the well-known tale of the blind men and the elephant (see Davids, 1911; Meier, 1982). Each person reaches a different conclusion about the nature of the beast as a result of exploring what is only a part of the whole. The other is a more modern saying: "If you wish to find water, it is better to dig one 60-foot well than to dig six 10-foot wells." These parables point to the importance of breadth and plurality of approaches, as well as depth and intensity of approach, to appreciate or access the abundance of life's rich, yet sometimes hidden, treasures.

These guidelines have obvious applicability in clinical and other professional practices, as well as in research endeavors in psychology and in the other human sciences. The wisdom of these complementary approaches of breadth and depth, however, goes strangely unheeded in many clinical and

35

research projects. Too often, researchers cling to a single method or to a small number of methods with which we and our clinical or research subcultures have become familiar but that may not be the most appropriate for addressing the issues at hand. My aim, in this chapter, is to suggest ways to expand and extend our research and practical applications to learn more about ordinary human experiences and begin to develop new means of disciplined inquiry for exploring some of the more exceptional human experiences that we heretofore have ignored.

INTEGRAL INQUIRY: EXPANDING RESEARCH THROUGH COMPLEMENTARY QUANTITATIVE AND QUALITATIVE APPROACHES

As a first step in this endeavor, we as researchers can expand the range of questions to ask about our subject matter and recognize that there exist many research methods that vary greatly in their appropriateness for addressing different types of questions. In doing this, we are mindful of Carl Jung's (1993) statement: "Ultimate truth, if there be such a thing, demands the concert of many voices" (p. xiv), while also remembering the caveat of our British colleague John Beloff (1990): "If we are barking up the wrong tree then we shall not find what we are looking for no matter what kind of ladders we use" (p. 128).

Table 3.1 indicates four major types of questions researchers can ask about subject matter. These are the same types of questions for which we seek answers in our clinical work—in the contexts of both particular clients or larger classes of clients. The four types of questions, and the research methods that best serve them, are arrayed along a continuum from the more qualitative to the more quantitative and from the more idiographic to the more nomothetic. The four clusters of questions and methods also correspond nicely to the familiar research objectives of understanding, explanation, prediction, and control. Of course, many of the methods can be used in multiple ways and can be tailored to suit more than one type of question or concern. Table 3.1 is subject to flexible rearrangements and modifications; by no means is it intended to represent a rigid classification of approaches. For example, *surveys* is listed in the left-most column of the table because surveys could be used to describe the experiences themselves of large numbers of respondents. To the extent that survey results—especially as they are conventionally used—may be treated quantitatively, however, the survey method also could be placed in the quantitative section of the table, perhaps as a precursor to the second column from the right (examining one variable quantitatively, rather than the relationships of two or more variables).

The four clusters of methods can be understood as complementary sets of tools useful for addressing different aspects of a particular research issue or human experience—four ways of "feeling the elephant" that is the issue being explored. It is possible to adapt these methods for use in exploring exceptional human experiences and topics appropriate to the developing field of transpersonal studies.

Transpersonal psychology is concerned with experiences and processes that extend beyond the personal or individual, that go beyond the usual limits of ego and personality. It studies consciousness and unusual states of consciousness; exceptional experiences; transegoic development; individuation; and spiritual experiences, growth, and transformation. It concerns itself with "the study of humanity's highest potential, and with the recognition, understanding, and realization of unitive, spiritual, and transcendent states of consciousness" (Lajoie & Shapiro, 1992, p. 91). It seeks to learn how people can become more whole through integrating the somatic, emotional, intellectual, spiritual, creative-expressive, and relationship and community aspects of their lives.

Causes and Outcomes

The cluster of experiment-like methods at the extreme right of Table 3.1 is well known to researchers. These methods are well suited for exploring causal questions and for assessing the effectiveness of various treatments or interventions. Of all the methods, these provide the greatest feelings of confidence in conclusions, and they yield the least ambiguous findings. For this payoff, however, they sacrifice depth of understanding and lose knowledge of the contexts, complexities, and richness of what is being studied. Their use can encourage superficial appreciations of artificial or incomplete forms of what researchers are seeking to study. Devotees of these methods mimic the approaches of the natural sciences in seeking to learn the universal laws that govern simple systems in isolated contexts, knowing and controlling relevant variables, and attempting to keep "everything else equal or constant." Most laboratory work in neuroscience, cognitive science, clinical and medical outcome research, and experimental parapsychology makes use of these approaches.

TABLE 3.1 Conventional Disciplined Inquiry Methods That Closely Match Four Major Types of Research Questions

		Continuum	
Qualitative — Quantitative			
Idiographic			Nomothetic
(Understand)	(Explain)	(Predict)	(Control)
Qualitative Methods		**Quantitative Methods**	
EXPERIENCE	CONCEPTUALIZATION	PROCESS	FRUITS
What is the experience of *x*? How is *x* perceived by the participant?	How can we conceptualize *x*? What are useful explanations or interpretations of *x*?	How does *x* unfold as a process? What are the concomitants of *x*? What sets the stage for the occurrence of *x*? What facilitates *x*? What inhibits *x*?	What are the outcomes, consequences, "fruits" of *x*?
Phenomenological Heuristic Narrative Life stories Case studies Feminist approaches Organic approach Interview Questionnaires Surveys	Theoretical Historical Grounded theory Textual analysis Discourse analysis Hermeneutic	Correlational Causal-comparative Field studies	Experimental Quasi-experimental Single-subject Action research

In transpersonal studies, these methods could be used to assess the outcomes, consequences, side effects, and other "fruits" of particular experiences (e.g., meditative conditions and altered states of consciousness) or of deliberate practices or training exercises (e.g., certain spiritual disciplines, special breath work, and particular ways of working with dreams). The experiment-like methods could be used to assess possible effects of engaging in specific forms of creative expression (such as working with self-produced mandalas) or of participating in rituals developed to ease passage through liminal conditions (e.g., when an individual disidentifies with an older way of being to reidentify with a newer way).

In our own work, my colleagues and I have made extensive use of experimental methods in exploring alternative, nonlocal modes of knowing and influence. In series of experiments, we have learned how persons are able to access information, hidden at remote locations, through direct knowing for which they are prepared through psychological and psycho-physiological procedures (Braud, 1975, 1978, 1982). We also have found that persons are able to directly influence random or labile inanimate or animate systems (e.g., radioactive decay-based random event generators, small animals, human red blood cells in test tubes, the sympathetic nervous system activity of distant persons, and distant persons' concentration/attentional skills), mentally and at a distance, through processes of atten-tion, intention, and visualization (Braud, 1990, 1992, 1993, 1994a, 1994d; Braud & Schlitz, 1989, 1991; Braud, Shafer, & Andrews, 1993a, 1993b; Braud, Shafer, McNeill, & Guerra, 1995). These latter studies provide reliable empirical evidence for human potentials or abilities beyond those that are mediated by conventional sensorimotor processes or conventional energetic and informational exchanges. Variations of these same abilities are frequently described within many, if not all, of the various spiritual and wisdom traditions.

An important concept within transpersonal psychology is interconnect-edness. The *trans* in *transpersonal* conveys two aspects of that connected-ness. One meaning of *trans* is "beyond"; it implies the existence of, and connectedness with and relationship to, something beyond the individual. Another meaning of *trans* is "through"; this implies a connectedness among the various aspects of oneself, as well as a connectedness of oneself with others and with all of Nature. It is difficult to understand how direct knowing of events remote in time or space, or direct mental influence of remote animate and inanimate systems, can occur without presupposing a profound interconnectedness among people and also between people and all of animate and inanimate Nature. This interconnectedness has impor-tant implications for our understanding of who we really are, of our individuality, of our true selves; from these implications flow other, ethical implications for appropriately interacting with others and with our envi-ronment.

The visible parts of trees in a dense forest seem to be separate entities until one looks beneath the surface of the earth and finds the extensive, interconnected root systems that bind the trees together. The peaks of mountains shrouded in mist seem isolated and unconnected until the mist melts away, revealing the common lower continuities that previously had been obscured. These two metaphors help us appreciate aspects of the interconnectedness that is emphasized and studied by transpersonal psy-chologists. The concept is beautifully expressed by the 13th-century Persian mystical poet Jelaluddin Rumi (1984):

I've heard it said there's a window that opens
from one mind to another,
but if there's no wall, there's no need
for fitting the window, or the latch. (p. 10)[1]

Process, Concomitants, and Modulating Factors

Leaving the laboratory to explore everyday life occurrences, we can move to the familiar methods described in the second cluster from the right in Table 3.1. Here, we observe interrelationships among naturally occurring events (a correlational approach) and look for additional but as yet unknown, and possibly causal, differences between individuals or groups that are already known to differ in some other way (a "causal-comparative" approach; see Borg & Gall, 1989, pp. 535-571). In making this move, we gain advantages through including a far greater number of events to study as well as naturally occurring events that cannot be duplicated readily in the laboratory. The price we pay for this gain is a loss in certainty about our findings. Causal conclusions become risky, and hosts of extraneous and possibly confounding variables arise.

In transpersonal contexts, correlational and causal-comparative strategies could be used to explore research questions such as the following: Which preexisting characteristics might discriminate persons who have or do not have near-death experiences under comparable circumstances? Is there a relationship between the "density" of deliberate transpersonal practices and spontaneously occurring transpersonal experiences and the nature of one's recovery from childhood sexual abuse (Schellenberg, 1997)? How do sense of humor and spirituality relate to freedom from stress and presence of positive life satisfaction and well-being in HIV-positive and HIV-negative males (Maas, 1998)? What are the concomitants—in physical and psychological health and well-being, meaning in life, and personal and spiritual growth and transformation—of disclosure-facilitated assimilation of exceptional human experiences such as mystical, unitive, "psychic," and death-related experiences (Palmer, 1998)?

Conceptualization

We use the approaches of the next cluster in Table 3.1 to conceptualize and theorize about findings or about the particular issues being investigated. Historical considerations can help contextualize the issue and provide additional types of explanations. Hermeneutic methods can be used to explore latent, hidden meanings and can yield more complete interpretations. The risks of such methods are uncertainties about the validity of interpretations and the possibility of empirically empty generalizations, or self-consistent and seemingly valid theories or models that can be tested and possibly falsified only with great difficulty, if at all. The needed reality tests in this cluster of methods are not always available or sought.

Some of the methods within this cluster (e.g., theory and model building and the historical method) are familiar to psychologists. Other methods (e.g., grounded theory, textual readings, discourse analysis, and hermeneutics) originated in disciplines other than psychology, have been imported into psychology only recently, and are still relatively unknown to conventional psychological researchers. (See Harré & Stearns, 1995, and Smith, Harré, & Van Langenhove, 1995a, 1995b, for information about these and related new methodological approaches within psychology.)

A conceptual, theoretical approach is appropriate for developing and testing models or theories of human psychospiritual growth and development, such as those proposed by Underhill (1911/1969), Maslow (1968, 1970), Wilber (1990), Washburn (1990), and Ruumet (1997). Historical methods could explore the nature of mystical experiences through the ages, whether there have been temporal changes in the character of the "perennial wisdom," and factors that may have been involved in the many migrations of Eastern spiritual teachers to the United States at the turn of this century, and so forth.

Experiences Themselves

We move to the cluster at the extreme left of Table 3.1 to gain the greatest appreciation of experiences themselves and of the ways in which the actual experiencers perceive and interpret their experiences and the events in their lives. Here, we can explore in great depth and intensity; here, we can dig a 60-foot well. Here, we gain richness and completeness of description, a view from the inside, an understanding of the contexts in which experiences and events occur, and an appreciation of the complex, dynamic, and often subtle ways in which events and experiences come together and play themselves out in the lives of particular individuals. In return for these gains, we pay the price of reduced certainty about the actual referents and sources of experiences and events and become uncertain about the contributions or importance of particular perceived interrelationships or connections among the experiences and events. Unless contrasts or comparisons are introduced or considered, how can we know whether we are really describing what we think we are describing? But these questions and concerns reveal the importing of particular ontological and epistemological approaches, assumptions, biases, and values into this realm. These questions are natural, useful, and answerable when we are working in the right-most parts of Table 3.1; are they appropriate, however, in the left-most reaches of Table 3.1? In gaining a description (a rich, thorough, "thick," and deep "snapshot") of a complex system, we seem to give up certainty about specific subcomponents and their causal interplay. Indeed, we may ask whether concepts such as component or cause are even appropriate in this new context.

There appears to be an interesting dance between richness and fullness of description, and certainty as to source, referent, and process. Rich description and certainty seem to be contraries or complements—neither can be reduced to the other, and both are necessary to a complete understanding of the whole. This dance of the complements reminds us of similar dances between various complements in physics, such as light-as-particle and light-as-wave. Physicist friends say that they use the term *complementary conjugates* to describe these yin-yang processes. The root of *conjugates* implies playing together. Complements play or dance together. This dance too often is seen as a conflict or battle in which the two fight with or oppose one another. This interpretation or judgment encourages either/or thinking in which one feels compelled to favor one or the other. How strange to favor one partner in a dance or to think that the dance could happen with only one dancer. Again, we can turn to Rumi (1983):

> *Never in truth does the lover seek*
> *without being sought by his beloved*
> *No sound of clapping comes from one hand*
> *without the other hand.* (Vol. 3, lines 4393, 4397)[2]

We have come full circle. The richness, synthesis, and subjectivity of Table 3.1's left-most cluster need the discrimination, analysis, and objectivity of the right-most cluster to make the dance complete. Each of the four clusters provides a set of questions and approaches useful for appreciating a particular aspect of an entire issue or experience that we are seeking to investigate. For the outcome of our research to be faithful to the whole of what we are studying, we would combine methods and questions from all parts of Table 3.1 and blend the different views to form a more complete picture. This approach is true to the etymology of the word *research*, which has to do with circling around again. Table 3.1 helps us recognize and remember what is included with great density and what is excluded in each method or cluster of methods. It can provide leads for enriching what we already are doing to make accounts of our investigations more complete and more balanced.

Storytelling and Story Listening: Experiences Revisited

In exploring Cluster 1 (the left-most cluster of Table 3.1) more thoroughly, we find that something most interesting and magical may begin to happen for those engaged in these forms of research. The conventional boundaries between research, practical application, and personal growth and transformation can melt away. As we provide our research participants (or *coresearchers*, as they are more appropriately called) opportunities to describe their experiences and life stories—typically in the form of in-depth, semistructured, or unstructured interviews—three things begin to happen at once. First, the interaction becomes a research session by providing new information and knowledge that can contribute to the development of our discipline. Second, it also becomes a clinical session by offering the participants/coresearchers an opportunity to learn more about themselves, more fully integrate and assimilate materials, and work through important issues more thoroughly than before. This is especially likely if relevant and important topics have been chosen for the research project. Stated somewhat differently, the opportunity to tell one's story and to speak one's own voice has *healing power.* Third, hearing the stories of participants/coresearchers and working together with them on the issues addressed in the research project can result in change and transformation in ourselves as investigators. We can do our own work and progress in our personal and spiritual growth and development in the context of conducting research. All three processes occur simultaneously, and each feeds the others in synergetic ways.

There is undeniable evidence that recognizing, owning, honoring, and sharing personal experiences, especially an individual's more unusual or previously unvoiced experiences, are beneficial to physical health and psychological well-being. All counseling, psychotherapeutic, and spiritual guidance traditions are based on this truism. I call your attention, however, to six particular sets of findings to concretize this concept.

James Pennebaker and his coworkers have been studying the psychological and physiological correlates of confession, self-disclosure, and confiding of significant experiences. They have found that even relatively brief disclosures of personal and traumatic experiences (especially those that have been kept secret from others) are associated with improvements in health and well-being as measured by various psychophysiological indexes, symptoms, physician visits, and immunological reactions (Berry & Pennebaker, 1993; Harber & Pennebaker, 1992; Pennebaker, 1995; Pennebaker, Barger, & Tiebout, 1989; Pennebaker, Hughes, & O'Heeron, 1987; Pennebaker, Kiecolt-Glaser, & Glaser, 1988; Pennebaker & Susman, 1988). Although processes of catharsis, extinction, and disinhibition undoubtedly play important roles in Pennebaker's results, perhaps the most important health-facilitating aspect of disclosure is that the process allows reconceptualizations or cognitive changes as the experiences are shared and explored from new and different views. Certain experiences no longer are shut off and isolated from the rest of a person's experiences. The previously ostracized experiences can return to the fold, and the increased wholeness resulting from these new integrations favors greater well-being. Mishara (1995) proposes a phenomenological explanation for the results of Pennebaker's research projects, suggesting that the healing factor in such writing or talking cures is the changed relationship of the participant to his or her past painful experience, facilitated by the narrative act itself; there is a change in the participant's total bodily attitude and in his or her entire being or sense of self.

Ian Wickramasekera (1989) has found that the majority of his patients who present somatic complaints have either high or low hypnotic susceptibility. Those who are highly hypnotically susceptible tend to report parapsychological and other unusual experiences. As the patients discuss these experiences and assimilate them more thoroughly into their lives, they experience remission of their somatic symptoms.

Herbert Otto (1967) conducted group work in which participants recalled and shared their "Minerva experiences" (MEs), which he defined as *"a network of highly formative and growthful experiences, having strongly positive affective components and playing a dominant role in the genesis of personality resources, and thus significantly affecting personality development*" (italics in original; p. 119). Otto viewed MEs as similar to, but more general than, Maslow's (1963) "peak experiences" (p. 117). Otto was especially interested in MEs occurring during the first 18 years of people's lives. These MEs tended to involve significant relationships with others; experiences related to achievement or recognition; nostalgic experiences; and experiences associated with religion, music, nature, animals, or food. These experiences, which might be viewed as the opposites of traumatic experiences, appeared to have long-lasting, beneficial influences on the participants' later attitudes, strengths, and self-concepts. Recalling and disclosing MEs in small-group contexts were associated with new insights, powerful upsurges of energy, resurgence of interests and desires to further develop skills and abilities, and enhanced self-images and ego-supportive values. Some participants identified their work with MEs as a turning point in their development (Otto, 1967, p. 123).

Thomas Driver (1991) has discussed the important and transformational concomitants of confessional performance and self-revelation. Rhea White (1993a, 1993b) has pointed out the relevance of Driver's ideas to exceptional human experiences and has indicated that through acknowledging and confessing our own experiences, we may grow in understanding them. In addition, disclosure may somehow increase the reality of our experiences to ourselves, to others, and perhaps to the physical world as well. I have made similar points about the benefits of confession and profession of unusual experiences in a prior paper (Braud, 1994b).

An obvious place in which to observe the power of disclosure is in dreamwork. As individuals move along the continuum of being aware of their own dreams, paying increased attention to them, recalling them, recording them, sharing them with significant others, sharing them with groups of people, associating to them, elaborating them, amplifying them, dramatizing them in the form of drawings and other creative expressions, and acting them out, their dreams' reality and impact increase. Montague Ullman's work (Ullman & Zimmerman, 1979) with small dreamwork groups indicates some of the benefits that can occur through the more public sharing of previously private experiences.

Contributing to the appeal and power of the various feminist research approaches (e.g., Nielsen, 1990) are their emphases on the voices of the Others, providing opportunities for unassimilated *others* (other persons and other experiences that have not been valued or privileged within the dominant culture) to speak their own stories with their own voices and opportunities for these voices to be listened to and honored. Unassimilated others result in separation and fragmentation, "dis-ease" of the individual and of the greater group, and an incompleteness of worldview. Assimilating others, through storytelling and story listening, facilitates integration and wholeness, health and well-being of the individual and of the greater group, and the framing of a more adequate and more complete worldview. Encouraging and attending to a pluralism of voices within feminist research approaches are emancipating, empowering, and health facilitating.

The sorts of impacts mentioned above are most likely to occur when a researcher uses the methods to the left of Table 3.1, but the methods to the right of Table 3.1 can be used to assess and document the impacts and confirm that they actually occur. This provides still another illustration of how the different methods can cooperatively support one another.

Feminist research approaches emphasize characteristics of the research enterprise that typically are neglected in more conventional treatments of the nature of scientific research. Accessible treatments of these complementary qualities of inquiry may be found in Shepherd (1993) and in Ullman (1995). An appreciation of the flavor of these qualities can be gained from the chapter titles and subtitles of Shepherd's book *Lifting the Veil: The Feminine Face of Science*. In these chapters, she deals with topics of feeling (research motivated by love), receptivity (listening to nature), subjectivity (discovering ourselves through the experiment), multiplicity (webs of interaction), nurturing (a long-term approach), cooperation (working in harmony), intuition (another way of knowing), relatedness (a vision of wholeness), and social responsibility of science (research that has significant impacts).

The organic research method, described in Chapter 6, builds on and extends feminist research. It emphasizes the sacred, inclusive, subjective, experiential and contextual, transformative, transpersonal, individual, and understandable features of the investigative endeavor. This approach, usually in combination with compatible feminist, phenomenological, and case study methods, has already been employed in several doctoral dissertation projects at the Institute of Transpersonal Psychology, where the approach was developed (Ettling, 1994; Newton, 1996; Safken, 1997; Shields, 1995; Spencer, 1995; Taylor, 1996). The organic approach has been used to explore topics such as the creative arts, embodiment, and transformation; experiences of the interstices or "the space between" in the body disciplines of Aikido and fencing; Sufi stories as vehicles for self-development; beauty, body image, and the deep feminine; transpersonal aspects of painting; and women's experience of the "descent into the underworld" and the path of Inanna. Some of these projects are described in Part III of this volume.

Alternative Ways of Knowing

Within the feminist, organic, and narrative approaches to research is a common emphasis on hearing and honoring the voices of the other person, particularly the previously unempowered person or the member of a previously unempowered group. The heuristic research approach, as developed by Clark Moustakas (1990) and his colleagues, also emphasizes a plurality of voices. Some of the voices are those of different persons whose varied inputs are valued in the research effort; these are the voices of interviewed participants, of the investigator herself or himself, and of others who have researched or written their own views of the experience being studied. Still other voices, however, represent different modes of knowing and of expressing one's knowing. Thus, the heuristic researcher is not limited only to data generated within the discipline of psychology but explores, as well, findings from the other human sciences, from the humanities, from the arts, and from the various spiritual and wisdom traditions—anything that bears on the experience being researched and that promises to contribute to a full and rich depiction of the studied topic. The heuristic researcher also values his or her own tacit knowledge— intuitive and body-based knowings that are difficult to put into words. The heuristic method has much in common with the creative process. Indeed, a creative synthesis, to which many attributes of the researcher can contribute, is part of the final outcome of the research project (see Wendy Rogers's contribution to Part III).

Heuristic research yields perhaps the richest and most satisfying description of an important human experience to which the researcher has devoted extensive and deep attention for a long time. A prototypical example of the heuristic approach is Moustakas's (1961) classic study of the experience of loneliness, in which he deeply immersed himself in as many aspects of the experience as possible for a lengthy period.

Two additions to the heuristic method would make the picture even more complete. Within the approach, places are not provided for direct social action or for conceptualizing and theorizing about the experiences being studied. The final presentation of a heuristic research project can be sufficiently complete, accurate, moving, and impelling to lead to subsequent social actions by those who read and resonate to the findings of the report. Such follow-up responses themselves could be studied—either by an addition to the method itself or by other, complementary methods. Aspects of action research, in which investigators study and evaluate what they do as they provide an actual service to a community (typically in the form of a new or already existing service program), could be added to a heuristic project to study aftereffects or consequences. Certain aspects of the feminist research approach also could be added to provide an additional dimension of social change.

Although theorization and conceptualization are played down by heuristic (and phenomenological) researchers—in favor of heeding Husserl's imperative, "Back to the things themselves" (cited in Valle, King, & Halling, 1989, p. 9), or in this case, to the experiences themselves—there is no reason to avoid thinking about findings and experiences as well as simply providing rich and deep descriptions of them. Thinking and interpretation may indeed interfere with experiencing per se, and it may be necessary to bracket the former so they do not interfere with or distort the latter. At some point, however, thinking, interpreting, conceptualizing, modeling, and theorizing can be unbracketed and brought back into the fold to yield a more complete account of the topic. In Jungian terms, researchers need not leave their thinking function forever at the door while inviting the sensing, feeling, and intuiting functions inside for the feast. After all, thinking is an experience, too, and thoughts, interpretations, and meanings are parts of the contexts in which other experiences take place.

Some Bolder Additions and Extensions

There are many ways of knowing and of working with and expressing that knowing, yet research enterprises typically have attempted to explore only narrow ranges of a wide spectrum of possibilities. Clues that may help us expand our research practices, and hence enlarge our store of public knowledge, are found in diverse traditions.

For example, Origen (185-254 C.E.) recognized three approaches to scriptural meanings and interpretations: seeking literal, concrete meanings (*somatikos*); developing meanings through intellectual, logical, and associational means (*psychikos*); and seeking spiritual, allegorical, symbolic, and metaphorical meanings (*pneumatikos*); see Latourette (1975, p. 150), Nigg (1962, p. 46), and Temple (1990, pp. 33-34). If we heed the suggestion of recent researchers that a vast variety of subject matters (not only literal documents but also life stories, lives, and experiences) can be considered as texts to be interpreted and understood, then perhaps we can apply analogues of Origen's three methods to this endeavor.

Ibn Al Arabi (1981; 1164-1240 C.E.) recognized three forms of knowledge: through information, through experience, and through being. He likened the first form to knowing a fruit through reading about it, the second form to knowing a fruit through direct experience of its qualities (its weight, texture, odor, and taste), and the third form to consuming and assimilating the fruit into one's being (Schneck, 1980). Analogues of these three forms of knowing could be incorporated into present-day research.

Bonaventura (1217-1274 C.E.) and Hugh of St. Victor (1096-1141 C.E.) recognized at least three realms of being and three ways of accessing these realms. They used the metaphor of three eyes to describe three modes of knowing. A physical, sensory realm is accessed by the *eye of the flesh;* a mental realm of ideas, thoughts, and images is perceived by the *eye of the mind;* and a transcendental or spiritual realm is known through the *eye of the spirit* (see Bonaventura, 1259/1953). Perhaps analogues of these three eyes could be used in our research.

More recently, Reason and Heron (1995) have suggested four forms of knowledge: *propositional* knowledge (knowing about something, expressed in statements and theories), *practical* knowledge (knowing how to do something, expressed in a skill or competence), *experiential* knowledge (gained through direct face-to-face encounters with persons, places, or things), and *presentational* knowledge (through which tacit knowing is translated into imagery and then symbolically expressed through movement, sound, color, shape, line, poetry, story, and drama). As researchers, we can provide formal places for each of these knowings in our research designs and reports.

To extend Bonaventura's metaphor, we can view our typical research efforts as observing the world through one eye, processing and interpreting what we perceive with one brain, and expressing what we have learned through one mouth. The one eye is the sensory eye of perception of external, sensory information; typically, we restrict even this information to visual and auditory information. The one brain is the left-hemispheric, verbal, linear, analytical processing of information. The one mouth is the mouth of verbal expression through linear prose. In working with questionnaires or with depth interviews (even within alternative approaches such as phenomenological, feminist, and heuristic procedures), we collect vast quantities of words from articulate participants. As investigators, we then process, filter, organize, cook, and distill those words while in an alert, active state of consciousness, using primarily our word-serving left hemi-sphere. We express what we have learned by outputting still other words and delivering these in learned treatises to our readers who receive these words and add them to their own stores of words and verbal concepts. It is possible to expand each of these phases of research and, in doing so, to enlarge both what we can learn about our topic and the research enterprise itself.

The heuristic approach has already opened up all three channels. It welcomes the addition of bodily based knowing (obtained through a technique known as *focusing;* see Gendlin, 1978), intuition, and tacit knowing. It includes incubation periods in which materials are allowed to "process" themselves in different ways, leading to "aha" or illumination experiences in which the pieces come together in new ways and in which novelty may arise. It encourages augmenting the linear prose report with other forms of expression such as poetry and artistic productions.

It is possible to go even further than this, however, in expanding research procedures and in developing a more complete, integral methodology for transpersonal and other studies. Steps in this direction were taken recently by students at the Institute of Transpersonal Psychology in their doctoral dissertation work. Dorothy Ettling (1994) added two nonverbal treatments of her data—emotional and intuitive appreciations of the materials—to the usual intellectual inductive analysis in which themes are extracted from interview transcripts. She allowed these other forms of knowing to arise as she listened to her tape-recorded in-depth interviews while in a meditative state. She also allowed nonverbal production to arise, creatively expressing her participants' stories in the forms of dance, drawings, sculptures, crying, and singing.

Alzak Amlani (1995) extended these nonverbal additions further by attending to visual, auditory, and proprioceptive images—and their emo-tional and intuitive meanings—that arose in him as he listened to each taped interview while in a meditative state. After incubating those impres-sions for several weeks, he recognized key archetypes associated with particular images and sensations. Connecting them with each participant's life story, Amlani found certain myths, stories, gods, and goddesses that mirrored the participants and their inner processes. In addition to the usual rational thematic analyses, he developed cross-cultural, mythic personifi-cations for each participant. After returning these mythic descriptions to the participants, Amlani reported that the participants found that the augmented descriptions rang true to them and that they often added accurate information beyond the information contained in the original transcripts.

Because she was interested in studying what happens when participants engage in a program of uninterpreted, nonverbal dreamwork, Nancy Fagen (1995) requested that each of her participants incubate a special dream, during the last week of her study, asking the dream itself to use its voice in commenting on the intervention process. In a final section of her dissertation, she presented a selection of such dreams, without any interpretations on her part, so that they might speak more directly to the reader, conveying an aspect of the process other than that conveyed by rational discourse. She included this as a supplement to more conventional work using standardized assessments, unstructured interviews, and special questionnaires.

Details concerning the methodological innovations of Ettling, Amlani, and Fagen may be found in their contributions to Part III of this volume and, of course, in the dissertations themselves.

A further extension of research "reporting" through inclusion of the nonverbal has not yet, to my knowledge, been formally tried or proposed. This extension would involve the deliberate employment of intention to invest one's research report with a capability of directly communicating additional content to the reader—nonverbally and "psychically." In principle, this should be possible. I am aware of a number of consistent anecdotes indicating that this already is taking place, albeit, most probably, in an informal, unconscious manner rather than as a result of a deliberate aim or procedure.

An Even Bolder Step: Knowing Through Becoming

Emotional, intuitive, and nonverbal expressive aspects can be added in greater density to research projects to make them more complete, more balanced, and more likely to tap all dimensions of what is being studied. But a researcher can take an even bolder step, as well, in the direction of a truly transpersonal methodology. Such a step involves paying full attention to *what is known directly by the eye of the spirit;* this type of knowing seems to require a change or transformation in the investigator's *being*. It requires that the investigator *become* what is being studied and to know it as *subject* rather than as object.

Evelyn Underhill (1915), a dedicated student of the mystical experience, expressed this same idea:

We know a thing only by uniting with it; by assimilating it; by an interpenetration of it and ourselves. . . . Wisdom is the fruit of communion; ignorance the inevitable portion of those who "keep themselves to themselves," and stand apart, judging, analyzing the things which they have never truly known. (p. 4)

We find similar expressions in the writings of scientists such as cytogeneticist Barbara McClintock, biologists Jonas Salk and June Goodfield, and physicist Albert Einstein:

I've often marveled that you can look at a cell under the microscope and can see so much! Well, you know, when I look at a cell, I get down in that cell and look around. . . . I found that the more I worked with them the bigger and bigger [they] got, and when I was really working with them I wasn't outside, I was down there. I was part of the system. I was right down there with them, and everything got big. I even was able to see the internal parts of the chromosomes—actually everything was there. It surprised me because I actually felt as if I were right down there and these were my friends. . . . As you look at these things, they become part of you. And you forget yourself. The main thing about it is you forget yourself. (McClintock, quoted in Keller, 1983, pp. 69, 117)

Very early in my life I would imagine myself in the position of the object in which I was interested. Later, when I became a scientist, I would picture myself as a virus, or as a cancer cell, for example, and try to sense what it would be like to be either. I would also imagine myself as the immune system, and I would try to reconstruct what I would do as an immune system engaged in combating a virus or cancer cell. (Salk, 1983, p. 7)

If you want to really understand about a tumor, you've got to be a tumor. (Goodfield, 1981, p. 213)

Only intuition, resting on sympathetic understanding, can lead to [these laws]; . . . the daily effort comes from no deliberate intention or program, but straight from the heart. (Einstein, quoted in Hoffman & Dukas, 1973, p. 222)

In much earlier times, we find similar ideas expressed in Patanjali's expositions of the *Yoga Sutras,* in descriptions of uniting with the object of inquiry in the form of complete absorption or *samyama* (see Taimni, 1975). In these are promises that different types of *direct knowing* can be achieved through the concentration, contemplation, and absorption of attention, consciousness, and awareness on different "objects"—that one can know directly by merging or becoming one with the object of one's intentionality. Similar ideas are part of the epistemologies of many indigenous peoples and of many spiritual, mystical, esoteric, and wisdom traditions. Certain meditative and contemplative practices may facilitate this type of direct knowing. Shear (1981) and Powell (1982, pp. 257-268) report the tantalizing findings of preliminary attempts to explore *samyama* in modern investigative settings. It also is useful to consider the various forms of direct knowing studied in parapsychology and psychical research as possible instances of this same principle of becoming what one wishes to know.

Purposes and Motives for Research

I suggest that there are three major motivations for conducting research. One of these is to learn as much as we can about the world, other people, and ourselves to predict and control. This aim may be in the service of security and adaptation. What is unknown, unpredictable, or uncontrollable can evoke apprehension and anxiety, whereas what is known, predictable, and controllable promotes feelings of safety and security. In this context, science and research in general have instrumental and utilitarian value. The research enterprise is seen as a series of problems to be solved. As in engineering, present or future practical applications are privileged. If we know underlying mechanisms, we can, potentially, change them or direct them in ways that are useful to us. The search for universal laws—a nomothetic approach—is quite consistent with these motivations; knowledge of principles of great generality increases the ability to predict and control. Anomalies and exceptions are threatening, and every effort is made to explain them away, incorporate them under a new rule, or show that they are unimportant. In nomothetic endeavors, it is clear that large and random samples are important because such samples not only facilitate the recognition of general principles but also more readily allow the detection of possible exceptions to rules than do smaller, more homogeneous, or biased samples. It is also clear that methodological strategies that allow deliberate interventions are valued—for example, experimental and quasi-experimental designs. Manipulation and control yield a type of knowledge that allows, down the line, further manipulation and control. This aspect of research and of science appeals to those for whom, as for Francis Bacon (1620/1955, p. 462), knowledge is power. In the interest of prediction and control, errors are unwelcome, and certainty is the major desideratum. Therefore, there are many safeguards to ensure certainty and to quantify findings and their accuracy to determine their degree of certainty (e.g., quantifications in general and statistical tests and decision rules in particular).

A second motivation for research is simply to understand the world, in the service of curiosity and wonder. The researcher seeks to know the many constituents that make up the universe and how those constituents interact. The world is like a puzzle—the researcher wishes to know what the pieces are, how they fit together, and what sort of picture begins to be revealed when sufficient pieces have been assembled and put in place. There is an interest in discovering nature's themes and variations. What remains invariant in the midst of variability? What are the islands of constancy amid seas of change? What is the nature of the order that emerges from chaos and disorder and that later may yield to disorder once again?

A third motivation for research is to appreciate the world, to delight in the myriad of entities, creatures, and events that a bountiful nature provides. This form of research is also in the service of wonder, but wonder of a slightly different sort—the wonder that accompanies discovery, surprise, delight, and awe. The productions of nature are more like works of art to be appreciated rather than problems to be solved. The unpredictable and the unexpected are as valued as—perhaps more valued than—the predictable and expected. Exceptions, anomalies, novelties, and variations are as valued as rules and well-established themes. White crows are of more interest than are the common black variety. Variety is a key word here. A satisfying research outcome is the presentation of a detailed map of some new territory or the revelation of some previously unknown trails and pathways in an old territory. In the human sciences, the researcher might simply wish to know the varieties of particular human experiences— what forms they take, what they are like in their depths, how they play out in people's lives, and what their accompaniments and outcomes are. The researcher may emerge with a topography of human experiences—a picture of how the experiences develop, disappear, transform, twist, and turn through life, how they cluster or do not cluster—but may not know with any certainty just how the experiences come about or which events cause other events. The researcher can present maps or parts of maps, however, and point out fine details of the terrain to others who wish to know what they might encounter should they decide to take certain journeys or, for those who already have embarked, what the remainder of the journey might bring. A number of book titles illustrate this essentially descriptive research strategy: *The Varieties of Religious Experience* (James, 1902/1958), *The Varieties of Psychopathological Experience* (Landis & Mettler, 1964), *The Varieties of Psychedelic Experience* (Masters & Houston, 1966), and *The Varieties of Sensory Experience* (Howes, 1991).

Some might argue that research of this third type is not especially interesting because it is merely descriptive and not sufficiently enlightening or explanatory. To such a criticism, I respond that *an explanation is essentially a description that satisfies.* An explanation of an event at level x is simply a description of events—and, often, hypothetical events—at another level, y. Explanations are themselves mere descriptions of what is occurring at other levels. A researcher's temperament, proclivities, and interests determine how many levels to take a new description from what is to be "explained" before reaching a level of satisfaction sufficient to earn the label *explanation.* My reaching for a cool glass of water can be explained by describing (a) the future outcomes of such an action; (b) the memories, intentions, and purposes that reside in my subjective domain; (c) the environmental and reinforcement histories relevant to similar prior actions and their consistent past consequences; (d) patterns of neural excitations in areas of my hypothalamus, occipital cortex, motor cortex, and other areas of my brain, bloodstream, and musculature; (e) biochemical patterns in various parts of my body; (f) particular patterns of collapse of quantum mechanical state vectors in various areas of my physical body; and so on. Descriptions all. I choose to emphasize those that satisfy me, and those I call "explanations." My descriptions may not be the same as those that satisfy others.

For researchers whose motivations are in line with the second (curiosity-serving) and third (appreciation-serving) approaches, sampling strategies are different from those of the first (prediction/control-serving) approach. Range of sampling is more important than representativeness of sampling. If a researcher is interested in the whole picture, or in the varieties of experiences that are possible within the big picture or pictures, the researcher may wish to sample extreme cases or interesting cases or cases that possess certain specific features of great interest to the researcher or to the research project. Emphasis shifts from large random samples to smaller *purposive* samples deliberately selected on the basis of certain criteria. Techniques of self-selection, researcher-selection, selection on the basis of nominators who have extensive knowledge of the characteristics of their nominees, and "snowball" and word-of-mouth techniques of participant solicitation and project advertising now become useful—in contrast to reliance on truly random or stratified random sampling. To study varieties of experiences or the furthest ranges of experiences or unusual or exceptional experiences, it is important to use sampling procedures that ensure that persons possessing these characteristics are included, and included in abundance, in the research sample. Sampling techniques that emphasize the central portion of some characteristics distribution—that is, those that emphasize a distribution region dominated by its mean and plus and minus one or even two standard deviations—are not as useful as those that allow for an abundance of outliers or atypical cases. What is atypical from the view of random or normal distribution sampling becomes typical from the view of the researcher's interest of the moment. To learn about white crows or about their life worlds, it is important to have lots of white crows in the sample; an abundance of black crows is not particularly helpful in such cases.

It is somewhat ironic that small, nonrandom, or convenience samples may also yield especially useful information for those interested in predict-and-control research strategies. If the researcher is interested in general, universal laws, then those laws should be followed by everyone; the researcher expects to be able to find indications of these laws in any and all research participants—in small, purposive samples as well as in large, random ones. Further, if reality is holographic in nature, then the researcher expects to discover interesting principles even in small samples. Such a holographic view is not limited to the perennial wisdom and to ancient hermetic and esoteric traditions that stress the "as above, so below" maxim. Similar notions are common to such diverse conceptualizations as the universal presence of gravitational attraction; attractive and repulsive tendencies in all physical, chemical, biological, and psychological systems; homeostatic and cybernetic principles in widespread systems; the holographic physical processes suggested by Bohm (1980); the holographic aspects of brain functioning proposed by Pribram (1971); and the mirroring, correspondence, and repetitious aspects of fractal geometry (Mandelbrot, 1982)—to name but a few. If reality and its operating principles are indeed holographic, this is a liberating and anxiety-relieving gift to those concerned with the adequacy and representativeness of their research samples. Findings that might be obtained with larger samples should be represented in small samples as well.

The three aspects of research described above appeal differently to researchers of different temperaments. Persons with strong needs for control and for certitude and who have tendencies toward doubt and skepticism will be more attracted by the predict-and-control aspects of research than will persons with less of those qualities and with a greater tolerance for ambiguity. The appreciative aspects of research will have greater appeal to those who value discovery above proof and who are comfortable with mystery and with various degrees of unknowing. William James (1907/1975) offered an early characterization of the two temperaments to which these aspects of research have differential appeal—what he termed the *tender-minded* and *tough-minded* philosophical types.

Mitroff and Kilman (1978) adapted Jungian typology and applied their conceptualization to social science methodology to better understand possible congruencies between research interests and styles and personality. They define the Analytical Scientist as the Jungian sensing-thinking type, the Conceptual Theorist as the intuitive-thinking type, the Conceptual Humanist as the intuitive-feeling type, and the Particular Humanist as the sensing-feeling type. These four types might be explored through the three aspects of science and research described above and also in connection with the four major types of research questions (those concerned, primarily, with outcome, process, conceptualization, or experience) discussed earlier in this chapter.

Stanley Krippner (1984) has applied the Mitroff and Kilman typology to the discipline of parapsychology. He illustrates the typology by naming individual researchers who, he feels, exemplify each type, and he recommends specific ways in which knowledge of a researcher's type might benefit the discipline as a whole. Some of the latter possibilities include help in judging the adequacy of researcher contributions, identifying likely strengths and weaknesses of students who intend to become researchers, recognizing one's own strengths and challenges as a researcher, and matching one's interests and strengths to particular research questions or methods.

PRINCIPLES OF INTEGRAL INQUIRY:
PRAXIS AND POSSIBILITIES

The research approach outlined in this chapter is called *integral* because its aim is to be as whole and inclusive as possible. This inclusivity applies to the overall approach and to each of its stages, as well.

The Focus of the Research

In following this approach, the researcher begins with a question of burning interest and importance—an area of inquiry that is heartfelt and significant. The meaning may derive from the relevance of the inquiry to important human or social issues, problems, challenges, or concerns. Often, the inquiry is directed toward something that has been directly experienced by the researcher—an important experience about which the researcher wishes to learn more. "How common or rare is my experience?" the investigator asks. "How is my experience similar to and different from those of others?" "What might have led me to have such an experience?" "Which factors are favorable to the experience, and which interfere with it?" "What has the experience brought with it; what were its outcomes?" "How might I have changed as a result of having had such an experience; how might others have changed?"

Depending on the interests of the investigator—and also on the personal and logistical resources available for the research project—one or more of these questions becomes the focus of the research. The researcher then seeks to find as complete an answer as possible to this burning question or set of burning questions using all relevant methods, approaches, information, and means of knowing, understanding, and expressing what has been learned. Contributing to the choices of question, methods, and modes of expression are considerations of the possible or desired outcomes of the research project itself. "Where will I be after having completed the research project, compared with where I am now?" "What will the research project have accomplished?" "How might my findings be useful—useful to whom and in which ways?" "Who is the audience for my findings?" "Whom do I wish to reach, primarily, and how might I best reach and communicate my findings to my intended audience?" Dwelling on such questions of aim and purpose will help the researcher choose the most appropriate means of formulating the research question(s), choosing the most suitable approach(es), conducting the research most efficiently, opening up to being informed by suitable aspects of the collected data, and presenting and communicating the findings in ways that are maximally understandable and significant to the intended audience.

Audience Considerations

A teleological element is involved with respect to the intended audience for the researcher's work. If the final outcome is kept in mind throughout each step of the research project, that aim will help inform every aspect of the work to optimize its appropriate completion. The form of the final research report will be determined by the nature of the intended audience and by what the researcher hopes to accomplish through doing the research. Does the researcher wish the work to have a social or political impact? If so, the relevance and prevalence of the issue addressed would be emphasized, along with the possible practical applications that could derive from the research project. Is the purpose to elucidate possible mechanisms or causal factors underlying experiences or events? If so, care would be taken to address potential artifacts and confounds, and a design should be chosen that would be convincing to thoughtful and skeptical readers. Some readers are convinced by certain types of data, collected only in certain ways, and presented via reasoned arguments. Other readers are convinced more by rich anecdotes or case study reports, in which an experience is allowed to come alive and speak forcefully with its own voice. For some—and for some things—presentation alone is a sufficient form of analysis or explanation. Philosopher Alfred North Whitehead remarked, "We have to search whether nature does not in its very being show itself as self-explanatory. By this I mean, that the sheer statement of what things are, may contain elements explanatory of why things are" (quoted in Burnshaw, 1970/1991, p. 287). As we shall see in the *sympathetic resonance* concept described in Chapter 4, simply confronting a full and accurate description of an experience may allow the reader to relive this experience with such completeness that the reliving carries with it its own explanation and understanding of its nature—an understanding from within.

Of course, the researcher need not choose only one type of audience or one presentation mode for findings. Multiple methods may be used within a research project to address several types of questions, and the findings can be reported in different forms in multiple reports—such as in journal papers, semipopular articles, books for the general public, lectures and workshop presentations, professional trainings, and seminars.

The Character of the Research Question

In developing the most appropriate research question, the researcher will ask herself or himself questions such as the following: How will the exploration of this topic contribute to my discipline? How might its outcome fill gaps in our knowledge? Could the answer to this question help clarify puzzling issues, lead to new conceptualizations, or suggest new practical applications? Might it help illuminate an area in which there are theoretical controversies?

Can the question be framed in such a way that its exploration will provide experiences during the research itself that benefit the research participants? How might the conduct of the research benefit me, as researcher? Is the question important enough to me to maintain my interest and enthusiasm for the period required for its exploration? Is the question too significant; does it tap an issue that is too close or too important to me? If, as researcher, I pick a question that too closely involves an issue I currently am working through in my personal life, I may be so over-whelmed by developments that my attention and energies are diverted from the research project, which requires a certain degree of detachment to ensure proper discernment, toward dealing with my own issues and feelings. Do I really want to spend weeks or months or years intensively studying this topic? If, in some sense, I *become* what I study during the research project, do I wish to invest so much of myself in this particular topic?

The researcher, ideally, will consider the magnitude of energy to be invested in exploring the research topic by researcher, participants, and those learning of and affected by its findings. Further, if such a high density of intentionality and attention is directed toward the study of a particular type of experience, might this not increase the likelihood, incidence, or prevalence of its (or of its polarity) occurring in the culture at large—either through conventional or more subtle means? If so, the researcher may wish to work with positive, joy-enhancing, growthful experiences—such as peak experiences, happiness, optimism, love, empathy, creativity, insight, or altruism—rather than with experiences involving stress, troubling symptoms, trauma, pain, anxiety, depression, or hopelessness.

Sources of Information and Inspiration

For help in formulating and fine-tuning the research question, and for learning about relevant findings and interpretations, the researcher can consult the obviously relevant, recent, primary research literature of the discipline but can also range more widely into more remote areas. Conventional research practice dictates remaining within the familiar territory of scientific research publications and not venturing out into the frontier land of nonscientific thought, where—in the parlance of ancient mapmakers—"there be monsters." The integral inquirer is not constrained by such advice, knowing that many relevant observations, useful ideas, and profound insights into human nature and human experience are to be found scattered throughout many areas of study.

In discussing the proper preparation for a "pure psychology," which he felt he was developing through his work on psychoanalysis, Freud (1917/1952a; 1926/1978) consistently emphasized the importance of studying areas within the humanities—literature, the history of civilizations, mythology, and the psychology of religion—for their relevant content and for developing capacities of thought useful for psychological work, in contradistinction to remaining tied to the findings and habits of thought of the medical and natural sciences that he felt were irrelevant to, and could even be detrimental to, what was demanded by the new psychological science. Addressing a medical audience in 1915, Freud (1917/1952a) made these remarks:

> Your training will have induced in you an attitude of mind very far removed from the psycho-analytical one. You have been trained to establish the functions and disturbances of the organism on an anatomical basis, to explain them in terms of chemistry and physics, and to regard them from a biological point of view; but no part of your interest has ever been directed to the mental aspects of life. . . . For this reason a psychological attitude of mind is still foreign to you, and you are accustomed to regard it with suspicion. . . . Now this limitation in you is undoubtedly detrimental to your medical efficiency. . . . [Psycho-analysis] must dissociate itself from every foreign preconception, whether anatomical, chemical, or physiological, and must work throughout with conceptions of a purely psychological order, and for this very reason I fear that it will appear strange to you at first. (pp. 451-452)

Just as Freud had to expand beyond the conventional medicine and natural science of his day to develop his system, so, too, do my colleagues and I feel the need to expand beyond the conventional sciences and psychologies of our time to find and develop approaches that more adequately address "the farther reaches of human experience." In developing such tools, we retain useful insights and methods from psychoanalytical, behavioral, humanistic, and cognitive schools of psychology, but we look for information and inspiration from the humanities, the arts, and the spiritual and wisdom traditions, as well.

Many have suggested studying the humanities both for their rich and relevant content and for the training in different forms of observation and thinking that they may provide. Here is just one representative statement of this view:

> Literature is a storehouse of observations. . . . Literature and history offer unending opportunities for cultivating the sensibilities of the productive observer. . . . The language of literature usually comes much closer to the varieties of experience than that of most of our experiments. For an example, see the last chapter of *Ulysses*. If our concern is the conduct of people in ongoing life situations, we could find no better preparation for the continuous shifting back and forth from magical and prelogical to logical thinking, from allusion and analogy to rational confrontation, from fantasy to self-differentiation. (Wyatt, 1967, p. 300)

The Supporting Atmosphere

As integral researchers, we may look to the events in our lives—to our ordinary and our extraordinary personal experiences—for additional inputs. Dreams may provide research ideas, as may those twilight states between waking and sleeping. Insights about moving ahead with or modifying research plans may arise spontaneously during reverie or effortlessly during times when our project plans are incubating. Our bodies may give us clues—in the form of aches, pains, tensions, or feelings of pleasure— whether our research plans are on track. Outside events—synchronicities, accidents, and auspicious or inauspicious happenings (see Chapter 4)—can comment on our planned or current work. We may have feelings that the universe is commenting, affirmatively or negatively, on our project. Researchers often have profited by attending to these sorts of unanticipated indications and lessons from other parts of themselves, from others, or from the universe and by heeding the advice implicit in such indicators, continuing or modifying research plans accordingly (see Chapter 7).

Journals, kept during all phases of research, may help us notice, keep track of, and interpret these less common indicators.

During a research effort, the momentum can carry over into our daily lives so that anything we do, experience, and read is seen for what it might contribute to our fuller understanding of what we are studying. Casually encountered events and thoughts may be seen to connect with and illuminate our research question. Books, quotations, snippets of information, comments from acquaintances and strangers—all these, if we are sufficiently attentive and open to them—begin to contribute useful new ways of thinking about our research issue (see, also, Chapters 4 and 7). When we direct a sufficient density of interest, intentionality, and attention toward a topic, the universe seems to join in, beneficently conspiring to provide additional pieces to the puzzle and helping us advance our thinking about the topic in question.

It is likely that the intentions of all research personnel play significant roles in molding the findings of virtually all research projects. Usually, these intentions are not explicitly recognized, and they operate informally and tacitly. It is possible, however, to augment the supporting atmosphere of a research project by bringing greater awareness to these intentions and by structuring them more deliberately and explicitly. Everyone involved in a research project (the researcher, the participant, and both acting together) can set special intentions (and perhaps even ritualize these at the beginning of the research project) for the "right" persons to appear in the research sample; for them to be able to know and to express the most useful material relevant to the topic being studied; and for the researcher to be able to receive, understand, and express new learnings in the most useful ways— ways that are useful to the participants, to the researcher, to future readers of the research report, to the field (the researcher's professional discipline), and to society as a whole. Novel uses of intention are described in Chapter 4 and in Sophie Arao-Nguyen's contribution to Chapter 9.

Questioning Assumptions

A fruitful research strategy, fully in line with the rationale of integral inquiry, is to continually question assumptions during all phases of research. Usually, assumptions cover only part of the story. Examining them more closely, and even reversing them completely—turning the assumptions on their heads—can yield the complementary, missing aspects of reality that the initial, partial assumptions kept hidden. A remark attributed to quantum physicist Niels Bohr has relevance here: "The opposite of a truth is a lie. The opposite of a profound truth is another profound truth." Commonly held assumptions can be turned 180 degrees to yield new research questions or interpretations of old or new findings. This practice enables the researcher to break out of automatic, narrowly constrained modes of thinking and begin to think more flexibly, fluidly, and creatively (see Chapter 4).

Modes of Knowing

The integral inquirer uses a pluralistic epistemology throughout the research effort—polling all facets of herself or himself (bodily reactions, imagery, emotions and feelings, intuitions, and aesthetic sensibilities, as well as cognitions) to learn about the research topic from as many perspectives as possible. The researcher not only polls herself or himself but also obtains reports of these diverse modes of knowing from all research personnel. Alternative states of consciousness could be facilitated in the research participants and in the researcher to promote forms of attention, knowing, and being that are not as accessible during ordinary, alert, waking consciousness. These states could be fostered during all stages of the research project and in all involved personnel. The reader of a final report could even be given state-induction instructions so that knowledge transfers mediated by state similarity (akin to state-dependent learning or memory) could be maintained even into the later phases of the research project. Creative uses of alternative states of consciousness in research are described by Rosemarie Anderson in Chapter 4 and in many of the contributions to Chapters 8 and 9 of Part III.

Expressing Findings

In addition to presenting research findings and conclusions in standard, linear prose, integral inquirers can consider alternative ways to express their results, interpretations, and conclusions. Some possibilities include poetic expressions, analogies, metaphors, tropes, symbols, imagery, humor, and various forms of artwork. These modes of expression provide possibilities of communication of nuances and entireties of experience that cannot be matched readily by ordinary descriptive language. "If we want to grasp the actuality of experience, we have to grant absolute relevance to the allusive and metaphoric quality of so much of our thinking, which the language of literature demonstrates with unsurpassed fidelity" (Wyatt, 1967, p. 300).

Findings could be presented in the form of stories, which have an especially rich, convincing, and compelling character. Again, Freud has something useful to say (Freud & Breuer, 1895/1957):

> It still strikes me as strange that the case histories I write should read like short stories and that, as one might say, they lack the serious stamp of science. I must console myself with the reflection that the nature of the subject is evidently responsible for this, rather than any preference of my own. . . . Detailed descriptions of mental processes such as we are accustomed to find in the work of imaginative writers, enable me . . . to obtain at least some kind of insight. (pp. 160-161)

Edith Sitwell (1961) made the following observation in considering the active role of the reader of poetry:

> The poet needs the collaboration of his [or her] audience. The reader must not sit back and expect the poet to do all the work. To read poetry with enjoyment entails the use of all the reader's powers of concentration, sensitivity and sympathy. (p. 118)

Although the comment was made in connection with the appreciation of poetry, presenters of research findings can learn from it. We can provide opportunities for greater reader involvement and interaction by providing the reader sufficient unprocessed or uncooked materials with which to work.

In connection with "the work of the reader," this Sufi story comes to mind. Someone said to Bahudin Naqshband, a Sufi teacher of the 14th century, "You relate stories but you do not tell us how to understand them." He said, "How would you like it if the man from whom you bought fruit consumed it before your eyes, leaving you only the skin?" (Shah, 1971, p. 137).

Exploring Validity

In testing the validity of research findings, not only can we rely on the familiar formal methods in research textbooks (i.e., the various procedures that help ensure internal and external validity, generalizability, and reliability) and on intellectual criteria for consistency, but we can note bodily, emotional, aesthetic, intuitive, and pragmatic indicators, as well. Clues from each of these areas can indicate whether our procedures, findings, and conclusions are faithful to what is being studied or whether we have gone astray. We can look for coherence or conflict among these indicators. Together, they can contribute to a measure of *experiential adequacy* of our research program, indicating the extent to which each facet of the project rings true in the experiences of all personnel involved in the research (researcher, participants, and those who receive our findings). Perhaps the most complete and straightforward approach to validity is the one suggested by Rosemarie Anderson in Chapter 4: the commonsense understanding of validity as "just telling the whole truth of what occurred in lived experience" (p. 72; see also, Anderson, Braud, & Valle, 1996, p. 17). The fruits of our research, both locally and nonlocally, can provide further indications of our findings' validity and authenticity. An extensive treatment of some novel, alternative approaches to validity can be found in Chapter 11.

Outcomes of Integral Inquiry

Integral inquiry welcomes and expects that those who participate in this approach will be changed. The approach encourages at least five types of transformation:

- The *professional discipline* is transformed by the knowledge gain that results from the inquiry.
- The *research participants* (coresearchers) are transformed as they learn more about themselves and understand and assimilate more about their present and past experiences because real and significant experiences are the topics of the research project.
- The *researcher* confronts, assimilates, and understands these same issues within herself or himself, and what is newly learned may have a transformative impact.
- The *readers* (audience) of the research report experience new learnings from appreciating the findings and from confronting and assimilating corresponding experiences within themselves.
- The views and practices of *society at large* can change if enough individuals are reached by the research findings or by applications or direct actions that derive from those findings.

From beginning to end, the plurality of possibilities and inclusiveness of integral inquiry permit deep and extensive knowings to arise and allow many more individuals to benefit from the research undertaking than would be possible from more restricted approaches. It is hoped that the inclusive and balanced nature of this approach can foster increments in wisdom, as well as in knowledge, in everyone touched by the research endeavor.

On Taking a Stand

Some may be uncomfortable with, or suspicious of, the inclusive stance of integral inquiry—feeling that advocates of such an approach may be trying to be all things to all people and not making needed choices. They may wish integral researchers to take a more definite stand on overarching issues and accept epistemological challenges such as those laid down by Denzin and Lincoln (1994) in their *Handbook of Qualitative Research,* to locate themselves more definitively in the context of a long development of traditional and nontraditional approaches and to take sides in the latest bout of the confrontation between quantitative and qualitative or nomothetic and idiographic advocates. They may contend, along with philosophers of science such as Kuhn (1970) and Feyerabend (1975), that paradigms are incommensurable and that premature attempts to integrate could lead to confusion rather than illumination.

To these potential criticisms, I respond that such views reflect adherence to an exclusive, either/or view in which one approach is generally privileged over another, without a discerning consideration of specific needs or purposes. The complementary view espoused by the integral inquirer favors, rather, inclusivity, integration, and discerning discrimination. The integral inquirer urges choosing particular tools for particular purposes— and choosing from among a large number of tools provided by different paradigms or approaches. In this view, there is no one best tool or approach or overall stance. Rather, there are tools and approaches that are more or less appropriate to different problems or purposes. There are many stances, each matching well or poorly a particular aim. This is the point of Table 3.1. For certain research goals, method x is ideal and method y is a poor fit, whereas for other goals, the values of the same methods reverse themselves. The researcher picks and chooses according to her or his aim, need, and the nature and suitability of the tool. It is unwise to think of one tool as generally better or worse than another. Imagine attempting to construct a house and an automobile with only a wrench or with only a hammer.

The incommensurability of paradigms may be true only if a researcher uses particular metrics or tries to apply one metric or framework to both paradigms, or—even more unwisely—commits the category error of trying to measure or explain one realm solely with the tools or concepts of another realm. (In addition, commensurability has, literally, to do with measurement and metrics, and commensurability becomes an issue only if the researcher is interested in measuring or in comparing measurements with one another for a given purpose.) Fit and appropriateness seem, again, to be the watchwords here—along with mindfulness of the contexts and limitations of, reasons for, and assumptions underlying one's interpretations.

NOTES

1. Excerpt from *Open Secret* (p. 10), by Jelaluddin Rumi (John Moyne and Coleman Barks, Translators), 1984, Putney, VT: Threshold Books. Copyright © 1984 by Threshold Books. Reprinted by permission.

2. Excerpt from *The Mathnawi* (Vol. 3, lines 4393, 4397), by Jelaluddin Rumi, in *The Sufi Path of Love: The Spiritual Teachings of Rumi* (p. 209), by William Chittick (Translator and Editor), 1983, Albany: State University of New York Press. Copyright © 1983 by State University of New York Press. Used with permission.

CHAPTER 4

INTUITIVE INQUIRY

A Transpersonal Approach

Rosemarie Anderson

Today, like every other day, we wake up empty
and frightened. Don't open the door to the study
and begin reading. Take down a musical instrument.
Let the beauty we love be what we do.
There are hundreds of ways to kneel and kiss the ground.

—Jelaluddin Rumi (1995, p. 36)[1]

As a field of research, scholarship, and applications, transpersonal psychology endeavors to understand and value human life in its fullest and most transformative expressions. Commonly regarded as the fourth expression of 20th-century psychology, transpersonal psychology seeks to delve deeply into the most profound and inexplicable aspects of human experiences, including mystical and unitive experiences, experiences of transformation, extraordinary insight, meditative awareness, altered states of consciousness, and self-actualization. Even in studying commonplace phenomena, transpersonal psychologists tend to explore the dimensions of human nature and experience that ordinarily are thought of as spiritual and ineffable and concerned with ultimate value. Having expanded steadily in the past 25 years or so, this innovative expression of psychology builds on and extends the hallmark eras of behavioral, psychoanalytic, and humanistic psychologies. The legacy of a little more than 100 years of psychological inquiry has been an enormous in-gathering of psychological knowledge, acquired by use of the methods of inquiry in psychoanalysis, behaviorism, and humanistic psychology. Much of this knowledge is well known, even taken for granted, in contemporary life. At the same time, rich experiences such as human love, imagination, intuition, and extraordinary experiences—such as those occurring in altered states of consciousness and mystical experiences—seem outside the purview of respectable psychological investigations. Largely abandoned by the psychologies of quantification in particular, vast domains of rich human experiences seem ignored by conventional psychology. Instead, profound experiences seem more the specialty of the poets, novelists, and playwrights who bring meaning and significance to their works through the language tools of metaphor, story, tall tales, legends, and drama.

As we turn from the end of the 20th century, a century of enormous change, and toward the beginning of the 21st century with its vast potential, it seems fitting and timely to bring imagination and intuition back into scientific inquiry. Psychology is, after all, the study of human behavior and experience, including their fullest expressions. Methods falling short of including "the farther reaches of human nature" fail to explore the fullness of being alive here and now in this extraordinary experience called daily life.

To explore the full dimensions of human awareness and experience, today's epistemologies and methods must be vigorous and dynamic. The field of transpersonal psychology has been exploring these rich dimensions of being human for more than 20 years. Regrettably, research in transpersonal psychology has often seemed stymied by reliance on the experimental methods it inherited from the dominant psychologies of the 1960s and 1970s, the context for its impetus. This chapter will present new ways (or perhaps nuanced but old ways) of exploring the nature of human awareness and experience. The essential qualities proposed here place attributes such as intuition, compassion, immediate apprehension of meaning, and service to society's disenfranchised persons as central to scientific or empirical inquiry in psychology.

It is recommended that investigators-researchers incorporate the features, skills, and procedures of intuitive inquiry into other forms of research, including conventional behavioral research. Much of what is proposed here is simply good science (if only we would do it). Doing research while being consciously aware of our intuitive processes is precisely what is proposed here. Therefore, although intuitive inquiry is a unique approach and can be followed formally, many of its properties can be readily appropriated into other approaches. The values of the field of transpersonal psychology encourage blending and borrowing between research methods and making choices that best suit the topic of inquiry and not necessarily any isolated research approach.

THE ESSENTIAL FEATURES OF INTUITIVE INQUIRY

The Heart of Compassion as Value and Principle of Validation and Consensus

Bringing the compassionate heart to scientific inquiry—to the way we, as researchers, ask our questions, set our hypotheses, devise our instruments, conduct our investigations, analyze our data, construct our theories, and speak to our readers (our audience)—brings a renewed intentionality to our sciences. Research informed by compassion is qualitatively different from emotionally detached research because our values and intentions frame the manner of our thinking and actions nonetheless: Better that compassion set our intentions.

Compassion allows us to ask the most significant questions and guides our hypotheses and speculations toward rich and expansive theories regarding the nature of the human experience. Compassionate listening allows our research participants to speak to us freely and honestly about the depth and value of their human experiences. Of course, it takes skill to learn to analyze data, yet compassion allows us to see the value and significance of the data as they shape themselves before us. And, finally, as we report our findings, compassionate writing is heartfelt, a vessel for others to hear ideas and theories already formed of compassionate listening, analysis, and synthesis of findings.

Examples abound. My students' and colleagues' research projects in topics such as reclaiming identity after abuse, the inward movement of beauty, the qualities of serenity and contentment in everyday life, the experience of addiction and its impact on long-term relationships, and mutuality in relationships have all emerged from personal experience and a desire to share and amplify the experience through study of the experiences of others. My own research on sacred weeping (Anderson, 1996) was born of a personal experience and desire to give voice to a life experience unexplored by contemporary science or by investigations into the nature of the mystical experience. My search for relevant descriptions that resonated with my own experiences was personal. It was a yearning to seek external validation and amplification of a rather common yet unspoken experience, an experience therefore unknown to consensual reality and consequent scientific discourse. My compassion and resonance with the experience allowed me to lean gently into the experiences of others for deeper understanding. This process was essentially introspective, heuristic, reflective, and enormously demanding in documentation and many cycles of reviewing the data and generalizations to themes. I doubt that I would have been able to see, far less understand and appreciate, the experience in others if I had not had the experience myself. Passion and compassion for the subject of inquiry have likely guided researchers throughout history. The principle of compassion as value and principle of validation makes this often implicit process in scientific inquiry more explicit and accessible.

From the viewpoint of everyday consensual discourse, validity concerns our capacity to relate accurately the fullness and richness of a given human experience. To portray something accurately is to relay it thoroughly and comprehensively. The intended listener, reader, or audience shapes the portrayal. Those experiences that seem sufficiently important to relate to others are often vivid, personal, and particular. Poetry, prose, and lyrics often speak artfully of these rich human experiences. Validity in conventional psychological empiricism, typically reduced to tests and measurements, often obscures and trivializes a commonsense validity of just telling the whole truth of what occurred in lived experience. Marshaled into operational definitions composed of Likert-scaling and Q-sorts and so on, descriptions of romantic love, grief and pain, or learning to trust again seem confused and constrained. The rich human experience is lost. Too often the richness and fullness of common—not to mention unique and transcendent—human experiences have disappeared from experimental investigations.

As scientists and psychologists, we value rigor, precision, and clarity. Yet a new science of research psychology must also give hope and an expanding awareness of human life lived fully and richly. If compassion guides each step of the research process of asking, analyzing, and telling, the final research findings may be less honed to focused precision. Yet they will be fuller and richer and, from my view, more valid and generalizable as well.

Empirical validation in intuitive inquiry relies on the principle of sympathetic resonance, as articulated below.

Sympathetic Resonance as a Validation Procedure

The principle of sympathetic resonance in the scientific endeavor is best introduced with an analogy. If someone plucks a string on a cello on one side of a room, a string of a cello on the opposite side will begin to vibrate, too. Striking a tuning fork will vibrate another some distance away. The resonance communicates and connects directly and immediately without intermediaries except for air and space. The principle of sympathetic resonance introduces resonance as a validation procedure for the researcher's particular intuitive insights and syntheses. The principle suggests that research can function more like poetry in its capacity for immediate apprehension and recognition of an experience spoken by another and yet (surprisingly and refreshingly, perhaps) be true for the researcher, as well. The procedures, insights, data analysis, and synthesis of transpersonal research may begin to approach the borders of understanding and communication that seem more like poetry than like conventional empirical science as we have known it in the 19th and 20th centuries. Describing the richness and fullness of human experience may require the use of metaphors, similes, and symbols. The poetry of Jelaluddin Rumi, Emily Dickinson, and Rainer Maria Rilke are notable examples of poetry that speaks directly to the inmost Self. In describing the poetry of Rilke, Robert Hass, the American poet laureate, describes the poet's unique ability to whisper or croon "into our inmost ear":

> Rilke's special gift as a poet is that he does not seem to speak from the middle of life, that he is always calling us away from it. His poems have the feeling of being written from a great depth in himself. What makes them so seductive is that they also speak to the reader so intimately. They seem whispered or crooned into our inmost ear, insinuating us toward the same depth in ourselves. . . . It is also what makes him difficult to read thoughtfully. He induces a kind of trance, as soon as the whispering begins:
>
> *Yes—the spring times needed you. Often a star*
> *was waiting for you to notice it. A wave rolled toward you*

out of the distant past, or as you walked
under an open window, a violin
yielded itself to your hearing. All this was mission.
But could you accomplish it? Weren't you always
distracted by expectation, as if every event
announced a beloved? (Where can you find a place
to keep her, with all the huge strange thoughts inside you
going and coming and often staying all the night.)

Look at how he bores into us. That caressing voice seems to be speaking
to the solitary walker in each of us who is moved by springtime, stars,
oceans, the sound of music . . . It is as if he were peeling off layers of the
apparent richness of the self, arguing us back to the poverty of a great raw,
objectless longing. (Mitchell, 1989, pp. xiv-xv)[2]

So often the poetry of Rumi, Dickinson, and Rilke points in the direction
of immediate knowing. Meaning somehow passes directly from the writer
to the reader or listener, seemingly by pointing to an inchoate experience
already shared by both. Readers of a poem may recognize their own
experiences (or similar ones) expressed within it. This recognition is an
immediate type of sympathetic resonance. Analogously for the intuitive
researcher, research findings may present a pattern of descriptions rather
like a pattern of harmonics. Although the readers or listeners may not have
the exact arrangement of harmonics, the basic pattern is nonetheless
immediately apprehended and recognized as like their own.

Constructing the Social Context of Knowledge: Building Validity Through Circles of Sympathetic Resonance

In scientific validation, the immediate apprehension or recognition of a
researcher's insight analyses could be verified using conventional experimental, quantitative procedures. Validity of findings is thus formed through
consensus building, noting consonance, dissonance, or neutrality—
subgroup by subgroup—within a culture and across cultures.

The importance of defining the social and political context of research
findings has been emphasized repeatedly by feminist researchers and
epistemologists (e.g., Fonow & Cook, 1991; Nielsen, 1990; Reinharz,
1992a; Riger, 1992; Shepherd, 1993). Through the validation procedures

of consonant, dissonant, and neutral sympathetic resonance, subgroup by subgroup, a type of mapping of the validity of a research finding could be done. A modified sociogram could be constructed with concentric circles of resonance designating subgroups wherein the research findings are immediately apprehended and recognized or reacted to with dissonance or neutrality (e.g., an arising yawn). (A larger discussion of validity and of the validation procedures of consonance, dissonance, and neutrality appears in Chapter 11.)

The Personal Is Universal
(The Heuristic Contribution)

Building on heuristic methods advanced by Clark Moustakas (1990), intuitive inquiry positions the experience and interpretation of the researcher at the center of the inquiry regardless of whether the data themselves are qualitative or quantitative in nature, or a blend of both. For both the intuitive and the heuristic researcher, expressing a comprehensive understanding of experience seeks to speak directly to the inmost self of another. It is as if speaking our personal truths—however unique and passionate that may feel—transcends our sense of separateness and brings us suddenly, even joyfully together—at least for an instant. We are at the same threshold: a threshold of appreciating, knowing, and acknowledging an aspect of life we all may share. In this process, it also happens that we see more clearly how we are different, as described above. Some of the synthesized, particular experiences of others will seem vaguely familiar and understandable, yet remote and unknown, as well. Again, the unique and personal expression of the experience or phenomenon allows us to see another's expression as understandable and valuable, yet sometimes unfamiliar and unknown in a personal and experiential sense. A similar notion was expressed by the playwright Tennessee Williams: "If I try to make a universal character, it becomes boring. It doesn't exist. If I make the character specific and concrete, it becomes universal" (Roxanne Lanier, personal communication, November 1, 1996).

Like heuristic methods, intuitive research methods emphasize the unique and personal voice of the individual researcher and depend on the experiences and insights of the researcher at every phase of the research process. The depth of the researcher's intuitive understanding gives a universal voice and character to the research findings. Because the unique experience and voice of the researcher are essential to enlivening the research with depth and richness of inquiry and expression, this unique voice gives heuristic research and intuitive inquiry their fundamental character. The researcher's personal and permeating analyses of experiences such as romantic love, loneliness, solitude, resistance, and chronic pain speak to others individually and universally at the same time. It is as if we are being individually spoken to—from one person's individual knowing to someone else's knowing of the experience; therein, those aspects of the phenomena universally shared seem brightly obvious.

Although the heuristic method encourages intuition in the forms of flashes of insight and creative syntheses, intuitive inquiry advocates expanded states of intuitive awareness, including but not limited to various altered states of consciousness, active dreaming and dream incubation, mystical vision and audition, intentional imaging, kinesthetic and somatic awareness, and states of consciousness more typically associated with the artistic process than with science, in all phases of the inquiry. Such expanded states have the advantage of plumbing the depths of transformative experiences by being more aligned with them state specifically. Jonas Salk (1983), for example, describes his scientific endeavors, although subject to scientific verification, as having an "inverted perspective" (p. 7) of imagining himself a virus, a cancer cell, or the immune system. Barbara McClintock, a well-known corn geneticist, describes her insights as originating in having "a feeling for the organism" that created "the openness to let it come to you" (quoted in Keller, 1983, p. 198).

From the individual researcher's point of view, the researcher intuitively "leans into" an experience that is clearly present, although perhaps not well articulated, in human experience. Clark Moustakas (1990) describes the process as

> an unshakable connection exists between what is out there, in its appearance and reality, and what is within me in reflective thought, feeling, and awareness. . . . Moffitt (1971, p. 149) captures this kind of seeing and knowing in his poem "To Look At Any Thing":

> *To look at any thing*
> *If you would know that thing,*
> *You must look at it long:*
> *To look at this green and say*
> *"I have seen spring in these:*
> *Woods," will not do—you must*

Be the thing you see:
You must be the dark snakes of
Stems and ferny plumes of leaves,
You must enter in
To the small silences between
The leaves,
You must take your time
And touch the very place
They issue from.

In Moffitt's sense, as a researcher I am the person who is challenged to apprehend the meaning of things and to give these meanings ongoing life. I provide the light that guides the explication of something and knowledge of it. When I illuminate a question, it comes to life. When I understand its constituents, it emerges as something solid and real. (Moustakas, 1990, p. 12)

The Personal Is Political
(The Feminist Contribution)

From the feminist critique of research (e.g., Fonow & Cook, 1991; Nielsen, 1990; Reinharz, 1992a; Riger, 1992; Shepherd, 1993) and from other liberation social movements (e.g., Boff, 1993; Gutierrez, 1990, 1994), we have gained valuable insight into the intricate interconnectedness of the personal and political aspects of everyday life. At minimum, it would be intellectually embarrassing, at the end of the 20th century, to disconnect what we do in the research laboratory from the implications of our methods and findings, to engage in any investigation of human behavior that does not analyze the sociopolitical context in which the behaviors and phenomena take place, or to contend that how we do what we do—with research participants, our analyses, and communications to the wider public—in the name of research is separate from our behaviors and beliefs in all other aspects of our lives, including our families, friends, communities, and world politics at large. Adrienne Rich, a contemporary American poet, presents this insight eloquently (quoted in Gelpi & Gelpi, 1993):

When the Civil Rights movement came along in the late fifties, early sixties, I began to hear Black voices describing and analyzing what were the concrete issues for Black people, like segregation, like racism, it came to me as a great relief. It was like finding language for something that I'd needed a language for all along. . . . At the same time, I was thinking a lot about something that wasn't being talked about at the time very much. I was thinking about where sexuality belonged in all of this. What is the connection between Vietnam and the lover's bed? If this insane violence is being waged against a very small country by this large and powerful country in which I live, what does that have to do with sexuality and with what's going on between men and women, which I felt also as a struggle even then? (p. 263)

For the feminist researcher, all actions are political and at their best—and I'll add most conscious best—have the power to emancipate, liberate, enliven, and energize human life and possibilities for all people, especially those who are socially and politically disadvantaged. The truly personal and inner are manifested in some way by us in our world—and, if commonly shared, manifested by others. Personal and enlightened intuitive inquiries into the nature of commonly held experiences such as loneliness, oppression by ideologies, reclaiming the self after abuse and rape, the anger of cancer, and so on are important in understanding the inmost dimensions of human experiences as well as their social and political consequences. What is inside is outside in the reflective and expressive sense.

Central to the feminist and liberationist critique of political and scientific discourse is the absence of the actual voice of poor and disenfranchised persons from research studies and social analysis in general. In writing about Emily Dickinson's life and poetry, Adrienne Rich expresses the liberating power of giving voice to the voiceless in contemporary poetry (quoted in Gelpi & Gelpi, 1993):

The poet's relationship to her poetry has, it seems to me—and I am not speaking only of Emily Dickinson—a twofold nature. Poetic language—the poem on paper—is a concretization of poetry of the world at large, the self, and the forces within the self; and those forces are rescued from formlessness, lucidified, and integrated in the act of writing poems. But there is a more ancient concept of the poet, which is that she is endowed to speak for those who do not have the gift of [poetic] language, or to see for those who—for whatever reasons—are less conscious of what they are living through. It is as though the risks of the poet's existence can be put to some use beyond her own survival. (p. 194)

How we treat the stranger and what happens between lovers are, in the end, scarcely separate from the happenings between countries in the worldwide political arena. Rigid patterns of behavior between people and ideologies saturated within a culture (e.g., stereotyped sexual behaviors) become analogues, or rather holograms of recycled patterns, of a people's actions in national and international affairs (e.g., Vietnam), as well.

The Interconnectedness of Scientific Insight

Bringing together the principle of the "personal is universal" from heuristic methods and the "personal is political," we come full circle. The interconnectedness of what is personal to what is political to what is universal draws a complete circle. At the risk of sounding theological, it seems rather trinitarian, in the original meaning. That is, what is particularly sacred in human life is also manifested in the individual and community aspects of our lives and in the unity that brings us together. Engaging in research that delves into the depths of human experience demands compassion and understanding for the richness of human expression and possibilities and the interconnectedness of the personal-political-universal circle of our endeavors, especially our research endeavors. From the view of personal preferences, the "personal is universal" contribution of heuristic methods and the "personal is political" contribution of feminist and liberation analyses are rather like two sides of the same coin. In my own experience in teaching, the "personal is universal" is readily appreciated by my introverted colleagues but not by the extraverts. On the other hand, my extraverted colleagues readily grok the "personal is political" and not the other.

Trust the Ritual: The Discipline of Procedures and Protocols

It seems appropriate to think of research procedures and protocols as a ritual, that is, a carefully designed form intended to reveal many layers of meaning. Once procedures are set in place, they are followed with care and precision. Modifications are made cautiously, with the intent to further a fuller explication of the topic and with an increased sense of urgency to document any changes made. Inherently, or through time, good methodologies, like good road maps, generate trust. The methods will guide the process of revealing the essential nature of an experience that seems to come to life through gentle and intuitive inquiry.

In trusting the ritual of the protocols, my colleague doctoral students and I have been delighted and surprised at how the procedures have allowed us to move more profoundly into the nature of the experience studied—often with quite unexpected results. An introspective and intuitive perspective is demanding and rigorous. Nonetheless, this perspective sustains a process that helps to thoroughly permeate the nature of an experience. Seemingly, the sheer intent and concentration converge to create a unified momentum. There is even the sense that following the procedures, especially in times of confusion and discouragement, allows the researcher to relax even more completely into the sustaining process of the investigation.

The Element of Delight and
Surprise in Scientific Inquiry

Most research, in my experience, entails delight and surprise. Hunches lead to new insights. Thoughts in the night and intuitions, although not particularly thinking about anything, lead to new ways of looking at old problems. The nature of intuitive methods sets the methodological stage for new ideas to happen. They often do.

The Function of Compassionate Knowing
(Soft Wisdoms of the Heart) in Scientific Inquiry

For Barbara McClintock, knowing a thing requires loving it. While looking through her microscope during research on corn fungus, she found that her perspective altered dramatically:

> I found that the more I worked with them [the viruses] the bigger and bigger [they] got, and when I was really working with them I wasn't outside, I was down there. I was part of the system. I was right down there with them, and everything got big. I even was able to see the internal parts of the chromosomes—actually, everything was there. It surprised me because I actually felt as if I were right down there and these were my friends. (quoted in Keller, 1983, p. 117)

In spiritual traditions throughout the centuries, true and encompassing intelligence is reported to have these same qualities. To know persons, we must love them first and look at the world from their perspective. To know any thing, we must love it and become its friend.

Compassionate knowing has a softness. It is as if what is observed yields itself to our knowing. There is no intrusion, no object, and no subject. Aspects of the experience studied that do not belong to the depth of the experience fall away. Those aspects that give amplitude and fullness to the experience studied begin to cohere in their complexity and interrelatedness (interbeingness). By loving, and through living thoroughly the experience studied, the researcher looks around from inside the experience and notes what is there. The researcher then searches from inside the experience until the essential qualities of the experience come to life as the researcher's own experience. Gradually, the entire panorama of the experience comes more clearly into view.

The Human Voice: Unique and Particular

For the purposes of research inquiry in psychology, clear and personal language describing human behavior functions in two significant ways.

1. When spoken clearly in words, heretofore unclaimed aspects of our experiences suddenly seem more solid and real. Claiming our memories and experiences gives our spoken words their emancipating qualities. Energy and tension are released. Subliminal memories and experiences tip above the threshold of our awareness challenging assimilation and integration in the present.

2. Conversely, as Abraham Maslow (1966) put it, "There is no substitute for experience, none at all" (p. 45). Eloquent metaphors and brilliant psychological conceptualization also can obscure, minimize, and trivialize the experience being examined. There is an inherent quality to human experience that is irreducible to words, descriptions, symbols, metaphors, and so on. Although symbols and metaphors, for example, may come closer in aiding a person to understand the experience, they still are *not* the experience itself. As Maslow emphasized, descriptions, symbols, and metaphors are useful only if the individual has had the experience (or one akin to it) already. A particularly apt example of the irreducibility of human experience is that of extreme pain. Although some descriptions may come close, none are the pain, nor do they reproduce it. This particular point

has been emphasized, repeatedly, by liberation theologians who have noted that pain has a shrill honesty that few can ignore.

What are researchers to do? We can stay as close as possible to the voice of the person(s) describing the pain, joy, grief, sadness, sorrow, and all other especially rich human experiences. We can be accurate. We can stay close to the behaviors, or to the phenomenon itself, and avoid collapsing categories that reduce complexity and importance. We can use poetic tropes, such as metaphors and symbols, to point to the experience that eludes words while never forgetting that the words, metaphors, and symbols are not the experience. We can keep a beginner's mind, stay humble, and always remember that the inmost capacities of the Self are enormous.

INTUITIVE RESEARCH SKILLS

Intuitive inquiry attempts to honor the expansive nature of human experience, particularly as understood in the field of transpersonal psychology. Studying rich human experiences warrants comprehensive methods, that is, methods of inquiry that engage logic and analysis as well as our capacities for imagination, intuition, and alternative states of consciousness. Borrowing and expanding on the methods of heuristic research (Moustakas, 1990) and certain aspects of phenomenological inquiry (e.g., Valle & Halling, 1989; Valle & King, 1978), intuitive inquiry as a distinct research approach seeks to bring these more comprehensive capacities of human awareness into *conscious* application in the conduct of research in the social sciences. In addition, in the interests of seeking methods that best facilitate exploring a particular topic of investigation, it is hoped that intuitive inquiry, or some of its distinctive properties, will be combined with other qualitative and quantitative methods. Although blending methods requires more rigor— especially in documenting procedures and analyses—it may nonetheless best serve a particular investigation. Ultimately, collaborative research using many research approaches, distinctly or in blends, and many sources of data contributes to the best and most thorough understanding of human experience.

Intuitive research skills advance a threefold purpose: (a) to allow the intersubjectivity of researcher, participants, and anticipated audience to influence the gradual unfolding of the research inquiry, (b) to assist the researcher in exploring thoroughly the landscape of a particular facet of human experience, and (c) to impart creatively the character of the experience without diminishing it in the telling.

Reflective Listening

In intuitive inquiry, the researcher listens reflectively to her or his own experience and the experience of others. Having chosen a particular facet of human experience as the topic of inquiry, the researcher first thoroughly explores and records the features of her or his experience, or the motivations for undertaking the particular study if the study does not issue from autobiographic experience. Second, throughout the investigation, the researcher uses the results of that inner reflection as an interactive template to listen to the experiences of others. This interactive template changes as the inquiry proceeds. As a natural consequence of this cycle of reflective listening, the researcher's understanding expands to include unique as well as integrative features of the experience studied. Third, the researcher's capacity for reflective listening facilitates a similar process in the participants. In research design, the researcher's capacity for reflective listening allows her or him to model and support the type of exploration desired of the participants. At a theoretical level, the researcher's capacity for reflective listening initiates a field of sympathetic resonance that facilitates the capacity of all participants to listen to the depths of their experiences. As the research proceeds, the researcher develops a deepening appreciation and understanding of the topic of inquiry. As the researcher's awareness of the dimensions, qualities, and wholeness of the topic expands, the field of resonance available to successive participants correspondingly increases.

Indwelling

Indwelling is a term borrowed from heuristic research and is artfully described by Moustakas (1990):

> Indwelling refers to the heuristic process of turning inward to seek a deeper, more extended comprehension of the nature of meaning of a quality or theme of human experience. It involves a willingness to gaze with unwavering attention and concentration into some facet of human experience in order to understand its constituent qualities and its wholeness. To understand something fully, one dwells inside the [visible and obvious] and [invisible and essential] factors to draw from them every possible nuance,

texture, fact, and meaning. The indwelling process is conscious and deliberate, yet it is not lineal or logical. It follows clues wherever they appear;
one dwells inside them and expands their meanings and associations until
a fundamental insight is achieved. (p. 24)

Indwelling on a particular facet of human experience often becomes a
preoccupying feature of the researcher's daily activities. The researcher
becomes the eye of the inquiry. Everything may become raw material for
scrutiny: relationships, dreams, bumper stickers, newspaper articles, chance
encounters, casual conversations, and synchronistic events such as a drop-
in visit from a least favorite relative. So compelling is the process, the
researcher constantly looks for information that clarifies, expands, focuses,
and rips apart her or his understanding of the topic of inquiry. In my
research, especially on the work of the nature of symbols, I sometimes feel
as though I am continually scanning my life experience—books, billboards,
newspapers, and word images—to nuance, amplify, and lay waste my
understanding. Some of the most productive encounters are the most
confusing and bewildering. Compelling and arresting images may become
paths for greater understanding. This research encounter is expanded in
the concept of "trickstering."

Trickstering

In indigenous cultures worldwide, tricksters open gateways of awareness
and insights. Tricksters are playful, mischievous, and sometimes outrageous.
Particular to culture, coyotes, ravens, fairies, leprechauns, and pookas (a
very Irish goblin) gift humans with insight, usually in the context of making
us feel foolish. Coyotes play tricks. Ravens steal and turn the stolen goods
into something else. Fairies appear as lovers. Leprechauns give us gold that
disappears. Pookas gleefully take us for a riotous ride. An auspicious
bewilderment!

In research, especially transpersonal research, auspicious bewilderment
may signal the beginning of renewed understanding. Contradictory stories
and examples move us deeper into the intricacies of the topic of inquiry.
Nuances that do not fit generate reconceptualization. Confusion takes us
in an unanticipated direction. Paradox challenges our assumptions, and so
on. The research project will take longer, require more work, and probably
cost more money, and it will also be more complete and useful in the end.
Weeks, even months, of feeling auspiciously bewildered—which, by the

way, is different from depression—are not unusual for a transpersonal researcher. Although bewildered, the researcher should stay with the process as it is. It is usually worthwhile even to exaggerate, dramatize, or extend the features of what bewilders, to look deeper. Dreamwork, drawing, dance, authentic movement, storytelling, and other expressions of the imagination may bring the creative, nonrational aspects of experience into synthesized awareness. If it gets to be too much, the researcher may rest, sleep, take a break, or gently put the research project (or that aspect of the project) on the back burner for a while, not allowing it to dominate activities, and return to the project again when refreshed.

More dangerous to transpersonal research is thinking we know what we are doing, being overly confident that we are on top of it, or having fixed ideas about the findings before we have finished collecting and analyzing the full complement of data. The nature of transformative experience often demands periods of confusion to be more fully understood. If we go for long periods of not being surprised, beware. Something might be wrong. Is the topic so well understood that there is nothing new to say? What is happening to contradictory information? Is the researcher bored? exhausted? otherwise preoccupied? on a tangent? in denial? avoiding the inevitable move to the heart of the topic? If so, being human is percolating its way into the researcher's research experience. No need for panic—the researcher can rest and come back when feeling refreshed and unwilling to spend energy going in the wrong direction.

Varying the Focal Depth

One of the most difficult features of skillful research for a beginning researcher to grasp is the degree of detail necessary for a particular investigation. How much detail—or depth of focus—best supports the topic of inquiry? When should the focal depth be varied? My initial understanding of focal depth stems from work in microscopy. In using microscopes in a laboratory, the use of varying focal depth to view various genetic structures more distinctly seemed immediately obvious. When I was a young scientist, changing the lens of magnification on my slide preparation from 10x (10 times the ordinary magnification) to 30x to 100x—and then switching to an electron microscope—was an intellectual revolution! Still, nearly 30 years later, it brings tears to my eyes. I was then and am now thrilled by the magnificence, complexity, and integrity of what revealed itself before my eyes, merely by rotating the lenses of my student microscope. One lens reveals the cellular level of activity, another the chromosomal, another the molecular, and so on.

Analogously, focal depth matters in studying human experience, although less obviously so. Changing focal depth makes a tremendous difference. Principles of organizations may change with different levels of depth. In my own research, and in working with beginning researchers, finding the best range of detail to suit a particular study is troubling and especially perplexing to articulate and teach. Determining focal depth and when to vary it may be one of those skills learned through the vicissitudes of trial and error, as I did. Yet understanding the subtleties of focal depth seems to distinguish professional researchers from the beginners.

In a transpersonal approach to research, determining and varying focal depth become even more difficult and less obvious. Transpersonal phenomena seem to yield subtle layers and more depth. At the same time, an overly detailed analysis can sometimes lose sight of the larger picture, as has happened in some early phenomenological analyses of transpersonal experiences (Miles Vich, personal communication, October 27, 1996). In my research on symbology, for example, not only did I access a range of sources, including archaeology, mythology, and legendary material, but also I often varied the focal depth to delve deeply into a micro feature or aspect of a symbol. This thorough immersion in minutiae was sometimes a dead end, but more often it unlocked doors to a more comprehensive understanding of the larger picture. In the research excursions in minutiae, I learned about the symbol and more. How the ancient people used and understood a particular symbol also helped me understand how they thought and imagined their world more generally. This movement to follow a trail of detail, rather like a detective novel, was an intuitive knowing of when to change focal depth, when to close in, and when to broaden out again. Much of what I appreciate now about these ancient cultures I learned by way of these intuitive forays into particularity, rather like moving from 30x magnification to the electron microscope and back again.

Ritualizing Intention

The researcher's intention to seek a comprehensive and compassionate understanding of a particular human experience affects all aspects of the inquiry. Researchers in the field of transpersonal psychology typically ritualize their intentions to choose topics that serve them and the wider community, to attract into the study the best possible participants, to create procedures that facilitate transformation for everyone involved in the research project, to analyze the data sensitively and fully, and, finally, to communicate findings comprehensively and transformatively to the future audience. If a researcher has explicit intentions, she or he may wish to design rituals that dramatize these intentions. Intentions are usually written out and spoken in ritual. A researcher, for example, may wish to set an intention to communicate fully and to facilitate transformation in future readers or audience. Bringing consciousness to intentions gives greater focus, coherence, and discipline to the individual phases of intuitive inquiry. Akin to setting up fields of morphic resonance (Sheldrake, 1988), setting intention creates a movement in consciousness in a particular direction.

Intersubjectivity of Researcher, Participants, and the Audience

At the heart of transpersonal research is personal and social transformation. The topic chosen for study, how the inquiry is planned, the unfolding of the data gathering, the discoveries of the analysis, and the final communication of the inquiry constitute a process of transformation in motion.

In intuitive inquiry, the researcher, participants, and audience eventually work together to give expression to a comprehensive understanding of a particular facet of human experience. Everyone involved is changed in the process. Through time, all contribute to communicating and to being influenced and transformed by the research inquiry. Whatever the topic, if it is compelling, its significance to the researcher, the participants, and audience is typically revealed layer upon layer, insight upon insight. The process continues in the lives of readers long after the inquiry has ended. Ideally, no one leaves unaffected by the significance of the experience studied.

Although it seems more or less obvious that researchers and participants influence one another, the interactive and transformative influence of the intended audience is often overlooked. Like other forms of writing and public speaking, scientific writing and presentations are also influenced by the intended audience. Science does not live in audience vacuum, either. In addition, most researchers, if they are honest, have an audience in mind whom they wish to reach and influence. In transpersonal research, researchers also hope to facilitate transformation in the audience, as well.

Intuitive inquiry intends to make this reciprocal influence or intersubjectivity of researcher and audience as conscious and explicit as possible.

Alternative States of Consciousness, Imagination, and Intuition

Intuitive inquiry recommends engaging alternative states of consciousness, imagination, and intuition as sources of data in each phase of the inquiry. For the most part, the states of consciousness and expressions have been only the subject of inquiry. Yet skillful use of them can help focus an emerging topic of inquiry, gain perspective in choosing the most suitable procedures for collecting data, assist participants in exploring the topic of inquiry, shift the data analysis to subtler aspects of the data, facilitate seeing patterns in data as the data analysis proceeds, and communicate artfully the full measure of the results by presenting artwork, music, poetry, symbols, and intuitive interpretations along with the traditional text presentation of the results.

The use of alternative states of consciousness, imagination, and intuition is essential to intuitive inquiry. The application of these creative processes is, therefore, discussed phase by phase in the following section.

PHASES OF INTUITIVE INQUIRY

Intuitive inquiry is a disciplined form of inward discovery. Like its forerunner, heuristic research, a comprehensive understanding of a particular facet of human experience ideally takes place in the awareness of the researcher as the inquiry proceeds. All the data are collected into the researcher's awareness and synthesized until a comprehensive understanding breaks through.

Selecting and Focusing the Topic of Inquiry

As is typically the case with all transpersonal approaches to research, intuitive inquiry investigates facets of human experience that are personally compelling to the researcher. Compelled by a topic, the researcher often feels pursued by it in her or his imagination, idle thoughts, and even dreams. In my research, most of my studies began as autobiographical. I had had the experience. In my research and that of colleagues, it often seems as though a particular topic is drawing, even compelling, our attention.

In conventional research, the researcher typically chooses a topic depending on scholarly interests, direction of the inquiry in specialty areas, and to some extent personal interests. In transpersonal approaches to research, intuition usually guides the "selection." Rather than choosing a topic, the researcher is selecting one that repeatedly attracts her or his attention. What often draws the attention and energy of graduate students does not even look like a research topic, at least initially. If the researcher closely observes what draws her or his attention, however, and deepens this focus through meditation and inner reflection, a manageable research topic often presents itself in awareness. It may take time. It may be perplexing and frustrating. Intuitive and imaginative information typically present right-hemisphere information, including symbols, pictures, music, or even vaguer indications of movement or shifts in consciousness. This information must be joined with the pragmatic and practical aspects of research inquiry to distill a topic suitable for inquiry.

A suitable topic for intuitive inquiry is

1. *Manageable.* If the researcher is a dissertation student, the topic (in my opinion) should be doable in a year. If a researcher has limited time, manageability means that the research inquiry can be completed within the time allotted, including periods of rest and relaxation.

2. *Clear.* Good research topics can be expressed easily in one sentence. The more a researcher understands a research topic, the simpler the basic statement of intent becomes.

3. *Simple and focused.* A simple and focused topic with significant implications for human experience is preferable to large, ambiguously defined topics.

4. *Concrete.* The research topic should be directly related to specific behaviors, experiences, or phenomena.

5. *Researchable.* Some topics are too grand or do not (yet) lend themselves to scientific inquiry.

6. *Active.* For a research topic to sustain the researcher's interest and energy, it should inspire the motivations and intellectual passions of the researcher.

7. *Essential.* A topic is essential when it signifies an experience of something still unknown (or seeking understanding). While an inquiry is just beginning, only the individual researcher can evaluate the potential and importance of a topic.

In summary, an ideal research topic is akin to a core search for the essence of a concrete, yet significant, human experience. This type of (re)search is a penetrating and comprehensive study of a clearly defined behavior, experience, or phenomenon that has personal meaning for the researcher. Particularity, depth, and involvement give intuitive inquiry (and all research) vigor and authority.

Collecting the Data:
Setting the Stage for the Experience
Under Investigation to Show Up

Two basic guidelines of designing a study are essential to intuitive inquiry. The first is general and applies to all research, and the second applies uniquely to transpersonal approaches, such as intuitive inquiry.

First, methods of research should be chosen to accommodate the topic of inquiry, rather than to follow the tradition within a field of study. In choosing methods, the essential question is this: Which method (or methods) best supports understanding the facet of human experience now being studied? Often, methods are chosen and imitated because they are readily available, easier to copy than create, or merely convenient. It is hoped that intuitive inquiry and other transpersonal approaches to research will give researchers the confidence and incentive to carefully select research approaches and methods, from among the many now available, and then creatively blend and synthesize these methods to suit the research project and the talents, skills, and values of the individual researcher.

Second, methods should set the stage for the phenomena being studied to show up! Creating a research design that closely reenacts, simulates, or generates the experience being studied is not new to psychological inquiry. Well-known procedures including reenactment, role play, psychodrama, and simulation, as well as newer procedures including creative and reenactment interviewing, storytelling, and narrative procedures, are possibilities. Challenging in a transpersonal approach, however, are reenacting, simulating, and generating transpersonal or spiritual experiences in the research participants—and perhaps the researcher—while collecting the data. Artful examples of using dreams as a source of intuition can be found in Mellick (1996). It becomes imperative to use intuitive and alternative states of consciousness as procedures, not merely as the topics of inquiry. (See Part III of this book for examples.)

Regardless of the actual methods used, the process of collecting data actively engages the researcher at many levels of awareness. It is quite possible, as Moustakas (1990) puts it, in describing heuristic methods, for the researcher to live "the question in waking, sleeping, and even dream states" (p. 28). All information gathered, formally or procedurally, informally, or intuitively, is considered potential data for analysis.

Incubating the Data

Incubation invites the creative process to do its work while the researcher rests, relaxes, and otherwise removes her or his focus from the research inquiry. The researcher "retreats from the intense, concentrated focus on the question" (Moustakas, 1990, p. 28). Rest and relaxation with ample open time to muse and do nothing are essential for the intuitive process to unfold naturally and spontaneously. So easy is it to minimize the importance of rest and relaxation that it may be necessary to schedule it. Empty space and time allow nonlinear brain activity to function more openly. Rather like suddenly remembering a childhood friend's name after giving up thinking about it, unexpected insights occur spontaneously and during activities unrelated to research, including while bathing, waking in the morning, dreaming, jogging, idling time away, meditating, and the like.

Incubating the data is an essential feature of intuitive inquiry. To proceed directly to data analysis without an incubating downtime for the new information to settle and shift in the awareness of the researcher undermines the intuitive process. The researcher may even wish to return to periods of incubation throughout the data analysis as well, especially if the analysis is lengthy or if the researcher feels stymied at any point.

Analyzing the Data

In intuitive inquiry, data analysis should accommodate the data that present themselves, rather than being immutably established at the outset of the study. If the data appear to be organized in key concepts and themes, qualitative content or thematic analysis applies. If the design allowed for focused descriptions of the constituents of one particular experience, phenomenological analysis applies. If the data are quantitative, various statistical procedures apply. If interview data resulted in long narrative or storytelling sessions, narrative and discourse analysis applies. If participants or the researcher suspects that thematic analysis would alter the unique voice(s) of those in the study, interviews or narratives can be presented intact to parallel the analysis. If data are deeply personal, reflective, and gathered from many sources, heuristic and hermeneutical analyses may apply. Many researchers blend the analytic procedures with beneficial results.

Intuitive inquiry, however, encourages incorporating intuitive processes and alternative states of consciousness as aspects of the data analysis itself. Examples of using dreamwork, creative expression, meditation practices, direct knowing, symbolic imagery, and various forms of intuition are found in Part III. In my research on sacred weeping, for example, I began using a hermeneutical approach to analyze ancient mystical texts on sacred weeping. I ended up using phenomenological content analysis to analyze the behavior descriptions found in the texts and hermeneutical, heuristic, and intuitive analysis to glean deeper meanings from the ancient texts. Specially, I simply could not comprehend and appreciate the meanings of the ancient texts without an inward and heuristic process, including extended meditation and concentration. Indeed, coming to a fuller appreciation of this particular experience would have been impossible if I had not had some of these experiences myself several years prior to this analysis.

Breakthroughs and Synthesizing the Findings

The most important feature of synthesizing data is the intuitive breakthroughs, those illuminating moments of insight when the data begin to reveal and shape themselves. Although breakthroughs about the topic may occur throughout the study, they often occur during the phases of incubation, analysis, and synthesis. In my experience, insights about particular aspects of the experience studied and about individual participants occur throughout the study, but overall patterns seem to reveal themselves only after individual participants or portions of the data have been analyzed. With all information freshly in mind, themes converge and patterns emerge. I usually work with a paper and pencil, drawing small and large circles—representing themes or stray ideas—and shifting the relationship and size of the circles, rather like a large Venn diagram. This process may go on for a few hours or several weeks with rest or incubation periods between work sessions. Other researchers work more verbally—bringing together ideas to form lists of interrelated themes, representative narratives, a sequence of developmental changes, or essential and irreducible features of the experience studied. Still other researchers ask the participants themselves to reflect on and synthesize each other's experiences.

Procedures for synthesizing data will vary with the inquiry and the researcher's skills. For intuitive inquiry, some of the most useful step-by-step procedures are those recommended for heuristic methods (Moustakas, 1990) and various forms of phenomenological inquiry, for example, Colaizzi (1978), Giorgi (1985), Moustakas (1994), Polkinghorne (1989), van Kaam (1959), and von Eckartsberg (1986).

Communicating the Findings
Through Sympathetic Resonance

Intuitive inquiry is completed in a creative expression of the findings, either in a conventional scholarly report, in creative synthesis, or in teaching. The researcher's task is to so richly portray the essence of the findings that a significant portion of the audience immediately apprehends and recognizes the experience as familiar. This audience response was introduced earlier as the principle of sympathetic resonance. It is expected, for example, not that a report on sacred weeping reproduce weeping in the audience but that many of the readers or listeners can immediately apprehend and recognize this experience of weeping from their own experiences or experiences they have closely witnessed.

Although not everyone is likely to apprehend and recognize the experience(s) portrayed, it is the researcher's responsibility to present the findings in as many forms or genres as necessary to maximize opportunities for sympathetic resonance to occur. With the technologies available now, laser disks, videos, recordings, and color photocopies of artwork can be included in scholarly reports. Incorporating these technologies may even be necessary to impart, in some measure, the rich and expansive nature of transpersonal and spiritual experiences. Intuitive inquiry aspires to honor these human experiences and their dynamic potential in every phase of research.

Honorable Closure

The final task of a research project is to celebrate the experience of the inquiry with honorable closure. Honorable closure completes the project by acknowledging the contributions that the researcher and others have made, recognizing without blame the difficulties and incompletions, making appropriate amends as necessary, expressing gratitude for the gifts of insight and delight, and celebrating the acts of generosity that allowed new understanding to unfold.

NOTES

1. Excerpt from *The Essential Rumi* (p. 36), Jelaluddin Rumi (Coleman Barks and John Moyne, Translators), 1995, San Francisco: HarperCollins. Copyright © 1995 by Threshold Books, Putney, VT. Reprinted by permission.

2. Excerpt from *The Selected Poetry of Rainer Maria Rilke* (pp. xiv-xv), by Stephen Mitchell (Editor and Translator), 1989, New York: Vintage International/Random House. Copyright © 1982 by Stephen Mitchell. Reprinted by permission of Random House, Inc.

CHAPTER 5

Transpersonal Awareness in Phenomenological Inquiry

Philosophy, Reflections, and Recent Research

Ron Valle
Mary Mohs

More than once when I
Sat all alone, revolving in myself,
The mortal limit of the self was loosed,
And passed into the nameless, as a cloud
Melts into heaven. I touch'd my limbs, the limbs
Were strange, not mine—and yet no shade of doubt
But utter clearness, and thro' loss of self
The gain of such large life as matched with ours
Were sun to spark—unshadowable in words,
Themselves but shadows of a shadow-world.
                    —Alfred, Lord Tennyson (1991, p. 328)

Phenomenological psychology invites us, as researchers, not just to an awareness of another perspective with a previously unrecognized body of knowledge but to a radically different way of being-in-the-world. In addition, this different way of being leads naturally to a different mode or practice of inquiry (i.e., the methods of phenomenological research). This chapter will compare phenomenological psychology to the more mainstream behavioral and psychoanalytic approaches (Valle, 1989), present the essence of the existential-phenomenological perspective (Valle, King, & Halling, 1989), describe the nature of an emerging transpersonal-phenomenological psychology (Valle, 1995), and present an overview of the transpersonal dimensions or themes emerging from seven recently completed empirical phenomenological research projects.

PHILOSOPHY AND APPROACHES IN PSYCHOLOGY

Existentialism as the philosophy of being became intimately paired with phenomenology as the philosophy of experience because it is our experience alone that serves as a means or way to inquire about the nature of existence (i.e., what it means to be). Existential phenomenology as a specific branch or system of philosophy was, therefore, the natural result, with what we have come to know as phenomenological methods being the manifest, practical form of this inquiry. Existential phenomenology when applied to experiences of psychological interest became existential-phenomenological psychology and has taken its place within the general context of humanistic or "third force" psychology; it is humanistic psychology that offers an openness to human experience as it presents itself in awareness.

From a historical perspective, the humanistic approach has been both a reaction to and a progression of the worldviews that constitute mainstream psychology, namely, behavioral-experimental and psychoanalytic psychology. It is in this way that the philosophical bases that underlie both existential-phenomenological and transpersonal ("fourth force") psychology have taken root and grown in this field.

In classic behaviorism, the human individual is regarded as a passive entity whose experience cannot be accurately verified or measured by natural scientific methods. This entity, seen as implicitly separate from its surrounding environment, simply responds or reacts to stimuli that impinge on it from the external physical and social world. Because only that which can be observed with the senses and quantified, and whose qualities and dimensions can be agreed to by more than one observer, is recognized as acceptable evidence, human behavior (including verbal behavior) became the focus of psychology.

In a partial response to this situation, the radical behaviorism of Skinner (e.g., 1974) claims to have collapsed this classic behavior-experience split by regarding thoughts and emotions as subject to the same laws that govern operant conditioning and the roles that stimuli, responses, and reinforcement schedules play within this paradigm. Thoughts and feelings are, simply, behaviors.

In the psychoanalytic perspective, an important difference with behavioral psychology stands out. Experience is recognized not only as an important part of being human but as essential in understanding the adult personality. It is within this context that both Freud's personal unconscious and Jung's collective unconscious take their places. The human being is, thereby, more whole yet is still treated as a basically passive entity that responds to stimuli from within (e.g., childhood experiences, current emotions, and unconscious motives), rather than the pushes and pulls from without. Whether the analyst speaks of one's unresolved oral stage issues or the subtle effects of the shadow archetype, the implicit separation of person and world remains unexamined, as does the underlying causal interpretation of all behavior and experience. Both behavioral and analytic psychology are grounded in an uncritically accepted linear temporal perspective that seeks to explain human nature via the identification of prior causes and subsequent effects.

EXISTENTIAL-PHENOMENOLOGICAL PSYCHOLOGY

Only in the existential-phenomenological approach in psychology is the implicitly accepted causal way of being seen as only one of many ways human beings can experience themselves and the world. More specifically, our being presents itself to awareness as a being-in-the-world in which the human individual and his or her surrounding environment are regarded as inextricably intertwined. The person and world are said to *co-constitute* one another. One has no meaning when regarded independently of the other. Although the world is still regarded as essentially different from the person in kind, the human being, with his or her full experiential depth, is seen as an active agent who makes choices within a given external situation (i.e., human freedom always presents itself as a situated freedom). Other concepts coming from existential-phenomenological psychology include the prereflective, lived structure, the life-world, and intentionality. All these represent aspects or facets of the deeper dimensions of human being and human capacity.

The prereflective level of awareness is central to understanding the nature of phenomenological research methodology. Reflective, conceptual experience is regarded as literally a "reflection" of a preconceptual and, therefore, prelanguaged, foundational, bodily knowing that exists "as lived" before or prior to any cognitive manifestation of this purely felt-sense. Consider, for example, the way a sonata exists or lives in the hands of a performing concert pianist. If the pianist begins to think about which note to play next, the style and power of the performance is likely to noticeably suffer.

This prereflective knowing is present as the ground of any meaningful (meaning-full) human experience and exists in this way, not as a random, chaotic inner stream of subtle senses or impressions but as a prereflective structure. This embodied structure or essence exists as an aspect or a dimension of each individual's *Lebenswelt* or life-world and emerges at the level of reflective awareness *as* meaning. Meaning, then, is regarded by the phenomenological psychologist as the manifestation in conscious, reflective awareness of the underlying prereflective structure of the particular experience being addressed. In this sense, the purpose of any empirical phenomenological research project is to articulate the underlying lived structure of any meaningful experience on the level of conceptual awareness. In this way, understanding for its own sake is the purpose of phenomenological research. The results of such an investigation usually take the form of basic constituents (essential elements) that collectively represent the structure or essence of the experience for that study. They are the notes that compose the melody of the experience being investigated.

Possible topics for a phenomenological study include, therefore, any meaningful human experience that can be articulated in our everyday language such that a reasonable number of individuals would recognize and acknowledge the experience being described (e.g., "being anxious," "really feeling understood," "forgiving another," "learning," and "feeling ashamed"). These many experiences constitute, in a real sense, the fabric of our existence as experienced. In this way, phenomenological psychology with its attendant research methods has been, to date, a primarily existen-

tial-phenomenological psychology. From this perspective, reflective awareness and prereflective awareness are essential elements or dimensions of
human being as a being-in-the-world. They co-constitute one another. One
cannot be fully understood without reference to the other. They are truly
two sides of the same coin.

TRANSPERSONAL/TRANSCENDENT AWARENESS

Some experiences and certain types of awareness, however, do not seem
to be captured or illuminated by phenomenological reflections on descriptions of our conceptually recognized experiences and/or our prereflective
felt-sense of things. Often referred to as transpersonal, transcendent,
sacred, or spiritual experience, these types of awareness are not really
experience in the way we normally use the word, nor are they the same as
our prereflective sensibilities. The existential-phenomenological notion of
intentionality is helpful in understanding this distinction.

The words *transpersonal, transcendent, sacred,* and *spiritual* represent
subtle distinctions among themselves. For example, *transpersonal* currently
refers to any experience that is transegoic, including the archetypal realities
of Jung's collective unconscious as well as radical transcendent awareness.
Although notions such as the collective unconscious refer to states of mind
that are deeper than or beyond our normal ego consciousness, *transcendent*
refers to a completely sovereign or soul awareness without the slightest
inclination to define itself as anything outside itself including contents of
the mind, either conscious or unconscious, personal or collective (i.e.,
awareness that is not only transegoic but *transmind*). This distinction
between transpersonal and transcendent awareness may lead to the emergence of a fifth force or more purely spiritual psychology.

In existential-phenomenological psychology, intentionality refers to the
nature or essence of consciousness as it presents itself. Consciousness is said
to be intentional, meaning that consciousness always has an object, whether
that intended object be a physical object, a person, or an idea or a feeling.
Consciousness is always a "consciousness of" something that is not consciousness itself. This particular way of defining or describing intentionality
directly implies the deep, implicit interrelatedness between the perceiver
and that which is perceived that characterizes consciousness in this approach. This inseparability enables us, through disciplined reflection, to

illumine the meaning that was previously implicit and unlanguaged for us in the situation as it was lived.

Transcendent awareness, on the other hand, seems somehow "prior to" this reflective-prereflective realm, presenting itself as more of a space or ground from which our more common experience and felt-sense emerge. This space or context does, however, present itself in awareness, and is, thereby, known to the one who is experiencing. Moreover, implicit in this awareness is the direct and undeniable realization that this foundational space is not of the phenomenal realm of perceiver and the perceived. Rather, it is a noumenal, unitive space within or from which both intentional consciousness and phenomenal experience manifest. From reflections on my experience, I (Valle, 1989) offer the following six qualities or characteristics of transpersonal/transcendent awareness (often recognized in the practice of meditation):

1. There is a deep stillness and peace that I sense as both existing as itself and, at the same time, as "behind" all thoughts, emotions, or felt senses (bodily or otherwise) that might arise or crystallize in or from this stillness. I experience this as an *isness* or *amness* rather than a state of *whatness* or "I am this or that." This stillness is, by its nature, neither active nor in the body and is, in this way, prior to both the prereflective and reflective levels of awareness.

2. There is an all-pervading aura or feeling of love for and contentment with all that exists, a feeling that exists simultaneously in my mind and heart. Although rarely focused as a specific desire for anyone or anything, it is, nevertheless, experienced as an intense, inner energy or inspired "pressure" that yearns, even "cries," for a creative and passionate expression. I sense an open embracing of everyone and everything just as they are, which literally melts into a deep peace when I find myself able to simply "let it all be." Peace of mind is, here, a heartfelt peace.

3. Existing as or with the stillness and love is a greatly diminished, and on occasion absent, sense of "I." The more common sense of "I am thinking or feeling this or that" becomes a fully present "I am" or simply, when in its more intense form, as "amness" (pure Being in the Heideggerian sense). The sense of a "perceiver" and "that which is perceived" has dissolved; there is no longer any "one" to perceive as we normally experience this identity and relationship.

4. My normal sense of space seems transformed. There is no sense of "being there," of being extended in and occupying space, but, similar to the previously mentioned, simply Being. Also, there is a loss of awareness of my body sense as a thing or spatial container. This ranges from an experience of distance from sensory input to a radical forgetfulness of the body's very existence. It is here that my everyday, limited sense of body-space touches a sense of the infinite.

5. Time is also quite different from my everyday sense of linear passing time. Seemingly implicit in the sense of stillness described here is also a sense of time "hovering" or standing still, of being forgotten (i.e., no longer a quality of mind) much as the body is forgotten. No thoughts dwelling on the past, no thoughts moving into the future—hours of linear time are experienced as a moment, as the eternal Now.

6. Bursts or flashes of insight are often part of this awareness, insights that have no perceived or known antecedents but that emerge as complete or full-blown. These insights or intuitive "seeings" have some of the qualities of more common experience (e.g., although "lighter," there is a felt weightiness or subtle "content" to them), but they initially have an "other-than-me" quality about them, as if the thoughts and words that emerge from the insights are being done to or, even, through me—a sense that my mind and its contents are vehicles for the manifestation as experience of something greater and/or more powerful than myself. In its most intense or purest form, the "other-than-me" quality dissolves as the "me" expands to a broader, more inclusive sense of self that holds within it all that was previously felt as "other-than-me."

Since the publication of these six qualities, we have come to recognize two additional dimensions or essential characteristics of transcendent awareness: (a) a surrendering of one's sense of control with regard to the outcome of one's actions and the dissolution of fear that seems to always follow this "letting go," and (b) the transformative power of transcendent experience, realized as a change in one's preferences, inclinations, emotional and behavioral habits, and understanding of life itself. This self-transformation is often personally painful because this power both challenges and changes the comfortable patterns of thoughts and feelings we have so carefully constructed through time, a transformation of who we believe we are.

These eight qualities or dimensions call us to a recontextualization of intentionality by acknowledging a field of awareness that appears to be inclusive of the intentional nature of mind but, at the same time, not of it. In this regard, I (Valle, 1989, 1998b) offer the notion of a "transintentionality" to philosophically address this consciousness *without* an object (Merrell-Wolff, 1973). As phenomenological psychologist and researcher Steen Halling (personal communication, July 25, 1988) has rightfully pointed out, consciousness without an object is also consciousness without a subject. Transintentional awareness, therefore, represents a way of being in which the separateness of a perceiver and that which is perceived has dissolved, a reality not of (or in some way beyond) time, space, and causation as we normally know them.

Here is a bridge between existential/humanistic and transpersonal/transcendent approaches in psychology. It is here that we are called to recognize the radical distinction between the reflective/prereflective realm and pure consciousness, between rational/emotive processes and transcendent/spiritual awareness, between intentional knowing of the finite and being the infinite. It is, therefore, mind, not consciousness per se, that is characterized by intentionality, and it is our recognition of the transintentional nature of Being that calls us to investigate those experiences that clearly reflect or present these transpersonal dimensions in the explicit context of phenomenological research methods.

FURTHER REFLECTIONS AND RECENT
RESEARCH ON TRANSPERSONAL EXPERIENCE

Following are our personal reflections on these dimensions as well as a description of recently completed phenomenological research in this area. Our purpose and hope in offering these reflections and information is to deepen our understanding of transcendent experience through the application of phenomenological research methodology and to facilitate the emergence of a new approach: *transpersonal-phenomenological psychology.*

This presentation is based on the following thoughts regarding the meaning of *transpersonal* in this context. On the basis of the themes that Huxley (1970) claimed to compose the *perennial philosophy,* I (Valle, 1989) presented five premises that characterize any philosophy or psychology as transpersonal:

1. That a transcendent, transconceptual reality or Unity binds together (i.e., is immanent in) all apparently separate phenomena, whether these phenomena be physical, cognitive, emotional, intuitive, or spiritual

2. That the individual or ego-self is not the ground of human awareness but, rather, only one relative reflection-manifestation of a greater transpersonal (as "beyond the personal") Self or One (i.e., pure consciousness without subject or object)

3. That each individual can directly experience this transpersonal reality that is related to the spiritual dimensions of human life

4. That this experience represents a qualitative shift in one's mode of experiencing and involves the expansion of one's self-identity beyond ordinary conceptual thinking and ego-self awareness (i.e., mind is not consciousness)

5. That this experience is self-validating

It has been written and taught for millennia in the spiritual circles of many cultures that sacred experience presents itself directly in one's awareness (i.e., without any mediating sensory or reflective processes) and, as such, is self-validating. The direct personal experience of God is, therefore, the "end" of all spiritual philosophy and practice.

Transcendent/sacred/divine experience has been recognized and often discussed, both directly and metaphorically, as either intense passion or the absolute stillness of mind (these thoughts and those that follow regarding passion and peace of mind are from Valle, 1995). In day-to-day experience, a harmonious union of passion and stillness or peace of mind is rarely experienced. Passion and stillness are regarded as somehow antagonistic to each other. For example, when one is passionately involved with some project or person, the mind is quite active and intensely involved. On the other hand, the calm, serene, and profoundly peaceful quality of mind that often accompanies deep meditation is fully disengaged from and, thereby, disinterested in things and events of the world.

What presents itself as quite paradoxical on one level offers a way to approach the direct personal experience of the transcendent, that is, to first recognize and then deepen any experience in which passion and peace of mind are simultaneously fully present in one's awareness. If divine presence manifests in human awareness in these two ways, and sacred experience is what one truly seeks, it becomes important to approach and understand those experiences wherever these two dimensions exist in an integrated and harmonious way. In this way, one comes to understand the underlying essence that these dimensions share rather than simply being satisfied with the seeming opposites they first appear to be.

The relationship between passion and peacefulness is addressed in many of the world's scriptures and other spiritual writings. These two threads, for example, run through the Psalms (May & Metzger, 1977) of the Judeo-Christian tradition. At one point, we read, "Be still and know that I am God" (Psalm 46, p. 691) and "For God alone my soul waits in silence" (Psalm 62, p. 701), and at another point, "For zeal for thy house has consumed me" (Psalm 69, p. 707) and "My soul is consumed with longing for thy ordinances" (Psalm 119, p. 749). Stillness, silence, zeal, and longing all seem to play an essential part in this process.

In his teachings on attaining the direct experience of God through the principles and practices of Yoga, Paramahansa Yogananda (1956) affirms, "I am calmly active. I am actively calm. I am a Prince of Peace sitting on the throne of poise, directing the kingdom of activity" (p. 6). And, more recently, Treya Wilber (quoted in Wilber, 1991) offers an eloquent exposition of this integration:

> I was thinking about the Carmelites' emphasis on passion and the Buddhists' parallel emphasis on equanimity. It suddenly occurred to me that our normal understanding of what passion means is loaded with the idea of clinging, of wanting something or someone, of fearing losing them, of possessiveness. But what if you had passion without all that stuff, passion without attachment, passion clean and pure? What would that be like, what would that mean? I thought of those moments in meditation when I've felt my heart open, a painfully wonderful sensation, a passionate feeling but without clinging to any content or person or thing. And the two words suddenly coupled in my mind and made a whole. Passionate equanimity—to be fully passionate about all aspects of life, about one's relationship with spirit, to care to the depth of one's being but with no trace of clinging or holding, that's what the phrase has come to mean to me. It feels full, rounded, complete, and challenging. (pp. 338-339)

It is here that existential-phenomenological psychology with its attendant descriptive research methodologies comes into play. For if, indeed, we each identify with the contents of our reflective awareness and speak to and/or share with one another from this perspective to better understand the depths and richness of our meaningful experience, then phenomenological philosophy and method offer us the perfect, perhaps only, mirror to approach transcendent experience. Experiences that present themselves as passionate, as peaceful, or as an integrated awareness of these two become the focus for exploring in a direct, empirical, and human scientific way the nature of transcendent experience as we live it. Here are the "flesh" and promise of a transpersonal-phenomenological psychology.

At this time, we are pleased that a more formal emergence of transpersonal-phenomenological psychology has already begun. All reported, each in its own chapter (in Valle, 1998a), seven recent research studies employing an empirical phenomenological approach have investigated experiences with transpersonal qualities or dimensions: "Being Voluntarily Silent" (Ourania Elite), "Being With a Dying Person" (Tom West), "Feeling Grace in Being of Service to the Terminally Ill" (Paul Gowack & Valerie Valle), "Being With the Suffering of Orphaned Children" (Patricia Qualls), "Encountering a Divine Presence During a Near-Death Experience" (Tim West); "Experiencing Unconditional Love From a Spiritual Teacher" (Craig Matsu-Pissot), and "Being Carried Along by a Series or Flow of Unforeseen Circumstances or Events" (D. Hanson & Jon Klimo).

Although we refer the reader to each of these particular reports for a list of the specific constituents presented in each study, a reflective overview of these results reveals an emerging pattern of common elements or themes. We offer these eleven themes as a beginning matrix or tapestry of transpersonal dimensions interwoven throughout the descriptions of these experiences, not as constituents per se resulting from a more formal protocol analysis. As we looked over the results of these studies, these themes naturally emerged, falling, even, into a natural order. Some are clearly distinct, whereas others appear as more implicitly interconnected. These themes are

1. An instrument, vehicle, or container for the experience
2. Intense emotional or passionate states, pleasant or painful
3. Being in the present moment, often with an acute awareness of one's authentic nature
4. Transcending space and time
5. Expansion of boundaries with a sense of connectedness or oneness, often with the absence of fear
6. A stillness or peace, often accompanied by a sense of surrender

7. A sense of knowing, often as sudden insights and with a heightened sense of spiritual understanding

8. Unconditional love

9. Feeling grateful, blessed, or graced

10. Ineffability

11. Self-transformation

Let us look at each of these themes in turn.

It seems that the transpersonal/transcendent aspects of any given experience manifest in, come through, or make themselves known via an identifiable form or vehicle. This theme was evident in all seven research studies, the specific forms being silence, being with the dying, being with suffering, near-death experience, being with one's spiritual teacher, and synchronicity. Transpersonal experiences can come through many forms including meditation, rituals, dreams, sexual experience, celibacy, initiations, music, breath awareness, physical and emotional pain, psychedelic drugs, and the experience of beauty. (Maslow's, 1968, description and discussion of peak experiences are relevant here as well as to a number of the themes discussed below.) We again use a musical analogy: Just as the violin, piano, flute, or voice can be an instrument for the manifestation/ expression of a melody, so, too, there are many ways in and through which consciousness reveals its nature.

The existential phenomenologist may interpret this as further evidence for the intentional nature of consciousness, that this is simply the way in which consciousness presents itself to the perceiver. There is also the view that consciousness is a constant stream of "energy" existing beyond the duality of subject-object (i.e., consciousness *without* an object) that flows through all creation, being both all-pervasive and unitive by its nature. Aware of the paradox implied in this perspective, Capra (1983) states,

> [The mystical view] regards consciousness as the primary reality and ground of all being. In its purest form, consciousness . . . is non-material, formless, and void of all content; it is often described as "pure consciousness," ultimate reality, "suchness," and the like. This manifestation of pure consciousness is associated with the Divine. . . . The mystical view of consciousness is based on the experience of reality in non-ordinary modes of awareness, which are traditionally achieved through meditation, but may occur spontaneously in the process of artistic creation and in various other

contexts. Modern psychologists have come to call non-ordinary experiences of this kind "transpersonal." (p. 297)

The next theme, intense emotional or passionate states, overlaps with the first in that these states can be considered a vehicle. Yet these states also stand alone, ranging on a continuum from being an instrument for transcendence to being a reflection of transcendence itself. Representing emotion as an instrument, consider the words of one of Qualls's coresearchers:

> I feel this deep, soul level kind of sadness. It speaks of the softness and the beauty of the human soul that suffers.

One of Tom West's research participants claimed,

> I was besieged by emotions that I'd never dealt with before.

And Hanson and Klimo report one response as,

> It was an exhilarating feeling, very powerful.

Qualities that characterize the latter side of the spectrum include joy, elation, bliss, euphoria, peace, and contentment. The following description from one of the protocols in Tim West's study addresses this:

> I never knew that such peace, such bliss could exist. . . . I felt the joy, the peace, the deeply loving, caring, glorious energy of that presence.

Elite quotes one of her participants as saying,

> I started to feel extremely happy—happier than usual. I'm usually a pretty happy person, but this state of not speaking made me feel very loving and very happy and quite contented with life and everything that was going on around me.

The third theme, being in the present moment, often with an acute awareness of one's authentic nature, appears explicitly in a number of the studies. Gowack and V. Valle report that this experience is described in all 12 of their coresearchers' descriptions. Responses from these coresearchers include,

Grace grounded me in the present and surrounded me as though always being part of my dominion, my environment.

Mentally, it is an experience of alertness at an elevated level. I feel merged with the moment, feeling the complete rightness of now. There is no sense of serving another, but only of being in this moment.

Elite describes her research participants as becoming involved with both the internal and external world in a deeper and more intense way and as seeing the present as playing a vital role in one's life. She quotes one of her participants:

There was this incredibly predominant sense of a tremendous amount of energy saved, on a moment to moment basis, from not having to talk. . . . I could be more directly in the experience and less in the words. . . . I could observe my own feelings and my feelings interacting with people with a heightened Awareness.

With Treya Wilber's thoughts on passionate equanimity in mind, is this not what is needed to be fully passionate about all aspects of life without clinging, without one's mind "hanging on"? If one is fully present, fully aware in each moment, there is no clinging, no attachment to what was or will be. There is, simply, a constant letting go into the next moment, into whatever is next.

Elite weaves this element of being in the moment with our next theme, transcending time and space:

When one is in the here and now, the ever present, one finds oneself nowhere (now-here) because all time (past, present, and future) is contained in the now. This is the point of timelessness . . . the timeless dimension of the Divine.

This theme is clearly illustrated in this description offered by one of Tim West's respondents:

I became Light. . . . It was infinite, and I was conscious of this eternity, yet there was no reference, just pure conscious awareness of vast eternity, eternal space, going beyond your conception of speed, beyond your conception of space, being aware of so much yet no time passed. And yet all time passed.

In the fifth theme, the researchers reported their participants as feeling connected in various ways to nature, people, or God. In this sense of oneness, there appeared to be an absence of fear. Gowack and V. Valle identified one of their constituents as the feeling of oneness or being connected to all human beings and to all there is. This experience was an exceptionally spiritual one for those who felt connected with God, the universe, a Higher Power, or the inner Self. Examples from their protocols include,

> I just suddenly found myself connected into and acting from a very "deep" place. I was aware of oneness.
>
> I combed his hair, washed his face, swabbed his mouth, all with the touch I would imagine belonging to an angel. I did not feel like I was important . . . but that I had transcended my usual self and was in touch with the sacredness of all things on this earth.

Stillness and peace are central to the next theme. One of Hanson and Klimo's coresearchers simply shared,

> I remember feeling very peaceful inside.

Gowack and V. Valle report one participant stating,

> I have had so many gifts from being with the dying. . . . I carry on caring for my friend, caring for myself. I work in a kind of stillness.

Referring again to Treya Wilber, she speaks of equanimity as being a key ingredient to feeling passion without attachment.

This stillness is often accompanied by a sense of surrender. Life experience tells us that surrender of this type (i.e., that implicit in peace of mind) evolves from letting go of, or surrendering, one's need to predict and control the events in one's life. In their study of "being carried along by a series or flow of unforeseen circumstances or events," Hanson and Klimo emphasize the role of surrender:

> Surrender is an important issue here as these subjects open to possibilities beyond the form of the desire that they are attached to.

One of their participants said,

> It was like not being in control of what was happening, but it was all right. I knew if I surrendered to it I could ride on the power of it.

Matsu-Pissot offers the following statement from one of the protocols in his study:

> [I am] getting where I'm not trying to control things as much.

The next three themes—a sense of knowing, with a heightened sense of spiritual understanding; unconditional love; and feeling grateful, blessed, or graced—present themselves as deeply interwoven, each one appearing most often in the context of the other two. Tim West's thoughts regarding his findings reflect this integration:

> This contact with the divine is characterized by such infinite power, loving acceptance, and complete immersion in feelings of well-being or safety that the experiencer emerges with a knowledge of ultimate reality which is at odds with what he or she has experienced in day-to-day life. The experience engenders intense feelings of gratitude, a sense of grace, and a sense of a private and personal communication with and acquisition of knowledge from a divine source.

This characterization is based on the words offered by his coresearchers, for example:

> What I bring from this [experience] is a sense of total understanding. There is this pure [unconditional] love that I want to radiate outward.

One of Tom West's research participants reflects this interrelationship of themes as well:

> He really afforded me the opportunity to see God in even broader ways than I've ever experienced God. . . . I could let go and say good-bye, and also say "thank you," with a tremendous, deep abiding sense of gratitude. That's just what gratitude is basically—it's the ability to be present to the love that's there.

Two coresearchers in Matsu-Pissot's study address these themes:

[This is] the experience of a love that acknowledges the expression of the truth of myself.

I felt blessed, protected, and this feeling seemed very permanent. . . . Those dear people who have given unconditional love to me still do so from the other side.

The 10th theme, ineffability, arose from the different researchers' statements regarding how difficult it was for their participants to describe their experience. One of the coresearchers from Tim West's study describes this aspect:

Being asked about my feelings when I experienced a divine presence, I am immediately at a loss for words. For my trouble with explaining what I felt is that I am truly speechless . . . as soon as I bring it out into words, they're so limiting; it brings it down and it tries to package something that is boundless, endless, and eternal.

Elite, in summarizing her findings, says:

The spiritual writings of the ages repeatedly describe its [silence's] essence as masked by paradox and riddles. Ironically, only silence itself can best describe the silent phenomenon. It can be described as the Sacred Silence— an ineffable experience indeed!

The last theme is in some ways the most powerful; it represents the personal mark these experiences left on the one who experienced them: self-transformation. The breaking down and re-forming of existing patterns of who we think we are is at the heart of spiritual development as a living process (e.g., Ram Dass, 1976; Watts, 1966). We present this as the last theme because it seems to be present in, and the culmination of, all the processes represented by the other 10, both individually and collectively. The selected words of the research participants from the different studies address this theme in different ways. One of Elite's coresearchers said,

There was very much a sense of rebirth that came out of the birthing, that came out of the struggle of those days.

One of Tim West's participants stated,

I'm not as judgmental, and I'm less interested in hanging out with or listening to the people who are judgmental.

A coresearcher in Matsu-Pissot's study said,

I'm able to deal with what happens on a better level; [I am] much more appreciative and [have] much less resistance.

And Qualls, as a researcher integrating and expressing her findings, concluded,

Suffering has the potential to transform the sufferer and/or caregiver, and offers an opportunity for the sufferer and/or caregiver to experience discovery and [personal] growth, and to give and/or receive compassion and love.

CONCLUDING THOUGHTS AND QUESTIONS

The findings of these seven phenomenological research studies, and the themes that they seem to share, have deepened our understanding of the nature of transpersonal/transcendent experience and appear quite consistent with what others have reported in this regard. In addition to Maslow's (1968) related work on peak experiences and the qualities suggested earlier (Valle, 1989), Grof (1985), for example, has done extensive research on nonordinary states of awareness. He identifies a number of characteristics common to these states including transcending space and time; the distinction between matter, energy, and consciousness; and the separation between the individual and the external world. Our impression of the descriptions that have emerged from self-investigations as well as the results reported from more formal analyses is that these nonordinary or altered states of awareness are often accompanied or followed by a deeper sense of spirituality and self-transformation.

Although the results of phenomenological research do, indeed, deepen our understanding of our experience, these same findings raise both new and ancient questions regarding the paradoxical nature of human experience and existence itself: Are we created or a manifestation of a greater essence? Is duality real, or are we missing the oneness in and of all things? Do cause and effect exist, or is everything happening in a spontaneous and simultaneous way? Are there a perceiver and a perceived, or do we not recognize the one Being? Does creative expression spring from passion or a deep inner stillness? Do we truly accomplish good things in the world, or is it "grace"? Is there an essence of life and reality or only what we perceive them to be?

Regardless of how we answer these questions or how each of us perceives life to be, there remains a *mystery,* the mystery of ultimate Reality. This mystery may be something we can "solve" with our minds, or it may, in the classic phenomenological sense, be a basic constituent of the experience of ultimate Reality itself. In any event, it seems to us that the very act of questioning emerges from a dualistic mind-set or ground, that is, "to question" implies by its nature both the one who questions and that about which one is asking. Whenever the mind attempts to understand the essence of the transcendent realm, it always ends in paradox.

Even with this paradox, and whatever its prereflective constituents may reveal themselves to be, there is undeniably a consciousness or awareness that simply *is.* With this "in mind," we leave the reader with the following more philosophical reflection. If one regards consciousness as intentional in nature, that is, that consciousness always *has* an object, then, in both reason and mystical experience, consciousness *is* the intended object as well. Intentionality is a quality of the mind, not consciousness. We are always, implicitly and unavoidably, connected with that which is *beyond.*

CHAPTER 6

ORGANIC RESEARCH

Feminine Spirituality Meets Transpersonal Research

Jennifer Clements
Dorothy Ettling
Dianne Jenett
Lisa Shields

> The greatest sacred stories are our own stories. This is because the Spirit tells our stories to us in the unfolding of our life journeys.
>
> —Meinrad Craighead (1993, p. 182)

A mutual desire to find a sacred and personal voice in our individual research projects brought us together four years ago. We have met weekly since that time to develop a methodology that uses the personal experience of the researcher and coresearchers to create a sacred work that offers transformation and healing to all who engage in it, researchers and readers alike.

Our work is a collaboration. Through the years, we have come to know how each of us contributes to the final product from our different creative styles. Jennifer is the scribe for this article, putting into words the concept of organic research that has grown into the center of our circle of four.

ONCE UPON A TIME:
THE STORY OF OUR NAMING

We felt terrible that we burned Lisa's big, beautiful blueberry muffins that day, but the four of us got so involved in our discussion that we completely forgot we had put them in the oven.

Lisa stretched out on the bed like a cat. There are cushions against the wall, but lying down is a lot more comfortable. Lisa's energy and luxurious beauty fool some people into missing her considerable depth.

Dianne coiled on the floor wearing something Indian, probably. Since her work in Kerala, India, began, we all depend on her for some mix of Western pragmatism with a freely offered struggle to move into acceptance of the unfathomable East in her daily life.

Dorothy sat across the room in the big Morris chair. She fools you, too. Although coming on as informed, contained, and competent, she also has a lot of experience with her own difficult and dark inner work.

Jennifer is the one who keeps things in order, loves words, gets fascinated by her own brilliant insights, and is awed by Dianne's ability to express her feelings. She lounged on the couch near the tape recorder.

Four years ago, at the beginning of spring quarter, Dianne and Jennifer came to the first meeting of their weekly women's group at the Institute of Transpersonal Psychology. They looked at each other across the altar spread on the floor, which had cookies and flowers and a cast stone Mama Goddess, and had to admit that their group had dwindled to two. That night they came to realize that it was research they cared about, and they decided to invite Dorothy and Lisa to join them.

So now, years later, we had set aside a weekend to sum up the experiences and discoveries that had come from our weekly discussions of how traditional research methods just didn't leave room for feminine creativity in our research work. We realized that a collective vision was beginning to emerge among the four of us, a vision of a new way to do research.

We were trying to name our vision, and we began, as these discussions often do, by wondering whether the transpersonal point of view emphasizes transcendent experiences at the expense of the day-to-day sacred.

Dorothy spoke. "Transpersonal for me emphasizes the crossing-over rather than the being-above, like it might cross over from *just* the personal into something *beyond* the personal."

Jennifer interrupted, "But does it *include* the personal?"

"You mean whether transpersonal means personal plus . . . ?" asked Dianne.

Lisa sat up and clowned, "We could call it Personal Plus! For those heavy flow days." We all shrieked and collapsed into luscious silliness. Barely able to speak through our helpless laughter, we went on to consider yoni research or vulva research or moon research.

"Seriously, though," Lisa continued, "this research starts with a seed and flowers into something. You start with the seed of your own story, gather the stories of your coresearchers, and then let whatever happens happen."

"Exactly," Jennifer agreed. "The word that keeps coming up for me is *sacred*. Even feminist methodology, which *does* have lots of what we are talking about, does not carry the idea of the sacred, which is primary for us."

Dianne looked thoughtful. "What's funny is I keep thinking about this moon metaphor. It finishes and it starts all over again."

"Oh, dear, we're back to moon research." We all began laughing again. We agreed that it is a powerful and suitable metaphor: feminine, changing, and mysterious. We joked about calling ourselves the Lunar Cowgirls.

Dianne got up. "It's also clear to me that many of the classic researchers or even the *feminist* researchers still have an idea about what they are going to find before they find it. They set out to *prove* something, which seems completely the opposite of what we are doing."

Dorothy agreed. "With my dissertation, I remember not knowing until I went to do the work, actually, what in the heck I was going to do with all of the data. I think I'd feel much more secure, now, to just jump right in there and see what happens."

Jennifer had a brainstorm. "I wonder if we couldn't call it something like *organic* research, knowing that it comes from our own process."

Lisa smiled. "Because then you can see it as coming from a seed that you nurture and water. That's perfect."

FIVE CHARACTERISTICS

Lisa's seed took root as we four, and a number of doctoral students at the Institute of Transpersonal Psychology, began to work with the concepts of organic research. A metaphor began to emerge.

To grow a healthy and productive tree, the gardener must first prepare the ground by loosening and fertilizing the soil. Then the seed can be planted. Underground, a complex root system develops. The tree sends up a shoot, and branches develop. Finally, the tree bears fruit, which contains tomorrow's seeds. We use this metaphor to describe the five characteristics of organic research.

Sacred: Preparing the soil
Personal: Planting the seed
Chthonic: The roots emerge
Relational: Growing the tree
Transformative: Harvesting the fruit

Sacred: Preparing the Soil

Before any seeds are planted, the earth must be spaded and broken up, old roots and stones removed, and fertilizer added.

Similarly, the ground of the research and the researcher must be prepared. Participation in the organic approach, either as researcher or as reader, calls for an expanded consciousness. This involves achieving an attitude that digs out old ways of thinking to allow for the sacred to emerge on all levels, from the everyday to the transcendent.

This approach is grounded in responsibility, reverence, and awe for the earth and all her inhabitants as well as for the mysteries of creativity. Doing this work requires honoring ourselves, our collaborators, our readers, and the context in which we work, as well as consciously keeping ourselves open to the gifts of the unconscious and the divine.

Dianne writes,

"The old organic world view, the vision that saw sacred presence in all of life, was made illegitimate in Western culture" (Starhawk, 1987, p. 7). We reclaim this vision of the interconnectedness of all which organic research often ritualizes. We use prayers in research, and give credence to synchronicities and dreams, understanding that they are gifts of knowledge.

I am interested in how the sacred images, stories, and rituals in Kerala, India, inform their wise social and political decisions, and I consciously ask myself the question, "How would this research look if it were sacred?" I surrounded myself with images of the snake for the year prior to doing research on the *naga,* or snake temples. As I began in Kerala, I did ritual for my photographic equipment, the film, the tapes, the books, and the computer. I blessed my tools with flowers and a prayer from my heart, thanking the women who had inspired me and who used their energy to write the books that had guided me and given me the information that I needed. I called on the Goddess Bhadrakali, protectress of Kerala, and the *nagas* for help.

Once I opened to this energy, I was suddenly invited to attend private rituals honoring the snake, was introduced to women who were on similar paths, and was led to obscure *naga* temples. I had no difficulty entering any temple, was graciously shown *sarpa kavus,* family snake groves by people who said that they recognized that I "was supposed to be there." As I was sitting in Manarasala *naga* temple, a stranger approached me and invited me to live with his family for several days to participate in the annual ritual of sacrifice and renewal to Bhadrakali.

Personal: Planting the Seed

After the ground has been prepared, the gardener plants the seed deep in the darkness of the earth.

This seed is the initial concept for the study, which comes from the researcher's profound personal experience. The researcher's story of her or his subjective experience of the topic becomes the core of the study. Unlike other research, which either ignores or dismisses the personal attitudes and experience of the researcher and which aims at objective observation only, organic research acknowledges the researcher's story as a point of beginning and as a filter for the other stories she or he will gather.

In her dissertation on women's experiences of psychospiritual descent, Nora Taylor (1996) begins with the story of her experience of the descent. We follow Nora from discontent to rage to healing. Nora gives us an intimate and detailed view of the experience that lies at the core of her research. In beginning with her own story, Nora emphasizes the importance of knowing her story to understand her research. She allows the reader to descend with her into the psychological underworld, and by doing it in such a personal way, she invites the reader to identify with the similarities and differences between Nora's story and her or his own.

Ginette Paris (1986), in this passage about the absence of personal feelings in poetry before Sappho, writes,

Today it seems self-evident that we may express personal feelings through poetry, literature, and song. But in an epoch when poetry was primarily a means of transmitting historical facts and collective myths, Sappho's description of her personal feelings seemed an audacity without precedent. (p. 48)

We feel that same "audacity without precedent" as we recommend including personal feelings in research, a practice alien to traditional methods. We also know that this encouragement of the personal voice of the researcher immeasurably deepens the research and increases its transformational potential for the reader.

Chthonic: The Roots Emerge

When the ground has been prepared and the seed has been planted, the gardener must trust that what happens underground will be successful. The seed splits open, and roots begin to emerge. This process follows the rules of nature, not those of the gardener. Even after the plant has emerged into the light, the invisible root system continues to grow unpredictably in the dark and to affect what happens above ground.

Similarly, organic research has a chthonic, underground life of its own. Although the research begins with responsible intent, the methodology often evolves and changes during the research because of synchronicities, dreams, intuition, or other manifestations of inner knowing. The researcher is urged to pay attention to expressions of the unconscious throughout the research process. Like roots, this realm cannot be controlled and is one that offers much richness to the evolution of the research.

Lisa writes,

As I was developing the method for my dissertation about beauty, body image, and the feminine (Shields, 1995), I had a dream that related to the questions I would use for the interviews. The dream went as follows: *I am looking at a photograph of a beautiful woman. The photograph is spliced together from two separate photographs; one is the most unattractive photograph, and the other is the most beautiful. When spliced together, the two separate photographs create the most beautiful photograph of all.* I interpreted this dream to relate to the questions I was going to use in the interviews. I decided on two questions for each of the interviews: (a) tell me about a time in your life in which you felt beautiful, and (b) tell me about a time in your life in which you felt unattractive.

Relational: Growing the Tree

A thin white stem with one leaf appears above ground, and the gardener can begin to see the progress of the plant. It grows gradually into a trunk with multiple limbs and branches and knotholes and leaves.

The personal stories of the coresearchers are branches that connect to the main trunk as they relate to the core story. The researcher and the coresearchers work together in face-to-face interviews to allow the stories to emerge in full color. Context is important; stories communicate not only to the thinking brain but also to the body, the heart, and the soul.

Dorothy writes,

> Last year, Robin Clark and I collaborated in a study with women living on the U.S./Mexico border in El Paso and Juárez (Ettling & Clark, 1996). They were participating in various programs of a women's center that were aimed at personal empowerment and collaboration across the border. We used a dual approach of personal interviews and group discussion to elicit the meaning of their involvement and what it had done for them.
>
> In using this methodology, we involve the women in designing the research. The women, themselves, corroborate the findings. Together, we create sacred space in which to do our work. As a result of my practice with this methodology, I realize that I no longer choose to do research with women that is not experienced as beneficial to them at some level.

Transformative: Harvesting the Fruit

Every spring, the tree flowers and bears fruit that is harvested for pleasure and for food. Seeds from the fruit may be planted back in the earth to grow new trees.

The fruits of organic research include transformation of the researcher, the coresearchers, and the readers, so far as each is willing to engage in both the conscious and unconscious aspects of the work and so far as each is willing to be changed through their involvement.

Lisa writes,

> The three of us—myself, along with my mother and grandmother as coresearchers—have felt closer to one another since the week of interviews and conversations (Shields, 1995). An incredible amount of trust made itself evident in the open and honest communication. All three of us have felt an

increase in intimacy. My grandmother states she feels more confident about herself and her future. Even when we're not around, she feels close to us. My mother feels that the interviews helped her come to a deeper understanding of her assertiveness and the overpowering aspect of her personality. I feel seen as a woman instead of as a daughter or granddaughter to these two important women in my life. We came to a very deep understanding of our differences as women. My mother and I had an incredible healing during the week of the interviews.

CONNECTIONS WITH AND ACKNOWLEDGMENTS OF OTHER RESEARCH METHODOLOGIES

For four years, organic research has been slowly emerging from the conversations, teaching, writing, and daily life of the four of us. During the early years, Dorothy and Lisa completed dissertations that contain the beginnings of the organic approach.

Since then, nine other dissertations either have been completed or are in progress that use the organic method, usually in combination with other methods. We have learned immeasurably from these studies. They are examples of a method that previously existed only as a possibility. They have given form to our concept, and we are hugely grateful for their groundbreaking and exploratory work.

The ideas we present here seem to us to have grown from the depths of our psyches, but, in reality, much of what we present is not new. Among the influences on our work, feminist and heuristic methodologies have played the most prominent role.

Feminist Methodologies

Dorothy writes,

Over the past two decades, there has been a revolutionary emphasis given to the expression of women's experience in psychological research. As Carol Gilligan (1982) has pointed out, women have been missing even as research subjects at the formative stages of our psychological theories. With the advent of women scholars in the fields of biological and social sciences, in particular, who challenged the appropriateness and validity of this practice, recent research has opened the door for startling new perspectives in the areas of growth and development of women. These perspectives, which touch at the core of how women see themselves and are seen, are having a profound impact on the transformation of consciousness in Western civilization.

Feminist research is a validation of women's experiences, ideas, and needs. Issues are generated from the viewpoint of women's experience. Bettina Aptheker (1989) writes about how the feminine experience differs from traditional ways of thinking:

> [The] dailiness of women's lives structures a different way of knowing and a different way of thinking. The process that comes from this way of knowing has to be at the center . . . of a woman's scholarship. . . . The point is to integrate ideas about love and healing, about balance and connection, about beauty and growing, into our everyday ways of being. We have to believe in the value of our own experiences and in the value of our ways of knowing, our ways of doing things. (pp. 253-254)

Dorothy continues, "Feminist research further insists that the inquirer be placed on the same critical plane as the participant in the research. Knowledge is held to be jointly constructed by the researcher and the research participants."

The Heuristic Method

As we turn to a consideration of heuristic research, Clark Moustakas, founder of the method, and colleague B. G. Douglass (1985) describe it.

> In its purest form, heuristics is a passionate and discerning personal involvement in problem solving, an effort to know the essence of some aspect of life through the internal pathways of the self. . . . When utilized as a framework for research, it offers a disciplined pursuit of essential meanings connected with everyday human experiences. (p. 39)

This method is much more akin to organic research than are most traditional approaches in its willingness to involve the researcher personally, to search for data in the realms of the unconscious, and to be awed by the results.

The heuristic method, however, seems to stand closer to phenomenology than does organic research. Heuristic research tends to be about the experience of fear or courage or being close to nature, whereas organic research is more likely to be about how women experience their bodies or relationships or psychological descent. The heuristic approach seems to invite inquiry about existential issues, whereas organic inquiry leads to the investigation of how life is lived. Heuristic research is more masculine, theoretical, and inward focused; the organic research studies, so far, tend to be more feminine, grounded, and focused toward offering ways of interpreting and improving daily life or social reality. As men begin to use the organic research method, this may change.

THE METHODOLOGY IN ACTION

Instead of providing the researcher with a set of processes or procedures, organic research offers ways the researcher might position herself or himself to harvest the information that becomes available both from her or his own psyche and from the stories of the coresearchers and the context of the research. Following are nine concrete suggestions for the researcher who is seeking to develop a method from the organic methodology, many with examples of how they have been used in actual studies.

The Topic

The topic of an organic study is rooted in the story of the researcher's own personal experience. Lisa's dissertation (Shields, 1995) uses the image of the triple goddess to structure her study of the interweaving stories about beauty, body image, and the feminine—stories about herself, her mother, and her grandmother. Although traditional research frowns on the lack of objectivity in interviewing one's own family, the organic approach sees the inherent intimacy of this situation as an opportunity to travel deeper into the psyches of the coresearchers. Many readers report crying as they read Lisa's dissertation. Our belief is that because Lisa was working with such intimate material, the stories touch a deeper level of the psyche where connection precedes competition and thereby have a greater power to change both the participants and the reader.

Aspects of the Study

All aspects of the study, as it evolves, are recorded and reported in the researcher's own voice. Dorothy introduces her study of women on the U.S./Mexican border (Ettling & Clark, 1996) in a way that succeeds in inviting the reader into the context of the work:

> In the late '60s I arrived in the dry, dusty terrain of El Paso, Texas. Immediately struck by the stark beauty of the low mountains which loomed to the south, I felt the sense of ruggedness which pervades the environment. . . . I never lost my first love for this earth and its peoples . . . which is at once inviting and yet painful to experience. . . . Here, a tiny river symbolizes the immense chasm between those belonging and [those] *del otro lado,* between the welcomed and the stranger, between opportunity and destitution. (p. 1)

Choosing Organic Methodology

Choosing to work with the organic methodology presupposes a moderately high level of consciousness about the researcher's own psychospiritual development. Organic methodology originates with the profound inner experience of the researcher. The approach assumes some psychological sophistication and inner experience by the researcher as well as an understanding of the mechanics and meanings of her or his experience. Coresearchers' stories can be set alongside the core experience of the researcher so that the reader may identify with the material and learn from it.

Reverence

Organic research grows from a reverence for the sacred aspects of the topic, the method, collaboration with the coresearchers, the context, and the implications of the inquiry and may include nonrational and nonverbal ways of gathering and reporting data. Wendy Rogers (1996), in her heuristic and organic study of loss of fertility, writes about the importance of the sacred in her work.

> Throughout this study, I have relied heavily on my relationship with Spirit, a prayer practice, and ritual. . . . [A] ritual I performed to acknowledge the anniversary of my loss of fertility . . . prompted a shift in my beliefs about

my loss of fertility. I shifted from a view of myself as barren and lacking creativity to a view of myself as sacred because I draw breath—as a baroness. This ritual served as encouragement to perform rituals throughout the implementation of the research. (p. 209)

Unique Method

The unique method of each organic study depends on the creativity of the researcher and is expected to evolve during the investigation because of influences both from within the researcher's psyche and from the progress of the study. Lisa's study begins with a dream, and her method often changes direction because of subsequent dreams. Despite knowing she was traveling in unfamiliar and chthonic waters, Lisa continued to act on her dreams and intuitions during the day-to-day process of gathering and analyzing her data.

The Goal

The goal of organic research is personal transformation for the reader of the study, the coresearchers, and the researcher. Reflecting on her study of infertility, Wendy Rogers (1996) writes about its impact on her.

Over and over again, I was challenged to trust my intuition and, over and over again, I was rewarded with deeper insight into the essence of the experience of loss of fertility. I was also given greater access to a deeper level of integration of my own loss of fertility . . . [as well as] in embracing my own authority and powerful knowing . . . [and] in giving voice to my truths and experience. (pp. 210-211)

The Fundamental Technique

The fundamental technique of organic research is telling and listening to stories. Nora Taylor (1996) writes about the importance of the relational aspects of interviewing in her work:

I [am] interested in the relationship aspect of the research: in how we each affect each other, particularly in the one-to-one relationship of an interview. . . . Relationship does make a difference. What's going on within me, as the researcher, while I'm interviewing affects the storyteller.

It also affects the story because, ultimately, the story is filtered through me. (p. 120)

Analysis of Organic Data

Analysis of organic data may be done by the researcher, by the coresearchers, and/or in the mind of the reader. The most personal and chthonic analysis is done by the reader as she or he reads the stories and identifies with them on an archetypal level. This method is likely to be used by most organic inquiries. Other methods of analysis will probably be used as well.

The researcher may ask all the coresearchers to analyze the data by reflecting on the others' stories. The researcher will probably also choose to comment on the data by commenting on her or his personal reaction to the material as well as its similarity to or differences with her or his core story. This type of analysis also gives the readers a model for shaping their opinions about how they may relate personally to the data.

The more extraverted or academic researcher will also choose to make a direct analysis of what she or he feels is to be learned from the data—of the similarities, differences, patterns, and implications. This may be done in rational or intuitive or in verbal or nonverbal ways.

The Final Form

The final form of an organic study is personal, engaging, and informative. Jennifer writes,

> In a study of women's experiences of menopause, Pam Davison and I spent days in the Stanford medical library researching studies on the relationship between menopause, hormone replacement, foods, and disease. Our intent was to blend this medical information with women's and doctors' stories of their own experiences of menopause into a book that would appeal to the average, intelligent woman. Our study was written as the continuing story of our experience of doing the research. The subject comes alive for the reader as she or he experiences the discoveries about the literature, the women's experiences, and our own lives as a complete and chronological story.

Dorothy speaks for each of us when she writes,

I have begun to see personal transformation in a much less individualistic way. I have been moved by the value and the power of sharing this process with others. Personal transformation is the on-going process of becoming fully oneself and sharing that with others. Through it, one knows and experiences connectedness and unity with all that is. It is the path of a consciously chosen spiritual journey.

CHAPTER 7

BECOMING MORE HUMAN AS WE WORK

The Reflexive Role of Exceptional Human Experience

Rhea A. White

The recesses of feeling . . . are the only places in the world in which we can catch real fact in the making, and directly perceive how even events happen, and how work is actually done.

—William James (1902, p. 492)

Since 1952, when I had a near-death experience, I have been interested in unusual, nonordinary experiences with qualities similar to my experience, which led me into parapsychology at the Duke University Parapsychology Laboratory in 1954. From then until 1989, I was identified with parapsychology, and I still am closely connected with it. Nevertheless, my interest in all forms of exceptional experience, not just psychic ones, has taken me beyond it, aided in part by the *exceptional human experience* (EHE) autobiography technique (to be described). Since 1989, I have been formally studying EHEs (White, 1990).

The ideas of many others have gone into the development of the concept of EHE. (For a history of the term, see White, 1990.) This concept has since evolved, and I have expressed its most recent explication (White, 1996c, 1997).

An EHE does not often spring forth full-blown. Rather, an EHE generally starts out as an *exceptional experience* (EE), that is, an anomalous one—one whose existence is considered questionable or impossible—in Western consensus reality. EEs are psychic, mystical, death-related, and strange encounter experiences that raise eyebrows.

Exceptional experiences are often shrugged off as oddities. Some people find them frightening and dismiss them. Some who have EEs are considered strange or even mentally ill—certainly deluded. Sometimes they are.[1] These experiences, however, can touch the experiencer in personal and significant ways that cannot be dismissed as ideas of reference. Rather, they seem to catalyze a process that eventually can lead to the realization of the person's higher human potential. Lives, worldviews, and even identities can be transformed. When this process of transformation is initiated, the EE becomes an exceptional *human* experience. Thus, all EHEs are exceptional experiences, but not all exceptional experiences are EHEs. EEs, in themselves, point the way to new possibilities of human knowledge. EHEs occur when the experiencer relates to and is connected with that knowledge and its source in a transformative way. EEs spotlight new areas of the unknown to be explored. EHEs are experiences of dynamic interaction and connection with that unknown.

In this chapter, I emphasize EEs and EHEs that can institute scientific innovations. Although hard scientists such as Kekulé (Bernd, 1978) and Poincaré (1913) have publicly recognized the EEs that served as catalysts for their research, they are exceptions. Usually, when scientists receive insights in nonordinary ways, they set out to verify those insights by empirical data and rational inference. If they succeed in their verification, as Kekulé and Poincaré did, they make no mention in their research reports of how they obtained the idea that was the actual impetus for the research. Moreover, in the physical sciences, rarely have these unacknowledged EEs changed the researchers themselves. I suggest that breakthrough insights in the psychological and social sciences are more likely to implicate the researcher, and others involved, than in the physical sciences.

Transpersonal psychology, especially—because it promotes firsthand study of various techniques for altering states of consciousness and the new levels of meaning and knowledge associated with them—is perhaps the discipline best situated to explore and use EHEs and to help others understand them. Humanistic and existential-phenomenological psychologists, because they sometimes explore what Maslow (1971) called *being cognition,* as well as self-actualization and other means of realizing human potential, may also encounter EEs/EHEs and could help extend the range of Western consensus reality to include them.

I do not think these experiences will be able to aid us in realizing our human potential until we first learn how to cooperate with the process involved. Without the key element of cooperation, these experiences will occur only sporadically, momentarily providing a spark that can only go out if we do not tend it. The first step in cooperating is to honor these experiences by maintaining an open stance toward them, welcoming their occurrence, making an effort to become familiar with the folklore and scientific findings of each type as it occurs, and helping colleagues and research participants to do the same. Finally, existential-phenomenological, humanistic, and transpersonal psychologists sometimes encounter EHEs in the natural course of their work. Such encounters place them in a special position to honor these experiences by writing and speaking, both publicly and professionally, of the experiences' role in their life and work, and by including mention of them in reports of research in which they act as facilitator rather than as subject. Occasionally, this is done, but more often, these experiences (if referred to at all) are described only in memoirs (e.g., Loewi, 1960). Standard research protocol would be enriched if broadened to include reporting the source of insights and ideas,[2] even when the empirical basis is questionable from the viewpoint of Western consensus reality, and especially when the research reported offers empirical verification of the "exceptional" key insight. Reflexively, if the insight forwards the research, it behooves us as researchers to honor the source of the insight.

The type of research referred to in this chapter is *creative research*— leading-edge investigations aimed at consolidating the researcher's *personal* creative insight, not investigations into the creative insights of others, unless the researcher has genuinely identified with them. EHEs are most likely to occur when the researcher is on the growing edge of the "known and accepted" and is attempting, through research, to discover what previously has not been captured or realized in the discipline. As the alchemists knew, scientists working at the boundary between the known and unknown (especially in the human sciences) are likely to—or may need to—advance their own process of self-realization for their work to proceed because they must go by a way that is unique and individual. Briggs (1990) uses the metaphor of the creator as alchemist who creates him- or herself as he or she discovers and becomes involved in the research. It is unlikely that we as researchers will get a foothold in the unknown merely by building a plank bridge by means of logical inference, based on data already gathered, although we need to make all the educated guesses possible. But when we have done all we possibly can, it is likely we still will fall short, unless some form of EE/EHE comes to the rescue. If it does, we must realize, beforehand, that it will not necessarily "make sense." It is our job as scientists to take this odd-looking puzzle piece and move it around, and perhaps even reshape it, until it fits the hole we are trying to fill or until it provides the plank we require to move forward.

As Kremer (1988) points out in regard to experiences associated with finding one's "tale of power" (a means of recognizing one's calling or, in his felicitous phrase, one's "personal trajectory"), such experiences will deviate from the "collective expectations of daily reality" simply because "they have the power of uniqueness stemming from a movement into the individual's creative center" (p. 35). Kremer's tales of power are mediated by or consist of various EEs as is the case with breakthrough science insights. Kremer notes that they have "a crazy edge to them . . . the price to be paid for stepping out of the collective consensual reality. We do not expect to find the crazy edge in cultures that provide a supportive framework" (p. 35). This is *not* the case, however, in Western, industrialized societies.

OVERVIEW OF EXCEPTIONAL HUMAN EXPERIENCES

EHEs form a large group of many types of experiences that heretofore have primarily been studied individually or in association with only a few other types. I am considering all of them as members of a single class to see (a) if any generalizations can be drawn that apply across the whole class and (b) if looking at them as one class can shed light on specific types of EHEs. I have identified 150 EEs (White, 1996b) that are potential EHEs and have provisionally classed them in the following five broad categories.

Mystical Experiences

Mystical experiences were once considered a type of religious experience, but increasingly they are reported and studied within a nonreligious context, in which they are referred to as peak experiences (Maslow, 1971), as flow experiences (Csikszentmihalyi, 1990), as a form of epiphany in literature (Holman, 1972), and in sports as being "in the zone" (Murphy & White, 1995). Grof and Grof (1989) class them as a type of spiritual emergence, and many are transpersonal experiences.

The secularization of mystical experiences may have been promoted by transpersonal psychology, which, although it often retains the religious context, also views the experiences as an aspect of human psychology, whereas in the Middle Ages many were regarded as supernatural. Sir Alister Hardy (1979) set out to collect religious experiences but ended up with many that were profound but not especially religious.

Leonard George (1995) points out that since the 1600s, a mystical experience has been "characterized by the feeling that, despite the apparent diversity in the world, everything forms a unity" (p. 186). He refers to Stace's observation that the unity is not simply perceived, but "it is sensed as certain knowledge, compared to which the apparent separation of objects in the world seems illusory" (p. 186). I am suggesting that both mystics and nonmystics perceive the same worlds, and neither is viewing an illusory one. As Steven Rosen (1994) has noted, it is not a case of either/or but of both/and. He therefore uses the image of the Möbius strip, which faces first one way and then the opposite, but either way, it is the *same* strip. He has also introduced the term *nondual duality* to characterize this paradoxical reality.

Psychic Experiences

Psychic experiences are forms of extrasensory perception (ESP; clairvoyance, telepathy, and precognition) and psychokinesis, that is, being able to influence organisms or objects at a distance without sensory contact. If taken at face value as *human* experiences, they provide an inside view that humans literally may not be separated from others, especially from those with whom we are intimate, by distance or time. When confronted by psychic experiences, the Cartesian-based impulse is to explain them away, but it may be more constructive and life potentiating to realize we live in a world in which they can occur. With general acceptance of, or at least an openness to, the *possibility* of psychic experiences, more people might be aware of them and be more likely to report them.

Death-Related Experiences

This category consists of several types of experience ranging from a mystical sense of immortality to what is commonly referred to as near-death experiences and deathbed experiences: experiences in which people "see" and "meet" with deceased loved ones and, in some cases, with people about whose death the experiencer is unaware ("Peak in Darien" cases). Also included are accounts provided by mediums; telephoned, videotaped, and tape-recorded communications from the dead; and older forms of post-mortem communication such as raps, Ouija board, and other automatisms, the most recent being the mirror-visions induced by Moody (1993). All these experiences, in one way or another, erase the awareness of death. (It can be countered that death remains a physical reality, but even if it does, this form of knowing can be beneficial in that death loses its sting while one is alive.)

Encounter Experiences

This category includes experiences of observing and sometimes inter-acting with seemingly substantial or partially substantial apparitions; alien beings; and cultural-specific beings, such as the "Old Hag" phenomenon of Nova Scotia, the "phantom hitchhiker," and even Elvis Presley. (The latter may seem laughable, but Moody, 1987, has reported some interesting experiences associated with the deceased Elvis.) Also classed here are encounters with UFOs, angels, religious figures, apparitions, weeping or bleeding statuary, crop circles, and other anomalous phenomena/experi-ences that can become EHEs. This category of exceptional experience is valuable because it expands our grasp of what may be possible and the range of our potential for interaction.

Exceptional Normal Experiences

These experiences of knowing, being, and doing are at the outer limit of experiences viewed as "normal" in Western societies. They are not considered anomalous, but they generally go beyond the limits of what the individual experiencer or perhaps even any member of the human species has known. Some people therefore find it hard to accept them. Many of the concomitants associated with the more unusual EHEs are present in these experiences, such as tears, goose bumps, a crisis of identity, and feeling "wonderstruck." For example, former distance runner Mike Spino (1977) describes a 6-mile training run he made on a muddy, slippery road. He ran the first mile in 4½ minutes and was amazed at how effortless it had been. He reports,

> During that run I experienced my own encounter with death—for some-where down that road I had felt the wind blowing flesh from my body until there was nothing left to resist the sweep through space. Something else had taken me, something grand and inexorable and powerful beyond anything else I had known. Then, when the run was over, I seemed to shrink back into my own body, and I . . . wept as I tried to decide "who I was"—the one who had run the race or the usual Mike Spino? (p. 127)

Spino (1971) writes that his running mate, who accompanied him on foot and by car, later said "he could feel the power I was radiating. He said I was frightening" (p. 224).

When individuals are living at the limits of their capacity, let alone that of human capability, EEs tend to occur. Examples are the ghostly presences and the sense of immortality that accompanied Lindbergh on his flight to Paris or Bob Beamon's paradigm-shattering long jump in the 1968 Olympics—not bested until 1991 (see Murphy & White, 1995, for this and many examples). Included in this group are extraordinary dreams; inspiration of all types; aesthetic and literary experiences; witnessing or encountering art, architectural, religious, historical, and other cultural relics, music, and literature; and the performance of noble acts—or other exceptional human performances. All these experiences can engender a sense of our own larger being in bodily and emotional forms of knowing that enrich our lives, and they may also enrich our research.

THE EPISTEMOLOGICAL FUNCTION OF EHES

Human intelligence functions best when it is actively open to many possibilities not considered to exist according to Western consensus reality. Any type of EHE can be seen as a way of extending human knowledge beyond the bounds of our bodies, our conscious minds, and any instruments researchers have devised. The creative "aha" experience itself is exceptional, and it obviously functions in the service of extending knowledge. But each type of EHE, in its own way, connects the experiencer to aspects of self or environment that cannot be made, given the person's situation, in any other way. Realizing and consolidating new insights and connections constitute a process that underlies all research. EHEs promote viewing the world in new, more connected ways at the levels of both the individual life view and the worldview.

EHEs can aid in extending research parameters. They can present new insights to investigate and ways of interpreting research results. They can enable researchers to become aware of data and connections of possible relevance they might not notice otherwise and to conceive of ways to extend research into new areas by conceptual and methodological innovations.

EEs can serve an epistemological function either first- or secondhand. In the former, experiencers take their experiences seriously, take them to heart, and sooner or later are transformed or at least greatly changed by them. An aspect of this transformation is that they see reality in a new way. They have gained a form of double vision (White, 1994c). They can still see the world from the viewpoint of consensus reality, but they also are constantly aware of another seemingly more life-affirming and self-potentiating way (see White, 1994a, 1997, for details). In the special case of scientists, this places them in an optimal position to extend consensus reality, at least in their own field, in the direction of the new views they have glimpsed.

This process may be observed secondhand by reading autobiographical accounts by those who have had EHEs, or EHE autobiographies (White, 1994a, 1994c, 1995b), or by studying individual experiences from their triggering circumstances through the phenomenology of the experience itself and its aftereffects. In this way, observers can see how others fared who entered the process initiated by an EE. Reading cases and autobiographies enables readers to glimpse general patterns, regardless of the type of experience, that may indicate that something is happening here. Even if readers are not convinced, they may come away more open to such experiences.

Because there seems to be no end to the human potential that can be explored, once the process initiated by an EHE is under way, it is helpful to find ways of consolidating and integrating the fund of new insights that have been tapped. Two possible ways of doing this follow.

WRITING AN EHE AUTOBIOGRAPHY

To catalog, expand on, integrate, and even recall EHEs, it is useful to write an *EHE autobiography*. This exercise is the opposite of writing a curriculum vitae, which records all the objective life data such as birth date, schooling, degrees, honors, positions held, writings, and other accomplishments, each item of which can be verified by other people. The curriculum vitae may even be written by someone else.

An EHE autobiography, however, can only be written by *you*.[3] It is a record of the highlights of your subjective life—of your exceptional experiences: of places, people, events, visions, dreams, and encounters that profoundly affected you, often in unaccountable ways. An EHE autobiography is about the *wonder side* of your life—the experiences associated with wonder and awe—and those that made you question the adequacy of the Western worldview to account for EEs.

You need to chronologically record all the altered states you have experienced and the EEs you have had in or out of those altered states. Such states also will be anchored to certain persons, places, or activities, and these should be described; the aim, however, is not to describe events, as such, but rather how the events affected you subjectively, how they may have influenced you since they first occurred, and how they could affect you in the future.

You may have experienced certain types of EHEs several times so that no single one stands out—such as déjà vu and being uplifted by music, surfing, hiking, art, or nature. Give a generalized description, placing it chronologically according to when you think the first such experience occurred. Also indicate the number of times and the frequency with which you have had that type of experience.

Once you have your time line in place, and your EHEs situated along it, try to connect as many of the experiences as you can. Note those that had the same feeling tone or seemed to suggest the same meaning, raised similar questions, or concerned the same quandaries or revealed similar ways of opening. Add your current associations to these experiences, although many occurred long ago. Note especially any ways in which the experiences changed your view of yourself, your view of others, your life view, or your worldview.

In this way, you develop the life line of your inner EEs. Try to sense that line as you write and as you reread what you have written (also an important part of this technique). As you do so, you may recall related experiences. You cannot write your EHE autobiography in one sitting. You need to come back to it for weeks, rereading it once a day for at least three days each week, and recording any new experiences, associations, connections, or meanings that arise. Write them down before they slip away again.

When you think you have remembered and recorded all that you can, add a final section about their possible import for you today and in your future. You should find yourself aware of possibilities of "being and doing" you have not imagined before. It is important that you then try to act on some of these new possibilities or, failing that, to at least witness to some of your insights by sharing them with others. This will help consolidate them in your memory and awaken new levels of interpretation and meaning. Once you have written your EHE autobiography, it is unlikely that you will ever forget the experiences. Continue to take time out, occasionally, to add to your EHE autobiography and to reread it, so that new connections and possibilities will be given the opportunity to arise.

WRITING A SCIENTIFIC EHE AUTOBIOGRAPHY

A scientific EHE autobiography is a log of EEs related specifically to research and work. Many EHEs tend to be about the experiencer's calling in life. A sense of vocation is itself an EHE. Many people go through life not even aware that they have a calling, perhaps because they have not remembered or worked with their EHEs.

Weber (1958) was one of the first to write about the vocation of a scientist as a response to a call, which he characterizes as the " 'personal experience' of science," adding that "without this strange intoxication . . . without this passion . . . you have no calling for science and you should do something else" (p. 135). Vocation is experienced as if coming from beyond the conscious mind, which could implicate many sources: the personal unconscious, in the interest of self-integration; the deep unconscious—which elsewhere (White, 1997) I have proposed is the self of all things, or the All-Self—in response to the need of the human species to become more conscious and connected; Gaia, the soul of Earth, in response to her need to be saved from the ravages of greed, need, and supertechnology; or even the universe itself, calling out to move the process of evolution forward, just as it may have called the dust of our planet to life. Or, it could be that persons are living out some deep ancestral memory buried until now in unconsciousness or possibly are responding to a basic desire from even before birth.[4]

EHEs can help us as researchers become aware of one or more of these possibilities and their application to our chosen professions. A powerful motivational source could be a revered teacher who awakens the desire to do research. Such teachers usually seem larger than life—they are charismatic—and the magical charism they have for us is, itself, an EHE. It is fortunate to encounter even two or three such persons in a lifetime. Some EHEs that may be related to specific research projects may have predated those projects by months or even years. In these ways of questioning and exploring and remembering, you need to work out what brought you to your work and why you engage in it. The answers may not be readily apparent, and even when you think you know what the answers are, with the passage of time, you may discover other facets or deeper levels of understanding.

Presumably, everyone who is engaged in research has access to a computer. I recommend that you open a file for your EHE explorations. It can be a tool you will want to add to and use throughout your career. For those who may want to write your biography, it will be an invaluable resource. It will also be useful to future students interested in following up on your research leads, ideas, and insights.

Your computer file should consist of several parts, the first being your EHE autobiography. The second should be your scientific EHE autobiography, which records all the significant experiences related to your work. Every time you engage in a new research project, open a new file to record experiences and insights that occur specifically in connection with it. For each project, give consideration to your motivation for engaging in it, the research methodology, analysis of results, the bearing of this project on future research, and how it affected you. In each part, the important points to note are not the objective ones, which will be described in the formal report. Here you will record your subjective reactions and feelings about each stage of the research and especially any EEs of your own or of anyone else associated with the project. If an EE occurs, it will be useful to have relevant accounts from several persons associated with the research.

The focus of this scientific EHE autobiography should be the senior investigator or doctoral candidate or whoever primarily conceived the research project. It will be useful, however, for all involved to write their personal project autobiographies, as well. Some of those involved may think other approaches or methods of analysis should be used, or they may interpret the results differently, or they may be conscripted for the research and have little interest in it. All these motivations and responses may influence the research itself, and it is good to have records of them. Even the participants could be asked to write mini-autobiographies on why they opted to participate, what they experienced as participants, and any EEs they may have had before or during the project.

EXCEPTIONAL EXPERIENCES MOST LIKELY TO OCCUR IN THE RESEARCH CONTEXT

Any EE has the potential to shed light on research, but I will consider those that are most likely to do so (beginning with those closest to Western consensus reality, but even common experiences such as hunches can be far out). All the following experiences can be seen as forms of inspiration, although some may not generally be thought of as such because of their anomalous character. Hallman (1963) has noted five necessary conditions for creativity that can be viewed as aspects of the creative process. They are openness, nonrationality, originality, connectedness, and self-actualization. The first four apply also to EEs, whereas all five apply to EHEs.

Dreams

Many dreams have been recorded that assisted innovations in science and technology. But some dreams, especially of those who are engaged in human consciousness research, involve the whole being of the scientist and presage a major change of approach (e.g., see Rosen, 1992). These are EHEs. Berry (1990) has suggested that in our dreams and revelatory visions, we can get in touch with the universe itself and get from it (which we ourselves are) a sense of direction for our lives and work (p. 211).

Lucid Dreams

If dreams are helpful in providing scientific answers, lucid dreaming should be even more helpful because the dreamer is conscious. LaBerge (1985) describes a dream of his that was becoming a nightmare. It concerned a lecture he was to give at an upcoming scientific meeting. The dream became lucid and motivated him to prepare much sooner than he had planned but just in the nick of time for the conference (pp. 172-173).

Hunches

Hunches generally concern specific aspects of research such as selecting one research assistant rather than another, when both are equally qualified; choosing a specific test from many others measuring the same variable and that are equally valid and reliable; or even choosing a subject area as indicated by a strong inner urge or feeling of rightness rather than by rational choice. For example, early in his scientific career, Otto Loewi (1960, in LaBerge & Rheingold, 1990) had a hunch about the nature of the nerve impulse. Because he could not come up with a way of verifying his hunch scientifically, he forgot it. Seventeen years later, he dreamed, two nights running, of an experimental design that enabled him to verify his earlier hypothesis of chemical transmission. Loewi's dream-suggested experiment allowed him to discover what was later identified as acetylcholine, a major neurotransmitter. For this work he shared the 1936 Nobel Prize for physiology and medicine (pp. 170-171).

Hypnagogia

Hypnagogic (during the twilight state of consciousness encountered on going from waking to sleeping), and especially hypnopompic (during the twilight state of consciousness encountered in going from sleep to wakefulness), imagery is often associated with new ideas. (See Mavromatis, 1987, for an overview.) Edison (Bernd, 1978) is said to have capitalized on this when he was at an impasse in his work. He would take a nap in his chair, holding a steel ball in each hand. On the floor, on either side of his chair, he placed flat pans. When he fell asleep, the balls dropped out of his hands and landed on the pans, thus waking him up, often with an idea that would break the impasse (pp. 28-29).

Visions/Hallucinations

Tesla (in Inglis, 1987) depended on visions bordering on hallucinations for his ideas and inventions, saying he experienced as complete "a mental state of happiness" as he had ever known while in those states. He writes: "Ideas came in an uninterrupted stream. . . . The pieces of apparatus I conceived were to me absolutely real and tangible in every detail, even to the minutest marks and signs of wear" (p. 90). In a well-known case, Henri

Poincaré (1913) had tried hard for 2 weeks to prove that what have since become known as Fuschian functions could not exist, but Poincaré did not succeed. Then one night, contrary to his custom, he drank coffee and could not sleep. As he lay in bed, "ideas rose in crowds; I felt them collide until pairs interlocked . . . making a stable combination. By the next morning I had established the existence of a class of Fuschian functions" (p. 387).

Empathy

Empathy is important in research with humans and is not considered exceptional, but at its limits, it can shade into what is close to, if not identical with, telepathy or ESP. Physician/researcher Alex Comfort (1984) astutely notes that the only way physics can communicate its revolutionary change in worldview, in which that which we have taken to be objective can be seen as a construct, is by making world models that have empathic appeal (which he defines as "those which coincide with feelings"), which helps people to incorporate them (p. xvi). He observes, "By empathy I mean incorporation going beyond intellectual assent. We know the earth is spherical, and many actually have flown around it, but not until astronauts saw it *ab extra* can its roundness be said to have been empathized" (p. xviii). For several of those astronauts, the experience of actually seeing the earth from space was a life-changing EHE (see White, 1987, for examples).

Similarly, the wonders we, as researchers, experience in exceptional experiences help us empathize in ways that can forward our work and aid us in communicating our findings to others. Nobel prize biologist Barbara McClintock spent her life studying maize, and such was her empathy with her participants that she studied each plant from the time it was a seedling so that she could say, "I don't feel I really know the story if I don't watch the plant all the way along." Of each plant in the field she said, "I know them intimately, and I find it a great pleasure to know them" (cited in Keller, 1983, p. 198). She received the Nobel prize for her work on the tiny chromosomes of red bread mold. She told Keller that they got larger and larger as she worked with them under the microscope. Here she combined empathy and visualization to such a pitch that I call it *magnified vision.* Although she examined molecules under an actual microscope, what she saw was far larger than the magnifying capability of her instrument. She said that when she was "really working with them" she experienced herself not as outside but as part of the system. I was right down there with them, and everything got big. I even was able to see the internal parts of the chromosomes. . . . It surprised me because I actually felt as if . . . these were my friends. (Keller, 1983, p. 117)

ESP

Various automatisms, especially map dowsing, seem to involve ESP and have been used to locate geological deposits (Bird, 1979). Remote viewing and other forms of ESP have been used in geology, archaeology, and anthropology. Jones (1979) reports on research with psychics who were able to find archaeological sites and "reconstruct physical, cultural, and historical environments" (p. 253) by "reading" or "psychometrizing" artifacts. The psychics described some buried artifacts and the cultural context of a site in detail by scanning a photograph of it and provided "accurate identifying information about a cultural situation by handling non-diagnostic rubble from the particular site" (p. 253). Jones published the psychics' transcripts so readers can draw their own conclusions.

ESP in Interspecies Communication

McClintock communed with plants. Interspecies communication is an important EE that may eventually open doors to understandings unguessed at present. Mishlove (1993, pp. 237-239) reports on some experiments/ experiences he and others had in trying to communicate with and heal Dondi, a dolphin, partly from a distance. He also describes the dolphin-human EE of Wade Doak, who believes he communicated with a dolphin by telepathy. Biological research would be transformed if we could develop interspecies communication, which is now itself an EE or EHE.

Out-of-Body Experiences

In an out-of-body experience, veridical information sometimes is obtained of a person, place, or object at a distance while the experiencer feels in the body at the distant site. Out-of-body experiences indicate that humans can have access to places outside our bodies, not simply by clairvoyance but with the sense of "being there." This may be highly important in the space age. There are reports of attempts of two psychics, Harold Sherman and Ingo Swann, to explore the planet Mercury while out-of-body and/or using ESP (Mitchell, 1975; Sherman, 1981). Some of their findings were later confirmed by Mariner space probes.[5]

Synchronicity

Synchronicity is a subjectively significant coincidence between an inner state, usually of need, and an unaccountable outer event that corresponds to and/or answers the need. Because they cannot causally be accounted for, synchronicities are EEs; when they are also personally significant, they can be EHEs. A common role played by synchronicity in the research process is in turning up needed information sources not otherwise available. Vaughan (1979, pp. 95-96) presents an instance reported by parapsychology writer-researcher D. Scott Rogo, who, when writing about obsession, knew he needed to include the work of Titus Bull. Rogo, however, knew nothing about him and had nothing concerning him at hand, despite possessing a well-stocked personal library. Having written Bull's name and just one sentence, Rogo decided to go to Los Angeles and check bookstores, but it was too early, and they were closed. He then went to a park in a rundown section of Los Angeles that he had been to perhaps five times. When he got out to walk, Rogo recalled a bookstore he had once visited that was not well stocked with books on parapsychology. Going in and finding nothing of interest, he was walking out when he noticed some magazines in disorder on the floor. For some reason, he stopped. Under the magazines, he saw something yellow, which reminded him of the color of the *Journal of the American Society for Psychical Research* in the 1920s and 1930s. He pulled the publications out, and there in the unlikeliest of places were some back issues of that journal for the years 1928 through 1934, including eight lengthy reports about the work of Titus Bull. These reports gave him all that he needed to complete the chapter on Bull in a week.

CONCLUDING REMARKS

Many of the examples I have given are often cited. Few, I imagine, were honored at the time of their occurrence or when the research findings they led to were reported in technical journals. Although it is doubtful whether the research would have been conducted had the experiences not occurred, they are considered folklore, unscientific, unreliable, "lucky"—relegated to the underside of the research process. The point of this chapter is to illustrate that these insights and inspirations *should* be honored as they deserve—that they deserve to be put in the forefront. If this were done, researchers would have many fresh new examples to study, numbers of them recorded soon after they occurred. If, as most do, they require verification, they should be recorded *prior to* that verification. This circumstance points to the need for *insight banks,* possibly under the aegis of the various scientific and professional societies associated with each discipline, to enable scientists to centrally record the exceptional experiences relating to their research, as they arise.[6]

Needed are fresh cases in greater detail than ever before. The value of these dreams, visions, and encounters is not only in the information or ideas they provide but also in how we, as scientists, respond to them. If we were to honor them as they deserve, not only might our knowledge be transformed, but reflexively, so might we, which could lead to even more startling breakthrough insights. Correspondingly, research would not exploit its subject matter but would empathize with it and, as it progresses, make many connections rarely glimpsed before. This enrichment would help promote the growth of peace and of life on earth, which should be the ultimate aim of every vocation and certainly of paramount concern to science.

NOTES

1. Part of learning the lore of a specific EE is to become educated concerning the ways we can delude ourselves about an experience. Experiencers need to be aware of counterexplanations for seemingly psychic events, encounter phenomena, and death-related EEs— especially possibilities such as subliminal perception, suggestion, cryptomnesia, illusion, and even deliberate hoax. Useful books to check or read for this purpose are George (1995), Neher (1980), Reed (1988), Schick and Vaughn (1995), and Zusne and Jones (1982, 1989).

2. To practice what I preach: This is the third version of this chapter. Each time, I began with a formal outline but spontaneously—as if from over my left shoulder and accompanied by a sense of humming and warmth in my left ear—came unbidden ideas, sentences, and phrases I otherwise would not have thought of that I much preferred to my own plodding and boring text. I was in a slightly altered state of being "high" and in a "state of flow" in which I was more amanuensis than deliberate writer. I became more conscious of connections than usual, and I feel this is reflected in what I eventually wrote. To be sure, I went through 14 rewrites to arrive at the present version, during which I added supplementary material and smoothed out some of the writing until I was pleased with the result. But whether or not I should be realistically pleased depends on the reader's response, whose opportunity to respond one way or the other was made possible, in part, by those two "watchers of the threshold," William Braud and Rosemarie Anderson!

3. I will purposely use the pronoun *you* in much of the following text to emphasize that the EHE autobiography is an individual and personal process.

4. As I perceive it, the call today is the call for all life to become conscious, and to know that it is conscious, and for it to sing with consciousness with all other life forms.

5. For the first installment of an annotated bibliography on outer space EHEs, see White (1996a).

6. I have an arrangement for people to record their EHEs on-line, via bulletin board and e-mail, so this concept unquestionably is doable. To check it out, contact

`http://www.publishingarts.com/ehe.html`.

PART III

APPLYING THE PRINCIPLES
SELECTED EXAMPLES

Each of the contributions in Part III exemplifies one or more of the basic principles of the transpersonal research methods proposed in Part II. The examples have been carefully selected from among the many fine doctoral dissertations and master's theses (from the Residential and Global Programs, respectively) at the Institute of Transpersonal Psychology (Palo Alto, California). Part III is divided into three chapters to exemplify alternative ways to approach the three basic steps in the research process: Encountering and Collecting Data (Chapter 8), Engaging and Confronting Data (Chapter 9), and Expressing and Communicating Findings (Chapter 10).

Since 1992, we have been actively and increasingly encouraging alternative approaches to research among our doctoral and master's students, as discussed in the preface. This dynamic process has been accelerating in the past few years. We cannot adequately express our gratitude to our students for their willingness to engage research as a transformative process itself. It is challenging enough to complete a master's thesis or doctoral dissertation, let alone study spiritual and mystical topics. Studying spiritual and mystical topics ought to be enough, let alone engage the methodology imaginatively and allow it to transform the researcher in the process. All our students are foolishly wonderful, and it is a delight to invite their creative contributions. All their research has been completed since 1994. These contributions, therefore, represent a leading edge in the development of a transpersonal perspective for understanding spiritual, mystical, and other phenomena; the incremental elaboration of theory; and (most important for our purposes here) the development of alternative ways to study these phenomena.

The evolution of the transpersonal research methods presented in this book is a story of many people working together. Along with other colleagues and students, our goal as transpersonal researchers is to generate and nurture ideas and methods that innovatively "grow" the field, like seeding and tending young plants in a greenhouse. All of us—together with our beloved research projects—are the young plants. Neither of us has ever had a graduate student in transpersonal psychology who did not love his or her research topic, because the topic was deeply related to the researcher's life experience and he or she honored the experience in itself. Our work has been to help create research methods that so honor life experience that they similarly prompt our affections.

A few cautionary remarks to the reader are warranted. Our primary interest in including the research contributions is to illustrate through example the basic principles and features of the transpersonal research methods proposed in Part II. We are aware, however, that some of the topics of investigation are controversial. Probably the most controversial are investigations into the nature of channeling and shamanic journeying. Our selection of research examples has been guided by our desire to be comprehensive and to direct the reader's attention to research methods that have been rigorously and efficaciously applied from a practical research view. One or both of us have been directly involved in each of these research projects, and we are familiar with the integrity of these research applications beyond the final thesis or dissertation itself.

Each of the 13 short contributions to Part III emphasizes specific, concrete examples of methodological innovations, rather than the specific findings that issued from the use of the new methods. For more information about the subject matter and findings, the reader is urged to consult the full reports from which these sections were condensed. Full references for the dissertations summarized in Chapters 8, 9, and 10 may be found in the reference section at the end of this book. The dissertations themselves may be obtained through Interlibrary Loan from the Institute of Transpersonal Psychology Library or through University Microfilms Inc. (UMI; 300 North Zeeb Road, P.O. Box 1346, Ann Arbor, MI 48106-1346; 313/761-4700).

CHAPTER 8

ALTERNATIVE WAYS OF KNOWING (ENCOUNTERING AND COLLECTING DATA)

In a discussion with a colleague, this question arose: What would the *ideal* Institute of Transpersonal Psychology dissertation look like? Because our graduate program emphasizes six facets of human experience—bodily, emotional, intellectual, spiritual, communal, and creatively expressive aspects of our humanity—the obvious first answer was that the ideal dissertation might attempt to address these six areas in each major phase of the dissertation work. Generalizing this idea further, a metaphor began to form. Most conventional dissertations, and research projects in general, tend to deal with only a narrow band of the spectrum of possibilities. Such projects observe reality with *one eye,* process what is learned through *one brain,* and express their findings with *one mouth.* The one eye is the eye of the conventional senses through which we survey the external world. The one brain is a left-hemispheric, logical, analytical, interpretative approach to working with the data we have collected. The one mouth is the expression of our findings through the writing of linear, scientific prose. These approaches yield relatively narrow slices of what may be known about reality. The constraints imposed by conventional quantitative research methods narrow the slices even further. Newer qualitative approaches open the filters somewhat. Yet even here, constraints remain. We explore research issues by framing our questions in words, listening to the abundant words our participants give us in reply, process and think about the collected words using our linguistic skills and word-based rationality, and then express our findings to others using still other words. It is not far from the truth to conclude that qualitative research is nothing but glorified word processing.

Surely, there are ways of expanding the nature and number of the eyes, brains, and mouths we use in our research. Initial steps in these directions are presented in Chapters 8, 9, and 10. In the first of these chapters, we indicate some of the many creative ways in which researchers might become *polyoccular*—ways to encounter and collect data using several eyes, several alternative ways of knowing. In these extensions, new sources of information are explored. We broaden our methods by asking questions of different aspects of ourselves, of our participants, and of the world and by listening to replies in new ways. We invite different phenomena to reveal themselves in their own ways, in their own languages, and we resist the strong temptations to mold, translate, or interpret those different languages into or by means of the external-sensory and word-based rational language that is our well-practiced default mode.

Nancy Fagen invites her research topic—nonverbal dreamwork—to speak in its own way, using its preferred language of images and symbols. She does this by augmenting conventional quantitative and qualitative methods through a novel procedure in which her research participants incubate dreams, at the conclusion of her study, that are asked to comment on the study and on the participants' experiences in the study in their own, nonverbal manner. She deliberately resists the temptation to verbally interpret what she receives.

How might we prepare our research participants, and prepare ourselves as researchers, to be more attentive to and sensitive to information and knowledge that might come to us through nonverbal means? How might we get more direct reports from the phenomenon we are studying, asking the subject matter itself to comment on or teach us about itself, using its own preferred means?

There has been great popular interest, and moderate academic interest, in *channeling*, in which persons transmit information from sources perceived as paranormal. Even in the most extensive research studies of this phenomenon, the channel's own inner experience has been strangely neglected. In Kathleen Barrett's project, conventional phenomenological interviewing and analysis procedures are used to explore the channeling experience from the view of the channel. A methodological innovation is the application of the same techniques to novel interviewees—the ostensible *sources* of the channeled information.

Kathleen Barrett invites her participants to make known what they have learned from unusual sources. Here, we already see the challenge of expanded inquiries of this sort: Her participants are forced to mold their knowings into words through which they express this knowing to themselves, to the researcher who interviews them, and to the reader who finally reads Kathleen Barrett's words. How might we become more skilled at asking new types of questions of new phenomena of study in new ways? To whom or to what might we ask such questions, and how might we do this? How do we know when we have received valid answers from the processes we are questioning in new ways and asking to reply through novel means?

Sharon Van Raalte breaks new research ground by exploring direct knowing, intuitive diagnosis, and paranormal knowing in the context of shamanic journeying in a therapy practice. She documented the process of undergoing a shamanic journey at a distance on behalf of a behavioral psychiatrist. Reports of the contents of the shamanic journeys were reported to the therapist who then shared them with the individual clients. In the full report, from which this section is abstracted, the entire process of journeying and the interactions between the researcher and psychiatrist are documented in depth.

The more general questions raised by this report are these: How can we help ourselves, our research participants, and the readers of our eventual reports become more sensitive to their own processes of direct knowing, so that these might become additional sources of potentially accurate and useful information about ourselves and about the world at large? How might we set the stage or prepare ourselves so that paranormal information is more accessible? What are the factors that facilitate or impede such knowing? Could the induction of nonordinary states of consciousness in our participants, ourselves, and our readers help increase access to such information? Can we become sufficiently practiced in looking for and accessing such knowledge so that we can distinguish wheat from chaff, signal from noise, and valid from invalid paranormal information? Can we learn to recognize internal reference points or indicators of accurate paranormal impressions that might help us distinguish these from irrelevant mental noise, idle wishes, fears, apprehensions, and projections? Can we teach such skills to others? How might we weight such information along with more conventional information about our research topics?

Sheila Lynn Belanger extends a qualitative thematic analysis of her research participants' experiences of shamanic journeying by adding two expressions of her intuitive awareness, as researcher, of the participants' experiences. Each participant completed a questionnaire about his or her experiences during a shamanic journey, and this information was analyzed for themes. With each participant's themes in mind, Belanger creates a *touch drawing* to express and amplify her understanding of the symbolic level of each participant's experiences. Thus, several alternative modes of knowing are explored at once—the direct knowing or paranormal functioning of the research participants, similar processes in the researcher, the researcher's tacit and bodily knowing (as expressed in the drawings), and the knowing conveyed through symbolic processes in participants and researcher. Using the information from the qualitative thematic analysis and the imagery of the touch drawing, Belanger creates a *haiku* to synthesize each participant's experience of shamanic journeying.

Genie Palmer provides an exceptionally complete and well-balanced example of the integral inquiry approach described in Chapter 3; the study is also informed by heuristic research considerations (Moustakas, 1990). The project illustrates how a great variety of complementary quantitative and qualitative research methods can be integrated to study several aspects of a research issue simultaneously. The quantitative methods include descriptive statistics, correlational matrices, and analyses of variance performed on both standardized and original assessments. Qualitative methods include qualitative content and thematic analyses of materials collected from questionnaires, journal writings, educational group work, and in-depth semistructured interviews. The research takes place in the context of studying changes that occur in meaning; health and well-being; and personal and spiritual growth, development, and transformation as persons devote attention to, disclose, and assimilate their exceptional human experiences (EHEs; see Chapter 7) in areas of mystical experiences, paranormal experiences, death-related experiences, encounter experiences, and exceptional normal experiences. Not only do the research participants evidence alternative modes of knowing in these experiences themselves, but the researcher includes her own EHEs in all phases of her research project and deliberately makes places for many alternative forms of knowing as she collects, works with, and presents her findings. This research resembles a self-similar, fractal landscape made up of different modes of knowing, each of which, in turn, contains the same multiple modes of knowing, and so on. The project also contains features of the other four novel research approaches described in Chapters 4 through 7. It represents a truly integral inquiry, informed by many complementary methods; types of literature (from spiritual writings through physiological studies); and ways of acquiring, working with, and expressing information.

IMAGES AND SYMBOLS

Nancy L. Fagen

I designed a research project for the purpose of studying the experiences, accompaniments, and perceived effects of working with one's dreams using creatively expressive, nonverbal methods. The project included a balance of quantitative, qualitative, nomothetic, and idiographic methods. Sixty research participants engaged in dreamwork for 6 weeks. They recalled, recorded, and elaborated their nocturnal dreams using conventional verbal techniques of writing and journalizing. Half of the participants ($n = 30$) were assigned randomly to a new intervention condition that involved augmenting the verbal dreamwork with creatively expressive, nonverbal techniques. These participants elaborated their dreams by drawing, sketching, and painting their dream images, in addition to their usual verbal work. Thus, two groups were constituted—a conventional group that used only verbal dreamwork methods and a nonverbal group that used both verbal and nonverbal dreamwork techniques. The possible effects of these nonverbal dream elaborations were assessed in four ways.

The first way was a quantitative assessment, using Shostrom's (1976) standardized instrument, the Personal Orientation Inventory (POI), an operationalization of Abraham Maslow's (1968, 1970) qualities of self-actualization. This assessment was given to all participants at the beginning, and again at the end, of the 6-week study. Scores on the major scales and subscales of this instrument were analyzed using analysis of variance procedures, for group (conventional versus nonverbal) and assessment time (pretest versus posttest) effects. An examination of scoring patterns on a standardized assessment tool was included in this phase of the work for researchers interested in nomothetic findings.

A second component of the research project involved a special question-naire I constructed (the Dream Research Measure Questionnaire or DRMQ), which was included to satisfy my curiosity about the participants' self-perceived changes in particular aspects of their lives and in particular types of dream-related experiences. As is done with the POI, the scores on this instrument were analyzed quantitatively.

A third research component included in-depth, semistructured inter-views of six participants selected from the nonverbal dreamwork group. This qualitative, idiographic component was included to learn about the experience of doing nonverbal dreamwork from the words of the partici-pants themselves. This research component was devoted to the interests of the participants in that it allowed them to tell their own stories about their participation in the study and to do this via their own voices in a relatively free and unstructured setting. These interviews were treated using qualita-tive content analysis methods.

The fourth research component was a novel one in which the process being studied—nonverbal dreamwork—was asked to describe itself, using its own "voice." Toward this end, near the conclusion of the study, participants in the nonverbal dreamwork group were asked to incubate a dream with the intention that the dream itself would "comment on" and summarize, nonverbally, that participant's experience throughout the study; the incubated dream was also "asked" to comment, in its own way and in its own voice, on the study as a whole. This unique component of the study provided a "report from the dreamworld itself" and was included as a novel transpersonal methodological extension. Several of these incubated dreams were presented in the research report. Because I wished the dreams—especially their nonverbal elaborations, that is, the drawings of the dream images—to address the reader directly, I deliberately refrained from any interpretations of these dream reports. To convey a sense of this novel mode of data collection and data presentation, I include two such uninterpreted reports from the dreamworld. Figures 8.1 and 8.2 present incubated dreams' nonverbal answers to requests to comment on the process of nonverbal dreamwork and on this research project as a whole. Following the nonver-bal dream presentations are the comments, by the respective dreamers, about their dreams and dream images. The reader is invited to relax, to simply observe and be with the two dream images, and to let them speak to the reader in their own ways.

Figure 8.1. The Siamese Twin Puppets: A nonverbal presentation from a dream incubated for the purpose of "commenting" on the research project.

The Siamese Twin Puppets (refer to Figure 8.1)

It's mid-day. I'm sitting on the floor of a semi-small room alongside an ex-roommate, one whom I haven't seen for some years. We are having an informal discussion or session with a therapist I know who does dreamwork. It seems significant that she is having this discussion with us. She casually speaks to us about each of our shadow sides, about the duality of each of our lives. She holds up this hand puppet made from a material that looks like papier-mâché. The puppet serves as a prop for her discussion, as it is a sort of Siamese twin, attached at the arms. Between the two puppets is a strip of material—black. With the exception of clothing color, each puppet is exactly alike.

We all discuss the experience of the meeting and reflect on how each of us is so different today. I remember thinking how different my path has been compared to my ex-roommate's. We are strangers, yet she is, or was, part of what I guess is my own shadow. She, too, has changed.

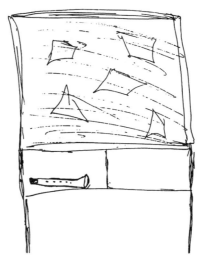

Figure 8.2. Beautiful, Sad Sounds: A nonverbal presentation from a dream incubated for the purpose of "commenting" on the research project.

Beautiful, Sad Sounds (refer to Figure 8.2)

I am in a room with some other people. In front of us is a free-standing glass case. Enclosed is paper of various shapes. We are supposed to look at this from all sides and draw the shapes we see.

I look at them but can't really make out any clear shapes. Everyone else is excitedly drawing. I stand back refusing to even try, feeling stupid and frustrated. I sit down.

Underneath the case is a cupboard with some unusual instruments. There is a small, silver, flute-like instrument. I pick it up and start playing very softly. Beautiful, sad sounds come from it.

NOVEL INTERVIEWS

Kathleen Barrett

How does a researcher conduct an interview with a small part of the collective unconscious, a disembodied being, an aspect of someone's unconscious mind, or an inner guide with human limitations? Channeled entities, often described as one or more of the above (Bennett, 1994; Fiore, 1987; Jung, 1977; Spangler, 1988), are known for their propensity to converse with humans. In client "readings," séances, channeled lectures, and channeled books, invisible sources willingly describe life before birth and after death and offer great quantities of advice on how to conduct the physical life in between. Because of their nonphysical nature, an interview with one of these sources requires the cooperation of a third party, a "channel" who receives messages from the invisible source and relays them to the listener.

The objective of my research project on the *experience* of channeling (Barrett, 1996) was to obtain a complete understanding of the subjective experience of the phenomenon, as perceived by its participants. To achieve this, I held a series of interviews with nine experienced channels and their sources. In addition to the primary goal of obtaining a phenomenological description of the channeling experience, I wanted to explore many other aspects of the phenomenon, such as the nature of the source, the perceived purpose of channeling, and the authenticity of the experience itself.

Each interview focused on my basic research question: "What is your inner experience of channeling?" After listening to each channel's description of his or her experience, I asked the channel to act as liaison for my interview with the channel's source. I then asked the source to describe its experience of being channeled, encouraging it to include "feelings, thoughts, sensations, impressions, circumstances, and any other aspects of your experience that I may not have sufficient knowledge to ask about." After obtaining as many details as possible about its subjective experience, I then asked six additional questions of each source: (a) Who are you? (b) Why are you communicating with people in this way? (c) Where are you, and what are you doing when you are not involved in channeling? (d) What qualities does this person possess that led you to choose and retain him or her as a channel? (e) Do you communicate through channels other than this one? If so, why; and who are the others? and (f) How has channeling changed your existence?

Although I realized that each source may be a part of the channel's psyche, I always addressed it as a separate, independent being. There were several reasons for doing so: Because each channel spoke of the source as a separate being, it seemed counterproductive to appear to negate the channel's perspective. Even if each source were indeed a part of the channel's unconscious mind, it would still resemble a separate being in that it would be unknown to the conscious mind. Also, each source seemed to have its own viewpoint, personal history, and body of knowledge that differed from those of the channel; in this sense, each source presented itself as a separate, autonomous being.

Conversations with the sources occurred in two forms. Some were one-on-one exchanges, with the source speaking directly through the channel, using the first person. Others were three-party conversations in which the channel reported the source's answers using the third person.

For first-person channels, I always addressed the source directly and proceeded as though the channel were not present. In these instances, I found it useful to imagine the source as a separate being, hovering somewhere near the channel. Although the channel's ears and voice were essential instruments in these conversations, it was surprisingly easy to ostensibly converse with another being in this way because the source often spoke as though from a different historic era or from a greater perspective than that of the channel.

For third-person channels, I often addressed the channel directly. The opportunity to speak directly to the channel helped deepen my under-standing of the channel's interior experience as well.

During the source interviews, I always had the feeling that my link with the interviewee was rather delicate, as though the conversation could be interrupted at any moment by the slightest difficulty in the channel's ability to remain in an altered state. I found myself attempting to compensate for this impression of fragility by making extra efforts to ensure good commu-nication. For example, I expressed appreciation and encouragement in response to many of the source's answers.

I was also aware of an invisible barrier to direct communication in that the source's perceptions and responses were limited to those understood by the channel, who was, after all, in an altered state of consciousness. I felt as though I was speaking through a membrane that hindered clear or spontaneous communication. In response, I maintained a gentle conversa-tional style and pace, to avoid overtaxing either channel or source. I was alert to the importance of proper timing.

To further ease the interview process for channel and source, I avoided asking confrontational-sounding questions. For example, instead of asking the source, "Who are you?" I often restated it as, "If people say you are a part of [the channel's] mind, what would you say to that?" A gentle, flexible style seemed to work best with my tenuous, removed interviewees.

I will admit to holding the notion that a significant portion of the answers may have come from the channel's conscious mind. I had decided beforehand to assume each channel's authenticity and honesty because each one was experienced and respected for his or her channeling abilities, yet I was aware of my desire to reduce any level of performance anxiety, in case the channel was indeed "faking it" for my sake.

In general, I used standard interview techniques, attempting to adhere to the topic and to strive for complete and accurate answers. I attempted to avoid leading questions because the phenomenological method of analysis is dependent on spontaneous answers.

It was unnecessary for me to describe my research project to the sources; they uniformly indicated they already were aware of my research. In the few cases in which I was able to interview two sources for the same channel, I asked the same questions of each source. In these double-source interviews, the answers of one source amplified, without contradicting, those of the other.

Of course, I made mistakes and learned through experience as a result. In one instance, a source reported that because feelings are experienced in the body, and he did not have a body, he therefore did not experience emotions. In the next source interview, I began a question with, "Although this is probably not an emotional experience for you . . ." I was immediately corrected by the source:

Emotions are more than the capacities that exist within the physical reality. There are mind levels which increase our ability to have feelings and gather emotive responses to experiences as we evolve and grow. I am most certainly not removed from my emotions in this process.

In interviewing the sources as well as the channels, I felt as though I needed to collect as many details as possible despite my own assorted reactions. In effect, I was unable to maintain the desired objective outlook during each interview and found myself grappling continuously with proprioceptive responses toward the channel, the witnessed experience of channeling, and the source. My skepticism was always present, whispering such things as, "She is just acting," or "He may be delusional," or "She can't be serious!"

Yet I found myself trusting several channels. What triggered the difference in responses? There were three toward whom I had a positive reaction: I was previously acquainted with one channel and knew her to be a spiritually aware person; in another case, both the channel and her sources were friends of mine who had provided prior opportunities for me to witness their channeling activities; the third channel gave me a spontaneous reading during the interview, the accuracy of which convinced me that something quite real was happening. My personal experience with each of the three had established a feeling of trust. This parallels the "knowledge by acquaintance" described by Michael Grosso (1994) as a recommended way to leap beyond perpetual skepticism. Yet skepticism seemed to foster the integrity of the investigative process by prompting me to elicit as much data as possible from all participants, so that my later analysis would be based less on my degree of acceptance of the witnessed experience than on the collection of recurring themes given by all participating channels and sources.

In general, the channels were clearly inexperienced in transmitting information about their sources and often gave answers that were abbreviated and vague, with a marked absence of detail. The sources were certainly more accustomed to giving readings for clients than to providing information about themselves. Yet in a few interviews, the source provided an ample volume of information that sounded relatively specific.

My overall outlook had been that some channels are authentic, and others are not. Perhaps my perspective influenced my expectations and, later, my conclusions, that some channels, and their sources, were more convincing than others. My approach, however, was to use all the information provided to understand a process that seemed quite real for the channel and, on some occasions, for me as well.

Interview results from the sources were remarkably uniform in certain areas. Each source reported feeling a long-term, kindred, or multilifetime relationship with its channel, and most sources considered themselves to be separate, autonomous beings. Almost all reportedly adjusted their vibrational frequency to achieve communication with the channel. Sources also described how, during the transmission of information to and through the channel, they made efforts to cooperate with the channel in a team effort to achieve an accurate transmission and presentation. Some reported focusing intently on receiving the questions and sending the answers. Others emphasized their efforts to protect the channel's body and mind during the transmission. Most sources said their channeling activities were the fulfillment of a commitment previously made, often before the channel's birth. All reported a positive outlook about channeling, including feelings of satisfaction and joy, and the perception that their activities are intended as a helpful service to humanity.

DIRECT KNOWING

Sharon Van Raalte

Bringing shamanism and psychiatry together grew from the experience of my own search for healing. During a crisis in my life, I sought the help of a psychiatrist and benefited greatly from his cognitive-behavioral approach. Our interaction gradually had less to do with my cognitive and behavioral reframing than with my search for spiritual meaning, which eventually led me to in-depth studies with Michael Harner at the Foundation for Shamanic Studies and with the Institute of Transpersonal Psychology. My emerging spiritual language and the psychiatrist's cognitive language differed greatly, and yet sometimes his "brain" talk and my "soul" talk produced moments of mutual understanding. A desire to find a common understanding and vocabulary led to this project. My research attempts to introduce a shamanic approach as complementary to the work of contemporary psychiatry. In collaboration with the psychiatrist, I studied the effects of shamanic journeying at a distance on behalf of some of his clients (Van Raalte, 1994).

Because shamanic work is, by its nature, subjective and participatory, I chose a qualitative framework to reveal the interaction between shaman and patient. The psychiatrist selected participants according to his assessment of their openness to the idea of shamanic journeying on their behalf and obtained their permission before I began any shamanic journeying for them. The clients had little or no knowledge of shamanism. At the outset of the study, I was told the clients' first names and little else. In some cases, the psychiatrist indicated an interest in obtaining insights into the sources of their difficulties, but such direction was always abstract and without details. Together, we agreed on the wording of the journey question, leaving it open-ended to receive maximum information.

Using drumming tapes, I journeyed alone, at a distance, without clients knowing when or how I would work on their behalf. I then provided the psychiatrist with written descriptions of each journey, which he shared with the client, noting the reaction evoked by the client's reading of the journey. Later, I discussed with the psychiatrist how the information either confirmed what he already knew or provided new insights, and we worked together to formulate the next journey question.

Because the intention of the journeys usually focused on the source of the clients' present problems, what was shown was often troubling and even traumatic. For all the clients, the initial journeys revealed enough accurate information about events in their lives I could not have known that all were intrigued and wanted to continue learning from my journeys. When I later offered to teach them how to journey for themselves, all of them expressed interest. In the end, however, only two of four participants learned the basic journeying technique. I taught these two to journey to the Lower World to find a power animal. They journeyed easily and, although each found the single journey to be pivotal in the healing process, to my knowledge, neither one journeyed again. The other two clients, who also had expressed interest, did not follow through. The psychiatrist confirmed that avoidance was common to the life patterns of both these clients. It surprised him when they continued to be willing to receive even confrontational information from the journeys and to work with this material in therapy. He said they seemed touched that someone wanted to work on their behalf.

Through image and symbol, the shamanic journeys revealed levels of knowing that were often beyond what could be perceived or expressed by the clients or the psychiatrist. For example, Luke was dying from a brain tumor. An early journey suggested that I teach his wife, Suzanne, to work with him. Learning to journey to find her power animal proved to be helpful when it came time for her husband to die. At another point, I was journeying on a question for myself, when the focus abruptly changed. I found myself sitting with the couple in a boat that began moving to a farther shore. On the other side, Luke got out of the boat and went toward a group of people waiting to greet him. I had the sensation that the pain they had caused him in his life was washed away as they surrounded him with love. This classic shamanic experience (known as *conducting the souls of the dead*) had come unbidden. Only after I had reported this journey to the psychiatrist did I learn what had literally happened. In his delirium as he was dying, Luke had called out the name of his dead sister, with whom he had had a painful relationship. Drawing from the experience of her single journey, Suzanne knew what he was seeing and urged him to run to his sister.

Another participant, Ian, was fascinated by accurate references in my journeys to certain frightening childhood experiences, and he asked me to teach him to journey. As he journeyed to the Lower World to find a power animal, he became visibly moved, weeping as his experience unfolded.

Describing his journey afterward, he said that as he settled into the drumming, he began to see himself sitting in a dugout canoe. He looked down to see that he was naked except for a loincloth. Paddling down a river, he looked to the shore and could see tigers following him along the shoreline. He felt strong and virile. He brought the canoe to shore and, flanked on either side by tigers, he moved to a higher place where there was a throne. He realized that he was some kind of deity and that the throne was his. When he sat down and looked out, he saw his mother and his father. In a gesture of total love, he raised his arms and forgave them for all the pain he had ever received from them. With that gesture, they ascended to heaven, and his journey was over.

The psychiatrist's application of Ian's shamanic journey into the therapy came toward the end of the research project. To help Ian remove blocks in his process, he asked Ian to describe the place he was leaving, his destination, and the means of transfer. When asked to visualize where he wanted to go, Ian saw himself, standing naked on a beach with his tiger beside him, holding a spear and looking out over the water. In this case, Ian had integrated his single shamanic journey into personal myth, as a consequence of the collaborative work between the psychiatrist and me.

George was a client who did not journey, although he learned much from my journeys on his behalf. They were often difficult and, according to the psychiatrist, affected him deeply. I was troubled by repeated images in the journeys of implied incest, forced sexuality, attempted abortion, and the pathos of a blighted twin. The journeys helped George understand the source of many of his problems—a feeling of worthlessness, a tendency to sabotage himself, an inability to be still, a sense of someone else inhabiting his space, and denial and dysfunction in his family. The journeys also offered healing, as nature cradled him and helping animals surrounded him. The psychiatrist reported that George became calm, serious, and more willing to believe in himself as a result of the journey work on his behalf.

David did not learn to journey. My work for him revealed that his life had been co-opted early when he became the unwilling heir to the family business. My journeys were permeated with images of David trapped and suffocating, all passion stifled. The metaphor for his energy was a white-hot volcano, ready to erupt. The information collected in the journeys led the psychiatrist to suggest bodywork as a complement to therapy to help David contact and safely release this seething energy.

Although this analysis involved only four participants, the research suggests that clients may benefit when seemingly disparate disciplines, such as shamanism and psychiatry, work in concert. Clients not predisposed to believe in shamanism received relevant and valuable information that appeared to contribute to their well-being. Luke and Suzanne were guided gently through the final stages of the death process. Ian found a powerful image as a focus for healing. George was made aware of hidden information that was preventing him from finding balance in his life. David's images of smothered energy led the psychiatrist to suggest augmenting therapy with bodywork to help release anger.

Frequent conversations with the psychiatrist about ritual, belief systems, control, spirit, soul, faith, and ordinary and nonordinary reality were sparked by the journey work. Through time, we approached greater mutual understanding. The psychiatrist has remained open to the benefits of companion modes of healing and is currently exploring the uses of energy resonance, sound, and imagery in his practice. My ability to trust the shamanic process has been deeply strengthened. By demonstrating that each of us is connected to the mythic source around which the shamanic model grew, the study has confirmed for me that contemporary shamanism has a vital role to play in healing today.

KNOWING THROUGH ART

Sheila Lynn Belanger

This research is an experiential, transpersonal study of the healer archetype Chiron identified in astronomy, mythology, and the esoteric language of astrology (Belanger, 1995). The astronomical Chiron is a comet discovered in 1977 that orbits between the planets Saturn and Uranus. It exhibits qualities of both a comet and an asteroid, and its presence is catalyzing astronomers to shift their ideas about the nature of our solar system. The astronomical Chiron is also a bridge to expand our sense of reality. In mythology, Chiron is a centaur (half-human, half-horse) who is a healer for his people and acts as a bridge between intellect and instinct. Astrologers link the myth of Chiron to the celestial body named after it, thereby identifying the astrological Chiron as a symbolic healer who bridges between the personal ego and the transpersonal self. In this study, I use the process of the shamanic journey with the drum to explore this multidimensional figure.

Integrative Methodology

I created an integrative methodology that corresponds to and supports the topic of study—the subjective experiences of 15 participants as they did shamanic journeys to the figure Chiron. I integrated these three research methods: (a) a verbal qualitative analysis of themes present in the participants' shamanic journeys, (b) an artistic analysis with touch drawing to express and amplify my understanding of the symbolic level of each participant's experience, and (c) a poetic analysis with *haiku* to synthesize each participant's experience. Each of these is a different phenomenological window into the participant's journey experience. Just as the participants accessed an alternative view of their reality via an alternative state of consciousness, I also looked at their experiences from multilayers of consciousness. In so doing, I hoped to access greater levels of understanding of their spiritual processes.

Data Analysis

The four-step process for data analysis proceeded as follows:

Step 1: Descriptive Thematic Analysis. I analyzed each participant's questionnaire responses on the participant's experiences with the shamanic journeys to ascertain common and unique themes and processes. For example, themes included body movements, hearing music or chanting, or seeing an animal figure.

Step 2: Touch Drawing Analysis. I used the alternative state of consciousness technique of touch drawing. This highly intuitive, nonlinear art process is taught by Northwest artist Deborah Koff-Chapin (1996). The process of touch drawing involves covering a board with paint and placing a light-weight piece of art paper on top of the paint. Then placing the fingers gently on the unpainted side, the "painter" touches the paper to create an image. In touch drawing, the artist experiences the images emerging directly from the interior aspects of self. To deepen my understanding of each participant's experience, I created a piece of touch drawing art in response to reading each participant's data.

Step 3: Haiku Analysis. I then reread the thematic analysis for each participant and looked at the touch drawing I had created for him or her.

Uniting the two in my mind, I created a haiku poem to express my feeling about the two aspects of reality I had created for each participant.

Step 4: Bridging Analysis. The three sets of data were synthesized to offer an integrated presentation of the participants' experiences.

Personal Process During the Analysis

This integrative analysis suited the topic as the methodology became a type of shamanic journey itself, using visual, kinesthetic, and auditory channels of reality. For example, as I read through each participant's journey descriptions, I experienced images of the figures, colors, actions, and so on encountered by the participants. The process was primarily visual. The second analysis (touch drawing) was directly kinesthetic as my hands touched the paper in an intuitive response to reading the verbal descriptions of a participant's journey. The third analysis (haiku poem) was fast and spontaneous. Gazing at the touch drawing for a participant, I heard the corresponding haiku poem spoken in my head. Because it is in the medium of poetry, the haiku poem analysis is most efficacious when read aloud.

Critique of Methodology

This methodology is a promising one for researchers in the field of transpersonal psychology to use in exploring alternative states of consciousness. In general, I felt that the combination of verbal, qualitative analysis with touch drawing and haiku analyses worked extremely well in supporting the bridging focus of this study.

The three analyses developed into a smooth, sequential process. By preparing the verbal analysis first and spending some time immersing my consciousness in the participants' stories, I created a foundation for the touch drawing and haiku analyses. Both the art and poetic analyses flowed easily from the verbal work.

Each of the three types of data analysis offered a unique perspective on the participants' experiences. The verbal description allowed me to access a cognitive version of their process. The touch drawing was much more of an alternative state or intuitive experience. I felt that through the art, my unconscious self was offering another perspective on each person's process. The art analysis allowed me to intuitively merge with each person. Because of the intimacy of the process, it might support researchers who are interested in a more feminist or nonhierarchical approach to researcher-participant interactions. The haiku window on the journey experiences was like a quick, summary snapshot of the experience. It took me to a place that shared cognitive and intuitive qualities. In the entire data analysis process, the movement seemed to be from cognitive to unconscious-intuitive to a blending of cognitive and intuitive. By using multiple levels of my consciousness, a deeper understanding of the participants' experiences in an alternative state of consciousness became available, and this allowed a creative synthesis of complementary ways of knowing.

INTEGRAL INQUIRY

Genie Palmer

This section illustrates the integral inquiry approach described by William Braud in Chapter 3. The example is taken from my dissertation research on this question: How might *disclosure* of exceptional human experiences (EHEs) to self and to others promote *assimilation* of the experiences and, therefore, have an impact on well-being and spiritual growth and development? (Palmer, 1998).

Some benefits of disclosing traumatic experiences were described in Chapter 3 (pp. 44-46). Not mentioned there is work of Augustin de la Peña (1983) on automatization and boredom in relation to health and disease, which suggests that the normal automatization process of the brain leads to boredom and that this boredom can lead to disease and premature aging. According to de la Peña, as humans learn perceptual, cognitive, and motor skills through repeated experiencing, they become automated, and this allows more room in the central processor of the brain to learn new skills and information. The other side of this is that with increased automatization, there is a decrease in consciousness, leading to an increase in experiences of boredom, ennui, and loneliness.

The works of Pennebaker (e.g., 1995), Wickramasekera (1989), and de la Peña (1983) provide two threads of thought for the study of EHEs of the type described in Rhea White's Chapter 7. If—as Pennebaker and Wickramasekera suggest—repression of *traumatic* experiences produces increased psychological stress on the body, leading to the potential for dis-ease, then the repression of extraordinary events or EHEs could have the same effect because a common element in both is an act of repression or inhibition of appropriate expression of an experience. In addition, White (1994a) has suggested that EHEs "are those happenings in our lives that can pull us out of boredom and disconnection into a world of meaning and connection" (p. 139). EHEs may help release us from the boredom of everyday existence—release us, even if only for a few moments, from the automatization that holds the mind captive. Instead of the brain creating a disease process for "information-novelty" when there is an information deficit (boredom)—as de la Peña (1983) suggests—our need for novelty could be satisfied by working with EHEs. Learning to welcome, value, and give expression to EHEs could have a positive impact on our health and well-being.

Quantitative Aspects

In the tradition of integral inquiry, my research includes complementary approaches to studying the disclosure and assimilation of EHEs. In a more conventional, quantitative phase of the project, volunteer participants are assigned randomly to five groups. Group 1 (a *nonintervention,* control group) completes pre- and postassessments with no other planned activities. Group 2 (also a nonintervention group) writes a mindfulness daily diary, focusing on different areas of the body. Groups 3, 4, and 5 are *intervention* groups that learn to write their EHE autobiographies (see Chapter 7). Group 3 does its autobiography work in a solo fashion, whereas Groups 4 and 5 do their autobiography work in weekly educational group settings. I lead Group 4, and Group 5 is self-directed. Common to all three intervention groups are the disclosure procedures of creating an EHE life line, writing an EHE autobiography, and journalizing about old and new EHEs. In addition to this work, the participants in Groups 4 and 5 learn about and share their EHEs in a group setting; this adds a confessional (professing), performative component to their disclosure work.

Standardized assessments are used to measure certain characteristics of all participants before and after the 10 weeks of the study, including (a) the occurrence, frequency, and degree of profundity of life impact of EHEs; (b) the features of EHEs (using semantic differential scales); (c) degree of disclosure and assimilation (of experiences in general and of EHEs in particular); (d) aspects of spirituality; and (e) meaning and purpose in life. Analyses of variance and correlational techniques are used to evaluate patterns, changes, and comparisons of these variables for members of the five groups.

Qualitative Aspects

To balance the quantitative analyses just described, there are also qualitative treatments of materials derived from (a) selected EHE autobiographies and journal writings of participants in each of the three intervention groups, (b) questionnaire materials, (c) participants' reflections on their experiences during the 10 weeks of the study, (d) my reflections on the individual materials and on the group work, and (e) in-depth interviews of participants selected from each of the three intervention groups. These materials are analyzed using conventional qualitative, thematic analysis methods and are supplemented by meditative reflections gained through novel, intuitive procedures similar to those described by Ettling and Amlani (see pp. 176 and 179). For all these qualitative analyses, emphasis is on the meanings of EHEs, the life impacts of these experiences, and how these may be influenced by the disclosure and assimilation components of the study. Finally, the quantitative and qualitative findings are integrated and woven together in the form of a creative synthesis, similar to that described by Moustakas (1990).

Other Ways of Knowing

To my study's traditional ways of knowing that satisfy the intellect, I add other forms of knowing that appeal to the heart.

Learning to do the Sacred Labyrinth Dance provided me with a helpful metaphor for integral inquiry. Both the dance and the methodology have many varied, intricate steps. As a felt sense, the labyrinth dance illustrates the great variety of complementary steps and transformational qualities of this approach. As a visual image, the labyrinth symbolizes the extent and depth of this methodology. Labyrinths are powerful symbols that may have soothing effects because "as symbols, they are complete and balanced, and therefore satisfying" (Bord, 1975, p. 14). The labyrinth has been described as "at once the cosmos, the world, the individual life, the temple, the town, man, the womb—or intestines—of the Mother (earth), the convolutions of the brain, the consciousness, the heart, the pilgrimage, the journey, and the Way" (Purce, 1980, p. 29). As a symbol for integral inquiry, therefore, the labyrinth suggests that this methodology is more like a path or a journey—a healing journey into the center of the data, the center of the study, and the center of the Self that is complete, balanced, and satisfying for the coresearchers, the researchers, and the readers alike.

Nature continually supplies me with rich ways of knowing about my research topic. Early in my research, shortly after I began pondering the question, "How could I capture the essence of these experiences without disturbing them or causing them to disappear?" a hummingbird flew almost into my face, hovering at arm's length directly in line with my eyes. Stopping all movements, I carefully observed the bird. It was close enough for me to see clearly its beauty and to hear clearly its more subtle sounds. I stood as still as I could as this brilliant gem of a bird flew up and down my body length as if observing me as much as I was observing it. This lasted several seconds, and then the bird flew directly above and perched on a tree limb. I watched as the little bird fluffed its wings and slipped its long bill through its feathers, then I decided to move on and not disturb it. The moment I took a step, the little bird was back, flying in front of me, again flying up and down, and at one point almost landing on my shoulder. Shortly after that, a second hummingbird came, and the two birds flew off together. I stood there for several moments, awestruck by this encounter with nature. I felt the hummingbird had just given me a lesson in how to be with EHEs and how to study them. Like hummingbirds, EHEs are natural occurrences in our environment and are meant to be appreciated and enjoyed. If one tries to capture a hummingbird and cage it, it surely will die, for it can flourish only in its natural environment—and so it is with EHEs. This *hummingbird effect* continues to guide me in this research project; it helps me see how I might get closer to EHEs in a way that supports the experience and the experiencer yet does not seek to control or capture the experience.

EHEs are often difficult to put into words, possibly because of their ineffable nature or because we fear that words will alter the sacredness of the experiences. For these reasons, creative expressions in the form of metaphor, poetry, and drawings—produced by me as researcher and by the participants—appear throughout the dissertation to help bring clarity and ease of understanding and to introduce nonverbal elements for added meanings. My drawings will take the form of flowers because I find many similarities between EHEs and flowers. Some EHEs are like beautiful, fragrant roses that people stop to enjoy, taking in the loveliness of the moment and finding that sufficiently satisfying. These serve as wake-up calls, inviting us to pay attention to our world outside ourselves. Other EHEs are like squash blossoms that flower, are pollinated, and then bear fruit to eat. These are practical EHEs that help us in the everyday physical world. Still other EHEs are like honeysuckle flowers, filled with the sweet nectar that sustains the butterflies, bees, and hummingbirds. These are EHEs that nourish our souls.

Still another way of knowing involves the deliberate use of a meditative phrase employed with the intention of gathering the most useful information about EHE disclosure and assimilation and of imparting this knowledge most effectively to the readers of my research reports. While working on a pilot study for this project, I was drawn to the writings of Hildegard of Bingen. A book about her seemed to open naturally to a particular page, and as I glanced down, I saw the phrase, "for the usefulness of believers" (Fox, 1985, pp. 11-12). As I read the whole paragraph, I discovered that Hildegard, wishing to be a practical and helpful mystic and prophet, gave "usefulness" as the reason for writing her major work, *De Operatione Dei* (see Schipperges, 1965). This statement resonated with my work with EHEs because I have found the hallmark of these experiences to be their *usefulness*. Therefore, Hildegard became the patron saint of my dissertation. Meditating in her honor and using her phrase to ritualize intentionality continue throughout all phases of my work.

A final way of knowing used in this research project is one of the bolder approaches suggested by Braud—that of *samyama* (see p. 53). As I focus and amplify my intention and attention on my EHE subject matter—increasing my absorption in what I am studying—I may become what I am studying and know it from the inside, participating as fully as possible in the experience I am exploring.

Research, then, becomes something more than increasing knowledge about my given topic. It becomes a vehicle for my possible transformation, as a researcher, and for possible transformations of my coresearchers and readers as well.

CHAPTER 9

ALTERNATIVE WAYS OF WORKING WITH DATA (ENGAGING AND CONFRONTING DATA)

To continue with the metaphor introduced at the beginning of Chapter 8, the contributions of the present chapter represent attempts to work with *many brains* while interacting with a study's data. In each of the research summaries included here, the researcher attends to other sources of information in addition to external sensory information and works with that information through rational as well as arational means. The researchers become aware of, attend to, work with, and express information that arises from bodily, emotional, intuitive, and other sources. They do this chiefly while working with data that already had been collected in more traditional ways.

Before working with her material in conventional analytical ways, Dorothy Ettling entered a meditative state during which she attended to what her own emotions and intuitions suggested about her tape-recorded participant interviews. She listened to the tapes several times, each time attending to a different aspect or level of information—emotional, intuitive, rational, or specific content. She allowed metaphors and other forms of creative expression to arise in her—these conveyed meanings of the materials she worked with that could not readily be expressed in more linear, rational forms. She combined these alternative modes of knowing and expression with a more conventional thematic analysis and presentation of her results.

In his multiple case study research project, Alzak Amlani augmented conventional analytical theme-extraction methods with insights gained through attending to his emotional and intuitive reactions, as well as his visual, auditory, and proprioceptive imagery, while working with taped interviews in a quiet, meditative state. Next, he elaborated the resultant images by exploring their metaphorical, symbolic, and archetypal aspects, and he developed a cross-cultural, mythic personification of each of his research participants. These augmented descriptions added new and accurate information beyond what was contained in the original research transcripts.

In her phenomenological study of the inner experience of being-movement, Jan Fisher deliberately sought to reproduce in herself, as researcher, the same experience that she was studying in her research participants. She did this by engaging in being-movement many times during the various phases of her research project to stay as closely connected as possible with the phenomenon she was studying. She also had her participants engage in being-movement to be able to describe that experience more fully during the research interview. Both the research participants and the researcher were able to relate to and describe the experience *from the inside* (emically) throughout the investigation. Internal events (imagery, especially kinesthetic imagery) and direct knowings helped illuminate the research findings.

In her feminist, case study approach to issues of cultural isolation, assimilation, and integration among Filipino immigrant women in their journeys to wholeness, Sophie Arao-Nguyen describes how she treats her data intuitively to assess the ways in which her participants experienced change. Her participants used verbal as well as nonverbal means (through images arrayed on novel identity shields) in telling their stories to the researcher and to one another in group meetings. While working with the data, the researcher used nonordinary techniques of rituals, dreamwork, bodily knowing, creative expressions, and intuition to augment and inform the more conventional ways of working with the interview materials. Through these varied means, she achieved insights about her own story that helped provide a framework that applied more universally to the stories of her research participants as well.

The summaries of innovative research methods provided in this chapter suggest a number of more general questions. How might we and our research participants better access internal systems to learn more about a greater number of experiences of ourselves and of others? We are familiar with the content and the operating rules of our intellects. We are not as familiar with the languages of our bodies, feelings, and intuitions. These systems have their own governing principles—some unique, some overlapping those of other, more familiar, systems. By attending to these various systems in ourselves during all phases of our research endeavors, and by using what we learn to help familiarize our research participants and our audience with these alternative systems (learning to speak their respective languages), we can greatly expand what all of us can learn about a rich variety of human experiences.

LEVELS OF LISTENING

Dorothy Ettling

I have always been a person who loved learning. It took me almost 50 years, however, to honor how I learn as a woman. Rumi (1984) says,

> *Until we've kept our eyes and wanting still for fifty years,*
> *we don't begin to cross over from confusion.* (p. 15)[1]

Although I deeply respect and trust Rumi's wisdom, I now know that some insights about ourselves can be nurtured into awareness from childhood. One of these is the many ways we, as human beings, arrive at knowledge. These are not simply ways of being informed but ways of knowing from within.

In 1991, I faced the issue of writing my dissertation. My intention was to invite nine women into a personal exploration and sharing of their inner transformative journey. Each research methodology I considered offered possibilities, but each left something wanting. I was encouraged by the openness of phenomenological and narrative study approaches to simply seek the story. I was heartened by heuristic methods to include my own experience and process as part of the writing. But nowhere could I find the permission to go beyond the systematic study of the women's narrative. I knew there were other ways of finding and expressing the depth and meaning that these stories held, and I longed to include that richness. With the support of a visionary research director and a resourceful committee, I was able to develop a research methodology that honored intuition, rationality, creative expression, and systematic analysis that was founded on narrative. It was a methodology that fed my passion, held integrity for me, and, above all, honored different ways of knowing.

In my experience, women often tell their truth through sharing their personal experience in the context of a narrative. The narrative itself holds the wisdom and contextualizes it in a way that elicits a rich and unique tapestry, a virtual gold mine for research. Being invited to share one's story can be tremendously empowering. Hearing another's story is often the shortest and most profound entry into the recognition of the bonds we share as human beings.

I chose a narrative approach in gathering the data for the study because I believed that the material I sought would be most readily found in the women unfolding their life stories before me. I was not disappointed. Their stories were alive and full. Once we had found a place of trust and sacredness within which to share this experience, the interview was mutually enriching. To help create that sacred space, I found it was helpful to send a preinterview tape on which I reiterated the purpose of our time together and a simple reflection on honoring the experience. At the beginning and end of each interview, we engaged in ritual, spontaneously created by both of us, which helped set a tone for the importance and reverence for our time together. I now know that this additional piece is essential to my methodology. It encourages me and perhaps my coresearchers to be reflective and aware of our interconnectedness with all that is.

The format for the interviews was quite broad. I described transformation as the process of growing in awareness of the interdependence and oneness of all things, and I asked each woman to simply tell me of her spiritual journey in coming to know herself and what that revelation meant to her.

Each one was also invited to complement her story with creative arts, if she so wished. I suspected that these treasures of expression would add another layer to the story of her journey. Some chose to bring artwork or writing to our interview; others invited me to view some of their creative efforts in home, garden, workplace, or photos of children and family.

Two-hour interviews elicited a wealth of information. Once the tapes were transcribed, I entered into an arduous process of becoming informed and formed by their contents. The first phase of working with the data focused on intuition. I read each interview twice, attending to what I heard both from within myself and from the women. I also listened to each interview in three modes of intention: (a) listening for my own emotional reaction to the interview while in a meditative state, followed by a form of creative expression to integrate and conclude the experience; (b) listening for the emotional tone of the interviewee's voice and words; and (c) listening for content to attend to recurring words and themes. In both the listening and reading, I attempted to bear witness to what was spoken, allowing myself to be acted on by the material, rather than simply acting on it. At the completion of this intuitive analysis, I sat in quiet, allowing a metaphor to emerge within me that captured the overall experience of the woman's story. All the results of this were included in the dissertation.

In the second phase of working with the stories, I read them more systematically, seeking significant elements of meaning in each woman's process of personal transformation. I began by extracting words and phrases that pertained to personal change and growth, then attempting to discover the meaning of these phrases within the content and context of the woman's story. After grouping these statements of meaning, I articulated them as themes, relying almost exclusively on the words of the women themselves. Returning to the context of the whole story, I validated the themes and used them as a foundation to recapture the participant's story in a more concise way. Finally, using both the fruits of this analysis and the first intuitive phase, I wrote a description of the meaning of the experience of personal transformation for each woman.

I sent the entire results of my work with each woman back to her for validation and correction. After receiving their comments and making any necessary changes, I sat with all the material to see what would emerge. In lieu of a general description, frequently the final step in a phenomenological study, I chose to write a shared story. I thought this would better honor each woman and the process we had shared. Through it, I attempted to highlight some of the connections among the women's experiences while emphasizing the uniqueness of each one's personal story.

According to the women, the study did honor them and present their stories as journeys that became clearer in the telling. The process of sharing was, in itself, transformative for all of us. The women commented on the effect of "being heard" in a new place and the empowerment of seeing the spirals of their own lives. Their stories were filled with both ordinary and extraordinary events of life. Creativity played an important role in most of these women's lives, although it was described in many different ways. All had struggled—with family, church, community, or workplace—to continue to identify and name themselves as women, learning from their own experience and seeking the sacred in their lives.

For me, this research project literally changed my life. Convinced of the need for women's stories to be told, I now engage in research as a substantial part of my work. It was from that first seed of uncomfortable questioning about methodologies that several of us were prompted to work collaboratively for the past several years in developing organic research; that story is told in Chapter 6 of this book. Committed to working for action and social transformation, I now believe that life stories lead the way to new knowledge and to new policy. Confronted by my desire and love for learning, I now seek it more in the sacred wisdom of ordinary lives. As I reflect on my experience, I realize that I completed this project at age 54. Perhaps Rumi was right after all.

INTERNAL EVENTS
AND ARCHETYPES

Alzak Amlani

In a qualitative study, I explored the physiological, psychological, and spiritual changes and challenges associated with changing from the standard American diet to a three-phase living foods diet (Amlani, 1995). I interviewed 12 selected participants eating 80% or more vegetarian live foods for 18 months to 32 years and thematically analyzed their experiences using a computer-assisted, qualitative content analysis method. I also used a 100-item survey, incorporating the six areas of body, mind, emotions, spirit, community, and ecology, to elicit detailed self-perceived changes associated with eating primarily live foods. I introduced an innovative transpersonal-intuitive analysis that involved listening to the taped interviews in a meditative state while noting my visual, auditory, and proprioceptive impressions and sensations.

The Self as the Instrument

The researcher's personal qualities are critically important in qualitative research. The researcher's special sensitivities can suggest innovative approaches to the conduct, analysis, and reporting of a study. After setting intentions to allow creative and novel ways of interacting with the data to emerge in this study, I became further aware of my own intuitive inclinations. I remembered past incidents in which certain intuitive impressions had been highly informative. These were primarily visual images and proprioceptive (internal physiological) sensations that had occurred while conversing with friends or while practicing psychotherapy. Much of my training included Jungian and other forms of symbolic work, which greatly supported and helped refine and use these natural inclinations.

Developing the Method

Arnold Mindell's (1982) process-oriented psychology applies a nonverbal, contemplative mode to unveil personal and transpersonal insights and knowledge. Mindell refers to the body-mind-spirit complex receiving this information as the *dreambody*. The channels or *discrete carriers of information* (Goodbread, 1987, p. 24) of the dreambody include visual imagery, auditory impressions, proprioception, and kinesthesia.

My dominant *dreambody channel* is the visual. The second most dominant is the proprioception, or body sense. On the basis of work pioneered by Ettling (1994), I used the dreambody to attend to the tape-recorded data. I engaged in this transpersonal research in the following way.

Applying the Method

I first entered a meditative state by practicing 15 minutes of a traditional Yoga meditation technique known as "watching the breath." This assisted in stilling the body, quieting the mind, calming the emotions, and opening the subconscious and other channels (Mindell, 1982). Desiring to listen to the soul of the participant, I was preparing to listen *with* the soul (Braud, 1994c). After 15 minutes of quietude, I listened to the taped interview of each participant. I simply allowed and was mindful of any visual, auditory, or proprioceptive impressions that arose throughout the listening period. These were described and spoken into a hand-held Dictaphone the moment they arose. Remaining congruent with Johnson's (1986) *Inner Work* technique, I did *not* free-associate to the arising image or sensation. Immediately after each impression was recorded, my auditory attention returned to the listening of each interview. This form of intuitive treatment of the data was applied to the audiotapes of all interviews.

TABLE 9.1   Edited Condensations of Researcher's Imagery and Internal
Sensations During Meditative Listening to Two Interview Tapes

AIANNA		
Visual	*Auditory*	*Proprioceptive*
Bali, Fiji, Indonesia; holding a basket, picking fruit; African woman holding a child while working in the fields	Exotic; simplicity and close to the earth; not fitting into today's society	Grief felt in heart and gut; energy in the first and third chakra; grounded and connected to the earth

KATE		
Visual	*Auditory*	*Proprioceptive*
Woman in the Amazon; Kate dancing in a fire ceremony in a dark jungle; walking with a clay pot on her head; mandala of the earth	Men singing; flute and drumming; vessel of culture, diversity, and mother earth	None

Sorting the Data

Each interview elicited one to two pages of words, phrases, and sentences. These were transcribed and edited. The editing was based on the following criteria: (a) delete excess words, (b) choose impressions with the strongest resonance (Taylor, 1991), (c) choose impressions that endured through a larger portion of the listening, and (d) attempt to represent all three modalities—visual, auditory, and proprioceptive. Table 9.1 shows two samples of edited condensations.

Reflection on the Meditative Process

During each intuitive session, I experienced one or more of the following: (a) shifting from one-pointed attention to panoramic attention (samatha vs. vipassanna; Speeth, 1982), (b) getting immersed in the content or simply noting my own impressions, (c) having little material arise or being flooded at other periods, (d) activation of my own unconscious processes, (e) boredom and sleepiness, (f) stopping the tape to reestablish the meditative state, (g) moments of strong resonance with particular revelations, (h) moments of "one-mind," and (i) moments of penetrating the unfolding, archetypal mystery or *soul story*.

I noted that those participants who spoke of their own experiences in allegorical and metaphorical language more easily evoked my own symbolic process. I found myself maintaining a smoother, less obstructed flow of awareness and sensations while listening to participants who more readily reported and discussed their own psychospiritual process. Their openness facilitated an opening of my own inner channels. The brighter their light of awareness, the more internally visible and audible were my images and sensations. My experience of the intuitive analysis was qualitatively influenced by each participant's own content, style, level of awareness, and insight. I was not an independent agent acting on the material. The state of consciousness embedded in and emitting from the participant's words and story was interacting with my own body, mind, heart, and spirit. Once again, the theme of *intra-* and *interconnectedness* arose.

Incubation of Symbolic Impressions

As I began to reflect on the various intuitive impressions gathered from the meditative state, I realized that I was unknowingly forming a gestalt of the various symbols and metaphors. I began to wonder if these symbolic impressions suggested a theme or pattern that was subtle and less conscious. As I continued to let the material *act on me* (Ettling, 1994), I noticed a gradual unfolding of an archetype or perhaps a myth. My curiosity naturally led me to interface these perceptions and related questions with the participants' actual stories, their content analysis, and my face-to-face experiences of them during the interviews. I easily remained in a slightly altered state—an open, reflective, and dreamlike state. Again, I simply allowed another level of material to emerge, without expectation or limits.

The words *archetypes, myths, gods,* and *goddesses* echoed in my mind. It soon became evident that some of the images I had gathered during the initial meditative period were mythic and archetypal. I remembered two vividly: "men sailing across a turbulent sea" and "a mother holding an infant." Bolen (1989) writes about the meaning of such cross-cultural representations:

> Archetypes are preexistent, or latent, internally determined patterns of being and behaving, or perceiving and responding. These patterns are contained in a collective unconscious—that part of the unconscious that is

not individual, but universal or shared. These patterns can be described in a personalized way, as gods and goddesses; their myths are archetypal stories. They evoke feelings (proprioception) and images (visual), and touch on themes that are universal and part of our human inheritance. (p. 6)

I questioned whether some of the universal symbols and impressions I had noted could tell me something about the *depersonalized dream* (Campbell, 1968) or myth underlying the participants' stories. Could they possibly provide me a fuller, deeper, transpersonal grasp of their life journeys? After exchanging these ideas with a colleague well versed in Jungian thought and symbolism, I consulted *An Encyclopedia of Archetypal Symbolism* (Moon, 1991) and other sources.

Using the method of waiting for an "Aha!" insight, or a "click" or "resonance" with the material as suggested by Bolen (1984), Johnson (1986), and Taylor (1991), respectively, I began to link the various symbolic impressions with myths, archetypes, gods, and goddesses. As I connected them with each person's life history, I developed and wrote a cross-cultural, mythic personification of each participant. Following is a one-paragraph sample taken from a 1½ page depiction of 1 of the 12 participants.

Kate/Artemis

Icons of numerous indigenous cultures flooded my awareness while intuitively attending to Kate's story. Primitive images of forest, fire, and ceremony personify the "Greek goddess of wildlife." Armed with a silver bow, Artemis roamed the wilderness, mountains, meadows escorted by her band of nymphs and hunting dogs. Known to the Romans as Diana, she is the personification of an independent spirit. This is Kate. Born in Wales, she grew up in nature and has always been captivated by rituals of the Celts and Native Americans. She came to America alone in her early 20s, began her conscious spiritual quest in her 30s, and in her 40s has traveled and lived in South America, the Far East, and Europe. She has now moved to the wilderness practicing and teaching permaculture. Bolen (1984) underscores, "The archetype she represents enables a woman to seek her own goals." (p. 49)

Reflection on Mythic-Archetypal Elaborations

Desiring to be true to the intuitive material, I chose only those archetypes that had strong resonance with the various visual, auditory, and proprioceptive impressions. I was quite amazed to notice how certain archetypal patterns expressed through the characteristics of the gods and goddesses strongly clicked with particular participants. At other times the descriptions fit, but there was no resonance or "Aha!"

This final stage of the intuitive treatment of the data allotted me a deeper, empathic appreciation of each live foodist's *waking dream* or *personal my-thology* (Feinstein & Krippner, 1988). It returned the entire study and its significance to the individual's personal and unique quest for self-reali-zation. A concern throughout the reporting of the themes was the possible loss of each individual participant within the amorphous data. I found this extension of the transpersonal methodology to more fully honor each participant in a purely mythological-transpersonal context and manner. Greek and Indian mythology provided a rich context for each person. It was apropos at the close of the study after the numerous phases, dimensions, and developmental years had been reported and discussed. The perspective reawakened the mystery, wonder, and fascination that no amount of conventional analysis could fully uncover and explain.

KNOWING THROUGH MOVING

Jan Fisher

The central question of my study was this: What is the experience of being-movement? (Fisher, 1997). To investigate being-movement, I defined being-movement as any type of dance/movement practice that allows the mover to move in an undetermined, nonstructured, freestyle manner, with the attention focused inwardly and on the experience of the movement. Some examples of being-movement forms are Gabrielle Roth's shamanic movement (e.g., Albert, 1990), Authentic Movement (e.g., Chodorow, 1988), and Emily Conrad-Da'oud's Continuum (e.g., Shaffer, 1987). Six experienced practitioners of being-movement, two from each of the above disciplines, were asked, "What is your experience of being-movement?" Phenomenologi-cal, feminist, and intuitive inquiry were used to work with the transcripts and discover the nature of the experience of being-movement.

My intent in this study was to stay as close as possible at all times to the actual experience of the phenomenon being studied, according to both feminist and phenomenological research principles. By including being-movement throughout the research process, I honored the nonverbal, prereflective nature of the experience itself, the unique experience of each participant, and the contextual nature of the phenomenon. In accordance with feminist research principles, I treated each individual interviewed as fully participating in the study and myself as coparticipant in the phenomenon being studied (e.g., Shepherd, 1993). Coparticipation of participants and researcher was accomplished by using the actual practice of movement throughout the research process and by using intuitive inquiry for working with the data.

Being-movement itself was therefore an integral part of the interview process. First, in the screening interview, the participant engaged in a 15-minute being-movement session, while I observed. This served the dual purpose of grounding the study in the context of being-movement and of providing verification that the potential participant was engaging in the subject of the study (an important aspect of phenomenological research, e.g., Wertz, 1984). Second, I included movement prior to the actual interview. Directly before the interview, I moved for 30 minutes, while the participant observed. Following my movement, the participant moved for 30 minutes, while I observed. Then, I arranged the materials for the interview, and we spent a moment in silence to recollect our experiences of being-movement before I turned on the tape recorder and began the interview. Following the interview, I went home and engaged in another movement session, in response to the interview. In this way, being-movement was involved at all stages of the interview process.

By moving prior to the interview, as researcher, I hoped to stay as closely connected to the material as possible and facilitate my own understanding of the experience of being-movement. My movement also set the context for the interview, connecting the participant to the experience of being-movement and creating a safe place for full participation. In my own experience, establishing a context for safety and surrender is an essential component of the experience of being-movement. By moving prior to the interview, I also hoped to establish a coparticipative relationship with the participant, a prominent feature of feminist methodologies, so that I was on an equal footing with the participant and not distanced from the subject of study or from the participant.

I requested that the participant move prior to the interview to reestablish the experience of being-movement for the participant and to ensure that the interview would reflect as closely as possible the participant's actual experience of being-movement, as opposed to recollection or mental reflections. The moment of silence prior to the actual interview also brought the participant closer to the actual experience of being-movement and reestablished the context of the interview after the interruption of the recording logistics.

By moving after the interview, I hoped to maintain the context of being-movement at all points of the study. My initial movement response to the interview, as researcher, reflected the essentially nonverbal, nonanalytical nature of the experience of being-movement. This movement session was the purest, most true reflection of the results of the interview because it took place within the context of being-movement and within the context of a relationship between researcher and participant.

Because movement does not leave a visible trace, I included three creative responses to each of the movement sessions: (a) I produced a creative response after my preinterview movement session, (b) the participant and I produced a creative response after the participant's preinterview movement session, and (c) I produced a creative response to my postinterview movement session. These creative responses—which took the form of prose, sculpture, and drawings—are included in the presentation of the data (sometimes as photographs) and provide an accessible but nonlinear, intuitive, and uninterpreted representation of the experience of being-movement. During data analysis, the creative responses were viewed as nonanalytical reminders of the actual being-movement experience.

Being-movement was included throughout analysis of the interview transcripts, as well. One set of results was obtained using only being-movement and my intuitive summaries of the transcripts. That is, after transcribing the actual interview, I reviewed all the creative responses relating to that participant and engaged in a 30-minute being-movement session. Then, I read the transcript of the interview directly following the movement session and wrote a summary of the transcript from an entirely intuitive place. For each participant, this intuitive summary was about a paragraph in length and reflected an intuitive, immediate, nonanalytical summary of the transcripts. I performed this procedure for each transcript and for the group as a whole. These unanalyzed, intuitive summaries are an integral part of the presentation of the data and support the conclusions regarding the nature of the experience of being-movement.

Being-movement was also included at various stages of the phenomenological analysis of the interview transcripts. Before beginning the phenomenological analysis for each participant and for the group as a whole, I reviewed all the creative responses to the various movement sessions for that participant and engaged in a 30-minute being-movement session. Whenever I stopped working for a period, I again reviewed the creative responses to the movement sessions before returning to work. In a practical and manageable manner, these steps maintained my work throughout the data analysis in the context of the experience of being-movement.

Another aspect of intuitive inquiry was used during phenomenological data analysis. After completing the phenomenological analysis of all six transcripts and preparing the phenomenological descriptions, I created a mandala incorporating all the results. For each participant, I performed a spontaneous movement ritual around the mandala and then reviewed the phenomenological description and made my final revisions. In this way, my phenomenological analysis incorporated the intuitive aspects of being-movement and the experience of being-movement itself in the final stages, creating a full circle in which being-movement formed the beginning and the end. I used a similar procedure to create the final phenomenological description for the experience of being-movement for the group as a whole.

After including being-movement in all aspects of my research procedures, from screening interviews to data analysis, the phenomenological analysis of the experience of being-movement revealed 28 higher-order themes that represent the components of the experience of being-movement, as follows: affected by internal and external, body sensing, choice/ surrender, development over time, different experience of reality, emotions, empty mind, energy, heightened awareness, higher emotions, imagery/hallucinations, inner focus/attention, interconnectedness, intuition, just being, meaning, paradox, personal unconscious, physical aspects, pleasure, rightness, self, space, spirit, surrender, timelessness, transformation, and variety.

SETTING INTENTION
AND ASSESSING CHANGE

Sophie Arao-Nguyen

Using the methods of feminist research and multiple case studies, my inquiry explored the processes involved in Filipino immigrant women's journeys to wholeness (Arao-Nguyen, 1997). Specifically, the research question was "How do Filipino immigrant women respond to the impact of immigration to the United States, whose culture is different from their culture of origin?"

John Berry's (Berry, Kim, Power, Young, & Bujaki, 1989) four acculturation attitudes of separation, assimilation, marginalization, and integration, and Carol Christ's (1980) individuation process for women, which includes nothingness, awakening, and new naming, were used as conceptual models. Ten Filipino immigrant women, including me, as researcher, participated in the study. All 10 women were between 20 and 40 years of age at the time of immigration, had resided in the United States for at least 5 years, were resident in the Bay Area, and were willing to commit at least 10 hours to the study.

The research design involved preinterview and postinterview gatherings at my home, where dinner was served at each meeting to enable the participants to establish relationships and a sense of community and to network with each other. During the preinterview gathering, an identity shield exercise was introduced as a source of creative expression to explore and reflect on the process of acculturation through the use of words or symbols. The identity shield consists of three parts. The left upper quadrant pertains to the things that strike the participant about her culture of origin, whereas the right upper quadrant describes what strikes her about American culture. On the base of the shield, she incorporates what she wants or expects from both cultures. The materials used were crayons and the identity shield instrument. Participants were invited to share their identity shields with the group, after which a group identity shield was put together by including common themes from the individual shields. The purpose in doing the group shield was to allow the group members to discover their commonalities and uniqueness.

Between the gatherings, individual semistructured interviews were conducted at sites chosen by the participants. The interview was started with a discussion of the woman's identity shield, and five topics were explored— her purpose for coming to the United States, the losses she experienced when she moved to the United States, the opportunities she took advantage of to improve her quality of life, events or situations that triggered her transformation and growth, and her dreams or future goals.

A postinterview gathering was convened to finalize discussion around the group's identity shield, to elicit participants' overall reactions to their participation in the study, to give participants a chance to incorporate their personal insights and learnings from the study into their lives by doing an individual action plan (using a things-to-stop, things-to-start, things-to-continue format), and to brainstorm and discuss the group's action plan.

The 10 individual profiles of the participants were included in the findings. Each participant profile consisted of a demographic description of the participant, her identity shield and its description, her story, her individual themes as gleaned from her story, her reactions to the interview and to the study as a whole, and her individual action plan. A group profile also was prepared. The group profile included a demographic description of the group, a group identity shield and its description, a glimpse of the group process, collective themes, reactions to the overall study and to being part of it, and the group's action plan. Categories and emergent themes were woven together to formulate the stages involved in the Filipino immigrant women's journeys to wholeness.

To demonstrate what I learned from transpersonal psychology, I included rituals and transpersonal practices, and I tapped my intuition to help me in my research project.

Selection of Participants

I created an altar at home and invoked the Great Feminine to lead me to the right participants. I offered the names of 20 women whom I had contacted and who expressed interest in participating in the research. In the end, 9 participants came to the preinterview meeting. I was the 10th participant. Later comments from the participants regarding how well the group interacted and how well the study progressed suggest that the early ritualizing of intention for the "right participants" may, indeed, have been useful in drawing appropriate and compatible participants into the study.

Using Intuition

When I started my research, I accessed the intuitive part of me and agreed to create rituals that would enable me to enter into my creative space. Instead of feeling discouraged when schedules and deadlines were not met, I allowed circumstances to speak to me so I could accept the changes wholeheartedly even before understanding the full import of the dynamics involved in my research. My dreams guided me in uncharted terrains and territories of the research, and by externalizing the dream motifs into collage form, I was able to access their meanings. There were moments when I would be overcome with new insights and new ways of looking at the stories, and my tears would water the seeds that were planted in my mind so they could bloom and come to fruition. I experienced an aliveness in body, mind, and spirit that I had experienced only in deep meditation before. Examples of these "moments of grace" were when I realized that the title to my own personal journey was an appropriate description of the stages involved in the women's journeys overall; when, after writing the women's stories, the appropriate titles to their stories would pop out from nowhere; and when the questions I had asked during the interviews "matched" the three stages involved in the journey.

Attending to the
Culture of the Participants

During the pre- and postinterview group meetings, the first part of the agenda was to have dinner together. Eating together is a practice that is embedded in Filipino culture. Food not only is symbolic of physical nourishment but also is an offer of friendship, fellowship, and kinship. Eating together initiated the process of bonding. Once the bonding occurred, there was a shared feeling of commitment to the project and a desire by the participants to give the best of what they could give to the project. The process of bonding occurred at the first meeting and was deepened at the second meeting. The support system that the participants claimed they had lost was recreated at these group meetings. The first meeting enabled them to trust the process and therefore facilitated the telling of their stories during the interviews. The second meeting allowed them to incorporate their insights and learnings into their present lives as well as to establish some form of "psychic closure" before saying their good-byes.

Individual and Group Shields

The purpose of including the individual identity shield in the study was to enable the participants to pause from their business of living and take a look at where they are now in their process of transformation and growth. The group identity shield also allowed them to reflect on how they can integrate the values they have chosen to retain from their culture of origin and the values they have adopted from the new culture. It enabled them to consciously reflect on what they wanted from both cultures, resulting in a blending and integration of values.

Individual and Group Action Plans

Individual action plans were initiated at the postinterview meeting to allow the participants to incorporate their learnings from the research study into their personal lives. Examples of their learnings are "continue to assert rights as an individual, parent, woman"; "reclaiming my own power and authority"; "pass good Filipino and American values and practices to my children"; "stop judging myself and my life"; and "continue heartfelt, open, and honest exchange with others."

"Giving back to the community" was presented to the group as a culminating activity of the research. Although most of them were already giving back to the community through their individual volunteer work in sociopolitical action and personal and family transformations (Comas-Diaz, 1994), I proposed a group action plan to make use of the synergy that was produced by the research so that this group of immigrant women with professional status could make a difference in the Filipino community. We began brainstorming possible projects, but the group members were not ready to decide on the scope and focus of the group action plan. Instead, the group agreed to come out with a directory of participants for networking purposes. Business cards exchanged hands. Group members agreed to get together again to continue the process that had begun.

At present, group members are continuing with their individual volunteer work. I am calling a third meeting (not part of the original design) to present my findings, and I hope that toward the end of the meeting, the participants will return to the task of planning for the socialization process to continue so that even as the research project will come to an end, the gatherings will go on, and the process of empowerment will continue to affect the lives of the participants and of the community. As a result of this research project, I plan to lead workshops and retreats for women of color to help them come to a better understanding of what they have been through, where they are now, and where they want to go in the future, using the stages of the journey to structure the workshops and retreats.

NOTE

1. Excerpt from *Open Secret* (p. 15), by Jelaluddin Rumi (John Moyne and Coleman Barks, Translators), 1984, Putney, VT: Threshold Books. Copyright © 1984 by Threshold Books. Reprinted by permission.

CHAPTER 10

ALTERNATIVE WAYS OF PRESENTING RESULTS (EXPRESSING AND COMMUNICATING FINDINGS)

Presenting research findings to diverse audiences may not be a challenge unique to the field of transpersonal psychology. Nevertheless, the popularity of transpersonal topics requires transpersonal researchers to be unusually creative in responsibly and comprehensibly reporting their findings to a wide, and often diverse, readership or audience.

Traditionally, research accounts are written for peers and published in professional journals. The readership or audience is clearly defined. We, as researchers, are writing for people much like ourselves, and, assuming that readers are knowledgeable in the field and subspecialty, our report writing is precise and to the point. We expect research accounts to be explicit and thickly packed with information, typically including a review of the relevant literature, detailed description of the methods and procedures, results and analysis, and a discussion of the implications of the findings for theory and future research. We can more or less count on our readers accurately understanding our terminology and logic and interpreting our report more or less as we intended. Despite the almost telegram-style writing of most professional journals, we often appear to communicate rather well, at least among professional peers.

But these scientific circles are small. With the mushrooming of subspecialties in academic disciplines, most of these accounts circulate within a specific group of researchers in closely related areas of interest.

Communicating in small circles primarily among peers is not a luxury transpersonal researchers can afford. As in a few other fields of study, the topics researched by transpersonal researchers, such as alternative approaches to health and wellness, mystical and unitive experiences, self-actualization and transcendence, and issues of ultimate values, are profoundly interesting to the general public. Many transpersonal researchers are wary of presenting their findings to the general public for fear of misinterpretation or even ridicule. Nonetheless, if they have something important to say, it is foolish—and perhaps irresponsible and unethical—to maintain a close-in dialogue among other transpersonal professionals and in any way screen the findings and their implications from the general public. It is also, candidly speaking, more profitable to publish trade books than professional books (such as this one, for example); therefore, there is a real and creative tension in the field between publishing in professional journals or books and publishing in alternative journals and trade books for the general reader. Transpersonal researchers already, and will no doubt continue to, present research findings in creative ways to the general public. Writing for professional colleagues is relatively easy. The audience is clearly defined. Writing for the general public, however, is fraught with challenges. Who is the audience? Imagining who might read our books is a bedeviling experience. Transpersonal researchers writing for the broad and pluralistic readership are challenged to communicate findings responsibly, comprehensively, and in a manner congruent with the intrinsic values of the field—and perhaps values intrinsic to a particular study or researcher.

The research examples in this chapter provide creative approaches to presenting research findings. Depending on the topic, the researcher's choices, and the intended audience, a variety of writing styles, formats, and modes of creative expression are chosen to present their research findings with greater depth and integrity.

To study the effect of physical beauty on a woman's sense of self, Lisa Shields employs a blend of feminist, heuristic, and organic approaches. In her dissertation, her voice as the writer is distinguished from the voices of her participants (her grandmother, mother, and herself) by different type-faces and font styles. An italicized font is used for the voice of her dreams, which play a significant role in guiding the unfolding steps of the research. Instead of the traditional format of report writing, the various sections, such as the literature review and presentation of results, are woven throughout the dissertation in a more narrative style.

Using heuristic research methods, Wendy Rogers explores the experience of the loss of fertility occurring during the childbearing years. The final phase of a heuristic research project is a creative synthesis of the findings that requires a comprehensive integration of the researcher's experience of the essential qualities of the research topic. Wanting her creative synthesis to offer the reader an interactive experience of these essential qualities, she creates an oracle, and an accompanying guidebook, from an intuitive perception of the participants' experience of the loss of fertility during the childbearing years. In the dissertation and continuing workshops, readers and participants are invited to take part in the oracle and to consider their own experiences of loss and feelings of barrenness or lack of creativity.

In a study exploring the interstices of space in the context of tournament sabre fencing or the demonstration of Aikido, Susan Newton asks 10 women who are senior practitioners to reflect on their experience of the space between one's self and another in the practice of these kinesthetic arts. Using a blend of heuristic, phenomenological, and feminist approaches, she invites each practitioner to reflect on the descriptions provided by the other research participants. Rather than thematically synthesizing the descriptions herself, she allows the practitioners' reflections on each other's descriptions to provide a series of iterative cycles successively approximating the essential qualities of the experience of the space between things in the practice of sabre fencing and Aikido. Like Lisa Shields's presentation, her dissertation describes the evolving process of the research rather than following the traditional format.

To study the transpersonal dimensions of painting, Linda Bushell Spencer asked artists to fully tell their stories without interruption, judgment, or critique of any sort from the researcher. Unique about her research is the unexpected outcomes of having participated in the study and her report of these outcomes as part of the presentation of her findings. Not only did artists report changes in themselves and in their art as a result of having told their stories and reading those of the other artists, but the artists on their own initiative gathered to continue the dialogues that had been so beneficial to them.

Several aspects of research examples in Chapters 8 and 9 warrant a retrospective comment here, as well. In Nancy Fagen's investigation of dreams through creative expression, she includes line drawings of dream images, along with the participants' brief commentaries, in her dissertation. Readers of her dissertation are encouraged to let the images "speak" in their own nonverbal language. Similarly, in Jan Fisher's study of being-movement, her intuitive "snapshot" interpretations of each participant's movement are presented intact, to add an uninterpreted dimension to her rigorous phenomenological analysis. Moreover, she encourages the dissertation reader to engage in being-movement as he or she reads the research findings to directly connect to the nonverbal, kinesthetic dimensions of the experience. As illustrated in these specific examples and throughout most of the research examples in Chapters 8, 9, and 10, an analysis of data is often accompanied by a parallel presentation of the participants' stories, artistic expressions, quotes, and so forth. By presenting the participants' experience and expressions in their own words or images, the nonverbal—and perhaps state-specific—transpersonal dimensions of meaning are expressed and more easily available to readers.

We encourage readers to read these research examples with a spirit of exploration. In the contexts of presenting research findings to both professional peers and the public, what creative possibilities might we explore to more comprehensively present the multidimensional aspects of human experience?

INTEGRATED, FEMINIST WRITING

Lisa Shields

I had spent much of my life plagued by feelings of low self-esteem because of negative feelings about my appearance. I come from a line of beautiful women—my mother, my grandmother, and my great-grandmother. Believing that my appearance did not meet the expectations of my family, I thought I was the ugly duckling in a flock of swans.

Throughout Western history, beauty in women has been a means of gaining access to power and financial security. Even in the liberated period of the late 1900s, physical attractiveness is an important aspect of women's status. Wanting to have a deeper understanding of its significance in my life, I chose beauty as the topic of inquiry for my research.

Yet I had no clear idea of the methodology I would use. I found myself drawn to the feminist approaches to research. In many feminist approaches, the subjective voice of the researcher is an important aspect of the research. The permission to include my story, my voice, and my experience within the research was exciting to me. I had two of the essential elements for my dissertation—the subject (beauty and body image) and a foundation of the methodology (a feminist approach). The third element was my connection to Jungian theory. I have interpreted Jungian theory to define the feminine as the nurturing, relational, connective aspect of Eros in contrast to the masculine component as the hierarchical, discriminating, individualistic aspect of Logos. The feminine and masculine are present in both men and women.

In the midst of attempting to put these three elements into a dissertation topic, I joined the organic research group. Because of my being in this group, my dissertation grew into an extremely subjective inquiry of beauty, body image, and the feminine. Through this organic process, my research grew to be a personal exploration of my female lineage. The process was organic, as if it had a life of its own. I let the process follow its own course without attempting to control it. Instead of taking an objectifying and masculine stance that dominates, separates, and controls, I attempted to maintain a subjective, feminine position that holds, allows, and receives.

Another organic aspect of my dissertation process was my trust in the unconscious. This process in organic research is named the *chthonic*. The seed ideas for the research are left underground or in the unconscious. It is in this subterranean landscape that dreams reside. My dreams guided me in the choice of my coresearchers, the questions I would use, and how to write and organize my dissertation. My dreams also coached me to follow my intuitions.

The outcome of this chthonic process was a creative methodology. I had only three participants in my study—myself, my mother, and my grandmother. Each of us interviewed the other two persons, at two times, asking two questions: (a) Tell me about a time in your life when you felt beautiful, and (b) tell me about a time in your life when you felt unattractive.

I spent a week with my grandmother and mother. It was a week filled with stories. When the initial interviews were complete, the three of us continued conversations about beauty, body image, and the feminine throughout the week. I carried a tape recorder wherever we went, collecting data during car trips, meals, and even visits to the women's room. I collected 15 hours of dialogue. With each story came a deeper understanding of the history of the women in my female lineage and how being beautiful was important to each. Neither my mother nor my grandmother had college degrees. They married young to potentially successful men, as my great-grandmother had done before them. Being beautiful and marrying well were a means of financial security.

In writing my final results, I wished to hold these stories and conversations sacred, not wanting to dissect nor analyze the stories themselves. I wanted to maintain the holding-containing aspect of the feminine in working with the data I had collected. Wanting their voices to be heard within the presentations of the findings, I kept the conversations in their original forms. Specific conversations or stories were inserted throughout to illustrate concepts that pertained to the chapter topics.

In presenting the findings, I used different typeface styles to distinguish my voice as the writer in contrast to the dialogue. I used an italicized font when describing a dream. Feeling that the three voices also needed faces, I included photographs of my female lineage.

The traditional psychology research report format—introduction, literature review, methodology, results, and discussion chapters—was too linear, dissecting, and separating. The format did not keep to the organic flow I was trying to maintain throughout my dissertation process. I included the content of each of the conventional chapters, yet I used different formats, titles, and positions in the text. For example, my methodology section was titled, "The Story of My Research."

The most important aspect of my research was the transformational change that occurred in each woman's life and in her relationship to the other coresearchers. Because each coresearcher interviewed the others, feelings of trust and equality were present during the interviews. The egalitarian format allowed each woman to drop into herself more authentically as a woman—beyond the context of the familial relationships. All coresearchers felt more seen and understood as individual and separate women. At the same time, each coresearcher experienced a strengthening of the mother-daughter-grandmother bond. The week was a transformational experience that lasted beyond the boundaries of the research. It has been almost 2 years since my mother, grandmother, and I spent a week together conducting interviews. Our relationships to each other have been significantly enhanced and deepened since that week, and that deepening continues.

Because transforming the researcher, the participants, and even the reader is an important aspect of organic research, these outcomes were significant. It has been gratifying to hear that many women have been moved to tears when reading my dissertation.

I found my dissertation process was a wonderfully creative and transformative experience. Because of the expansive nature of transpersonal perspectives and methods, I felt I was given the latitude and permission to pursue novel approaches in research methods.

READER-INTERACTIVE CREATIVE SYNTHESIS

Wendy Rogers

I chose the heuristic research approach, developed by Clark Moustakas (1990), to explore the experience of the loss of fertility during the childbearing years. The stages of heuristic research are completion of unstructured interviews or dialogue meetings in which the stories of the experience or phenomenon being studied are gathered, development of an individual portrait of each woman's experience, development of a composite portrait, selection of two or three exemplary portraits, and design of a creative synthesis. This discussion will focus on the creative synthesis.

Creative synthesis, the final phase of the heuristic research process, is an integration of the materials that reflects the researcher's personal knowledge, tacit awarenesses, intuition, and understanding of meanings and essences of the experience. The researcher arrives at creative synthesis through solitude and a meditative focus on the topic. She extends herself beyond a restrictive attention to the data and allows herself to be led to a comprehensive expression of the essences or essential qualities of the experience.

In the creative synthesis,

> The researcher as scientist-artist develops an aesthetic rendition of the themes and essential meanings of the phenomenon. . . . There is a free reign [*sic*] of thought and feeling that supports the researcher's knowledge, passion, and presence; this infuses the work with a personal, professional, and literary value. (Moustakas, 1990, p. 52)

Although the creative synthesis is comprehensive, it is not intended to be the final word. It is a snapshot of the current understanding of the researcher and coresearchers of the essence of the experience. The heuristic method allows for the creative synthesis to take the form of a poem, song, narrative description, a story or tale, or a combination of these.

Of utmost importance to me was that the creative synthesis be experiential and interactive. I wanted the expression of the essential qualities of the experience of loss of fertility to extend beyond the written word on the page to bring full attention to it, to give it life and dimension, and to convey the spiral quality of the experience. I wanted the reader to interact with it rather than simply read about it.

I chose to create an activity that resembles an oracle. The oracle is composed of a set of 25 stones, a Celtic knotwork design painted on fabric, and a book titled *From Barren to Baroness: The Essential Qualities of the Loss of Fertility.*

I wanted the qualities of the experience to be tangible, so I selected stones as the messengers to deliver the qualities of loss of fertility. Stones were used to provide a tactile dimension to the experience. Each was selected so that it could be held in or across the palm of the hand. Attention was also given to their weight. A basket, or container, is needed to carry all the stones. In other words, they are a burden that cannot be ignored. Attention is needed to carry and move them about.

The essential qualities of the experience of the loss of fertility are painted on the stones. These were obtained through a ritual. After entering a meditative state, I focused my attention, individually, on my own experience and that of each coresearcher. I asked for three words that express the essential qualities of the experience for each woman. On completion, I reviewed the qualities, collectively, to ascertain whether they expressed the breadth and depth of the experience expressed by the women as a group. I feel confident that this was achieved. The essential qualities are listed in the order I received them in this ritual: surrender, love, freedom, awakening, sorrow, release, descent, partnership, identity, chaos, loneliness, mystery, spirit, expectation, loss, peace, judgment, blessings, breakthrough, vitality, sacred, retreat, solitude, and strength.

I, then, painted a quality on each stone. In alignment with the Viking tradition of rune-stones, I provided a blank stone to represent the unknown and unknowable. Thus, each set of stones contains 24 lettered stones (three qualities for each of eight coresearchers) and a blank stone, bringing the total to 25. Painting the qualities on stone gave them life and rooted them more deeply in the emotional, spiritual, and physical. Their creation guided me in shifting from a predominantly intellectual perspective to an integration of body, mind, and spirit.

To convey that this experience is a journey or path, I selected a visual characterization. I chose the design and found an artist to create it on fabric. The design is an example of traditional Celtic knotwork; the pattern is a Lindisfarne spiral knot. It was chosen for its spiral quality and because the image has no discernible beginning or end. The design is also intended to be a symbol of a process that is neither linear nor finite. We will never conceive naturally. Therefore, the journey is also lifelong.

The next step was to create the book *From Barren to Baroness: The Essential Qualities of the Loss of Fertility*. My goal was to impart the essence of each quality. Beyond that, I wanted to assist the reader in either solving the mystery of loss of fertility or plunging more deeply into its exploration. I imagined the reader, alternately, as one of my coresearchers or a woman who has experienced the loss of fertility or is anticipating the loss; as a friend, family member, or partner of this woman; or as someone who has no experience or association with this type of loss. I attempted, therefore, to communicate with the reader in a variety of ways. I employed descriptive text, quotes from the coresearchers, quotes from authors, paintings and collages, and poems written by me and one of the coresearchers.

In an effort to further enhance understanding, I listed words that are counterparts or associations of the word used to identify the quality. These words, in many cases, serve as links between the qualities. They are the thread that weaves each quality into the greater fabric.

The qualities of the loss of fertility are recognizable and known to many of us. Many who have interacted with the creative synthesis set have noted a connection between the qualities of loss of fertility and of other types of losses they have experienced. A woman may recall her own experiences of more tangible losses such as the death of a loved one or the end of a relationship. She is also encouraged to ask herself, "Have I ever felt barren or infertile?" She may be encouraged to reflect on these times and the feelings associated with these experiences. She may be encouraged to stop and think about her experiences of loss and to realize that the loss of fertility is similar and is a source of suffering and growth like the more tangible losses.

Thus, the oracle extends an invitation to others to connect with their experiences of loss and feelings of barrenness or lack of creativity. Making an intentional connection between the loss of fertility and other losses serves as a way to educate others and increase sensitivity to the impact of the loss of fertility. Use of the oracle establishes a connection between those who have experienced loss of fertility and those who have not—a connection that transcends the typical awkwardness and speechlessness.

The oracle offers others insight into my experience, invites them to make connections between their experiences and mine, and encourages us to put our thoughts and feelings about these experiences into words; it encourages us to tell and listen to our stories. In the telling and listening, we feel seen, heard, and acknowledged in our experiences of loss.

My interactions with the methodology and the completion of the study prompted numerous insights, significant events, and a deepening of my experience of loss of fertility. I was changed through the gathering of data and the telling and listening to the stories. I go so far as to say that I was transformed. The events that led to a revelation about my desire to have a child and my desire to love spontaneously and with an open heart are noteworthy and reveal the deepening of my experience and transformation.

I am curious about the potential of the creative synthesis set as an intervention tool and its effectiveness in facilitating healing. I imagine the set being used in clinical practice. For example, the therapist could set the stones and fabric design on a table in her office and organize the therapy session around the quality that is most significant to the client at the moment or the quality the client feels most closely represents her perception of current issue(s). The client might arrange the stones on the design in a way that represents the issues that are most pressing. Another approach might be to have the client create her own set of stones by identifying qualities of significance, gathering stones, and painting them.

ITERATIVE REFLECTIONS

Susan J. Newton

I have long been curious about the spaces between things, nearly as much as with the things themselves. Increasingly, I find I am more drawn toward space, to the interstices, as a place of potential, creativity, and spirituality. What happens there? How can I explore this area?

I am both a student of Aikido and a competitive fencer. Sparked by my experiences in both practices, I am curious about how others, senior to me in each practice, experience the space between themselves and their partners.

This project was designed to gather reports of specific experiences from senior practitioners in the body/mind disciplines of Aikido and fencing. Five women from Aikido, third- to fifth-degree black belt, and five women from fencing, nationally classified A or B, were my coresearchers, considered as experts in their fields. I asked them to describe, completely and concretely, their experience of a time when their usual way of perceiving, and moving, in the space between themselves and another shifted, and changed, in the intensely focused context of a major tournament (fencing) or demonstration (Aikido). Other questions were asked for context. My own experiences were woven into the overall picture through the questions I asked, as well as being more directly reported as part of each area of research into the specific practice contexts.

Why do I want to be there, in that space between? The sense of being part of a larger, expanded self draws me there. It seems I am moved into this more expanded mode by a shift or change of perspective, by being willing to let go of attachments, by becoming "lighter" on many levels. For me, the practice context functions as a way of both opening space and opening into the space between.

Which context, and how it is used, I suspected would influence how the experience may be held and worked with. I suspected that the development of attentional training is a major component of a practice context, at rest or in movement. I believe there to be developmental aspects to practice contexts, and I deeply honor the place of practice as access to transpersonal realms, where there is space for the whole of one's being, body, mind, and spirit.

Several methodological innovations are evident in my research. My chosen approach combined aspects of heuristic, phenomenological, and feminist research practice, with a transpersonal perspective. I worked with the others selected as coresearchers, rather than as subjects, and gathered materials through a participant-observer stance. My elected perspective encouraged respect for the many ways of knowing that are part of being in the world, in addition to the more traditional, rational mode.

I drew from heuristics in working with my own experiences and from phenomenology in working with those of others. With both methodologies, I was attracted to the emphasis on the experience itself as beginning point. Nevertheless, I was uncomfortable with the perspective that phenomenological research "studies the experiences people have of their bodies" (Polkinghorne, 1989, p. 45). To me, this speaks of a continuing dualistic approach to human experience.

I see the underlying principles of both transpersonal psychology and organic methodology as honoring experience as arising in the blend of body/mind/spirit, considered as facets of a whole, not split parts spliced together. In the words of Minh-ha (1989),

> Closure and openness, again, are one ongoing process: we do not have bodies, we are our bodies, and we are ourselves while being in the world. . . . We write—think and feel—[with] our entire bodies rather than only [with] our minds or hearts. It is a perversion to consider thought the product of one specialized organ, the brain, and feeling, that of the heart. (p. 36)

I found not only room for materials to present themselves in a manner of unfolding but also an honoring of the sacred and potentially transformative processes involved within the research process itself.

I intuitively, and deliberately, allowed the material to structure the form of presentation. Gathering of information and what grew from the inter-actions as the process of research unfolded were both honored. The form of reporting unfolded with the research process itself and does not follow the traditional format, although the usual aspects are addressed, albeit in different ways and places. For example, the literature review is woven into the document where it was most relevant to the flow of reporting.

My coresearchers each read and responded to the reports of the others. When I initially contacted the people I hoped to work with, prior to the actual interviews, I spoke of the format I planned to use. Each person who agreed to work with me knew that she had a choice of how she could be identified in the study. They also knew that each person would have the opportunity to review hard copy of the interview transcripts, to edit for clarification and correct spelling. In addition, each person would have the opportunity to read and approve for accuracy the abstracts I would create from the transcripts and be asked for their response to this material, which would be read by all the coresearchers as part of this project. This was agreed to, up front, prior to the actual interviews.

I clarified my personal context by asking myself: What are my assump-tions and preconceptions about the phenomenon in which I am interested? My requests of my coresearchers were informed from this process.

As with the heuristic approach, internal alertness and focused attention were part of what informed my creation of the abstracts, as well as honoring my own hunches and intuitive resonance with the material gathered in the interview process. As I worked with transcript material from the interviews,

I was aware that my own framing of what I was creating from what had been gathered was not so much that of a story as that of a report. Indeed, I saw what I was doing as creating an abstract of their reports, descriptions of their experiences.

The interviews were roughly 1 to 1½ hours in duration; each person was interviewed twice, and in one case, three times. The interviews were taped, and the tapes were transcribed by someone else. I then listened to the tapes, doing a word-for-word check for accuracy, and corrected the transcripts accordingly. This resulted in a database of nearly 600 pages of transcript material. I then abstracted and drew from this material those portions that seemed to me to speak most clearly to the questions I asked. Each person speaks in her own words. I added nothing but edited lightly for clarity. Each person reviewed what I created and approved it as accurately reporting her experiences and her reflections. All my coresearchers agreed to the use of their own names, so no pseudonyms are involved.

I expected the fruits of this research to emerge from responses to the abstracts of those interviewed as well as from my own experience of doing the study. Their observations, and my own, structure the analysis of the data.

Looking at orders of change within a given system, as well as across systems, may be useful in contexts other than the martial arts. Work in organizational development, conflict resolution, psychotherapy, and education might usefully apply information gleaned from the experiences of exploring the spaces between contexts. Conceivably, a ripple effect of changes embodied in a person might act as catalyst, influencing and expanding the range of possibilities for others in similar practice contexts and beyond into the larger community. I believe that the implications may be quite extensive and may address such questions as how to train for "performance" in many other contexts, how to invite grounded change, and how to then work with the fruits of these practices.

Also, to the best of my knowledge, the experiences of senior practitioners in two arts have not been reported in this way, much less the experiences of senior practitioners who are also women. This way was not compare/contrast but rather, "What is your experience of . . . ?"

Other variations from the research norm of practice are evident. The form itself is more open and reflects the interactive style of my engagement with the material, my own practices, and my coresearchers. In creating the overall structure, I invited and allowed the materials themselves to influence the form in which they appear. The presence of my coresearchers is direct and clear as they speak of their experiences, insights, and practices. The presentation of their reflections on reading the abstracts of the others in turn reflects the movements of dialogue and engagement with the research process itself.

Overall, I chose a stance of transparency in reporting my own sense of the unfolding research process and in allowing my coresearchers to be as present, throughout, as possible. Readers are invited to engage with and continue the process, drawing on their own experiences as connections and cross-connections may occur.

I suggest that there is consistency in how attention is used, in how mastery may be held, and in attitudes toward experiencing the space between the two practices. The space between may be experienced as a place of expanded awareness, a goal to be achieved or won, a place of transcending one's self, and a place in which one may achieve one's personal best.

Engagement of one's body, mind, and spirit in a practice may well have transformative potential beyond that of a practice that focuses primarily on one's physical performance. One's practice may be a vehicle for moving literally into a much less personal space. Here, there is much less ego involvement and less concern with one's self at moments of experiencing shift, and change of perspective, within the practice context. These experiences may then be held as positive and beneficial—as the fruits of one's practice that may occur in the experience of exploring the interstices, the space between one's self and another—in both a practice context and one's life.

At times, one may catch a glimpse or obtain a taste, in an embodied way, of that which is "through ego and self" and may be on the way to the transpersonal realms of experience. Moving through the interstices to that which is not said or done or even, perhaps, felt may serve as a way through the personality to the space of Self. In a similar way, going into and through the spaces between conceptual figures and images, form and technique, may lead into the ground of potential and being.

Exploring the interstices allows access to the experience of the spaciousness and potential that are inherent within this ground/space of becoming, which may well be transformative. Attention to one's experiences in a chosen practice context may provide the space for the exercise of what Jung termed the *transcendent function,* the unifying activity between consciousness and the unconscious. This in turn may profoundly influence one's being in the world.

UNPLANNED PARTICIPANT OUTCOMES

Linda Bushell Spencer

I address two issues: (a) the impact of an interview and (b) unintended opportunities and possibilities arising in a research setting. In conventional research projects, these may not be recognized or followed up.

It is important to realize the impact a research interview may have on a participant. It is not often that a person has the opportunity to tell his or her story to an attentive listener who does not interrupt, judge, or criticize. This experience can have a profound effect on the participant. For example, when Bob, who was interviewed about his art, was asked about the effect of the interview, he said,

> It was just what I needed. I was floating around in a boredom situation, and this [participation] provided me with the intellectual challenge that I needed. I was very lonely. The interview itself had as much benefit as my artwork ever did. The fact that you uncovered things, and opened doors, and that sort of thing was wonderful. When I started to dictate my life story, I realized I must have left half out of what was in my life. That really started me on a project. I ended up working about 2½ months on it. The first part of the project was a 2-hour audiotape. Then, I organized stacks and stacks of about 750 color slides onto videotape. After that was completed, I put together seven volumes of scrapbook material—newspaper articles, family photos, and thousands of photos—into a representative group. . . . I assembled all the pictures of the kids, including their different school pictures over the years. It's pretty much of a story. Then I got all my school year stuff put together. That goes all the way back to when I was in kindergarten up to college days. There's a whole section of my civic involvement all the way back to my youth center work in high school. There is some information of what I was doing during the war. Then there are all my greeting cards. They go all the way back to when I was 10 years old. In the last 10 years, I've done all the drawings of historical houses on the Christmas tour.
>
> As a result of all this exploring and encouragement of what I was doing, I ended up getting into a complete change in subject matter and an exploration of technique. These two pieces are very different from my previous work, and I've gotten more positive response to these two works than to anything I've ever done, to the extent that people flocked around

them. I took *Eliza* to the art association meeting, and it took first place. My next big challenge is to explore Impressionism. I have a subject in mind. It is an outdoor, graceful, garden stairway, and it was in the Castle Combe area of England.

As readers may gather from this unexpected response, the interview was just what Bob needed to jump-start his life. As researchers, it is important that we follow up on our interviews. Just as this interview had a wonderful effect, another may stir up unwelcome emotional materials in a participant. A case in point was Helen, a woman who takes medication for severe depression, who gave this response to the same question:

I've always viewed my life as good and bad, black or white—fragmented. My immediate reaction after the interview was the line was straighter, more connected. I have a place in the world. The line is angled upward. It was a positive, reaffirming feeling. A quick high. I felt as if I was seeing the big picture I had never seen before from a new perspective. Then I felt not as sure about things as I thought I did, and I felt numb and drained—quiet for the rest of the afternoon.

About a week after the interview for this study, Helen forgot (perhaps intentionally?) to take her medication when she traveled to Los Angeles; she was without medication for three nights. She visited her physician, telling him that she was feeling "pretty good" and that she did not care to continue the medication. She had taken medication for a long time and wanted it out of her body. He cautioned her that it takes about 10 days, even 14 days, to come down. She said, "There was really nothing he could say, because I had made up my mind. I was in there on a Tuesday, and by Saturday I was a mess. I was feeling suicidal, and I talked to him on the phone." Helen was depressed and unclear as to what to do when he asked if she felt she needed to resume the medication. He said, "I think you really need to go back on medication, but if you want to wait another week, keep calling me, that's fine."

Helen chose to abstain, but by Monday she was really depressed; she had been without medication for longer than a week. Given her family history, the doctor believed Helen's illness might be hereditary and that she needed to resume her medication. She notes,

It's taken me a good week to 10 days to get back on track again. I'm taking a new medication called Effexor. I don't feel depressed, but I don't feel my old self again. I haven't really created anything in my studio. I've felt really depressed. I feel paralyzed. I'm not capable of doing anything. I go to bed, curl up in a fetal position, and wait it out somehow. The waiting period is shorter and shorter. When I do get depressed, I come out of it more quickly. Just now I'm feeling better. I'm just one of these people who need medication.

These examples indicate the extreme effects research interviews can have on people. Because of this, there are ethical as well as professional reasons for doing follow-ups.

When embarking on a research project, the researcher should be open to arising possibilities and opportunities that may not have been anticipated in the original research plan. During interviews in my study of art and trauma (Spencer, 1995, 1997), I was struck by the similarity between parts of the participants' stories and my own story, and as the process continued, by resemblances among the stories of different participants. As I transcribed and read each interview, I realized that I was experiencing a deep healing. Details of a participant's story would match what I had previously thought of as insignificant details of my own life. The number of my "Ahas!" increased as each story unfolded.

For example, I noticed that fire was mentioned in the stories of the artists who had been abused. Remembering the autumn when, as a young child, I set the back meadow on fire, I got goose pimples. I thought of sandplay therapist Dora Kalff's (1971) observation that when a child was ready to tell his or her secret, the child used fire in the sand or in other areas of life. I wondered what secret I had that was yet to unfold.

Personal insights crystallized, and I realized that if I was benefiting, perhaps the participants would also benefit from reading each other's stories. I encouraged this to happen. The story sharing among the artists demystified the process and afforded each participant an opportunity to relive his or her own story through the other stories. After reading each other's stories, some of the comments were the following. Jean said,

Saille had such a sadistic mother. . . . It really put me in touch with how cruel my mother was. For me that was really poignant. With Helen, I could really relate with her eating disorder, because I had a lot of those patterns and a lot of criticisms about my body from my father. That story made me realize that I've come a long way.

I went into a funk after reading Mari's story. I could really relate to having someone come up from behind you, then startling, and being hit when you weren't expecting it. I went into a trance when I got to that section. I know how she felt. I had the feeling I would die if I told. It's that feeling of not being believed that is so wounding.

Bob always seemed to be giving up himself for somebody else. I was moved that it was a male story and by the loneliness and the pain that he also experienced.

I could relate to Myrtle's healing because when I was in the wheelchair after foot surgery, I felt like I was grounded. The pain medication didn't work. I noticed that she used her art in the same way, to block the pain.

Mari said,

Saille's work provided me with a validation that I had previously not experienced in relation to my own work. I was deeply affected by her description of feeling spiritually connected or disconnected as directly related to her feelings of appropriateness of her art. Saille's comments suddenly brought all of my concerns together.

Saille said,

What Mari said that I liked was that the repetitive letters were part of her healing process, and when she began to evolve, then her art became more of an expression of who she was. In other words, the healing was one thing, and the next work was another thing. It sounds so simple, but to me it was profound. The sculpture is a reflection of who I am. It's more of a projection of the "perfected" Saille. It helped make the integration of all I do easier.

Mary said,

I felt connected in a lot of ways. I could fit in and then at the same time I was way out. I've always been close to the church, and it's hard to read how they left the church. There are some things that are so foreign and, in another way, are so close to me. Like one of the girls said she looked and saw a combination of the bricks and fence and grass and wanted to paint it. Well, that happens to me, too.

Myrtle said,

> My experience was feeling so fortunate to feel so all together. I feel like I
> know where I'm going. I'm not afraid. I've got a purpose in life. My
> misfortunes are behind me. I have a lot to be grateful for.

Story sharing can provide a valuable addition to some forms of research.
It can provide a transpersonal aspect that is not easily achieved with
traditional research methodology. Through story sharing, the artists in this
study met one another and became friends. One participant commented,

> You know, I usually hate get-togethers, but when you offered us a chance
> to meet each other, I was so excited it surprised me. I couldn't wait. They
> were strangers to me and yet I knew them intimately. It was wonderful.

PART IV

FURTHER EXTENSIONS

CHAPTER 11

AN EXPANDED VIEW
OF VALIDITY

William Braud

Validity has to do with whether one's findings or conclusions are faithful or true to what one is studying. In the realm of quantitative experimental and quasi-experimental research, a great deal of attention has been devoted to the various factors that might compromise the validity of one's conclusions regarding the probable source of an effect—that is, whether an effect is most likely contributed by the particular independent variable, treatment, or intervention that is being investigated or, alternatively, by some extraneous variable, artifact, or confound. A number of *threats to validity* have been isolated and named. These factors of *history, maturation, testing, instrumentation, statistical regression, mortality (attrition),* and *selection* have been identified and elaborated chiefly by methodologists Donald Campbell and Julian Stanley and their students and followers. Clever experimental designs have been developed to deal with each of these or combinations of these factors. Thorough treatments of these issues may be found in Campbell and Stanley (1963) and Cook and Campbell (1979).

In another quantitative area of psychometrics, or tests and measurements, a major focus of validity is whether an instrument or assessment truly measures what it purports to measure. Here, validity is explored by examining how well a measure of *x* correlates with other instruments or events that presumably reflect this same property, *x*. Measures of *concurrent, predictive, criterion,* and *construct validity* are used to help determine whether one is really studying what one thinks one is studying. These issues are treated well by Anastasi (1988) and by Nunnally and Bernstein (1994).

Also in the quantitative domain, statistical tests of equivalence or difference (e.g., *t* tests, analysis of variance, and nonparametric tests of dependence or independence), degree of relationship or covariation (e.g., bivariate and multivariate correlations and factor analysis), and magnitude or consistency of effects (e.g., effect sizes and meta-analytical techniques) serve as quantitative indicators and as decision tools for judging the presence, absence, or degree of each of these concerns. We recommend as statistical texts that are thorough and readable Siegel (1956) and Siegel and Castellan (1988) for nonparametric statistics, Howell (1992) for parametric statistical tests and concepts, and Rosenthal (1991) for meta-analytic considerations and examples.

Proponents of qualitative methodologies are just as alert to the possibility of error, excessive subjectivism, and delusion as are quantitative methodologists. They have developed safeguards against error in the forms of methods of establishing *trustworthiness,* including *credibility, transferability, dependability,* and *confirmability* (see Lincoln & Guba, 1985). Techniques other than statistical procedures are used to help ensure the trustworthiness of qualitative findings. These techniques include prolonged engagement, persistent observation, triangulation (of sources, methods, and investigators), peer debriefing, negative case analysis, referential adequacy, member checks, thick description, dependability and confirmability audits, and the reflexive journal.

We suggest that along with the familiar techniques and procedures mentioned above, other indicators of validity and trustworthiness are more consistent with the new research methods described in this book. Transpersonal psychology reminds us that in addition to our faculty of intellect, we possess, as well, facets of body, emotion, spirit, community, and creative expression. Each of these facets supplies clues and suggestions about issues of validity, and the facets themselves provide a convenient organizational scheme for discussing these clues.

LIMITATIONS OF PURELY
INTELLECTUAL APPROACHES

In the area of *intellect*, the indicators and rules for determining validity have been developed with great sophistication. The well-established principles of deductive logic, inductive inference, statistical inference, and scientific method are familiar to researchers, and there is no need to describe these here. By themselves, however, these methods are insufficient guides. The yields of these methods are dependent on the raw materials and considerations that go into them in the first place, and these inputs themselves ("facts" and assumptions) may be incomplete, distorted, or erroneous. The history of science reveals vividly how the facts, predominant cultural tools (and, hence, the predominant intellectual and scientific analogies, metaphors, models, and theories), and intellectual habits of one period provide conclusions about reality that are found, in a later time, to be limited or mistaken. The counterintuitive glimmerings of yesterday become the accepted actualities of today. "It is very interesting . . . that in modern physics the more logical you are, the more wrong you are. This shows very clearly the limits of our logic," says Lama Govinda, in dialogue with philosopher Renée Weber (quoted in Weber, 1990, p. 61).

Kurt Gödel's famous *incompleteness theorems* demonstrate that any formal, logical system sufficiently complex to include arithmetic can include true statements that cannot be deduced or proved from its components—that is, from within that system; in addition, all such systems contain statements whose truth or falsity cannot be determined from within that system—that is, such statements are undecidable. The implications of Gödel's theorems are that no formal system that is sufficiently complex to be interesting can be finitely describable, consistent, or complete within itself. (For further information about Gödel's theorems, see Dossey, 1989; Hofstadter, 1980; Nagel & Newman, 1958; Rucker, 1987.) Gregory Chaitin's theory, more general than Gödel's, implies that no system can explain any other system that is more complex (i.e., contains more information) than itself (see Rucker, 1987). We are reminded of related statements of the contemporary scholar of comparative religion Huston Smith (1992): "We can control only what is inferior to us. . . . Science can only reveal what is inferior to us" (pp. 199, 200). This, in turn, echoes an admonition of Seng-ts'an (c. 600 C.E./1980), the Third Patriarch of Zen, in the classic *Hsin-Hsin Ming* (*On Believing in Mind* or *On Trust in Heart*):

"To seek mind with the (discriminating) mind is the greatest of all mistakes" (p. 7). There are limitations to a purely intellectual approach to anything.

BODILY WISDOM

Let us look, then, to other aspects of ourselves, to see what they might offer. The body is an obvious place to look next for clues to validity, especially in light of the oft-quoted expression, "The body does not lie." Our bodies often provide indications of our true intentions or of aspects of the outer world of which we are otherwise unaware. Events or words can make us gasp, "take our breath away," and bring tears to our eyes. Students of nonverbal behavior (body language) point out how statements that interest us can lead us to lean forward or approach the source through sometimes subtle muscular movements, how slight evasive muscular movements reveal discomfort or mistrust, how yawns and sighs betray feelings of frustration or stress, how unconsciously wiping away imaginary tears reveals sorrow and rubbing the nose reveals dislike or disagreement, and how pupillary dilation signals interest. By observing our own behaviors—where our bodies have taken us or how they have delayed us—we can learn more about the balance of our intentions in ambiguous situations. Even (or especially) in children and in animals, bodily movements and selections can reveal somatic deficiencies—for example, of vitamins and minerals—and can provide unconscious access to substances that can correct deficiencies. This is the well-known *wisdom of the body*. We speak of having "gut feelings," of something "touching the heart," and of feeling something "in the pit of the stomach." Situations prompt feelings of chills and shivers up and down the spine or "make our hairs stand on end." It is possible that certain bodily reactions could provide indications of the truth or validity of statements or conclusions in research, and other reactions could signal that something is amiss. Such bodily reactions could be noted in the research participants, in the researcher, or in the readers of research reports, and they could serve as validity signals *to be used along with* more conventional indicators. A careful, systematic study of the bodily signals of validity and lack of validity would constitute an important research project.

But can we always trust such bodily indicators? Can the body lie? Some maintain that the body itself never lies, but that should we go astray, it is because we intellectually distort or misinterpret the body's wisdom. This may well be. Consider the following scenario, however, selected from literally thousands of similar ones that could be presented.

In a straightforward study of classical or respondent (Pavlovian) conditioning conducted in 1952 by E. Sh. Ayrapetyants and colleagues (cited in Razran, 1961, pp. 91-92), respiration, electrodermal activity, intrabladder pressure, and the subjective report of an urge to urinate were monitored in three patients with bladder fistulas into which calibrated inflows of air or physiological solutions could be introduced. Normally, of course, all response indicators would register graded responses to introduced physical pressure but never to a "neutral" stimulus such as the reading of a manometer (pressure meter). After a number of pairings of a high meter reading (conditional stimulus) with high physical pressure (unconditional stimulus), strong interoceptive conditioning occurred. Now, when the manometer and the air pressure were dissociated (without the patients' knowledge), so that sham readings could be presented, the patients' objective and subjective reactions followed the meter reading (the previously established signal) rather than the physical pressure itself. Thus, the patients began reporting intense urinary urges, accompanied by all or most of the aforementioned objective response indicators, when the manometer readings were high (equaling or exceeding the reactions displayed during the conditioning sessions), although the physical pressure inflows were minimal or totally omitted. On the other hand, low or zero readings failed to produce the urge to urinate and its physiological reaction accompaniments, even if the physical inflow was actually present and was double the value used in the training trials. In short, the bodies of these patients were responding to what was not present and not responding to that which was present.

Were their bodies lying? The answer seems to be that with respect to the *present* physical world, their bodies were lying. All instances of conditioning, learning, habit, and memory contain strong elements of untruth. In all these cases, our bodies are not being entirely truthful to present conditions. They are being true, however, to the more general context in which the learning took place: They are being true to their *histories*. The bodies of Ayrapetyants's patients were responding in a manner consistent with (truthful to) the prior stimulus pairings—they respond now to what was once a signal that was perfectly correlated with yesterday's reality. The response is faithful to a signal of yesterday and supersedes the reality of today.

Sigmund Freud (1910/1952b) clearly saw the importance of this general principle of remaining true to the past, rather than to a changed present, and made this insight the basis of his understanding of hysteria and other psychoneuroses.

> *Our hysterical patients suffer from reminiscences.* Their symptoms are the remnants and the memory symbols of certain (traumatic) experiences.
>   The memorials and monuments with which we adorn our great cities are also such memory symbols. . . . Charing Cross is the last of the [London] monuments, which preserve the memory of this sad journey [the funeral procession of Queen Eleanor]. . . . In another part of [London] you will see a high pillar . . . which is merely called "the Monument." This is in memory of the great fire which broke out in the neighborhood in the year 1666, and destroyed a great part of the city. These monuments are memory symbols like the hysterical symptoms. . . . But what would you say to a Londoner who today stood sadly before the monument to the funeral of Queen Eleanor, instead of going about his business with the haste engendered by modern industrial conditions, or rejoicing with the young queen of his own heart? Or to another, who before "the Monument" bemoaned the burning of his loved native city, which long since has arisen again so much more splendid than before?
>   Now hystericals and all neurotics behave like these two unpractical Londoners, not only in that they remember the painful experiences of the distant past, but because they are still strongly affected by them. They cannot escape from the past and neglect present reality in its favour. (p. 4)

Krishnamurti extended these notions even further, arguing that

> truth lies in the living present, in this moment, and must be discovered afresh in the present, in the eternal now. All forms of its accumulation or accretion—thought, memory, knowledge, time—destroy truth. . . . The past is overemphasized and becomes dominant, thus resisting creativity where it would otherwise be natural and appropriate. The past must be ready to die when it no longer fits, but it tends to hold one, and that is the trouble. (quoted in Weber, 1990, pp. 224, 95)

So, the body can lie and, like any other tool, can introduce error as well as truth. Bodily reactions also, however, can accurately reflect present realities in ways that are sometimes less filtered, distorted, or biased than those of the intellect. Albert Einstein (1954), for example, noted that in the creative moments of his research, "the words or the language, as they are written or spoken, do not seem to play any role"; rather, the elements in his "thought" were "visual and *of some muscular type*" (italics added; p. 36). In his creative moments, Einstein apparently thought with aspects of his body (his muscles) other than his discursive intellect. Bodily reactions could contribute not only to discoveries but also to validity assessments of the larger body of one's work.

EMOTIONS AND FEELINGS

Remarks of the preceding section apply, as well, to *emotional* reactions. These, too—as they occur in participants, researchers, and readers—can contribute important indicators of validity. Like the body, the emotions can "lie" on occasion and can also be misinterpreted. Therefore, emotional reactions should be assessed carefully and their contributions given appropriate weightings in any validity assessments. Yet emotions and feelings can offer unique indications of the validity of specific findings and conclusions and even of the success of an overall research program. If aspects of the research, or the entire research endeavor, provoke feelings of vitality, excitement, and joy in those involved in the research, those responses are promising indicators that the project is on target, that the subject matter being studied has not been violated or compromised, and that the research has not been reduced to a sterile enterprise. Feelings of aliveness—or, indeed, of a supervitality, a "survitality"—in the research personnel indicate a rich appreciation of what the researchers are studying. Being attuned to the emotional and feeling states of researchers, research participants, and even the readers or audience for the research reports can give immediate feedback about the success of a research endeavor. Such feelings can be summed, as it were, across these three groups of people to provide a sort of appreciation monitor for the work. When feelings of excitement, surprise, and delight are supplemented by feelings of awe and gratitude, researchers can be assured that they are being true to the experiences that are being explored and that their approach and findings are valid.

AESTHETIC CONTRIBUTIONS

Aesthetic feelings may serve as useful indicators of the validity of methods, findings, and conclusions, as well as any conceptual models or theories developed from the work. Much has been written, especially within the positivistic paradigm, about the need for *empirical adequacy* in all components of research. Definitions must be operational; methods and conclusions must be objective, valid, reliable, and generalizable; and theories must provide for the possibility of their falsification by subsequently collected data. Research should also possess *experiential adequacy*—in all its components. Each facet of a research project should ring true in the experiences of the various research participants. This applies to theory construction, as well. As is the case for all facts and all experiments, theories themselves are value laden. On confronting a theory, a researcher has certain personal reactions. These reactions may provide important clues about the theory's value or adequacy. Scientists seem to follow the tacit assumption that any theory that ultimately will be shown to be correct will also be one that possesses simplicity and beauty. An extreme statement of this assumption has been made by the highly esteemed physicist Paul Dirac:

> It is more important to have beauty in one's equations than to have them fit experiment . . . because the discrepancy may be due to minor features which are not properly taken into account and which will get cleared up with further developments of the theory. . . . It seems that if one is working from the point of view of getting beauty in one's equations, and if one has a really sound instinct, one is on a sure line of success. (quoted in Polkinghorne, 1987, p. 46)

Perhaps the compelling search for grand unified theories characterized by unity, parsimony, elegance, and simplicity is a search for beauty in disguise. We cannot help thinking of these well-known lines of John Keats (1988):

> *"Beauty is truth, truth beauty,"—that is all*
> *Ye know on earth, and all ye need to know.* (p. 346)

If Keats is correct, then the aesthetic features of researchers' work could serve as guides to their validity.

THE ROLE OF INTUITION IN VALIDITY

Dirac's mention of "really sound instinct" is a reminder of the importance of intuition in research and in theory construction. In an address celebrating Max Planck's 60th birthday (in 1918), Albert Einstein (1954) included these remarks:

> The supreme task of the physicist is to arrive at those universal elementary laws from which the cosmos can be built up by pure deduction. There is no logical path to these laws; only intuition, resting on sympathetic understanding of experience, can reach them. (p. 221)

A bit later in his address, Einstein continued,

> The state of mind which enables a man to do work of this kind is akin to that of the religious worshiper or the lover; the daily effort comes from no deliberate intention or program, but straight from the heart. (p. 222)

Intuition and sympathetic understanding can lead researchers not only to elementary laws but also to an appraisal of the validity of their work as a whole. Willis Harman (1992) recommends, as an additional test of the discernment of the trustworthiness of one's findings and conclusions, looking for an internal feeling of certainty, a noetic, intuitive, and persistent feeling that one's knowledge is true.

William James (1902/1958) considered *noetic quality* to be one of the four major features of the mystical experience:

> Although so similar to states of feeling, mystical states seem to those who experience them to be also states of knowledge. They are states of insights into depths of truth unplumbed by the discursive intellect. They are illuminations, revelations, full of significance and importance, all inarticulate though they remain; and as a rule they carry with them a curious sense of authority for after-time. (p. 293)

James adds that although the experience brings with it a strong sense of authority for the experiencer, this authority does not extend to those standing outside the experience; these latter do not have the duty of accepting such revelations uncritically.

An anecdote concerning one of James's noetic experiences makes the point that it would be unwise to put inordinate trust in any and all such revelations, even if they should seem, at the time of their occurrence, extremely profound. During one of his nitrous oxide adventures, James (1882/1956) had a profound noetic insight into the nature of reality, and he made a written note of this revelation. Later, in his more usual state of consciousness, he read what he had written. His revelation was, "There are no differences but differences of degree between different degrees of difference and no difference" (p. 297).

Although remaining alert to the possibility that not all noetic revelations will remain as authoritative, profound, or useful as they transiently appear to be, researchers would be unwise to ignore the contributions of strong insight and direct knowing to their set of validation tools. Empirical evidence already exists that it is possible to distinguish illusory perceptions from nonillusory ones during the act of perception itself. Perceptual illusions remind us of how we can be deceived about some aspects of reality; our ability to recognize these illusions, however, provides a corrective against such deception.

Richer (1978) found that participants evidenced different behavioral reactions and different phenomenological experiences when observing unfamiliar visual illusions, compared with controlled, nonillusory geometrical figures. The phenomenological findings indicated that the illusory figures generally did not appear real but were perceived as peculiar. Further, this peculiarity continued and even increased with prolonged observation of the illusory figures from different viewpoints. These simple results suggest revising the usual understanding of an illusory phenomenon as "that which appears real but is not genuinely real" (p. 131). It was unnecessary to use later external, objective operations to reveal the illusory nature of the initial observations. If false perceptions can give themselves away in this manner, it is not unlikely that a vast range of perceptions, judgments, and knowings also carry with them subjective indications of their validity or falsity. Thus, not only can individuals know directly (intuitively), but also they can know, simultaneously and without the need for external criteria, whether that direct knowing is or is not true.

Similar findings from parapsychological research support this contention. It is possible for participants to know when they are merely guessing about target events versus when they have accurately described the targets through paranormal means, concomitantly with those responses and before they receive conventional feedback about success or failure. Participants are able to make those judgments about their own accuracy in real time by means of *differential feelings of confidence* that occur as they make their responses. Scoring accuracy rates are higher for high confidence call trials than for low confidence call trials—when those confidence judgments were given long before conventional information (knowledge of results) was provided about the accuracy or inaccuracy of the initial responses (e.g., see Fahler & Osis, 1966; Honorton, 1970, 1971; Kanthamani & Kelly, 1974).

COHERENCE OF ASPECTS

Perhaps it is helpful to consider indications from intellect, body, emotions, aesthetic feelings, and direct knowing as votes from different constituencies, as it were, in the decision process whereby researchers evaluate the validity of their research work. The indicators supplied by different facets of the self also can be supplied by each person (researcher, participant, and reader) contributing to the research effort. By observing patterns among these various votes and voters, the researcher might arrive at a validity judgment based on a majority vote or, better, on an explicitly or tacitly recognized *consensus* or *coherence* of the various indicators.

Validity judgments of this nature probably are occurring continuously, and at a subconscious level, among all researchers; it might be argued that it is best that such combinations and guidances remain tacit. On the other hand, becoming more aware of these indicators—monitoring them more mindfully and tracking their consistencies and individual and combined records of success—may augment their use as decisional tools for assessing validity. For the more analytically minded, these various pathways toward validity could be formalized and systematically studied.

We distinguish intellectual, somatic, emotional, aesthetic, and intuitive modes of knowing merely as an aid to communication and do not wish to imply that these are as separate as we make them out to be. Although they may be discussed separately, and although they may become dissociated from one another, these five modes can be simply different aspects of the same process—different facets of one gem. Perhaps it is their completeness, coherence, and integration that we are seeking in our quest for validity. In this connection, it is helpful to consider two meanings of the word *intellect*. Today, in the strange manner we moderns have of turning original word meanings on their heads, we use the term *intellect* primarily as a descriptor of rational, analytical, discursive thinking. To the early Greeks, however, intellect (*nous*) had a much broader meaning. It denoted the largest manifestation of mind, and, used in much the same way that we use the term *heart* today, it encompassed the deepest core of one's being. Through *nous,* humanity's highest faculty, one could know the inner essences or principles of things by means of direct apprehension. *Nous* was distinguished from *dianoia,* or reason, which was only a part of the former (see, for example, Palmer, Sherrard, & Ware, 1983-1995, Vol. 1, pp. 357-368). As already mentioned, this is but one example of the myriad of modern terms whose original meanings have been turned upside down. In the fuller, original meaning of *intellect* is perhaps a greater approximation of *validity*—in its sense of multidimensionality and completeness.

The word origins of *validity* itself help illuminate the concept. Both *validity* and *value* have their sources in the Latin *valere*—to have worth or to be strong. Suggestions of value, importance, and ability to impel or compel are implicit in its meaning. The same word, *value,* is used to indicate something of worth and, further, to indicate a particular numerical quantity resulting from a measurement or a calculation (e.g., "let x have the value of such and such"). This marriage of the qualitative and the quantitative suggests including a similar blend of the two in considerations of validity. Validity can be not only a measure of objective consistency and fidelity but also a feature that is able to convey a strong subjective impression of significance. In the words of John Polkinghorne (1988), who has expertise in both mathematical physics and theology, "The test of the validity of [an] exercise . . . will lie in its ability to discern pattern, to offer coherent understanding of human experience at its most profound" (p. 96).

SYMPATHETIC RESONANCE REVISITED

All these thoughts have their places in the concept of sympathetic resonance, as introduced in Chapter 4. Resonance is an indicator of fullness and fidelity and is, therefore, an indicator of validity. To borrow analogies from acoustical physics, the response of a suitably prepared or predisposed system (e.g., a resonating note of piano A) to the call of another system (piano B) depends on the similarity of structure and operating rules of the two systems and the degree of fullness or fidelity of the call (the deliberate sounding of a note on piano B). We could speak of a complexity of emitted sound waves, rich in overtones and undertones (a symphony of sound), evoking a similar complexity of response. We could speak of thresholds of elicitation and of narrowness or wideness of windows of resonance. The experiential description would have to be sufficiently accurate and complete ("descriptively thick") for it to evoke a resonant response in a reader.

One of the mysteries of resonance has to do with the extremely narrow and precise *tuning* that is possible: One system will accept energy from another system only in a narrow frequency band. This, of course, accounts for the exquisite efficiency with which a radio or television tuner is able to faithfully reproduce complex information within one narrow area of the electromagnetic spectrum (one particular station or channel) while rejecting all other information that lies outside that narrow range. The receiver has resonant circuits that are quite selective—they respond to certain features as *signals* while rejecting others as *noise*. The response of a radio receiver is a trustworthy indicator of the presence of a particular signal and is able to reproduce that signal faithfully—just as a shattered wine glass or collapsed footbridge are faithful and impressive indicators of a particular pure and strongly voiced note or of a particularly strong and congruent marching pattern of a group of soldiers, respectively. So, too, a strong and full reaction in the reader of a research report can serve as a faithful (valid) indicator that the researcher, through the aid of the research participants, has accurately portrayed a particular signal experience well enough for the resonating reader to distinguish it and affirm it as a faithfully recounted experience.

The more universal the experience, and the simpler or purer the experience, the more readily detectable it is through reader resonance. More complicated experiences or experiences that are limited to only certain portions of the human population provide a greater challenge for sympathetic resonance because all the proper components or ingredients of the experience would have to be present in an experiential description. Nonetheless, a full resonant response remains latent in the reader—awaiting the requisite rich and true experiential account or interpretation. In these complicated or rarer cases, resonance—in the form of an endorsement through sympathetic understanding—is an excellent indicator that the research participants and the researcher have succeeded in accurately describing the essential features of a complex experience and have done so in necessary and sufficient detail.

Resonance could be used as a probe or an assay for detecting the presence of certain experiences or particular qualities of experience. By presenting a variety of rich experiential descriptions to different sets of

readers—to persons with different histories or sociocultural backgrounds—
researchers could discern patterns of sympathetic resonance and construct
sociograms of the types of responses (some consonant, some dissonant, and
some neutral). Studying the patterns of reactions (networks of resonance)
in different circles of participants allows three things, simultaneously: (a)
The patterns teach more about the nature of what is being studied; (b) the
patterns inform how the studied experiences interact with various personality, social, and cultural factors; and (c) the patterns provide indicators of
replicability, reliability, and generality of the findings. In such explorations,
researchers might encounter *degrees* of resonance. Validity need not be an
all-or-none judgment. Protocols need to be developed to help determine
criteria of validity, requisite levels in the various nodes of the resonance
net, and ways of integrating the validity votes from various sources and
dealing with possible discrepancies and conflicting indications.

An intriguing research question is whether rich experiential descriptions
are able to induce resonance in inexperienced as well as experienced
readers. Rich and thick descriptions are expected to serve as reminders to
persons who have already had experiences identical or similar to the ones
being described. But what about readers who have not yet had such
experiences? Can resonance occur in these cases, too? This is a rich field
for new empirical studies. In at least two cases, already in the literature,
something akin to resonance occurred in inexperienced readers. Both of
these involved unitive and mystical (or quasi-mystical) experiences, and
both episodes were triggered by poetry. Batey (1993) reports how a
unitive/mystical experience was triggered in himself following his reading
aloud of parts of William Wordsworth's long poem *The Prelude*. Similarly,
Zaehner (1961) attributed what he called a "natural mystical experience"
to his third reading of Rimbaud's poem, *"O saisons, o chateaux"* (O
seasons, o castles!), which he said "gave rise to an answering ecstasy in the
reader" (p. xiv). I (Braud, 1995a, 1995b) had a similar instance of timelessness that was triggered by Wilber's (1979) rich description of timeless
experience in his book *No Boundary*. Zaehner, at the time of his poetry-
evoked mystical ecstasy, was inexperienced and unprepared. Batey's and
my responses, however, are complicated because each, on a previous
occasion, had deliberately sought to elicit such experiences, thereby introducing the possibility of sensitization for the subsequent events (see Braud,
1995a, 1995b; White, 1995a).

ON OBSTRUCTIONS AND
MATCHING: IMPEDANCE

Another physical process, like resonance, might be helpful in considerations of validity. This is the property of *impedance,* which, in electrical circuits, is a measure of the circuit's resistance to the flow of alternating current. Analogous to impedance are the various filters or resistances that might exist in the research participant, researcher, or reader and might interfere with the faithful reception, processing, or expression of the essence of an experience. Attempting to remove such biases and seeking to provide as clear and pure a channel as possible are important goals of any form of inquiry. The *bracketing* process, emphasized to such a great extent in phenomenological inquiry, is one method of seeking to ensure a clearer researcher channel that is as free as possible from impeding and interfering preconceptions about the research topic. *Any* preexisting structures—not only cognitive ones but emotional and bodily ones, as well—can obscure and distort what the researcher is studying. Therefore, the bracketing process could be extended beyond cognitive bracketing in the researcher to include other levels of possible interference (e.g., somatic, emotional, and aesthetic) in the researcher, and all levels of possible distortion (intellectual, somatic, emotional, and aesthetic) in others involved in the research.

Deliberate strategies could be employed to reduce rigid structures, interferences, and noise sources in all research personnel and at all phases of the research process. Techniques that yield quietude and openness at many levels of functioning could be practiced by all research personnel (including researcher, participants, and the reader of the final report). These procedures might include, but would not be limited to, exercises for relaxation and quietude, autogenic exercises, and meditational techniques. In addition to these, special forms of intentionality and an open attentiveness could be cultivated in all personnel. The promotion of nonordinary states of consciousness (alternative states of awareness) could remove certain interfering structures or at least provide different sorts of structures or interferences that might tend either to cancel some of the usual biases or allow access to aspects of the data that might not ordinarily occur.

Another interesting feature of electrical circuits is *impedance matching.* Two electrical circuits can exchange current flow (energy)—can communicate with and talk to one another and, hence, share information—most efficiently when the two circuits have identical or similar impedances. Transformers typically are used to change the impedance of one circuit so that it more closely matches that of another. Analogous techniques could be used in which research personnel could attempt to adjust themselves at as many levels as possible to confront one another while in similar conditions (of body, intellect, and feelings) of being or speak to one another "from the same space." Deliberate adjustment techniques could be used to this end. Some of the brief research reports in Part III of this volume illustrate several of these possibilities—such as Dorothy Ettling's and Alzak Amlani's self-alterations for purposes of confronting the data themselves and Jan Fisher's procedure of having researcher and coresearchers engage in shared bodily exercises. Formal or informal rituals could be used to help research personnel converge on the same or similar (hence, "impedance-matched") states of "bodymind" for the duration of the research interactions. Note that with respect to the research analogue of impedance, there are two aims—reduction and matching. The former minimizes biases and enhances validity; it is related to the purity of the channel. The latter facilitates communication and resonance; it is related to the similarity of two channels. By actively using memory to recall experiences similar to the ones being described and to help evoke corresponding states in the "bodymind," readers can adjust themselves to maximally partake of the essence of the research findings being offered. Similar reinstatement strategies could be used by the researcher and the research participants to maximize accessing and communicating their experiences in the data collection phases of a research project. Techniques such as Drew's (1993) *reenactment interviewing*—using techniques borrowed from psychodrama— could be used toward this end. *Mutual* reenactment, in which the researcher joins the participant in reproducing a similar condition of bodymind during a research interview, might further enhance the process; as far as we are aware, such mutual reenactment has not yet been reported in a research context, although techniques that partially approach this are sometimes used in therapeutic contexts.

We recognize that we are working with analogies and metaphors here. We also feel, however, that there are processes in research that are truly homologous with the resonance and impedance properties of the physical world and that corresponding flows or resistances or sympathetic correlations can obtain in research if suitable operations are used. These possibilities themselves offer exciting opportunities for careful empirical study.

ENHANCING RESONANCE AND
COMMUNICATION OF FINDINGS

Ernest Keen has suggested four criteria for research reports that maximize communication of descriptions of studied experiences from researcher to reader; these are *vividness, accuracy, richness,* and *elegance* of the descriptive statements.

> Vividness is the quality that draws readers in, creating a feeling of genuineness. Accuracy is the dimension that makes the writing believable, creating a focus that enables readers to see the phenomenon as their own. Richness is the quality that deepens the description through colorful use of language, graphic depiction or shades of meaning, and detail, relaying something of the sensual-aesthetic tones of the phenomenon. Elegance is found in an economical use of words, disclosing the essence of the phenomenon through simple expressions that unify the description and give it grace and poignancy. (quoted in Polkinghorne, 1983, p. 46)

We feel that these four characteristics of research and report writing are ways of maximizing impedance matching and sympathetic resonance in the research personnel and, hence, are ways of enhancing validity.

Keen's four criteria remind us of the features of good stories or good art, in general. It makes sense that whichever qualities contribute to the making of good art or good stories would also be usefully incorporated into the means we use to express our research findings. This would help increase the likelihood that our findings would be appreciated by our audience and that the latter might be better able to resonate with our findings or conclusions. The four criteria of vividness, accuracy, richness, and elegance help ensure that art and stories are true to life and, hence, acceptable and believable (judged valid). But merely realistic art or storytelling is not sufficient to make a strong impression on the viewer or listener. Certain departures from slavishly veridical reproductions may enhance, rather than degrade, the expression's impact on the audience. A painting that is an exact, photograph-like reproduction of some scene may fail to produce a response in the viewer, whereas the painting of the same scene that exaggerates or distorts the subject matter in a novel and striking manner may provoke a profound reaction. Consider, for example, many of the French impressionist landscapes, Van Gogh's or Blake's depictions of familiar scenes or persons, or cubist or surreal renditions of common objects. While being untrue to certain features of the subject matter, these paintings are true to other aspects, which they highlight through exaggeration. Such works call attention to aspects of reality that we typically ignore, and the freshness of their messages can be extraordinarily compelling. Similarly, some of the exaggerations of folktales, fairy tales, legends, and myths make them especially memorable, convincing, and influential. Perhaps we might increase the effectiveness of our research reports by adding to them principles that we can learn from the study of the types of augmentations, deletions, and modifications that are used to such good effect by accomplished artists and storytellers who are able to create expressions that are truer than true and able to leave indelible imprints on our minds and hearts.

RESEARCH OUTCOMES:
PRAGMATIC CRITERIA

Another set of validity considerations involves *outcomes*. We can ask, with Harman (1992), how would the world be if everyone in the world behaved in accord with her or his findings—that is, what would be the *fruits* of such knowledge—and if everyone used the likelihood of positive action outcomes based on the findings as another indicator of their validity? We can ask, in more general terms, about the usefulness of findings and have those answers serve as validity indicators. This is, of course, an updating of the pragmatism of Peirce (1878), James (1907/1975), and Dewey (1929/1984) in which the pragmatic may serve as an indicator of meaning and of truth.

Polkinghorne (1992) has suggested *neopragmatism* as an important positive feature of an epistemology of practice: "The criterion for acceptability of a knowledge claim is the fruitfulness of its implementation" (p. 162). In the context of psychology, he emphasizes a psychology of practice and privileges knowledge that allows a practitioner to produce beneficial results in clients (a special type of "knowing how" rather than "knowing that"). Further, he recommends that "an epistemology of practicing knowledge must be based on the processes of expert practitioners, not the deliberative procedures and theoretically derived rules that constitute the practicing knowledge of novices" (p. 156). Novices base their practice on rules and procedures, external to themselves, that were taught them in their training. For expert practitioners, the chief source of knowledge is the practitioner's own experiences in working with clients, informed by knowledge of useful patterns and microtheories or templates constructed through extensive observations and trial-and-error learning of what does or does not work for particular clients. This neopragmatism is grounded in the particular experiences that a practitioner has in dealing with particularized and contextualized challenges in everyday practice.

THE VALUE OF THE OLD:
AGREEMENTS WITH ESTABLISHED TRADITIONS

Still another criterion for validity or trustworthiness has been offered by Harman (1992): One can check one's knowledge, findings, and conclusions against those of others through the ages—that is, compare these against a long-enduring tradition. Implicit in this criterion, although Harman does not make this point, is the idea that any long-standing tradition must have made contacts with reality that were sufficiently reliable and valid to ensure the longevity of that tradition. Certain traditions have survived, and survival is an indicator of intelligence and adaptation. Adaption, in turn, is related to an adequate mirroring of the realities in which the tradition is embedded.

THE VALUE OF THE NEW:
THE HEALTH AND GROWTH OF THE DISCIPLINE

A final criterion of the validity of our work as researchers is the state of health and the growth of the discipline to which this work is contributing. If our field of study shows signs of excitement, freshness, and vitality; if it is growing in its methods, findings, conceptualizations, and applications; and if those in the field are experiencing engagement and joy in their research endeavors, we can be sure that value and validity are in what we are doing. If, however, there are minimal advances in the content or methods of our field, redundancy and stagnation in our research and thinking, and feelings of boredom and burnout in our researchers, clearly something is wrong in our current approaches, and it is time to reexamine their validity and their value. Imre Lakatos (1978) used the terms *progressing research program* and *degenerating research program* to describe these two states of research affairs, and he described ways that can be used to determine

whether a given discipline is healthy, growing, and progressing or un-
healthy, stagnating, and degenerating. Lakatos's suggestions, however, are
narrowly constrained within the conventional epistemological framework
from which he writes.

TYPES OF TRUTH AND AN INTEGRAL
APPROACH TO VARIETIES OF VALIDITY

"Truth" has a variety of meanings. Adherents of a modern, Western,
scientific mind-set assure us that truth is agreement with a reality that can
be verified by our senses and validated through consensus. Postmodernists
contend that there is no such thing as an absolute reality or absolute truth;
rather, there are local sets of truths or realities that have been socially and
linguistically coconstructed or constituted by groups of individuals in the
service of economic and power motives (see, for example, Guba, 1990;
Kvale, 1992). Varied pathways to valid knowledge have been advocated.
For the American pragmatist C. S. Peirce (1877/1962), four such methods—methods of "fixing belief"—were those of holding firmly to previously held beliefs (the method of tenacity), of appealing to the views of
another established person or institution (the method of authority), of
basing beliefs on reasonable propositions (the a priori method), and of
determining beliefs on the basis of empiricism and consensus (the method
of scientific investigation). In earlier parts of the present chapter, we have
described other possible contributors to the validity of knowledge claims:
the evidence of reason, bodily and emotional indicators, feelings, the
aesthetic sense, direct knowing (intuition), the presence of sympathetic
resonance, pragmatic considerations, and the coherence or agreement of
multiple indicators.

Huston Smith (1995) identifies three aspects of truth. There is truth
applied to *propositions, statements,* or *assertions;* this is the primary
meaning of truth in Western cultures. Truth, however, may also be applied
to *things* and has to do with their ontological status, their genuineness,
their position in the "Great Chain of Being"; this aspect of truth is
emphasized in South Asia (India). In addition, there is truth applied to
persons—a pragmatic view in which an act or utterance is true if it furthers
a desired outcome, which is usually social harmony; this aspect of truth is
emphasized in East Asia (China, Korea, and Japan).

A consequence of a plurality of validity indicators is that certain indicators may be used as tests of the validity of still other indicators. Thus, one can test not only the validity of particular knowledge claims but also the validity of the *validators themselves*. For example, one may use conventional validation criteria involving empirically determined degree of overlap or degree of intersubjective consensus to assess agreements or disagreements among the bodily, emotional, aesthetic, or intuitive judgments of large numbers of people. Alternatively, one can apply bodily, emotional, aesthetic, and intuitive tests to conclusions that already have been reached using conventional, empirical, sensory/consensual criteria for assessing truth claims. A way to state this somewhat differently is that experiments could be conducted to test agreement of intuitively developed conclusions, and intuition could be used to test whether logico-empirical claims ring true. The process becomes multifaceted and reiterative.

An expanded, integral view of validity considers all indicators of truth. Each criterion supplies a particular perspective—a particular view of the whole. Each has something useful to offer. Each is true to certain aspects of the being and becoming of ourselves and of our world. Each ignores other aspects and is, therefore, incomplete—supplying only part of the picture or story of what can be known and experienced. For a deeper and broader appreciation, we can combine indicators, taking into account as many aspects or faces of truth as possible.

Once again, a quotation (cited earlier in Chapter 3) from Carl Jung (1993) comes to mind: "Ultimate truth, if there be such a thing, demands the concert of many voices" (p. xiv). A New Testament saying resonates with Jung's view: In Matthew 18:19-20 is the familiar statement,

> Again I say to you, that if two of you *may agree* [italics added] on the earth concerning any matter whatever they shall ask, it shall be done to them from my Father who [is] in [the] heavens. For where are two or three gathered together unto my name, there am I in [the] midst of them. (Interlinear Literal Translation of the Greek New Testament, 1973, pp. 50-51)

The Greek συμφωνησωσιν, translated here as "may agree," is a form of *symphonein* (to sound [with the voice] together), from which comes our term *symphony*. To combine the ideas of these two references: Where there is truth, there is the concert of many voices; where there is such a concert or symphonic agreement of voices, there is power, and magical things may happen.

AN INTEGRAL RESEARCH TEAM

We have been describing a variety of validity indicators that might be recognized, fostered, and balanced within individuals. It is, perhaps, too much to expect that such balancing can occur readily within any given person. The indicators are developed to unique degrees and in unique profiles in different individuals. Some of us have strongly developed our bodily or intuitive awarenesses, whereas others have not. Aesthetic sensibility or empathic (resonant) sensibility may be only poorly developed in some researchers yet quite strongly developed in others. The various validity indicators can be conceived as different sensitivities, faculties, abilities, or skills for which we are predisposed or prepared to different degrees—some remain latent, poorly exercised, and only weakly developed, whereas others are well prepared, dominant, and used with great facility. In view of such individual differences, it makes sense to capitalize on these strengths and weaknesses by constituting research teams composed of individuals with complementary sensitivities.

Rather than hoping to find a single researcher in whom four modes of knowing are strongly developed, we may find it easier to create a research team of four individuals, each of whom possesses unusual strength in one of the four modes. For example, a four-person research team could consist of four individuals who are especially gifted in their bodily, emotional, intellectual, and intuitive sensibilities, respectively. Adequate coverage, integration, balance, and coherence could then occur within the team as a whole, rather than (or as well as) within any one team member. In a section of Chapter 3, Jungian personality typology was mentioned as a way of matching researchers to different types of research questions. This same typology could be used to select members for research teams—a team could consist of four persons who have strongly developed sensing, feeling, thinking, and intuitive functions, respectively. Of course, alternative typologies could be used. The Jungian typology comes to mind as especially relevant because it is based, essentially, on differential epistemological sensitivities, and this is precisely what we are seeking in the design of an effective research team.

Once we have become aware of the importance of the researcher in any research project, it makes sense to attend as carefully to researcher characteristics and biases as we previously did to the characteristics of participants in our research samples. Similar issues of selection, representativeness, and other sampling considerations will arise with respect to investigators themselves and to research team members; appropriate protocols will have to be developed to deal with these issues. The perceptions, interpretations, and epistemological strengths and weaknesses of all persons involved in the research endeavor will have to be considered. This applies not only to research participants but also to investigators and to future consumers of the final research reports.

WHAT IS REAL?

The considerations of this chapter suggest a pluralistic epistemology. A pluralistic epistemology implies a pluralistic ontology. What is true or real for the body of one person may or may not be true or real for the mind of another person. Difficulties arise when one reality is privileged over all others.

In the Ayrapetyants study mentioned on page 217, to the conditioned participants, is a meter reading that falsely indicates intense air pressure more or less real than an accurate meter reading that indicates low or absent air pressure? Judged by physical criteria, the latter is more real; judged by physiological and psychological criteria, the former is more real. Research has demonstrated that persons respond to innocuous leaves as though they are allergens (evidencing skin allergic reactions) and respond to normally irritating leaves with no allergic skin reaction, if the persons have been suitably prepared through hypnosis or suggestions (see Ikemi & Nakagawa, 1962). A drug (ipecac or epicac) that normally *induces* nausea and vomiting can actually reduce these symptoms in patients who are told in advance that the medication will *inhibit* nausea and vomiting; the patient's expectancies not only override but reverse the typical effects of strong chemical agents (see Wolf, 1950). In these two instances, which is more real, the agent or drug, or the patient's mental expectation? Which criteria do we use in deciding?

The issue of the reality of mental events vis-à-vis physical events is highlighted by Marie-Louise von Franz's (1989) description of a conversation that took place during her first meeting with Carl Jung:

He talked about a crazy girl and said, "She was on the moon," and talked about it as if it had been very real. Being rational, I was indignant and said, "She hasn't been on the moon." Jung said, "Yes, she has." I thought, "That cannot be." I said, "That satellite of the earth there—which is uninhabited— she hasn't been there." He just looked at me and said, "She has been on the moon." (filmed interview)

To the physical scientist, the *real* is what is external and measurable, what can be accessed by the senses or physical instruments and verified by the senses or physical instruments of others. To human beings, inner events—that are unobservable from the outside—can be as real or more real than outer events, and they can have profound effects on our own lives, the lives of others, and on the physical circumstances of our planet. "Real is what has life" (Estés, 1992, p. 314). "Anything is real of which we find ourselves obliged to take into account in any way" (James, 1911, p. 101).

I (Braud) will share a technique that I have found helpful, personally, in dealing with issues of what is and what is not "real." Whenever I hear someone ask whether something is real or assert that it is real, I add, in my own thoughts, the adjective *physically*. Thus, *real* becomes *physically real*, and *reality* becomes *physical reality*. This simple reframing or qualification does two things at once. First, it indicates that we are considering a specific form of reality about which most of us share a great deal of consensus regarding what has or has not occurred or about what is or is not possible or likely. By limiting discourse to this realm, we can bypass certain complex issues and, perhaps, more readily agree or disagree about our claims. Second, and more important, qualifying *reality* by the adjective *physical* reminds us that there may be forms of reality other than the physical, and that in those alternative realities certain ways of knowing, doing, and being may or may not be possible or may occur in ways quite unlike those that occur in physical reality. Therefore, we are no longer satisfied to answer, simply and globally, yes or no to whether something is real. Instead, we qualify and specify our answer to indicate the *nature* of the "reality" in which we are claiming certain events to have or to have not occurred. Our consideration becomes more discerning.

What may not be real physically may nonetheless be real psychologically (in realms of imagination, meaning, or impact) or historically (as in the Pavlovian conditioning examples mentioned earlier) or in some of the alternative realities (the clairvoyant and mythic realities discussed by LeShan, 1976). The possibility of such pluralistic realities, in turn, reminds us that we may possess pluralistic means of knowing, doing, and being that are appropriate, adapted, or specialized for the different realities. These may be the different epistemic modes expressed metaphorically as different ways of seeing or as the different eyes of the senses, of the mind, of the heart, and of the soul or spirit alluded to in Chapter 3 and that are found in virtually all philosophical, wisdom, and spiritual traditions.

CHAPTER 12

ADDITIONAL SUGGESTIONS, ETHICAL CONSIDERATIONS, AND FUTURE CHALLENGES

Rosemarie Anderson
William Braud

In several sections of this book, we alluded to the similarities and differences of research, practical applications (clinical and others), and the researcher's psychospiritual path of growth and possible transformation. It may be useful to revisit, here, the distinctions and similarities among these areas when they are viewed, alternately, through the lens of the more conventional research paradigm and through the lens of the transpersonal research paradigm advocated in this book. We find that research, application, and self-transformation may be quite different things or the same thing, depending on what is studied, how it is studied, and the stance that is taken by the investigator or practitioner.

THE CONVENTIONAL PARADIGM

In the conventional research paradigm, topics frequently are chosen for their tractability to reigning quantitative, experimental methods devoted to the discovery of universal laws (a *nomothetic* aim). The chief purposes of research—and the criteria for determining the research's success and importance—are prediction and control. The topics must, necessarily, be relatively simple ones involving variables that can be readily isolated and controlled. In the service of such simplification and isolation, the research setting often becomes decontextualized, artificialized, and, unfortunately, frequently trivialized. For example, studies of perception, learning, memory, and cognition involve straightforward materials and tasks that can be presented, responded to, and mastered in relatively brief periods in simple, isolated settings that are estranged from the rich and complex dynamics and ambiguities that accompany these same processes in everyday life. Motivation, personality, and individual differences are limited to and reduced to scoring patterns on standardized assessments. The study of social interactions and relationship processes is restricted to those that can be easily simulated or modeled in a research setting.

The stance of the investigator is that of a separate, distanced, "objective" observer who strives to be as uninvolved as possible with the research participants and with what is being studied, in an effort to eliminate or avoid contamination by his or her biases or expectations. There is an attempt to remove the investigator from judgmental and decisional responsibilities through the use of automatic, impersonal decision tools provided by research designs themselves and by statistical outcomes. Subject matter, evidence, and conclusions are limited to what can be observed "from the outside," rationally processed, and communicated to others in straightforward, linear prose.

Such conventions of subject matter, method, and investigator stance do tend to distance research from practical applications—be they clinical, educational, wellness oriented, business oriented, or concerned with spiritual guidance or other human or transpersonal services. All these applications involve more significant and more complex issues and processes, a greater reliance on experiential, subjective factors, and a greater involvement of the practitioner. Persons working in one of the two areas—research and practical application—tend not to use or be familiar with what is done or known in the other area. For an illustration of one particular form of this split or fragmentation between research and practice, namely, between conventional research approaches and clinical work in psychology, one may consult a continuing series of articles and exchanges in the professional journal *American Psychologist* that demonstrate the persisting tensions within and between these two approaches (a sampling of these articles includes Barlow, 1996; Cohen, Sargent, & Sechrest, 1986; Goldfried & Wolfe, 1996; Hollon, 1996; Howard, Moras, Brill, Martinovich, & Lutz, 1996; Jacobson & Christensen, 1996; Morrow-Bradley & Elliott, 1986; Newman & Tejeda, 1996; Peterson, 1991; Sechrest, McKnight, & McKnight, 1996; Seligman, 1995, 1996; Strupp, 1996; VandenBos, 1996; for a summary of this debate, see, also, Polkinghorne, 1992). These same conventions (of subject matter, method, and stance) tend also to separate research from what is happening in the investigator's psychospiritual experiences, growth, and development.

THE TRANSPERSONAL PARADIGM

In the transpersonal paradigm, research is complemented by what is missing in the conventional paradigm. Methods of disciplined inquiry are expanded to include qualitative methods that can more appropriately and faithfully address rich, significant, and complex human experiences. Full description and understanding are valued as much as, or more than, prediction and control. Emphasis may be placed on understanding how processes and issues interact complexly and dynamically in the everyday life circumstances and life journeys of individuals (an *idiographic* aim).

The researcher is more interested in learning the laws (relevant factors and the patterns and interactions of these factors) of individual lives than in learning the laws of the world at large. Because the themes and variations of individual lives do reflect, mirror, and instantiate more general, universal principles and laws, however, a nomothetic end is reached nonetheless. In this case, the universal becomes known through the deep and intensive study of the particular and through a holographic process whereby even small but carefully chosen research samples reveal knowledge and principles that can be generalized validly to the population at large.

Because qualitative methods can address a greater and more complex range of experiences, research topics can be extended to include the same issues that are subjects of clinical and other practical applications—rich personal experiences (common as well as uncommon); important challenges and triumphs; complex interpersonal interactions; issues of meaning, purpose, and identity; and issues of personal and transpersonal growth, development, and transformation. The researcher can use wider lenses and a greater variety of lenses, and the researcher and the participant, together, may explore much wider and deeper windows of inquiry—emphasizing depths of experience and breadths of outcomes and aftereffects that could not be addressed through the more limited time frames and approaches of the conventional paradigm.

Any and all sources of evidence, ways of knowing, and ways of working with and expressing knowledge, findings, and conclusions can be brought to bear on the issues being researched. Both *emic* and *etic*, both subjective/experiential and objective/observational modes of knowing, are recognized and honored. There is an epistemological stance of what William James (1912/1976) called *radical empiricism*—a stance that excludes anything that is not directly experienced but includes *everything* that is directly experienced, by anyone involved in the research effort. Thus, the research participants' subjective experiences and self-perceptions are treated as valid data, as are the experiences and perceptions of the investigator. There is an important place for intuitive, tacit, and direct knowing; for various arational ways of processing information; and for a variety of forms of creative expression in conducting and communicating research.

The investigator becomes intimately involved in the research effort, realizing that both obvious and subtle communications, interactions, and interconnections with the research participants make a stance of objective detachment unrealistic and illusory. The participants, the investigators, and the readers of the eventual research reports become the real research instruments. Because there are no longer only automatic decisional tools—those provided by formal research designs and statistical indicators—the investigator bears increased responsibility for evaluating and weighing evidence; making judgments and decisions; and reaching conclusions based on her or his experience, sensitivities, and skills.

HOW RESEARCH, PRACTICAL APPLICATION, AND SELF-TRANSFORMATION CAN BE COMBINED

In the following discussion, clinical practice is used as an example of a form of practical application that can be combined with research. Although these comments focus on clinical practice, they can be applied, with the appropriate changes and adjustments, to other forms of practical applications, as well.

Clinical practice and research can be combined, or can become one and the same thing, if a clinical intervention becomes the object of the research, as in outcome or efficacy studies or in action research in which a researcher evaluates a clinical method or program that is already in place or is being tested. A practitioner who uses standardized assessment instruments in clinical practice can quantify these and study them systematically and formally. In clinical practice, the practitioner is always doing research more informally—observing relevant factors, finding patterns, noting what works or does not work with particular clients, forming ideas on the basis of interactions with clients, and testing these ideas with subsequent clients. Thus, clinical practice already contains many research components, and these could be augmented or emphasized more fully.

At its best, research can contain clinical components, as well. In the transpersonal paradigm, research and clinical practice are more similar than they are different. Because of the changes in topics studied, methods used, and investigator stance, it no longer makes sense to think of research, clinical practice, and the investigator's psychospiritual development as distinct areas separated from one another by firm boundaries. These boundaries dissolve and melt away. A research session remains that but also becomes an opportunity for clinical application and for transformation of the researcher. It is a clinical application because significant and highly relevant issues may be chosen as research topics and because qualitative methods (and even special additions to and variations of quantitative methods) can provide research participants with opportunities to work on personal issues and tell their stories, allowing opportunities for assimilating new understandings and new ways of knowing, doing, and being. The research is an opportunity for change and transformation in the investigator when the latter chooses topics that are personally significant and heartfelt and engages more fully in the research project. In addition, all these choices and processes provide opportunities for change and transformation in the readers of the research reports that eventually issue from the work. Research, clinical practice, and personal transformation exist in synergistic interrelationship, with each contributing to, drawing from, and informing the other.

A MODEL OF TRANSFORMATIVE INTEGRATION

We offer this preliminary model of important aspects common to research, practical applications, and self-transformation. We present and consider these five aspects separately and sequentially for ease of communication. In reality, the five aspects resemble the facets of a gem (Figure 12.1). They

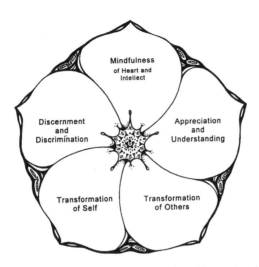

Figure 12.1. A Model of Transformative Integration: Five major features (facets) common to research, application, and self-development.

SOURCE: Original artwork by Winona Schroeter. Copyright © 1997 by Winona Schroeter. Reprinted by permission.

are integral parts of the whole—each becoming more or less prominent as the gem is turned and inspected from different viewpoints, each reflecting and refracting its companion facets. These five features may be viewed as phases of a process that brings knowledge, wisdom, and action. They also may be viewed as windows revealing certain aspects of a continuing, transformative process.

Mindfulness (of Heart and Intellect). The process begins with *mindfulness*—a fullness of attention, an evenly hovering attention, a presence, an awareness or awakeness. In certain Eastern esoteric traditions (see Amis, 1995; Kadloubovsky & Palmer, 1992; Palmer, Sherrard, & Ware, 1983-1995), there is a special term for this stance toward oneself and toward the world. The term is *nepsis,* and it could be translated as watchfulness or sobriety; it is the opposite of drunkenness or lacking in vigilance. Mindfulness involves a clarity of perception, a clear and undistorting mirroring of the fullness of what reality presents. It is an abiding awareness, an integral awareness, an expansive awareness. It is also a compassionate awareness— a compassionate awareness of actions, motives, and thoughts; a sweet and mellow feeling toward life and toward oneself, others, and all of nature.

Discernment. Accompanying mindfulness is *discernment*—a seeing to the heart of things, a seeing or knowing of what is not immediately evident. Discernment is an accurate discrimination with respect to sources, importance, pattern, and motives. In the tradition mentioned earlier, the term *diakrisis* (discrimination) is used for this process.

Appreciation and Understanding. With mindfulness and discernment come *appreciation* and *understanding.* These may be apperceived directly and affectively, without necessarily attributing meaning in a cognitive sense or providing a conceptual framework. This aspect is knowledge immediately grasped by the heart as right, moral, and good. Along with these may come a fullness and contextualization of experiences; there also may be a conceptualization, meaningful framework, or interpretation of experiences.

This process is akin to what is described by the Greek term *aisthesis.* Although aisthesis is typically taken to be synonymous with sense perception, the term has larger meanings, as well. Hillman (1995, pp. 47, 107) reminds us that at root, the term has to do with taking in, breathing in, gasping—a primary aesthetic response, a response of the heart. The term suggests a taking in or breathing in (inspiring) of the world—a taking in, taking to heart, internalizing, becoming intimate with. Aisthesis suggests a blending of sensation, perception, feeling, and imagination. Aisthesis suggests the intaking of the breath in wonder, in appreciation. It may be the heart's way of knowing, of understanding.

Transformation of Self. There is bringing of this heartfelt knowing to the head and to actions, too. Simultaneously, there are an integration, incorporation, and assimilation of what has been learned or experienced. There is a complementary bringing of knowing from head to heart, into lived experiences. One's being changes; there is transformation of the self, of the seeker, of the researcher, and of the practitioner. The esoteric term for this process is *metanoia*—a change of mind or heart that is synonymous with transformation.

Transformation of Others. As we communicate and share what we have learned or how we have changed with others, others are transformed as well. Through sharing, generosity, magnanimity, service to others, and compassionate abiding, this facet helps us create and sustain a benign and friendly world we can enjoy inhabiting. Not only may other individuals change, but smaller and larger groups, organizations, institutions, societies, and cultures—even the planet as a whole—may change, as well, in this fifth facet of the process. This is the social action component—the political component—of the process. Communications and sharings may contribute to changes and transformations in all participants in the project—including the reader of a report, in the case of a research or clinical project.

Aspects of this transformation of others are suggested by the Greek term *diakonia*. Diakonia involves service or ministering to others, or attending to a duty. Here, the service resides in presenting and making available what is helpful or needed for the change and transformation of others and of society at large.

ELABORATIONS AND
APPLICATIONS OF THE MODEL

These five facets are key processes for making progress and for avoiding delusions in life, in practical applications, and in research, and they appear to be identical processes in these three areas. They involve a fullness of attention to all that is happening and a careful discrimination of differences, similarities, sources, patterns, concomitants, outcomes, and facilitating and interfering factors. They include being mindful of when we are or are not confusing our wishes, expectations, desires, fears, apprehensions, and projections with what we are attempting to know as it is in itself. We are always doing research—in the sense of circling around issues, exploring more deeply, and finding out what is going on—but with different degrees of formality and care. The tools we use have different names and are directed toward different purposes in research, practical applications, and personal and transpersonal growth. We use these tools for *re-searching,* for looking again, looking more carefully and thoughtfully, and looking from several angles and perspectives at something of great interest to us. Research has much in common with *re-spect*—in which we also look again, look more fully and appreciatively at who or what is before us, honoring that person, thing, or event for what it is in itself and for what we may learn from this interaction.

This approach of mindfulness, discernment, appreciation, understanding, honoring, and respect is the opposite of an approach characterized by prejudice. In research, we are careful not to prejudge our data or findings or bias their collection, analysis, or interpretation on the basis of preexisting views or theories that may blind us to what the data really are telling us. The privileging of empirical findings over theoretical or rational expectations; the concern with internal validity and with threats to validity; and the practice, in phenomenological research, of *bracketing* (making explicit attempts to put aside expectations and biases during all phases of the investigation)—each of these is a stance against prejudice in the research domain. We learn more from the unexpected—the anomalies—than we do from what is expected. We welcome surprises because it is from surprises that discoveries are made.

In personal growth and development, we practice being alert to things as they are, rather than as we or others expect them to be. If we allow the five facets to act naturally within us, we are sensitive to our needs, to our particular path, and to which factors help or hinder our well-being and progress, rather than allow ourselves to be swayed, perhaps unwisely, by our expectations, assumptions, and presuppositions or those of others. We welcome surprises and what they may teach us about ourselves.

In the realm of practical application and social relationships, we meet each new individual with interest, enthusiasm, and respect—eager to hear, grasp, and learn from her or his unique story and particular way of being in the world. We attempt to hear the special voice and needs of that individual, unencumbered by preexisting expectations or biases—hoping to serve that person in the most appropriate way. Again, we welcome surprises.

ETHICAL AND POLITICAL CONSIDERATIONS

Knowledge contains the power to prosper good and ill ends both individually and collectively. Knowledge, then, begs ethical and political awareness. The few of any society having the time, energy, and societal support to conduct research suffer responsibility for the power inherent in perpetuating and creating knowledge and the power over others who follow directions and curry favor. Years ago, in the early 1970s—as a white, middle-class graduate student—I (Rosemarie Anderson) didn't *feel* powerful, but I was, relative to my undergraduate research participants. Typically, their participation was required as part of an introductory course. Yet more, they wanted to please me, and they complied with my directions and deceptions without overt complaint. I recall my discomfort with the imbalance of power. Yet my attempts to be considerate and egalitarian seemed only to increase my status as an authority. Outside the university, the gap in power between me and the research participants (we called them subjects then) was even wider. Privileged in my role as a scientist, my warrant to make decisions was rarely questioned. Although waves of feminist political critique were already rocking the culture, issues of equity within science itself were largely yet to be addressed. Early feminist research—then composed mostly of white middle-class women researching white middle-class women—can be critiqued as a perpetuation of a dominant social structure of values and a marginalization of others.

Largely because of the feminist and deconstructionist critiques of the past 30 years, however, researchers in the 1990s know more about the ideologies implicit in research and their pervasive effects. Will we now act more ethically and responsibly? We know that the focusing of research questions, the research setting itself, the relationship between researcher and participants, the power over resources, and especially the authority to shape the character of knowledge have political dimensions and effects. The prerogatives of rank and financial resources, and usually race, ethnicity, and social class, infuse all aspects of scientific discourse. Inequalities in power contextualize research in the physical sciences as well; the knowledge of the natural world lies close to the prerogatives of power. As researchers, we shape and define significant portions of consensual knowledge.

In transpersonal research, the demands for scrutinizing implicit ideologies and ethical review are higher. Frankly, the stakes are higher. Even with the best of intentions, portraying spiritual experiences and generalizing about the nature of transformative life experiences can easily lend itself to accounts biased in favor of the controlling ideologies of one culture (or subculture) and prejudiced against others. Already, world history is littered with accounts of the misuse of spiritual and religious authority.

What guidelines might we employ? How do we even learn to ask good questions of ourselves? How do researchers with a transpersonal orientation scrutinize cultural assumptions and remain open-minded in a pervasive spiritual sense? We propose the following set of propositions as an initial attempt to raise to consciousness pertinent ethical and political dimensions of research and of transpersonal research, more specifically. In preparing these questions, we acknowledge the work of Michael White (1993) for his deconstructive analysis of the politics of the therapeutic context.

ETHICAL AND POLITICAL RESPONSIBILITY

Among the great religious traditions of the world, it is commonly understood that making progress for the good of all people requires at least three essential characteristics: (a) a full recognition of our actions—and complicity in actions—that harm others and an expression of appropriate remorse; (b) an amendment of harmful actions and their consequences, including reparation of broken relationships and commitments; and (c) a change in future actions, including working for the common good. These basic characteristics are applied to the conduct of research, as follows:

1. Researchers recognize that all research carries with it the ideological assumptions of the researcher, reflective of his or her time in history and position of power within a culture and subcultures.

2. An honest evaluation is made of how these assumptions affect all phases of the research inquiry, including the choice of topic, methods and analysis employed, and generalizations extending from the analysis, as well as the choices made in properly presenting the results to the professional community and to the public.

3. As a result of this analysis, balancing points of view are considered and employed. Where balance is not completely feasible, researchers disclose their assumptions, as well as aspects of the research procedures and conclusions that favor the view of any one group, culture, or subculture over another.

4. When the researcher uses the experience of past research, each successive research inquiry is more balanced in empowering the silenced voices of society and thereby attempts to rectify the imbalances of past research and more fully explicate and understand the phenomenon being studied.

5. Taking seriously the power of knowledge in culture, researchers work individually and collaboratively to balance the hierarchical structures inherent in research and to create better structures for the benefit of all people.

To guide discernment of ideological assumptions implicit in research, we suggest that researchers recurrently ask themselves this question: Which societal voices are missing from this conceptualizing, method, data, analysis, synthesis, or theory? With much patience and goodwill, the pluralistic voices of any society and across societies will gradually result in more comprehensive and expansive portrayals of human experience. Rather it seem a cacophony at first than to privilege limitation and control. By empowering the various voices of the global community to speak in their own words of their own experience, new research approaches and integral theories may naturally and creatively arise.

ETHICS OF DIRECT KNOWING

Most transpersonal researchers acknowledge that it is possible to gain information about events remote to one's immediate surroundings. Several examples of direct knowing may be found in the parapsychological literature cited in Chapter 3, Chapter 7, Appendix C, and some of the research examples in Part III, notably Kathleen Barrett's interviewing of channels, Sharon Van Raalte's use of shamanic journeying on behalf of psychiatrist clients, Sheila Lynn Belanger's use of touch drawing to gain intuitive insight, Alzak Amlani's visual and proprioceptive modes of knowing, Jan Fisher's kinesthetic intuition, and Genie Palmer's work with exceptional human experiences. In all instances, research participants were aware of their involvement in the study. In particular, shamanic journeying was done only with the concurrence of the client and referring psychiatrist. Nonetheless, all forms of direct knowing and intuition require heightened ethical cautions concerning research participants' privacy and confidentiality of information. Direct knowing and intuition can also be incorrect (like anything else), and researchers' skills no doubt vary enormously. Moreover, because it is so easy to influence others when receiving the highly personal information so commonly sought in transpersonal research, researchers are well advised to evaluate transpersonal research using both the American Psychological Association's (1987, 1992) and the British Psychological Society's (1993) ethical guidelines for research with human participants and for clinical practice. Because transpersonal psychology at present remains a minority field, ethical considerations within institutions are reviewed by conventional ethics committees and supported by the values and mores of a small, interconnected community. As transpersonal psychology inevitably grows and expands into mainstream research communities, ethics will need to be delineated much more explicitly.

RESPECTING THE
LIMITS OF RESEARCH

Virtually anything can be researched to some degree. Conventional topics may be explored through conventional methods as well as through the newer methods described in this book. More unconventional topics—especially those of transpersonal relevance—may, likewise, be studied through both the conventional and the expanded research methods. In at least three instances, however, we recognize the potential inappropriateness of research in general or, at least, of particular forms of research.

When the Research Is Culturally Deemed Inappropriate. There are instances in which particular forms of research, or particular modes of inquiry, are not welcomed or not valued by the culture in which the methods would be applied. Wisdom and respect dictate honoring such attitudes and forgoing such unwanted research projects. Even if research, generally, is welcomed, specific ethical issues may arise surrounding particular components of a research project. For example, the use of informed consent forms may be viewed by potential participants as strange or even insulting because of their cultural patterns and mores. The researcher should consider the appropriateness or inappropriateness, as well as possible consequences, of introducing particular research components when their presence seems out of keeping with preferences and attitudes of the participants or the cultural context in which the research is conducted.

When the Research Is Personally Deemed Inappropriate. Occasions arise in which participants feel that research might violate, profane, or threaten to trivialize something that is held special by potential research participants. A specific example is found in a recently completed phenomenological study of the experience of being voluntarily silent.

> The researcher was unable to find Eastern Orthodox Christians who had had that type of experience. The ones who undergo silent retreats are monastics—Abbots, monks, or nuns. When asked to join the study they all responded in a similar manner; namely, that the experience of being silent for extended periods of time is not only too sacred to be put into words but also that once it is shared with others one can become arrogant, forgetful, etc. In other words, these Eastern Orthodox Christian monastics felt that *hesychasm,* or the state of being silent, is an experience only between oneself

and God and not an experience to be studied or analyzed. (Elite, 1993, p. 94)

In such instances, of course, the researcher does not venture to profane what is held sacred by another.

When Confronting the Ineffable. On occasion, a researcher confronts the numinous, the ineffable, or simply an object or experience of such power or profundity that inquiring into it in any way, or even attempting to describe or comment on it, seems obviously inappropriate or even impossible. There may be certain things that an investigator cannot research or would not even consider researching. Such things would be passed over in silence. Alternatively, a researcher might deign to study them quite indirectly, knowing that conclusions would concern only their shadows or reflections—perfectly true to certain aspects of their source but recognized as partial and incomplete.

BEYOND POSTMODERN DECONSTRUCTION

A thorough treatment of the intricacies of postmodernism and deconstructionism is beyond the scope of this book. Fortunately, an excellent treatment of these issues and of their possible impacts on psychology already is available (Kvale, 1992).

Rather than attempt to summarize the various arguments and counterarguments presented in Kvale (1992), we will describe an alternative postmodern proposal offered by Griffin (1988). Griffin characterizes the familiar form of postmodernism as *deconstructive* or *eliminative* postmodernism that

> overcomes the modern worldview through an anti-worldview: it deconstructs or eliminates the ingredients necessary for a worldview, such as God, self, purpose, meaning, a real world, and truth as correspondence. While motivated in some cases by the ethical concern to forestall totalitarian systems, this type of postmodern thought issues in relativism, even nihilism. It could also be called ultramodernism, in that its eliminations result from carrying modern premises to their logical conclusions. (p. x)

Griffin proposes another form of postmodernism that, by contrast, can be called *constructive* or *revisionary*. This alternative form seeks to overcome the modern worldview not by eliminating the possibility of worldviews as such, but by constructing a postmodern worldview through a revision of modern premises and traditional concepts. This constructive or revisionary postmodernism involves a new unity of scientific, ethical, aesthetic, and religious intuitions. It rejects not science as such but only that scientism in which the data of the modern natural sciences are alone allowed to contribute to the construction of our worldview. . . . The term *postmodern*, however, by contrast with *premodern*, emphasizes that the modern world has produced unparalleled advances that must not be lost in a general revulsion against its negative features.

From the point of view of deconstructive postmodernists, this constructive postmodernism is still hopelessly wedded to outdated concepts, because it wishes to salvage a positive meaning not only for the notions of the human self, historical meaning, and truth as correspondence, which were central to modernity, but also for premodern notions of a divine reality, cosmic meaning, and an enchanted nature. From the point of view of its advocates, however, this revisionary postmodernism is not only more adequate to our experience but also more genuinely postmodern. It does not simply carry the premises of modernity through to their logical conclusions, but criticizes and revises those premises. Through its return to organicism and its acceptance of nonsensory perception, it opens itself to the recovery of truths and values from various forms of premodern thought and practice that had been dogmatically rejected by modernity. This constructive, revisionary postmodernism involves a creative synthesis of modern and premodern truths and values. (pp. x-xi)

This constructive approach is elaborated in Griffin's (1988) *The Reenchantment of Science*. A similar stance is developed in Smith's (1992) *Beyond the Post-Modern Mind*. Spretnak's (1993) *States of Grace: The Recovery of Meaning in the Postmodern Age* critiques both modernity and deconstructive postmodernism from an ecofeminist perspective and indicates the values to be gained from the various wisdom traditions. The key features of these stances are inclusiveness and integration. These are precisely the features of the methods and approaches advocated in the present book. We wish not to throw out forms of inquiry practiced in the past or in the present—nor their findings—but rather to keep and perfect those that are most useful for our particular purposes; to use them appropriately; and to extend, expand, and complement them, as needed, so that they might contribute even more effectively to a more complete apprehension and appreciation of ourselves and of the world around us.

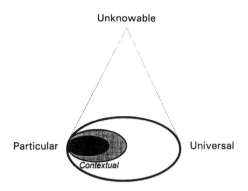

Figure 12.2. A Model of the Possibilities of Knowing: The apex of the cone represents the unknowable. The dashed lines indicate that aspects of the unknowable may be reflected in the known. The darker (umbral) and lighter (penumbral) shaded areas around the darkest point (the particular) indicate, respectively, the more local and less local contexts of the particular.

Recognizing the biases, limitations, and excesses of each, we value contributions from premodern, modern, *and* postmodern systems of thought.

Particularly useful contributions of postmodernism and deconstructionism include (a) the recognition that aspects of "reality" may be psychologically, socially, and politically constructed to various degrees; (b) the reminder that a plurality of voices—of particular persons, constituencies, ways of knowing, and criteria of legitimacy—testify for or against specific knowledge claims; (c) the reminder that some of those voices are privileged, whereas others are marginalized; and (d) the proposal that previously marginalized and deprivileged voices be encouraged to speak and that they be listened to and heard with attentiveness and respect.

A CONE OF KNOWING

Figure 12.2 presents a model of the possibilities of knowing. We suggest that there exist some things that cannot be known (and, perhaps, can never be known), others that may be known with great certainty and universality, and others that may be known only as particulars or understood only with qualifiers, limitations, or contextualizations. For example, certain topics— such as the nature or qualities of the divine or even the experience of transcendent reality—are not only ineffable but outside the spectrum of research because even transpersonal researchers must restrict themselves to experiences inside the human realm of knowing. Other experiences evidence repeatable, even universal, patterns. In the vicinity of unique particularities are regions of knowings that are common to given contexts, localities, or networks—strongly influenced by or reflecting those different contexts in which they are embedded and, for the most part, unrepeatable outside the contexts that inform and lend meaning to them.

If we use a metaphor of language, the unknowable (at the cone's top) speaks to us tacitly or inherently, if at all. Its is the language of silence appropriate to experiences of emptiness, of the ineffable, unspeakable, and nameless. The universal knowings at the right speak in a language known and understood by all—a species of Esperanto. Knowings in the shaded areas to the left—those in the umbra and penumbra of the individual point (the smallest darkened ellipse)—speak in different languages, dialects, or accents—recognizable to different degrees, or not at all, depending on one's degree of familiarity with the language or one's degree of membership in the culture, context, locality, or network in which the specific tongue is spoken. The language of the single point is singularly idiomatic, idiosyncratic, an idiot language, in the root sense of *idios*—one's own, private—a language of one.

To cover the large elliptical area as fully as possible, one must become polylingual. Or, to shift the metaphor, one must *move*—from point to point, from one perspective to another, from a universal (nomothetic) stance to a particular (idiographic) stance, and to everything in between, back and forth, again and again. To know as much as possible of what may be known, one must move constantly—one must dance. Especially for those with a kinesthetic intuition, the shifting can be particularly informative. The nature of movements, the shifts in position, taken to catch varying points of view, may speak directly to the character of the connection between particular understandings and universal principles. Moreover, to remain wedded only to a particular stance is to miss a great deal—to risk equating one's familiar room with the entire mansion.

These three situations—the completely knowable, the partially knowable, and the unknowable—may be present in all disciplines or forms of inquiry. The prevalence of each, however, may vary from discipline to discipline. Perhaps, as we move from the natural sciences, to the human sciences, to the transpersonal and spiritual sciences, we encounter, in turn, great densities of those three respective forms of knowing. It seems to us that spiritual experiences, for example, often have a bold uniqueness about them, and researchers are often reluctant to generalize across certain experiences. Personality penchants aside, generalizing seems to strip the particular stories of meaning. Curiously, however, universals sometimes seem more obvious, even glaring, here than in studies involving more everyday experiences—as if organizing principles are more distantly removed from the immediate experience. Because these final observations are themselves matters of intuitive judgment, giving examples is impossible, and we offer these impressions in the hope of generating discussion and study.

CONCLUSION

The far-reaching goal of research is the *good society,* in which kindness, peace, and compassion preside. Living, as we now do, in a global society composed of many cultures, religions, languages, and traditions, the good society on a global level requires—even begs—a vision of what will bring us together. This vision is inevitably spiritual, for none other will help us transcend our individual and cultural limitations and vanities. Who are we (the authors) to know what this vision might be? We are reminded of Jelaluddin Rumi's (1995) words and our closing prayer: "Out beyond ideas of wrongdoing and rightdoing, there's a field. I'll meet you there" (p. 36).

APPENDIX **A**

SYNOPSES OF
FIVE TRANSPERSONAL
APPROACHES TO RESEARCH

This appendix summarizes the major features of the five transpersonal approaches to research that are presented in greater detail in Chapters 3 through 7.

1. INTEGRAL INQUIRY

Essence: The world of human beings and their experiences is multileveled and complex, and to provide a faithful account of that world, research approaches must be correspondingly multifaceted and pluralistic. In integral inquiry, the researcher explores a research question that has great meaning to the researcher and to the research participants. This, in itself, guarantees that the findings also will be salient, significant, and useful to future readers of the research report (audience) and will help advance the knowledge base of the scholarly discipline in an important way. The nature of the research question(s) determines the choice of the most suitable research methods. The researcher may choose from an array of conventional methods that have been optimized to address, respectively, four major types of research questions: (a) How might we describe, as fully and deeply as possible, the nature of a particular human experience, and how

256

closely can we come to a sympathetic understanding of what it is like to have such an experience? (b) How might we conceptualize or explain that particular experience, historically or theoretically? (c) What are the developmental time course and "atmosphere" of that experience—that is, which factors have set the stage for its occurrence (facilitating or impeding its occurrence), and what are its accompaniments, concomitants, or correlates? and (d) What are the consequences or outcomes of that particular experience—especially its important impacts on the life of the experiencer?

Table 3.1 of Chapter 3 is helpful in selecting the most appropriate methods for exploring these types of questions. Next, the methods chosen may be expanded or extended to include alternative forms of knowing, alternative ways of working with the data, and alternative ways of expressing findings; these extensions may take place in the research participants or in the researcher. Examples include accessing and honoring one's tacit knowledge, bodily wisdom, emotions and feelings, intuitions, and direct knowing or paranormal access to otherwise inaccessible information; working with findings not only through the rational processing of ordinary waking consciousness but also through other representations and modes (e.g., imagery, proprioception, and direct apprehensions) that may occur more readily in nonordinary states of consciousness (e.g., meditative states and hypnoidal states); and expressing findings not only in linear prose but via alternative communication styles such as stories, nonverbal presentations, artwork, poetry, metaphor, myths, or symbolic modes. Reader-interactive modes of data presentation are also possible (e.g., presenting certain raw data to the reader along with instructions for working with the information in certain consciousness states and developing interactive CD-ROM presentations of all major steps of the research project). Important places are given to processes of intentionality at all phases of the research: (a) being informed by information from a vast array of sources (not only current professional literature of the discipline but also older and more tangential literature, information and approaches from other disciplines, spiritual and wisdom traditions, and one's transpersonal sources—e.g., dreams, intuitions, exceptional experiences, synchronicities, and inner guidance); (b) questioning assumptions, identifying hidden assumptions, and turning assumptions on their heads; (c) considering a variety of validity indicators; and (d) expecting and valuing the research project's ability to help change or transform the research participants, the researcher, the reader (audience), the professional discipline, and society at large.

Strengths: The approach permits extensive and intensive studies of a topic; allows understandings from a variety of perspectives to emerge; recognizes and honors alternative forms of knowing, doing, and being; promotes change and transformation in all persons involved in or touched by a research project; and helps dissolve the usual artificial boundaries between research, clinical and other practical applications, and personal and transpersonal growth and development. There is a strong emphasis on appreciating complements, transcending apparent dichotomies and contradictions, tolerance for ambiguity, and ability to live with and comfortably hold paradoxes.

Weaknesses: Because integral inquiry can be so broad, there is the danger of attempting to do too many different things and thus dilute the quality and depth of particular aspects of the research. Adequate practice of the method requires extensive and intensive experience and preparation of the researcher, along with familiarity and sensitivity to many modes of knowing and alternative ways of being in the world.

Illustration: What can a plurality of research approaches and personal experiences tell us about the nature and meaning of psychic experiences? (Braud, 1994a, 1994c).

Resources: Schumacher (1978); Smith (1976, 1992).

---

2. INTUITIVE INQUIRY

Essence: Building on heuristic, phenomenological, and feminist research methods, intuitive inquiry is a qualitative approach to conducting research. It is uniquely suited to exploring experiences considered complex and subtle. Intuitive inquiry uses transpersonal skills, such as intuition and alternative states of consciousness, as core methods of inquiry. Intuitive inquiry may be blended with other research approaches, especially qualitative methods, to provide rich portrayals of experience. Essential features of the method include compassion as a sustaining value in research, sympathetic resonance and circles of sympathetic resonance as validating procedures for research findings, the ritualistic nature of carefully following procedures and protocols, the role of compassionate knowing in scientific inquiry, and the importance of particularity (the researcher's voice and the participant's voice especially) in communicating the unique and yet potentially universal nature of the experiences studied. Research investigations are enriched and expanded by applying a variety of modes of intuition and states of consciousness to every level of inquiry, including choosing a compelling research topic, collecting data from a wide variety of sources, incorporating the researcher's insights, analyzing data through a variety of intuitive modalities, and interactively communicating results to an intended audience(s). A variety of innovative concepts are proposed, including the role of reflective listening to self and others, "trickstering" as a means to enliven research, the subtleties of varying "focal depth" in exploring complex experiences, ritualizing intention to guide and sustain the research endeavor, and the importance of the intended audience in all aspects of the research inquiry.

Strengths: Intuitive inquiry provides support for incorporating the full dimensionality of human knowing into the conduct of research.

Weaknesses: Using intuition and alternative states of consciousness in research is especially subject to the biases and prejudices of the researcher and therefore requires verification from independent researchers. The method expects researchers to be psychospiritually integrated and to have well-developed intuitive skills.

Illustration: Anderson's (1996) research on sacred weeping; Safken's (1997) research on Sufi stories.

Resources: Anderson's (1998) research on psychological and oracular significance of Celtic symbols.

---

3. ORGANIC RESEARCH

Essence: Organic research is a method that has grown from heuristic and feminist approaches to research. At its core is an emphasis on the transformative power of inviting, listening to, and presenting individual participants' stories about important aspects of their lives, using the participants' own voices and words as much as possible. The topic of an organic study is rooted in the story of the researcher's personal experiences. All aspects of the study, as it evolves, are recorded and reported in the researcher's own voice. Choosing to work with this method presupposes a moderately high level of consciousness about the researcher's psycho-spiritual development. Organic research grows from a reverence for the sacred aspects of the topic, the method, collaboration with the coresearchers, the context, and the implications of the inquiry. It may include nonrational and nonverbal ways of gathering and reporting data. The unique method of each organic study depends on the creativity of the researcher and is expected to evolve during the investigation in response to influences from within the researcher's psyche and from external events that have impacts on the progress of the work. The goal of organic research is personal transformation for the reader of the study, for the coresearchers, and for the researcher. The fundamental technique of organic research is telling and listening to stories. Analysis of organic data may be done by the researcher, the coresearchers, and/or in the mind of the reader or audience for the final research report. The reader is expected to do some or much of the work of "digesting" or making sense of the findings. A great deal of predigesting or processing of the data by coresearchers or researchers is discouraged.

The final form of an organic study is personal, engaging, and informative. The developers of the organic research method describe it using the metaphor of a tree that grows from seed to fruit. As the earth must be prepared before planting a seed, participation in the organic approach requires a reverence for the *sacred* in all aspects of the work. The seed for the study, which comes from the researcher's deeply held *personal* experience, is planted in the sacred earth. Before any growth is seen above ground, the seed absorbs warmth and food from the dark, wet earth so it can sprout and grow. Similarly, an organic study honors the *chthonic* or unpredictable and uncontrollable aspects of the methodological process. Just as the thin, white sprout is fed by the sun and rain, the investigation depends on a *relational* method as the researcher gathers stories from the coresearchers. The fruit of the study contains the *transformative* seeds that offer healing changes to the researcher, to the coresearchers, and, ultimately, to the readers.

Strengths: The method honors the transpersonal and the sacred, it explores topics that are of great meaning and significance to the researcher and coresearchers, and it acknowledges and supports the healing power of telling and listening to stories. There is great freedom in letting the research process be guided by the exigencies that develop during the study, unhampered by strict preexisting structures governing what is to be done and how the work is to be accomplished.

Weaknesses: In emphasizing an idiographic approach, and one in which there is minimal interest in extracting themes or commonalities across stories, the organic method plays down the importance of nomothetic findings that can help grow the knowledge base of one's discipline. The organic research method may become indistinguishable from the writing of a novel. Yet one wonders about the use of distinguishing novels from conventional research reports, especially in quality of understanding and potential impact.

Illustration: What is a woman's experience of "descent into the underworld"? (Taylor, 1996).

Resource: Clements (1994-1995).

---

4. TRANSPERSONAL-PHENOMENOLOGICAL INQUIRY

Essence: Building on years of experience with phenomenological inquiry as applied to a wide variety of existential and transpersonal experiences (Valle, 1998a; Valle & Halling, 1989; Valle & King, 1978), Ron Valle and Mary Mohs bring an understanding of transpersonal awareness to an existential-phenomenological philosophy and its application as phenomenological methods of inquiry. This integration is described as an emerging transpersonal-phenomenological psychology. It is proposed that transpersonal awareness is "prior to" any prereflective structure of a particular experience. Therefore, transpersonal awareness is not of the phenomenal realm of perceiver and perceived but rather of a noumenal, unitive space from which both intentional consciousness and phenomenal experience manifest in life. When transpersonal awareness presents itself in awareness, these experiences can be explored using empirical phenomenological research methods. A preliminary analysis of seven recent phenomenological studies of experiences with transpersonal qualities identified 11 common themes interwoven throughout the descriptions of these experiences: transpersonal awareness manifesting through the vehicle of a given experience, intense emotional or passionate states, being in the present moment, transcendence of space and time, expansion of boundaries and sense of connectedness, stillness or peace, sense of knowing, unconditional love, feeling graced, ineffability, and self-transformation.

Strengths: By positioning transpersonal awareness within existential-phenomenological philosophy and phenomenological inquiry, transpersonal-phenomenological inquiry is unique among transpersonal methods in providing a strong philosophical framework and well-articulated methods. Strengths of phenomenological approaches to research cited in Appendix B apply to this method.

Weaknesses: Because this method is building on phenomenological method of inquiry, the weaknesses of phenomenological approaches to research cited in Appendix B apply to this method as well. The method is best suited to research topics that can be clearly, and somewhat narrowly, defined.

Illustrations: Studies of transpersonal phenomenological experiences by Ourania Elite, Tom West, Paul Gowack and Valerie Valle, Patricia Qualls, Tim West, Craig Matsu-Pissot, and D. Hanson and Jon Klimo, cited in Valle (1998a).

Resources: Valle (1989, 1998a).

---

5. INQUIRY INFORMED BY EXCEPTIONAL HUMAN EXPERIENCES

Essence: Rhea White urges investigators to include more personal materials in their research reports—indications of the experiences that actually informed the work: the dreams, hunches, and similar experiences that actually led to the insights that were more formally explored in the research projects. She suggests that researchers honor, access, study, and report their personal experiences because these are more likely to result in deeper knowing and actual changes in being that can, in turn, allow still other forms of knowing and inspirations for, and understandings of, more extended and creative research programs. She urges investigators to explore, especially, the class of experiences she calls *exceptional human experiences* (EHEs) because these experiences are extremely rich in life-changing impacts and in providing bridges to other ways of knowing and other realities. The EHEs are mystical and unitive experiences, psychic experiences, unusual death-related experiences, encounter experiences, and exceptional normal experiences. She gives procedures for studying these experiences in the forms of EHE autobiographies and scientific EHE autobiographies.

EHEs that are particularly likely to occur in research contexts and provide useful information and insights include nocturnal and lucid dreams, hunches, hypnagogic and hypnopompic (twilight state) imagery, visions and hallucinations, empathy, psychic functioning, out-of-body experiences, and synchronicity. She suggests that these experiences be invited, noted, and recorded as they occur; be recognized, honored, and studied for their own sakes—and not merely for any useful or verifiable information that might derive from them; and be included systematically in formal research reports and be made available in database formats so that others might study and profit from them. She suggests that EHEs, through their transformational effects on the experiencer, can promote personal, experiential shifts in the paradigm in which the researcher is working, allowing a change in being or becoming in the investigator. This new way of being—and its associated changed perspective to the inside of the new paradigm—can allow new forms of knowing and insights that are unavailable to investigators who distance themselves from their own EHEs or from the topics they are studying.

Strengths: This approach encourages an intimate and thoroughgoing involvement of the researcher in the process of investigation. It recognizes the importance of tacit knowing and other forms of personal knowledge of researcher and coresearchers. It calls attention to a class of significant experiences that generally have been ignored or devalued and about which there is considerable misinformation and misapprehension. It calls attention to a different way of knowing—knowing through being—in which one becomes what one studies and knows it more intimately and more deeply from the inside.

Weaknesses: In its great emphasis on exceptional human experiences and on living and working from within a new, experiential paradigm, there is the risk of downplaying the importance of nonexceptional experiences and the use and value of more traditional approaches to research.

Illustration: What is the experience, and what are the accompaniments and consequences, of writing an exceptional human experience autobiography? (White, 1994d).

Resources: White (1994b, 1997).

SYNOPSES OF SIX RELATED RESEARCH APPROACHES

Following are summaries of six approaches to research that share important commonalities with the new methods presented in this book.

---

1. PHENOMENOLOGICAL APPROACH

Essence: The phenomenological approach aims to develop a complete, accurate, clear, and articulate description and understanding of a particular human experience or experiential moment—a rich, deep "snapshot" of an experience that includes qualities at many levels of experience (i.e., bodily, feelings) but especially at prereflective levels. It achieves its goal through the use of a special investigator stance and approach and through specialized methods of participant selection, solicitation of information, systematic data treatment, and assembling of interview components into a final report.

Strengths: The phenomenological approach provides a rich and complete description of human experiences and meanings. Findings are allowed to emerge, rather than being imposed by an investigator. Careful techniques are used to keep descriptions as faithful to the experiential raw data as possible; this is accomplished by extreme care in moving step by step and in being ever mindful not to delete from, add to, change, or distort anything originally present in the initial "meaning units" of the participant transcripts. The investigator attempts to "bracket" presuppositions and biases to hold them in consciousness through all phases of the research and minimize their influence on the findings.

Weaknesses: The method depends on the articulate skills of the participants who provide the information; logistical and generalization issues are connected with this. The language and terms employed in existential-phenomenological philosophy and phenomenological inquiry are usually obtuse. Conclusions depend on the particular participants chosen for the study. In its orientation toward a particular time frame or moment, the method may miss information about broader periods or about the development (time course) of an experience. In focusing on a rich description of an experience, the method may miss information about what led up to that experience, what its outcomes or consequences might be, and what the concomitants and other factors associated with the experience are. There is little interest in conceptualizing the experience or in "explaining" it.

Illustration: What is the experience of the decision process of a woman trusting herself in making a spiritual commitment that is contrary to the wishes of a significant person? (Andras, 1993).

Resources: Aanstoos (1984); Colaizzi (1978); Drew (1993); Giorgi (1983, 1985); Moustakas (1994); Polkinghorne (1989); Spinelli (1989); Tesch (1990); Valle and Halling (1989); van Kaam (1969); von Eckartsberg (1986).

---

2. HEURISTIC RESEARCH

Essence: This method, developed by Clark Moustakas and his coworkers, aims to provide a comprehensive, vivid, accurate, and essential depiction of an experience derived from the investigator's rigorous and intensive self-searching and from the explications of others. The topic is familiar and significant to the investigator. The investigator totally and lengthily immerses herself or himself in the process of understanding the experience from all possible perspectives. The method emphasizes identifying with the focus of inquiry, self-dialogue, tacit knowing, intuition, focusing (accessing bodily knowledge), and maintaining an internal frame of reference. The stages of the heuristic research process are similar to those posited for creative expression: initial engagement, immersion, incubation, illumination, explication, and creative synthesis. To help the reader appreciate the experience that is being described, rich and evocative individual, exemplary, and composite depictions or portraits are prepared.

Strengths: The method recognizes the importance of personal knowledge and of the tacit knowing of the researcher. The method yields a direct, intimate, inclusive awareness of the many aspects of an important experience. There is total involvement of the researcher, and all forms of knowing yield inputs into the study—the researcher's experiences, the reports of others, published findings, insights from novels and poetry, and insights from the researcher's dreams and other states of consciousness.

Weaknesses: The process is difficult, lengthy, and consuming. The method does not emphasize conceptualization or theorizing about the experiences studied. Social or political action is not emphasized directly, but this has, indeed, followed from the actions of others who have been exposed to and deeply moved by the method's experiential descriptions.

Illustration: What is the experience of loneliness? (Moustakas, 1961, 1972, 1975).

Resource: Moustakas (1990).

---

3. FEMINIST APPROACHES

Essence: Feminist approaches represent attempts to correct androcentric biases in findings, methods, and scientific philosophy through the use of more feminine methods that stress relatedness, connectedness, nonseparation, and participation.

Strengths: The approaches are correctives for androcentrically biased methods, approaches, and findings. They emphasize interdependence of investigator and participant. They keep present the historical and social backgrounds of researcher and participants. They recognize values within the research context. They promote egalitarian relationships between researcher and participants. The approaches are a reminder that many assumptions and methods of science are masculinely biased and ignore important feminine qualities and approaches to knowing and understanding. There is a strong emphasis on the personal and the political.

Weaknesses: If presented in extreme forms, these approaches can be just as biased, incomplete, and unwise as the androcentric extreme to which they are reactions. There are many forms of the feminist method or approach and, hence, many confusions. Conceptualization and theorizing are downplayed.

Illustration: What are the challenges to, and qualities of, the individuation process in African American women? (Morrill, 1994).

Resources: Nielsen (1990); Reinharz (1992b); Riger (1992); Shepherd (1993).

---

4. EXPERIENTIAL RESEARCH METHOD

Essence: Developed by Barrell and his coworkers, this approach has three major aspects. In the experiential method proper, research participants notice an immediate experience or relive a past one, write about the inner experience using present tense and first person, repeat this procedure with a number of additional related instances of the experience in question, and ask themselves about commonalities among the various instances of the inner experience; there emerge individual descriptions of the inner qualities of the experience. Next, group work (akin to group phenomenological work) can be done in which a group searches for common qualities among the individual experiences that had been described by group members. Finally, in a quantitative extension, the common descriptions can be quantified to test (via more conventional research methods) certain experiential hypotheses about actual lived facts of human experience—for example, "a feeling of uncertainty is necessary but not sufficient for anxiety."

Strengths: The approach emphasizes direct experience, self-awareness, and an understanding of the structure of experience. The method can be extended to include group consensus of the common qualities of important experiences, and it also can yield quantification and hypothesis-testing possibilities. Thus, the method may provide a bridge between human science approaches and more traditional research paradigms.

Weaknesses: By focusing on experiential elements only, other aspects of "experience"—more broadly conceived—escape treatment. Because much of the work is done by participants who follow written formats in relatively short individual or group meetings, more intensive or extensive materials may be missed.

Illustration: How can the experiential method be used to learn more about the experience of pain and its emotional and physiological accompaniments? (Barrell & Price, 1975; Price, Barrell, & Gracely, 1980).

Resources: Barrell, Aanstoos, Richards, and Arons (1987); Price and Barrell (1980).

---

5. COOPERATIVE INQUIRY

Essence: In cooperative inquiry (as developed by Reason and Heron), the person is viewed as a fundamental spiritual entity who has a distinct presence in the world and who can cause his or her own actions. All research participants in the research project are coresearchers and all researchers are "cosubjects"—each person fully participates in all aspects of the research project—its focus, design, conduct, and interpretation. There is truly a community of inquiry in which people engage together in cycles of action and reflection (consciousness in the midst of action); this is called *critical subjectivity.* The research cycles repeatedly through phases of propositional knowing (knowing about something), experiential knowing (through direct, face-to-face encounters), practical knowing (knowing how-to skills and competencies), and presentational knowing (aesthetic expressions of experiences) as groups of persons with focused interests meet and interact. Success in the method requires additional skills in group work, attentional skills, and emotional competence; these skills are developed through extensive practice. The validity of what emerges depends on the mature discernment of the coparticipants. Validity is enhanced through development of discriminating awareness, research cycling, divergence, and convergence, authentic collaboration, playing a Devil's Advocate falsification role, management of unaware projections, a balance of action and reflection, and a willingness to experience periods of chaos as a way to have new and creative structures emerge.

Strengths: The approach is rich in aspects of participation, collaboration, and the use of many alternative forms of knowing, working with information, and expressing knowledge. It values both action and reflection and involves persons deeply in learning about and doing things about significant issues in their lives. It allows many voices to be heard—both between and within people.

Weaknesses: The approach is demanding, and it is not well known or widely practiced outside the United Kingdom.

Illustration: Can cooperative inquiry have a practical impact in integrating holistic and complementary medical practices with conventional medical treatments? (Heron & Reason, 1985; Reason, 1995).

Resources: Heron (1992); Reason (1988, 1994); Reason and Heron (1995).

---

6. PARTICIPATORY RESEARCH

Essence: Participatory research (as proposed by Henryk Skolimowski) is the art of empathy, of communion with the object of inquiry, of learning to use *its* language, of *using* its language, of talking to the object of inquiry, of penetrating from within, of indwelling in the other, of imaginative hypothesis that leads to identification, and of transformation of one's consciousness so that it becomes part of the consciousness of the other. The researcher prepares the ground for participatory research by preparing her or his consciousness; meditating on the form of being of the other; reliving its past, its present, and its existential dilemmas; supplicating to it for permission to enter it (just the opposite of cutting it with a surgical knife); praying to the other to let the researcher in (prayer as a form of empathic energy); and dwelling in the other on compassionate terms. Participatory research demands the development of compassionate consciousness. It explores how the various sensitivities of the researcher can be used to explore self and other and how the sensitivities of what is explored may help reveal itself to the researcher. Participation implies empathy and entering the territory of the phenomena studied on their own terms.

Strengths: Participatory research emphasizes the importance of the consciousness of the researcher, the need for compassionate consciousness in research, and the need to tune consciousness to the uniqueness of the phenomena being investigated. The method helps researchers see how, through the human mind, the universe appreciates itself.

Weaknesses: The method is in its earliest stages of being elaborated and, as such, is chiefly prospective; there are no firm indications yet of the power of the approach in concrete situations.

Illustration: The Nobel-prize winning cytogenetic work of Barbara McClintock (previously cited elsewhere in this book) made use of principles similar to those proposed by Skolimowski (see Keller, 1983, 1985).

Resources: Skolimowski (1994, 1996).

SYNOPSES OF 17
CONVENTIONAL METHODS
OF DISCIPLINED INQUIRY

These summaries of 17 more familiar research methods or approaches may be used to address four major types of research questions (see Table 3.1 in Chapter 3 of this book). The first four approaches are useful for evaluating outcomes or consequences of various treatments or interventions. The next three approaches are useful for examining an unfolding process or for studying the naturally occurring interrelationships among several processes or factors. The next four approaches are appropriate for conceptualizing, explaining, or interpreting actions, experiences, or events. The next three approaches are appropriate for arriving at full and rich descriptions of experiences. This appendix concludes with three specialized approaches with unique purposes and unique methodological features. These special-purpose methods serve particular content areas of research. For each of the 17 approaches, one or more citations are given; these resources can be consulted as illustrations of the approaches or as sources of additional information about the respective methods. We deliberately have chosen transpersonal examples in illustrating each of the approaches.

These methods are arrayed (in Table 3.1) according to "good fits" with four major types of research questions; other arrangements are possible, however, and the present arrangement should not be taken as one that is rigidly fixed or even the best arrangement. For example, case study approaches are superb for tracking the unfolding of a process in time, and questionnaire assessments could be used to provide quantitative data for intervention or correlational studies. The 14 general approaches can be used in various creative ways or combinations to address the four major types of research questions. *Don't let them become part of a rigid system of classification or categorization. Rather, let them dance fluidly and flexibly in the service of your burning questions.*

---

1. EXPERIMENTAL DESIGNS

Essence: The experimental design has long been considered the apotheosis of scientific research methods. Independent variables are carefully operationalized and carefully manipulated in well-controlled situations. Dependent variables are carefully measured. Extraneous factors are eliminated or carefully assessed. Outcomes are subjected to well-recognized statistical analysis procedures. The designs themselves and their statistical outcomes provide automatic decision tools for determining the presence and magnitudes of various effects.

Strengths: Experimental designs have great status in the scientific community. They may provide extensive knowledge of and control of variables. Properly followed, experimental protocols can allow a researcher to make causal statements with a degree of certainty that is not possible with other approaches. Carefully following the recipe of a particular experimental design by another investigator can result in good replication outcomes. An experimental design is excellent for demonstrating the existence of an effect or a phenomenon in cases in which most artifacts or confounds are eliminated.

Weaknesses: To make them tractable to experimental manipulation and measurement, events that are studied usually must be simplified and brought into the laboratory. Thus, such events are removed from their natural, significant contexts. This can result in an artificiality, superficiality, and (unfortunately, often) triviality in what is actually studied. Treating events in isolation loses their context and their complex interactions with other events. Many important human processes cannot be readily reduced to forms that are amenable to experiments. There may be a problem in generalizing experimental findings to real-life situations. Experiments can be limited in providing an adequate understanding of important human processes and problems.

Illustration: Can reliable changes in anxiety, depression, and self-esteem levels be observed in practitioners and recipients of intercessory prayer? (ÓLaoire, 1997).

Resources: Borg and Gall (1989); Howell (1992); Huck, Cormier, and Bounds (1974); Siegel and Castellan (1988).

2. QUASI-EXPERIMENTAL DESIGNS

Essence: Quasi-experimental designs are similar to experimental designs, with one major difference: In true experimental designs, participants are assigned randomly to the various conditions. In quasi-experimental designs, such random assignment is not possible; rather, preexisting ("intact") groups are used. Quasi-experimental designs are used when circumstances disallow randomization—for example, assignment of one educational class to one condition and assignment of another entire class to another condition.

Strengths: The strengths are the same as those of experimental designs.

Weaknesses: The weaknesses are the same as those of experimental designs. In addition, the researcher must be much more careful in drawing conclusions about the effects of variables because extraneous factors associated with nonrandomized participants (e.g., preexisting differences among different intact groups) may exert great, but unknown, influences.

Illustration: What are the effects of a sustained mandala-making practice on the self-concepts of middle school students? (Stein, 1996).

Resources: Campbell and Stanley (1963); Cook and Campbell (1979).

3. SINGLE-SUBJECT DESIGNS

Essence: These designs are associated most closely with Skinnerian and behavior modification traditions. A variable or intervention is systematically introduced and withdrawn (often with many repetitions) in a single participant or a single group, and the consequences are observed.

Strengths: Baseline behaviors or activities are established well enough so that the immediate effects of interventions can be discerned straightaway without the need for statistical analysis. There is experimental, rather than statistical, control of variability. This allows direct studies of consequences of interventions or variables in individual cases. The approach is valuable for studies of behavior modification. It is useful when few participants are available. Results can be immediately obvious and compelling.

Weaknesses: Effects obtained with one participant may or may not be generalizable to other participants. The procedure is time-consuming and involves lengthy work with each participant or with a sufficient number of participants to reach trustworthy conclusions. There may be difficulties with shifting baselines; nonreversible baselines; and residual aftereffects of applying, withdrawing, or reversing variables. Ethical issues arise concerning withdrawing effective interventions.

Illustration: Is it possible to apply behavioral principles of schedules of reinforcement as helpful adjuncts to spiritual work?

Resources: Barlow and Hersen (1984); Kazdin (1982); Kratochwill (1978); Sidman (1960).

---

4. ACTION RESEARCH

Essence: In action research, the researcher has a role as an agent of social change. The researcher becomes actively involved as a facilitator and monitor of the effectiveness of a program that can have community or political consequences. One "studies what one does" and "does what one is studying."

Strengths: The approach can facilitate positive social change while allowing careful assessment of this change and of the factors that may be responsible for it, resulting in a congruency of life aims and research. Action research is practical, political, participative, collaborative, egalitarian (in that the perspectives of project participants have as much value as those of the researcher), emancipatory (in that participants are themselves responsible for important aspects and changes in the program being studied), and critical (in that the program is carefully evaluated).

Weaknesses: The investigator is not neutral and may bias outcomes or interpretations. Greater logistical and administrative support is usually required for action research than for less "practical" research projects.

Illustration: Which practices and principles are most and least effective in helping persons raise their consciousness with respect to issues of global ecology?

Resources: Argyris (1970); Carr and Kemmis (1986); Elliot (1991); Stringer (1996); Whyte (1991); Zuber-Skerritt (1992).

5. CORRELATIONAL APPROACHES

Essence: Correlational designs provide statistical methods for determining which variables covary and allow measurement of the degree to which two or more variables are interrelated. The major types of correlational analyses are bivariate correlations (Pearson and Spearman), establishing correlation matrices (in which each variable is correlated with all other variables), multiple regression analysis (in which a criterion variable is predicted on the basis of several predictor variables), discriminant function analysis (in which a categorical variable is predicted from several continuous variables), canonical correlation (in which several continuous variables are predicted from several continuous predictor variables), and factor analysis (which mathematically determines clusters of features that tend to go together or not go together on the basis of correlational patterns).

Strengths: This approach encourages examining many variables simultaneously and studying the interrelationships among many variables. Direction and degree of covariation can be quantified. Multivariate methods can provide good accounts of relationships because they deal with a great number of possibly important variables and their patterns of intercorrelation. Correlational methods allow predictions to be made and verified. There need not be any deliberate interventions or manipulations because qualities already existing in participants, in situ, are studied.

Weaknesses: It is difficult to conclude causality from correlations. In the service of this method, complex activities and processes might be broken down into overly simple components. There is some artificiality in defining and measuring variables.

Illustration: How is job satisfaction related to various measures of transpersonal self-concept (using regression analysis and factor analysis)? (Crafton, 1996).

Resources: Aiken and West (1991); Cohen and Cohen (1983); Howell (1992); Peduhuzar (1982).

6. CAUSAL-COMPARATIVE STUDIES

Essence: This approach involves searching for other ("causal") differences among groups already known to differ in some characteristic of interest. Group statistical methods (*t* tests and analysis of variance) are used to compare the presence or absence, or degrees of presence, of factors that may account for already known differences.

Strengths: The method may be used to uncover important factors that "cause" differences of interest. It may be used for naturally occurring, already existing groups. It may be used when actual manipulation of variables is not possible or feasible.

Weaknesses: It may be unwise to conclude causality because the real "cause(s)" may be among unmeasured factors. There are a lack of control and lack of knowledge of all important variables. Rival hypotheses and extraneous factors are more difficult to eliminate here than in experimental designs. The method cannot deal well with complications caused by events being multiply determined—caused by more than one variable or through complex interactions of variables.

Illustration: What are the patterns of self-esteem profiles in different groups of registered staff nurses, nurse managers, associate degree nursing faculty, and nursing students? (Snider, 1995).

Resources: Borg and Gall (1989); Howell (1992); Huck, Cormier, and Bounds (1974); Siegel and Castellan (1988).

---

7. NATURALISTIC AND FIELD STUDIES

Essence: In this approach, observations are made of a process as it occurs under natural conditions. The researcher may play the role of an outsider observer (not part of the process being studied) or may be a participant observer whose identity as a researcher is either known or unknown to other participants.

Strengths: This approach allows an investigator to observe "the real thing," rather than a more indirect or simplified indication or analogue of the actual process. The possibility of less distortion of what is studied and less artificiality can allow a greater understanding of the events, processes, and contexts involved. The approach allows the researcher to be flexible and sensitive to nuances. Because of a greater involvement in the actual process, a greater number of variables can be studied, and these can be studied for long periods. The approach is excellent for discovering something new, for being pleasantly surprised in research.

Weaknesses: There is less control. The investigator might miss unobserved but possibly important factors—that is, the participants' inner worlds are not visible (although they may be accessible via interviews, etc.).

There is an increased risk of subjectivity, observer bias, or being fooled by those being observed.

Illustration: What can a method of participant observation reveal about the practices, changes, and transformations that occur in a graduate transpersonal psychology program devoted to whole-person learning and psychospiritual development and transformation?

Resources: Jorgensen (1989); Lincoln and Guba (1985); Lonner and Berry (1986); Spradley (1980); Webb, Campbell, Schwartz, Secrest, and Grove (1981); Willems and Raush (1969).

---

8. THEORETICAL APPROACH

Essence: The heart of this approach is to develop and test higher-level theories, models, or conceptualizations in an attempt to integrate sets of findings or to explain and understand various phenomena or processes.

Strengths: The approach allows explanation and prediction. It allows the development of testable, falsifiable hypotheses and encourages new research. It interrelates and integrates previously unrelated findings. It is highly valued by the scientific community. Theories may help identify underlying mechanisms. The approach encourages feelings of understanding, closure, satisfaction, and security.

Weaknesses: Theories may be self-consistent yet incorrect. They may leave out important factors. Theorizing is difficult to do well because it requires a vast store of information, creativity, and critical thinking. Holding particular theories may blind a researcher to other, equally important, alternative understandings.

Illustration: What is the process of psychospiritual development, and its possible stages, as seen in persons throughout the ages who have had profound mystical and unitive experiences? (Underhill, 1911/1969).

Resources: Denzin and Lincoln (1994); Kuhn (1970); Popper (1968).

---

9. GROUNDED THEORY

Essence: Grounded theory (as developed by Glaser, Strauss, Corbin, and their coworkers) is an attempt to develop a set of strategies for conducting vigorous qualitative research. It uses inductive strategies for analyzing data. The researcher begins with no preexisting theory, hypothesis, or expectation of findings but rather permits a theory to emerge directly from the data—that is, the theory is grounded in the data. The aim of the approach is not only to describe well the topic of study but also to develop adequate theoretical conceptualizations of findings. The researcher begins with individual cases (chosen purposely or theoretically, rather than "randomly"), collects and analyzes data simultaneously, conceptualizes from the beginning, and allows findings and conceptualizations to grow together and cross-fertilize. One data collection episode (usually an interview) builds on the prior collections and the conceptualizations that have been developed up to that point. The researcher gathers "thick" data and makes the meanings of the participants explicit. The researcher continues this process until reaching "saturation" (is no longer learning anything new). The researcher's conceptualizations are guided by his or her theoretical sensitivity (based on unique skills and experiences).

Strengths: The method provides rigorous, systematic, and specific procedures (such as coding and memo writing) that help guarantee the development of theory that starts with and remains close to the qualitative data that are being collected. Researchers can check, refine, and develop their ideas and intuitions about their findings as the data are collected. The method has been used often in many disciplines and for the investigation of many topics.

Weaknesses: Most grounded theory works have stopped short of the professed aim of producing actual substantive, formal theories from which specific hypotheses can be developed and later tested. Usually, the work stops at a prior level of creating rich, conceptual understandings of specific lived human experiences.

Illustration: What are the qualities of self and identity in persons with chronic illness? (Charmaz, 1987, 1990, 1991, 1994).

Resources: Charmaz (1995); Glaser and Strauss (1967); Strauss and Corbin (1990).

10. HISTORICAL AND
ARCHIVAL APPROACHES

Essence: These approaches attempt to understand past events on the basis of careful and exhaustive study of extant documents, artifacts, and oral records related to the issues, events, or historical processes being studied.

Strengths: This is the only way of studying past events that are no longer available for study by present-oriented methods. The approach helps researchers understand the factors that may have contributed to past events, and these may, in turn, help illuminate present and future occurrences. Researchers may use knowledge of past mistakes to avoid similar mistakes in the present or future.

Weaknesses: Many conflicting interpretations are possible. Not all important factors may be known or understood. Historical or archival data may be incomplete or conflicting. Understanding of a unique, nonrepeating event may not be helpful in predicting or understanding subsequent events. Historical and archival analyses are difficult to do well and are time-consuming.

Illustration: How has the metaphor of light been used in various spiritual traditions, and how might the concept be useful to those seeking spiritual growth and development?

Resource: Chase (1995).

---

11. CONTENT ANALYSIS, TEXTUAL ANALYSIS, AND HERMENEUTICS

Essence: A variety of quantitative (content analysis) and qualitative methods (textual analysis and hermeneutics) can be applied to the interpretation of contemporary and historical texts. Content analysis involves systematic identification (and sometimes a systemic analysis) of predetermined categories within a text (or record of human actions), such as prose, music, speeches, audio and video recordings, or observations. Textual analysis and hermeneutics have been more frequently employed in literary analysis or exegetic analysis of sacred texts. Typically, a textual or hermeneutical analysis involves a careful analysis of the structure of implicit meanings within a text or record of human action. This analysis attempts to explicate (a) the meaning of the text for the initial audience, and possibly successive audiences, who have received the text or (b) the meaning of actions for the participants directly involved or affected. Layer upon layer, the meanings recorded in the text or recorded actions are uncovered through a careful examination of historical context, semantics, literary type and structure, societal and socioeconomic conditions, and so on. Having reconstructed as best as possible the original meanings, a formal hermeneutical analysis attempts to interpret these meanings for contemporary audiences.

Strengths: These methods are a rigorous set of procedures for exploring and interpreting the meaning of texts or record of human actions.

Weaknesses: Nonverbal factors, or other nonrecorded expressions, may be missed, resulting in incomplete or misleading understanding of intended meanings. Textual meanings are not pregiven but emerge with investigator influence. Text actors, for example, may not agree with derived interpretations.

Illustration: What is the meaning of mystical texts describing the gift of tears or sacred weeping? (Anderson, 1996).

Resources: Kvale (1983); Myerhoff (1992); Packer (1985); Packer and Addison (1989); Palmer (1969); Romanyshyn (1991); Thomas and Chambers (1989).

---

12. NARRATIVE AND DISCOURSE ANALYSES

Essence: Wide spectra of narrative and discourse analyses are now available. Generally, narrative analysis tries to tell the story or narrative, as the participants or community tells the story. Following the story line, with all its variants, is essential to the analysis. A formal analysis of semantic, linguistic, or textual structure may be presented as well. Discourse analysis presupposes that people use language to construct versions of reality and to perform social actions. A variety of procedures have been developed to identify common discourses and their functions.

Strengths: Narrative and discourse analyses allow the narratives or the discourses embedded in language to be told sufficiently and clearly, for what they are. Discourse analysis is a particularly effective tool for revealing the legitimization of power. Because a wide variety of narrative and discourse analyses are available, a researcher can choose the one best suited to the purposes of the study.

Weaknesses: Many narrative and discourse analyses available are highly technical and not in agreement with one another, conceptually or procedurally.

Illustration: What might a discursive approach teach us about an exotic "goddess possession" episode in India? (Much & Mahapatra, 1995).

Resources: Bruner (1990); DeConcini (1990); Drew (1993); Edwards and Potter (1992); Goldberg (1982); Harré and Stearns (1995); Howard (1991); Josselson and Lieblich (1993); Merriam (1988); Mishler (1986); D. Polkinghorne (1988); Potter and Wetherell (1987); Riessman (1993); Rosenwald and Ochberg (1992, 1994); Sarbin (1986); Spence (1982); Stroup (1981); Tappan and Packer (1991); Wetherell and Potter (1992).

13. CASE STUDIES AND LIFE STORIES

Essence: A case study is a detailed examination of a single participant, group, or phenomenon. In a multiple case studies project, several case studies are reported together, and features common to the cases are discussed; unique features of some cases are also reported and discussed. Cases may be presented in intact form or can be analyzed to find important themes or other salient features. Materials for preparing a case study are usually gathered via in-depth semistructured interviews or questionnaires. Life story materials typically are gathered through a series of oral reports.

Strengths: These approaches study "the real thing." They are especially useful in learning how complex processes dynamically interact in people's everyday lives. Factors that are measured more superficially through standardized assessments can be examined in greater detail and depth by case studies. The approach permits acquiring in-depth information from a small number of cases. The approach is ideal for the study of unique events, persons, or groups. Rare, extreme, diverse, typical, or especially interesting cases can be selected and studied.

Weaknesses: Often, cases are presented from the interviewee's perspective, so they are really accounts of important factors as self-perceived and self-interpreted by the interviewee. There are possibilities of subjective distortions, omissions, additions, or inaccuracies resulting from biased recall, observation, or reporting. Findings for one case may or may not be generalizable to other cases.

Illustration: How do exemplary aged women experience self-transcendence, spirituality, and meaning in their lives? (Gross, 1995).

Resources: Merriam (1988); Stake (1995); Yin (1993, 1994).

14. INTERVIEWS, QUESTIONNAIRES, AND SURVEYS

Essence: Research participants give unstructured, semistructured, or structured self-reports of the absence, presence, or degree of various experiences, behaviors, attitudes, cognitions, emotions, feelings, and so on. Surveys typically are administered to large numbers of participants using more structured formats, whereas interviews and open-ended questionnaires typically are used in deeper explorations of smaller numbers of participants.

Strengths: The researcher can collect large amounts of data quickly and efficiently by using these methods. These are effective means of learning important things about the lived worlds of human participants. There is the possibility of standardizing the data collection protocol. An interviewer can explain, probe more deeply, and facilitate the uncovering of information that would not be accessible through more superficial methods.

Weaknesses: Structured, standardized questionnaires, surveys, and assessments can, themselves, be superficial. Because these are administered during a specific time window, they can miss greater sweeps of time and also can miss the dynamic processes and social contexts that ordinarily are associated with what is being studied.

Illustration: Can a valid and reliable assessment instrument be developed for the study of spiritual bondedness and exceptional love relationships? (Young, 1992).

Resources: Fowler (1993); Mishler (1986); Sudman and Bradburn (1982).

---

15. META-ANALYSIS

Essence: Meta-analysis is the quantitative analysis of the findings of a large body of similar studies. Just as statistics can be applied to participants as the units of analysis in individual studies, so too can statistics be applied to studies themselves to provide a more "objective" alternative to the usual narrative or qualitative literature review.

Strengths: The findings of similar studies can be summarized in a quantitative manner. The various findings, as summarized by test statistics, are converted to a common metric—the *effect size.* These effect sizes can be examined statistically for consistency and for departure from mean chance expectation (effect size of zero) as a way of assessing replicability of findings in particular research areas. Effect sizes (related to the actual strength of obtained effects or differences) and their homogeneity, rather than levels of statistical significance, are emphasized. By appropriate subgroupings of studies, moderator variables can be identified and their influence assessed directly; new factors that might account for variability in study outcomes can be discovered in this way. Flaws in studies can be studied statistically to learn whether these actually influence study outcome. It is possible to estimate the number of null, unreported studies languishing in file drawers that would be necessary to cancel obtained effects. A binomial effect size display has been developed as an appealing way to present the practical import of a study or group of studies.

Weaknesses: Meta-analyses merely summarize what already has been done. Summarized studies may have undetected weaknesses or flaws. It is not surprising for small and possibly insignificant effects to accumulate to "significant" levels. Researchers should be wary of the "garbage in, garbage out" motto and also of the "bundle of sticks" analogy in which any one study may be weak but, grouped together with other weak studies, yields a strong and firm indication. It is not always easy to interpret what is really the case. Researchers can ignore important but "uncoded" features of summarized studies. Meta-analysis can trivialize research and lead to false confidence in indications of real or important effects that may be illusory. Required statistical information for preparing meta-analyses is not always available in every one of the studies the researcher wishes to summarize.

Illustration: What can meta-analysis tell us about the reality and reliability of psychic functioning occurring under conditions of relaxation and sensory restriction? (Bem & Honorton, 1994).

Resources: Glass, McGaw, and Smith (1981); Hedges and Olkin (1985); Rosenthal (1991, 1995); Wolf (1986).

---

16. PARAPSYCHOLOGICAL ASSESSMENTS AND DESIGN ISSUES

Essence: Specialized methods are used for exploring exceptional human abilities such as telepathy, clairvoyance, precognition, and psychokinesis.

Strengths: Special designs rule out artifacts such as sensory cues, rational inference, and chance coincidence. These designs are useful for demonstrating the existence or presence of these phenomena in the absence of artifacts or confounds. They permit process studies—that is, how these phenomena are related to other physical, physiological, psychological, social, and spiritual factors. The methods are appealing to the scientific community.

Weaknesses: Psychic processes are simplified, artificialized, and often trivialized to make them amenable to these laboratory methods. The methods may limit understanding of the nature of these processes in their full, spontaneous form. Events are robbed of their natural context and their meaning to the persons involved. Naturally occurring experiences are played down. Psychic phenomena are forced into prestructured molds that involve, essentially, how well the "sixth" sense can simulate the more familiar senses and motor systems; this looking only for sensorimotor redundancy may keep researchers unaware of less familiar forms of knowing, doing, or being that psychic processes might provide. Laboratory studies are unappealing to many practitioners of these processes. Field studies are rich in unknown and difficult-to-assess confounding factors; these make valid conclusions difficult.

Illustration: In which contexts do synchronicities or significant coincidences occur in everyday life, and can their incidence be influenced by means of an intentional "incubation ritual"? (Escoffon, 1994).

Resources: Edge, Morris, Palmer, and Rush (1986); Krippner (1977-1982, 1984-1994); Kurtz (1985); White (1992, 1994a); Wolman (1977).

---

17. PHYSIOLOGICAL AND BIOMEDICAL ASSESSMENTS AND DESIGN ISSUES

Essence: Specialized methods and instrumentation are used for measuring somatic concomitants or outcomes.

Strengths: These methods provide objective and reliable measures and procedures. They are highly valued by the scientific and medical communities. Findings obtained through these methods may have great relevance to medical knowledge and practice.

Weaknesses: These approaches may emphasize physical and physiological processes at the expense of experiential, cognitive, emotional, and behavioral processes. Obtained results may have statistical significance, but are they large and consistent enough to have practical significance?

Illustration: What are the electroencephalographic and subjective concomitants of shamanic drumming? (Maxfield, 1991).

Resources: Ader (1981); Andreassi (1989); Barrett (1995); Cacioppo and Tassinary (1990); Fried and Grimaldi (1993); Greenfield and Sternbach (1972); Martin and Venables (1980); Prokasy and Raskin (1973); Sidowski (1966).

CENTERS FOR
TRANSPERSONAL STUDIES

This is a partial listing of institutions that emphasize graduate-level training in transpersonal studies and in related areas. Research approaches consistent with the methods described in this book are being developed and pursued at these centers. More complete listings of transpersonal schools and programs may be obtained from the Association for Transpersonal Psychology (P.O. Box 3049, Stanford, CA 94309, http://www.igc.org/atp/) or by consulting recent issues of *Common Boundary* magazine.

Atlantic University
P.O. Box 595
67th St. & Atlantic Ave.
Virginia Beach, VA 23451
(804) 428-3588

California Institute of Integral Studies
9 Peter Yorke Way
San Francisco, CA 94109
(415) 753-6100

Institute of Transpersonal Psychology
744 San Antonio Road
Palo Alto, CA 94303
(650) 433-9200

John F. Kennedy University
12 Altarinda Road
Orinda, CA 94563
(510) 254-0105

Lesley College
29 Everett St.
Cambridge, MA 02138
(617) 349-3700

Naropa Institute
2130 Arapahoe Ave.
Boulder, CO 80302
(303) 546-3572

Ontario Institute for Studies in Education
University of Toronto
252 Bloor St. W.
Toronto, Ontario, Canada M5S 1V6
(416) 923-6641

Pacifica Graduate Institute
249 Lambert Rd.
Carpinteria, CA 93013
(805) 969-3636

Rosebridge Graduate School of Integrative Psychology
1040 Oak Grove Road #103
Concord, CA 94518
(510) 689-0560

Salve Regina University
Holistic Counseling Program
100 Ochre Road
Newport, RI 02840
(401) 847-6650

Saybrook Graduate School
450 Pacific, 3rd Floor
San Francisco, CA 94133-4640
(415) 433-9200

Sonoma State University
Department of Psychology
1801 E. Cotati Ave.
Rohnert Park, CA 94928
(707) 664-2585

Southwestern College
P.O. Box 4788
Santa Fe, NM 87502
(505) 471-5756

State University of West Georgia
Carrollton, GA 30118
(914) 967-6080

SUNY Empire State College
617 Main St.
Buffalo, NY 14203
(716) 853-7706

The Union Institute
440 East McMillaan St.
Cincinnati, OH 45206
(513) 861-6400

REFERENCES

Aanstoos, C. M. (Ed.). (1984). *Exploring the lived world: Readings in phenomenological psychology* (Studies in the Social Sciences, Vol. 23). Carrollton: West Georgia College.

Ader, R. (Ed.). (1981). *Psychoneuroimmunology.* Orlando, FL: Academic Press.

Aiken, L. S., & West, S. G. (1991). *Multiple regression.* Newbury Park, CA: Sage.

Albert, M. (1990, November/December). Urban shaman. *Yoga Journal,* 71-73.

American Psychological Association. (1987). *Casebook on ethical principles of psychologists.* Washington, DC: Author.

American Psychological Association. (1992). Ethical principles of psychologists and code of conduct. *American Psychologist, 47,* 1597-1611.

Amis, R. (1995). *A different Christianity.* Albany: State University of New York Press.

Amlani, A. (1995). *Diet and psychospiritual development: Physiological, psychological, and spiritual changes and challenges associated with lacto-ovo, vegan, and live foods diets.* Unpublished doctoral dissertation, Institute of Transpersonal Psychology, Palo Alto, CA.

Anastasi, A. (1988). *Psychological testing* (6th ed.). New York: Macmillan.

Anderson, R. (1996). Nine psycho-spiritual characteristics of spontaneous and involuntary weeping. *Journal of Transpersonal Psychology, 28*(2), 167-173.

Anderson, R. (1998). *Celtic oracles: A new system for spiritual growth and divination.* New York: Random House, Harmony Books.

Anderson, R., Braud, W., & Valle, R. (1996, April). *Transpersonal psychology: Qualitative and quantitative approaches to research.* Paper presented at the 76th annual meeting of the Western Psychological Association, San Jose, CA.

Andras, J. (1993). *A phenomenological investigation of: The decision process of a woman trusting herself in making a spiritual commitment that is contrary to the wishes of a significant person.* Unpublished doctoral dissertation, Institute of Transpersonal Psychology, Palo Alto, CA.

Andreassi, J. L. (1989). *Psychophysiology: Human behavior and physiological response* (2nd ed.). Hillsdale, NJ: Lawrence Erlbaum.

Aptheker, B. (1989). *Tapestries of life: Women's work, women's consciousness, and meaning of daily experience.* Amherst: University of Massachusetts Press.

Arao-Nguyen, S. (1997). *Ways of coming home: Filipino immigrant women's journeys to wholeness.* Unpublished doctoral dissertation, Institute of Transpersonal Psychology, Palo Alto, CA.

Argyris, C. (1970). *Intervention theory and method: A behavioral science view.* Reading, MA: Addison-Wesley.

Athenian Society for Science and Human Development and the Brahma Kumaris World Spiritual University. (1992, January). *Report on the second international symposium on science and consciousness.* Athens, Greece: Author.

Bacon, F. (1955). Novum organum [The new instrument]. In *Selected writings of Francis Bacon.* New York: Modern Library. (Original work published 1620)

Barlow, D. H. (1996). Health care policy, psychotherapy research, and the future of psychotherapy. *American Psychologist, 51,* 1050-1064.

Barlow, D. H., & Hersen, M. (1984). *Single case experimental designs: Strategies for studying behavior change* (2nd ed.). Elmsford, NY: Pergamon.

Barrell, J. J., Aanstoos, C., Richards, A. C., & Arons, M. (1987). Human science research methods. *Journal of Humanistic Psychology, 27*(4), 424-457.

Barrell, J., & Price, D. (1975). The perception of first and second pain as a function of psychological set. *Perception and Psychophysics, 17,* 163-166.

Barrett, K. (1996). A phenomenological study of channeling: The experience of transmitting information from a source perceived as paranormal (Doctoral dissertation, Institute of Transpersonal Psychology, Palo Alto, 1996). *Dissertation Abstracts International, 21,* R2503.

Barrett, P. (1995). Psychophysiological methods. In S. Breakwell, S. Hammond, & C. Fife-Schaw (Eds.), *Research methods in psychology* (pp. 160-173). Thousand Oaks, CA: Sage.

Barrow, J. D., & Tipler, F. J. (1986). *The anthropic cosmological principle.* Oxford, UK: Oxford University Press.

Batey, B. (1993). My experience of the transcendent and its integration into my life. *1993 Annual Conference Proceedings of the Academy of Religion and Psychical Research,* 16-18.

Belanger, S. L. (1995). *Bridging realities: The shamanic journey to the healer archetype Chiron.* Unpublished master's thesis, Institute of Transpersonal Psychology, Palo Alto, CA.

Beloff, J. (1990). *The relentless question: Reflections on the paranormal.* Jefferson, NC: McFarland.

Bem, D. J., & Honorton, C. (1994). Does psi exist? Replicable evidence for an anomalous process of information transfer. *Psychological Bulletin, 115,* 4-18.

Bennett, H. Z. (1994). *The lens of perception* (2nd ed.). Berkeley, CA: Celestial Arts.

Bernd, E., Jr. (1978). *Relax.* Orlando, FL: Greun Madainn Foundation.

Berry, D. S., & Pennebaker, J. W. (1993). Nonverbal and verbal emotional expression and health. *Psychotherapy and Psychosomatics, 59,* 18.

Berry, J. W., Kim, U., Power, S., Young, M., & Bujaki, M. (1989). Acculturation attitudes in plural societies. *Applied Psychology: An International Review, 38*(2), 185-206.

Berry, T. (1990). *The dream of the earth.* San Francisco: Sierra Club Books.

Bird, C. (1979). *The divining hand.* New York: E. P. Dutton.

Boff, L. (1993). *Liberating grace* (P. Hughes, Trans.). Maryknoll, NY: Orbis.

Bohm, D. (1980). *Wholeness and the implicate order.* London: Routledge & Kegan Paul.

Bolen, J. S. (1984). *Goddesses in everywoman.* New York: Harper & Row.

Bolen, J. S. (1989). *Gods in everyman.* New York: Harper & Row.

Bonaventura. (1953). *The mind's road to God* (G. Boas, Trans.). New York: Liberal Arts Press. (Original work written 1259)

Bord, J. (1975). *Mazes and labyrinths of the world.* New York: E. P. Dutton.

Borg, W. R., & Gall, M. D. (1989). *Educational research: An introduction* (5th ed.). White Plains, NY: Longman.

Braud, W. G. (1975). Psi conducive states. *Journal of Communication, 25,* 142-152.

Braud, W. G. (1978). Psi conducive conditions: Explorations and interpretations. In B. Shapin & L. Coly (Eds.), *Psi and states of awareness* (pp. 1-41). New York: Parapsychology Foundation.

Braud, W. G. (1982). Lability and inertia in psychic functioning. In B. Shapin & L. Coly (Eds.), *Concepts and theories of parapsychology* (pp. 1-36). New York: Parapsychology Foundation.

Braud, W. G. (1990). Distant mental influence of rate of hemolysis of human red blood cells. *Journal of the American Society for Psychical Research, 84,* 1-24.

Braud, W. G. (1992). Human interconnectedness: Research indications. *ReVision: A Journal of Consciousness and Transformation, 14,* 140-148.

Braud, W. G. (1993). On the use of living target systems in distant mental influence research. In B. Shapin & L. Coly (Eds.), *Psi research methodology: A re-examination* (pp. 149-188). New York: Parapsychology Foundation.

Braud, W. G. (1994a). Can our intentions interact directly with the physical world? *European Journal of Parapsychology, 10,* 78-90.

Braud, W. G. (1994b). Honoring our natural experiences. *Journal of the American Society for Psychical Research, 88*(3), 293-308.

Braud, W. G. (1994c). Reaching for consciousness: Expansions and complements. *Journal of the American Society for Psychical Research, 88*(3), 185-206.

Braud, W. G. (1994d). The role of the mind in the physical world: A psychologist's view. *European Journal of Parapsychology, 10,* 66-77.

Braud, W. G. (1995a). An experience of timelessness. *Exceptional Human Experience, 13,* 64-66.

Braud, W. G. (1995b). Response to White's commentary on "an experience of timelessness." *Exceptional Human Experience, 13,* 67-68.

Braud, W. G., & Schlitz, M. J. (1989). A methodology for the objective study of transpersonal imagery. *Journal of Scientific Exploration, 3,* 43-63.

Braud, W. G., & Schlitz, M. J. (1991). Consciousness interactions with remote biological systems: Anomalous intentionality effects. *Subtle Energies, 2,* 1-46.

Braud, W. G., Shafer, D., & Andrews, S. (1993a). Further studies of autonomic detection of remote staring: Replication, new control procedures, and personality correlates. *Journal of Parapsychology, 57,* 391-409.

Braud, W. G., Shafer, D., & Andrews, S. (1993b). Reactions to an unseen gaze (remote attention): A review, with new data on autonomic staring detection. *Journal of Parapsychology, 57,* 373-390.

Braud, W. G., Shafer, D., McNeill, K., & Guerra, V. (1995). Attention focusing facilitated through remote mental interaction. *Journal of the American Society for Psychical Research, 89,* 103-115.

Briggs, J. (1990). *Fire in the crucible.* Los Angeles: Tarcher.

British Psychological Society. (1993). *The BPS code of conduct, ethical principles and guidelines.* Leichester, UK: Author.

Bruner, J. (1986). *Actual minds, possible worlds.* Cambridge, MA: Harvard University Press.

Bruner, J. (1990). *Acts of meaning.* Cambridge, MA: Harvard University Press.

Burnshaw, S. (1991). *The seamless web.* New York: George Braziller. (Original work published 1970)

Cacioppo, J. T., & Tassinary, L. G. (1990). *Principles of psychophysiology: Physical, social, and inferential elements.* Cambridge, UK: Cambridge University Press.

Campbell, D. T., & Stanley, J. C. (1963). *Experimental and quasi-experimental designs for research.* Chicago: Rand McNally.

Campbell, J. (1968). *Hero with a thousand faces.* Princeton, NJ: Princeton University Press.

Capra, F. (1983). *The turning point.* London: Bantam.

Carr, W., & Kemmis, S. (1986). *Becoming critical: Education, knowledge and action research.* London: Falmer.

Charmaz, K. (1987). Struggling for a self: Identity levels of the chronically ill. In J. Roth & P. Conrad (Eds.), *Research in the sociology of health care: The experience and management of chronic illness* (Vol. 6, pp. 283-307). Greenwich, CT: JAI.

Charmaz, K. (1990). Discovering chronic illness: Using grounded theory. *Social Science and Medicine, 30,* 1161-1172.

Charmaz, K. (1991). *Good days, bad days: The self in chronic illness and time.* New Brunswick, NJ: Rutgers University Press.

Charmaz, K. (1994). Identity dilemmas of chronically ill men. *Sociological Quarterly, 35,* 269-288.

Charmaz, K. (1995). Grounded theory. In J. Smith, R. Harré, & L. Van Langerhove (Eds.), *Rethinking methods in psychology* (pp. 27-49). Thousand Oaks, CA: Sage.

Chase, J. (1995). Historical analysis in psychological research. In G. Breakwell, S. Hammond, & C. Fife-Schaw (Eds.), *Research methods in psychology* (pp. 314-326). Thousand Oaks, CA: Sage.

Chodorow, J. (1988). Dance/movement as active imagination: Origins, theory, practice (Doctoral dissertation, Union Graduate School, 1988). *Dissertation Abstracts International, 49*(10), SECB, PP4530.

Christ, C. (1980). *Diving deep and surfacing: Women writers on a spiritual quest* (2nd ed.). Boston: Beacon.

Clements, J. (1994-1995, Winter). Organic research: An introduction. *ITP Dissertation Express Newsletter, 2*(2), 6-9.

Cohen, J., & Cohen, P. (1983). *Applied multiple correlation/correlation analysis for the behavioral sciences* (2nd ed.). Hillsdale, NY: Lawrence Erlbaum.

Cohen, L. H., Sargent, M. M., & Sechrest, L. B. (1986). Use of psychotherapy research by professional psychologists. *American Psychologist, 41,* 198-206.

Colaizzi, P. R. (1978). Psychological research as the phenomenologist views it. In R. S. Valle & M. King (Eds.), *Existential-phenomenological alternatives for psychology*. New York: Oxford University Press.

Comas-Díaz, L. (1994). An integrative approach. In L. Comas-Díaz & B. Greene (Eds.), *Women of color: Integrating ethnic and gender identities in psychotherapy*. New York: Guilford.

Comfort, A. (1984). *Reality and empathy*. Albany: State University of New York Press.

Cook, T. D., & Campbell, D. T. (1979). *Quasi-experimentation: Design and analysis issues for field settings*. Chicago: Rand McNally.

Crafton, D. (1996). *The relationship of a transpersonal self concept to job satisfaction*. Unpublished doctoral dissertation, Institute of Transpersonal Psychology, Palo Alto, CA.

Craighead, M. (1993). Drawing your own story. In C. Simpkinson & A. Simpkinson (Eds.), *Sacred stories: A celebration of the power of stories to transform and heal*. New York: HarperCollins.

Csikszentmihalyi, M. (1990). *Flow: The psychology of optimal experience*. New York: Harper & Row.

Davids, T. W. R. (1911). Does Al Ghazzali use an Indian metaphor? *Journal of the Royal Asiatic Society* (London), 200-201.

de la Peña, A. M. (1983). *The psychobiology of cancer*. New York: Praeger.

DeConcini, B. (1990). *Narrative remembering*. Lanham, MD: University Press of America.

Denzin, N. K., & Lincoln, Y. S. (Eds.). (1994). *Handbook of qualitative research*. Thousand Oaks, CA: Sage.

Dewey, J. (1984). The quest for certainty. In J. Boydston (Ed.), *John Dewey: The later works, 1925-1953* (Vol. 4, pp. 3-250). Carbondale: Southern Illinois University Press. (Original work published 1929)

Dossey, L. (1989). *Recovering the soul: A scientific and spiritual search*. New York: Bantam.

Drew, N. (1993). Reenactment interviewing: A methodology for phenomenological research. *Image: Journal of Nursing Scholarship, 25*(4), 345-351.

Driver, T. F. (1991). *The magic of ritual: Our need for liberating rites that transform our lives and our communities*. San Francisco: Harper.

Edge, H., Morris, R., Palmer, J., & Rush, J. (1986). *Foundations of parapsychology: Exploring the boundaries of human capability*. Boston: Routledge & Kegan Paul.

Edwards, D., & Potter, J. (1992). *Discursive psychology*. London: Sage.

Einstein, A. (1954). *Ideas and opinions* (S. Bargmann, Trans.). New York: Crown.

Elite, O. (1993). *On the experience of being voluntarily silent for a period of four or more days: A phenomenological inquiry*. Unpublished doctoral dissertation, California Institute of Integral Studies, San Francisco.

Elliot, J. (1991). *Action research for educational change*. Milton Keynes, UK: Open University Press.

Epstein, M. (1995). *Thoughts without a thinker: Psychotherapy from a Buddhist perspective*. New York: Basic Books.

Escoffon, D. (1994). *Synchronicity or meaningful coincidences: Quantification of feeling states, circumstances, and attributing causes, and an experiment with "synchronicity incubation."* Unpublished doctoral dissertation, Institute of Transpersonal Psychology, Palo Alto, CA.

Estés, C. P. (1992). *Women who run with the wolves: Myths and stories of the wild woman archetype.* New York: Ballantine.

Ettling, D. (1994). *A phenomenological study of the creative arts as a pathway to embodiment in the personal transformation process of nine women.* Unpublished doctoral dissertation, Institute of Transpersonal Psychology, Palo Alto, CA.

Ettling, D., & Clark, R. (1996). *Crossing the borders.* Unpublished manuscript.

European Transpersonal Association links groups from thirteen nations. (1997, Spring). *ATP Newsletter,* 4-5.

Fagen, N. (1995). *Elaborating dreams through creative expressions: Experiences, accompaniments, and perceived effects.* Unpublished doctoral dissertation, Institute of Transpersonal Psychology, Palo Alto, CA.

Fahler, J., & Osis, K. (1966). Checking for awareness of hits in a precognition experiment with hypnotized subjects. *Journal of the American Society for Psychical Research, 60,* 340-346.

Feinstein, D., & Krippner, S. (1988). *Personal mythology.* Los Angeles: Tarcher.

Feyerabend, P. (1975). *Against method.* London: Verso.

Fiore, E. (1987). *The unquiet dead: A psychologist treats spirit possession.* New York: Ballantine.

Fisher, J. (1997). *Dance as a spiritual practice: A phenomenological and feminist investigation of the experience of being-movement.* Unpublished doctoral dissertation, Institute of Transpersonal Psychology, Palo Alto, CA.

Fonow, M. M., & Cook, J. A. (1991). *Beyond methodology: Feminist scholarship as lived research.* Bloomington: Indiana University Press.

Fontana, D., & Slack, I. (1996, June). The need for transpersonal psychology. *The Psychologist,* 267-269.

Fowler, F. J. (1993). *Survey research methods* (2nd ed.). Newbury Park, CA: Sage.

Fox, M. (1985). *Illuminations of Hildegard of Bingen.* Santa Fe, NM: Bear & Company.

Freud, S. (1952a). A general introduction to psycho-analysis (J. Riviere, Trans.). In R. Hutchins (Ed.), *The major works of Sigmund Freud* (pp. 445-638). Chicago: Encyclopaedia Britannica. (Original work published 1917)

Freud, S. (1952b). The origin and development of psycho-analysis (H. W. Chase, Trans.). In R. Hutchins (Ed.), *The major works of Sigmund Freud* (pp. 1-20). Chicago: Encyclopaedia Britannica. (Original work published 1910)

Freud, S. (1978). *The question of lay analysis.* New York: Norton. (Original work published 1926)

Freud, S., & Breuer, J. (1957). *Studies on hysteria.* New York: Basic Books. (Original work published 1895)

Fried, R., & Grimaldi, J. (1993). *The psychology and physiology of breathing.* London: Plenum.

Gelpi, B. C., & Gelpi, A. (Eds.). (1993). *Adrienne Rich's poetry and prose.* New York: Norton.

Gendlin, E. (1978). *Focusing.* New York: Everest House.

George, L. (1995). *Alternate realities.* New York: Facts on File.

Gilligan, C. (1982). *In a different voice.* Cambridge, MA: Harvard University Press.

Giorgi, A. (1983). Concerning the possibility of phenomenological psychological research. *Journal of Phenomenological Psychology, 14,* 129-170.

Giorgi, A. (1985). Sketch of a psychological method. In A. Giorgi (Ed.), *Phenomenology and psychological research*. Pittsburgh, PA: Duquesne University Press.

Glaser, B. G. (1978). *Theoretical sensitivity*. Mill Valley, CA: Sociology Press.

Glaser, B. G., & Strauss, A. L. (1967). *The discovery of grounded theory*. Chicago: Aldine.

Glass, G. V., McGaw, B., & Smith, M. L. (1981). *Meta-analysis in social research*. Beverly Hills, CA: Sage.

Global Co-Operation for a Better World. (1990, January). *Report on an international symposium on science, technology, and the environment: A case for global co-operation*. Athens, Greece: Author.

Goldberg, M. (1982). *Narrative and theology: A critical introduction*. Nashville, TN: Abington.

Goldfried, M. R., & Wolfe, B. E. (1996). Psychotherapy practice and research: Repairing a strained alliance. *American Psychologist, 51*, 1007-1016.

Goodbread, J. (1987). *The dreambody tool kit*. New York: Routledge & Kegan Paul.

Goodfield, J. (1981). *An imagined world: A story of scientific discovery*. New York: Harper & Row.

Greenfield, N., & Sternbach, R. (Eds.). (1972). *Handbook of psychophysiology*. New York: Holt, Rinehart & Winston.

Griffin, D. R. (Ed.). (1988). *The reenchantment of science: Postmodern proposals*. Albany: State University of New York Press.

Grof, S. (1985). *Beyond the brain*. New York: State University of New York Press.

Grof, S., & Grof, C. (Eds.). (1989). *Spiritual emergency*. Los Angeles: Tarcher.

Gross, D. (1995). *Harvesting the wisdom of the elders: A study of the lives of seven exemplary aged women*. Unpublished doctoral dissertation, Institute of Transpersonal Psychology, Palo Alto, CA.

Grosso, M. (1994). The status of survival research: Evidence, problems, paradigms. *Noetic Sciences Review, 32*, 12-20.

Guba, E. G. (Ed.). (1990). *The paradigm dialog*. Newbury Park, CA: Sage.

Gutierrez, G. (1990). *The truth shall make you free: Confrontations* (M. J. O'Conell, Trans.). Maryknoll, NY: Orbis.

Gutierrez, G. (1994). *A theology of liberation: History, politics, and salvation* (C. Inda & J. Eagleson, Trans. and Ed.). Maryknoll, NY: Orbis.

Hallman, R. J. (1963). The necessary and sufficient conditions of creativity. *Journal of Humanistic Psychology, 3*(14), 14-27.

Harber, K. D., & Pennebaker, J. W. (1992). Overcoming traumatic memories. In S. E. Christianson (Ed.), *The handbook of emotion and memory: Research and theory*. Hillsdale, NJ: Lawrence Erlbaum.

Hardy, A. (1979). *The spiritual nature of man*. Oxford, UK: Clarendon.

Harman, W. W. (1991). *A re-examination of the metaphysical foundations of modern science*. Sausalito, CA: Institute of Noetic Sciences.

Harman, W. W. (1992). Science and religion. In J. Mishlove (Ed.), *Thinking allowed: Conversations on the leading edge of knowledge* (pp. 97-104). Tulsa, OK: Council Oak Books.

Harman, W. W., & DeQuincey, C. (1994). *The scientific exploration of consciousness: Toward an adequate epistemology*. Sausalito, CA: Institute of Noetic Sciences.

Harré, R., & Stearns, P. (1995). *Discursive psychology in practice*. Thousand Oaks, CA: Sage.

Heard, G. (Ed.). (1949). *Prayers and meditations*. New York: Harper.

Hedges, L. V., & Olkin, I. (1985). *Statistical methods for meta-analysis*. Orlando, FL: Academic Press.

Heron, J. (1992). *Feeling and personhood: Psychology in another key*. London: Sage.

Heron, J., & Reason, P. (Eds.). (1985). *Whole person medicine*. London: British Postgraduate Medical Federation, University of London.

Hillman, J. (1995). *The thought of the heart and the soul of the world*. Woodstock, CT: Spring.

Hoffman, B., & Dukas, H. (1973). *Albert Einstein, creator and rebel*. New York: New American Library.

Hofstadter, D. R. (1980). *Gödel, Escher, Bach: An eternal golden braid*. New York: Vintage.

Hollon, S. D. (1996). The efficacy and effectiveness of psychotherapy relative to medications. *American Psychologist, 51*, 1025-1030.

Holman, C. H. (1972). *A handbook to literature* (3rd ed.). Indianapolis, IN: Bobbs-Merrill.

Honorton, C. (1970). Effects of feedback on discrimination between correct and incorrect ESP responses. *Journal of the American Society for Psychical Research, 64*, 404-410.

Honorton, C. (1971). Effects of feedback on discrimination between correct and incorrect ESP responses: A replication study. *Journal of the American Society for Psychical Research, 65*, 155-161.

Howard, G. S. (1991). Cultural tales: A narrative approach to thinking, cross-cultural psychology and psychotherapy. *American Psychologist, 46*(3), 187-197.

Howard, K. I., Moras, K., Brill, P. L., Martinovich, Z., & Lutz, W. (1996). Evaluation of psychotherapy: Efficacy, effectiveness, and patient progress. *American Psychologist, 51*, 1059-1064.

Howell, D. C. (1992). *Statistical methods for psychology* (3rd ed.). Belmont, CA: Duxbury.

Howes, D. (Ed.). (1991). *The varieties of sensory experience: A sourcebook in the anthropology of the senses*. Toronto, Ontario, Canada: University of Toronto Press.

Huck, S. W., Cormier, W. H., & Bounds, W. G. (1974). *Reading statistics and research*. New York: HarperCollins.

Huxley, A. (1970). *The perennial philosophy*. New York: Harper & Row.

Ibn Al Arabi, M. (1981). *Journey to the lord of power* (R. Harris, Trans.). New York: Inner Traditions.

Ikemi, Y., & Nakagawa, S. (1962). A psychosomatic study of contagious dermatitis. *Kyushu Journal of Medical Science, 13*, 335-350.

Inglis, B. (with West, R.). (1987). *The unknown guest*. London: Chatto & Windus.

Jacobson, N. S., & Christensen, A. (1996). Studying the effectiveness of psychotherapy: How well can clinical trials do the job? *American Psychologist, 51*, 1031-1039.

James, W. (1902). *The varieties of religious experience*. New York: Random House.

James, W. (1911). *Some problems in philosophy*. New York: Longmans, Green.

James, W. (1956). On some Hegelisms. In *The will to believe and other essays in popular philosophy* (pp. 263-298). New York: Dover. (Original work published 1882)

James, W. (1958). *The varieties of religious experience*. New York: New American Library. (Original work published 1902)

James, W. (1975). *Pragmatism*. Cambridge, MA: Harvard University Press. (Original work published 1907)

James, W. (1976). *Essays in radical empiricism*. Cambridge, MA: Harvard University Press. (Original work published 1912)

James, W. (1977). Final impressions of a psychical researcher. In J. McDermott (Ed.), *The writings of William James: A comprehensive edition* (pp. 787-799). Chicago: University of Chicago Press. (Original work published 1909)

Johnson, R. A. (1986). *Inner work*. San Francisco: Harper & Row.

Jones, D. E. (1979). *Visions of time*. Wheaton, IL: Theosophical Publishing House.

Jorgensen, D. L. (1989). *Participant observation: A methodology for human studies*. Newbury Park, CA: Sage.

Josephson, B. D., & Rubik, B. A. (1992). The challenge of consciousness research. *Frontier Perspectives, 3*(1), 15-19.

Josselson, R., & Lieblich, A. (1993). *The narrative study of lives*. Newbury Park, CA: Sage.

Jung, C. G. (1965). *Memories, dreams, reflections*. New York: Vintage.

Jung, C. G. (1977). *Psychology and the occult* (R. F. C. Hull, Trans.). Princeton, NJ: Princeton University Press.

Jung, C. G. (1993). Foreword. In E. Neuman, *The origins and history of consciousness* (pp. xiii-xiv). Princeton, NJ: Princeton University Press.

Kadloubovsky, E., & Palmer, G. E. H. (Trans.). (1992). *Writings from the Philokalia on prayer of the heart*. London: Faber & Faber.

Kalff, M. D. (1971). *Mirror of a child's psyche*. San Francisco: Browser.

Kanthamani, H., & Kelly, E. F. (1974). Awareness of success in an exceptional subject. *Journal of Parapsychology, 38*, 355-382.

Kazdin, A. E. (1982). *Single-case research designs: Methods for clinical and applied settings*. New York: Oxford University Press.

Keats, J. (1988). Ode on a Grecian urn. In J. Barnard (Ed.), *John Keats: The complete poems* (3rd ed., p. 346). London: Penguin.

Keller, E. F. (1983). *A feeling for the organism: The life and work of Barbara McClintock*. New York: Freeman.

Keller, E. F. (1985). *Reflections on gender and science*. New Haven, CT: Yale University Press.

Koff-Chapin, D. (1996). *Drawing out your soul: The touch drawing handbook*. Langley, WA: Center for Touch Drawing.

Kratochwill, T. R. (1978). *Single-subject research: Strategies for evaluating change*. New York: Academic Press.

Kremer, J. W. (1988). Tales of power. In R. Heinz (Ed.), *Proceedings of the Fourth International Conference on the Study of Shamanism and Alternative Modes of Healing*, 31-48.

Krippner, S. (Ed.). (1977-1982). *Advances in parapsychological research* (Vols. 1-3). New York: Plenum.

Krippner, S. (Ed.). (1984-1994). *Advances in parapsychological research* (Vols. 4-7). Jefferson, NC: McFarland.

Krippner, S. (1984). A systems approach to psi research based on Jungian typology. In R. White & R. Broughton (Eds.), *Research in parapsychology 1983* (pp. 153-166). Metuchen, NJ: Scarecrow.

Kuhn, T. S. (1970). *The structure of scientific revolutions* (2nd ed.). Chicago: University of Chicago Press.

Kurtz, P. (Ed.). (1985). *A skeptic's handbook of parapsychology.* Buffalo, NY: Prometheus.

Kvale, S. (1983). The qualitative research interview: A phenomenological and hermeneutical mode of understanding. *Journal of Phenomenological Psychology, 14,* 171-196.

Kvale, S. (Ed.). (1992). *Psychology and postmodernism.* Newbury Park, CA: Sage.

LaBerge, S. (1985). *Lucid dreaming.* Los Angeles: Tarcher.

LaBerge, S., & Rheingold, H. (1990). *Exploring the world of lucid dreaming.* New York: Ballantine.

Lajoie, D. H., & Shapiro, S. I. (1992). Definitions of transpersonal psychology: The first twenty-three years. *Journal of Transpersonal Psychology, 24*(1), 79-98.

Lakatos, I. (1978). *The methodology of scientific research programmes* (Philosophical Papers, Vol. 1). Cambridge, UK: Cambridge University Press.

Landis, C., & Mettler, F. (1964). *The varieties of psychopathological experience.* New York: Holt, Rinehart & Winston.

Latourette, K. S. (1975). *A history of Christianity, Volume I: Beginnings to 1500.* New York: Harper & Row.

LeShan, L. (1976). *Alternate realities.* New York: M. Evans.

Lincoln, Y., & Guba, E. (1985). *Naturalistic inquiry.* Beverly Hills, CA: Sage.

Loewi, O. (1960). An autobiographical sketch. *Perspectives in Biology and Medicine, 4,* 17.

Lonner, W. J., & Berry, J. W. (1986). *Field methods in cross cultural research.* Beverly Hills, CA: Sage.

Lorimer, D. (1988, November). *Towards a new science: A critical appraisal of scientific knowledge.* Paper presented at the 17th annual conference on the Unity of the Sciences, Los Angeles.

Maas, C. (1998). *Sense of humor and spirituality as correlates of psychological well-being in HIV+ and HIV– males.* Unpublished doctoral dissertation, Institute of Transpersonal Psychology, Palo Alto, CA.

Mandelbrot, B. (1982). *The fractal geometry of nature.* San Francisco: Freeman.

Martin, L., & Venables, P. (Eds.). (1980). *Techniques in psychophysiology.* New York: John Wiley.

Maslow, A. H. (1963). Fusions of facts and values. *American Journal of Psychoanalysis, 23,* 117-181.

Maslow, A. H. (1966). *The psychology of science: A reconnaissance.* New York: Harper & Row.

Maslow, A. H. (1968). *Toward a psychology of being* (2nd ed.). Princeton, NJ: Van Nostrand Reinhold.

Maslow, A. H. (1969). The farther reaches of human nature. *Journal of Transpersonal Psychology, 1*(1), 1-9.

Maslow, A. H. (1970). *Motivation and personality* (2nd ed.). New York: Harper & Row.

Maslow, A. H. (1971). *The farther reaches of human nature.* New York: Viking.

Masters, R. E. L., & Houston, J. (1966). *The varieties of psychedelic experience.* New York: Dell.

Mavromatis, A. (1987). *Hypnagogia.* New York: Routledge & Kegan Paul.

Maxfield, M. C. (1991). *Effects of rhythmic drumming on EEG and subjective experience.* Unpublished doctoral dissertation, Institute of Transpersonal Psychology, Palo Alto, CA.

May, H., & Metzger, B. (Eds.). (1977). *The new Oxford annotated Bible with the Apocrypha: Revised standard version.* New York: Oxford University Press.

McLean, T. (1997, Winter). Establishing the Japanese Transpersonal Association. *ATP Newsletter,* 3-4.

Meier, F. (1982). The problem of nature in the esoteric monism of Islam. In J. Campbell (Ed.), *Spirit and nature: Papers from the Eranos yearbooks* (Bollingen Series Vol. 30, No. 1, pp. 166-170). Princeton, NJ: Princeton/Bollingen.

Mellick, J. (1996). *The natural artistry of dreams.* Berkeley, CA: Conari.

Merrell-Wolff, F. (1973). *The philosophy of consciousness without an object.* New York: Julian.

Merriam, S. B. (1988). *Case study research in education.* San Francisco: Jossey-Bass.

Mindell, A. (1982). *Dreambody.* Santa Monica, CA: Sigo.

Minh-ha, T. T. (1989). *Woman, native, other.* Indianapolis: Indiana University Press.

Mishara, A. L. (1995). Narrative and psychotherapy: The phenomenology of healing. *American Journal of Psychotherapy, 49*(2), 180-195.

Mishler, E. (1986). *Research interviewing: Context and narrative.* Cambridge, MA: Harvard University Press.

Mishlove, J. (1993). *The roots of consciousness* (Rev. ed.). Tulsa, OK: Council Oak Books.

Mitchell, J. (1975). A psychic probe of Mercury. *Psychic, 6*(2), 17-21.

Mitchell, S. (Ed. and Trans.). (1989). *The selected poetry of Rainer Maria Rilke.* New York: Vintage International/Random House.

Mitroff, I. I., & Kilman, R. H. (1978). *Methodological approaches to social science.* San Francisco: Jossey-Bass.

Moffitt, J. (1971). To look at any thing. In J. Mecklenberger & G. Simmons (Eds.), *Since feeling is first* (p. 149). Glenview, IL: Scott, Foresman.

Monette, D., Sullivan, T., & DeJong, C. (1990). *Applied social research: Tool for the human services* (2nd ed.). New York: Holt, Rinehart & Winston.

Moody, R. A. (1987). *Elvis after life.* Atlanta, GA: Peachtree.

Moody, R. A. (with Perry, P.). (1993). *Reunions.* New York: Villard.

Moon, B. (1991). *An encyclopedia of archetypal symbolism.* Boston: Shambhala.

Morrill, B. (1994). *Quest for wholeness: The individuation process of African American women: Seven case studies.* Unpublished doctoral dissertation, Institute of Transpersonal Psychology, Palo Alto, CA.

Morrow-Bradley, C., & Elliott, R. (1986). Utilization of psychotherapy research by practicing psychotherapists. *American Psychologist, 41,* 188-197.

Morse, J. M. (1991). *Qualitative nursing research.* Newbury Park, CA: Sage.

Morse, J. M. (1992). *Qualitative health research.* Newbury Park, CA: Sage.

Moustakas, C. (1961). *Loneliness.* Englewood Cliffs, NJ: Prentice Hall.

Moustakas, C. (1972). *Loneliness and love.* Englewood Cliffs, NJ: Prentice Hall.

Moustakas, C. (1975). *The touch of loneliness.* Englewood Cliffs, NJ: Prentice Hall.

Moustakas, C. (1990). *Heuristic research: Design, methodology, and applications.* Newbury Park, CA: Sage.

Moustakas, C. (1994). *Phenomenological research methods.* Thousand Oaks, CA: Sage.

Moustakas, C., & Douglass, B. G. (1985). Heuristic inquiry: The internal search to know. *Journal of Humanistic Psychology, 25*(3), 39-55.

Much, N. C., & Mahapatra, M. (1995). Constructing divinity. In R. Harré & P. Stearns (Eds.), *Discursive psychology in practice* (pp. 55-86). Thousand Oaks, CA: Sage.

Murphy, M., & White, R. A. (1995). *In the zone*. New York: Penguin Arkana.

Myerhoff, B. (1992). *Remembered lives*. Ann Arbor: University of Michigan Press.

Nagel, E., & Newman, J. R. (1958). *Gödel's proof*. New York: New York University Press.

Nalimov, V. V., & Drogalina, J. A. (1996). The transpersonal movement: A Russian perspective on its emergence and prospects for further development. *Journal of Transpersonal Psychology, 28*(1), 49-62.

Neher, A. (1980). *The psychology of transcendence*. Englewood Cliffs, NJ: Prentice Hall.

Newman, F. L., & Tejeda, M. J. (1996). The need for research that is designed to support decisions in the delivery of mental health services. *American Psychologist, 51*, 1040-1049.

Newton, S. (1996). *Exploring the interstices: The space between in the body disciplines of aikido and fencing*. Unpublished doctoral dissertation, Institute of Transpersonal Psychology, Palo Alto, CA.

Nielsen, J. M. (1990). *Feminist research methods: Exemplary readings in the social sciences*. Boulder, CO: Westview.

Nigg, W. (1962). *The heretics*. New York: Dorset.

Nunnally, J. C., & Bernstein, I. H. (1994). *Psychometric theory* (3rd ed.). New York: McGraw-Hill.

ÓLaoire, S. (1997). An experimental study of the effects of distant, intercessory prayer on self-esteem, anxiety, and depression. *Alternative Therapies in Health and Medicine, 3*(6), 38-53.

Otto, H. A. (1967). The Minerva experience: Initial report. In J. Bugental (Ed.), *Challenges of humanistic psychology* (pp. 119-124). New York: McGraw-Hill.

Packer, M. J. (1985). Hermeneutic inquiry in the study of human conduct. *American Psychologist, 40*(10), 1081-1093.

Packer, M. J., & Addison, R. B. (Eds.). (1989). *Entering the circle: Hermeneutic investigation in psychology*. Albany: State University of New York Press

Palmer, G. (1998). *Disclosure and assimilation of exceptional human experiences: Meaningful, transformative, and spiritual aspects*. Unpublished doctoral dissertation, Institute of Transpersonal Psychology, Palo Alto, CA.

Palmer, G. E. H., Sherrard, P., & Ware, K. (Trans. and Eds.). (1983-1995). *The Philokalia: The complete text* (Vols. 1-3). London: Faber & Faber.

Palmer, R. E. (1969). *Hermeneutics*. Evanston, IL: Northwestern University Press.

Paris, G. (1986). *Pagan meditations*. Woodstock, CT: Spring.

Parse, R. R. (1996). The human becoming theory: Challenges in practice and research. *Nursing Science Quarterly, 9*(2), 55-60.

Peduhuzar, E. J. (1982). *Multiple regression in behavioral research: Explanation and prediction* (2nd ed.). New York: Holt, Rinehart & Winston.

Peirce, C. S. (1878, January). How to make our ideas clear. *Popular Science Monthly, 12*, 286-302.

Peirce, C. S. (1962). The fixation of belief. In R. Davidson (Ed.), *The search for meaning in life: Readings in philosophy* (pp. 254-264). New York: Holt, Rinehart & Winston. (Original work published 1877)

Pennebaker, J. W. (1995). *Emotion, disclosure, & health.* Washington, DC: American Psychological Association.

Pennebaker, J. W., Barger, S. D., & Tiebout, J. (1989). Disclosure of traumas and health among holocaust survivors. *Psychosomatic Medicine, 50,* 577-589.

Pennebaker, J. W., Hughes, C. F., & O'Heeron, R. C. (1987). The psychophysiology of confession: Linking inhibitory and psychosomatic processes. *Journal of Personality and Social Psychology, 52,* 781-793.

Pennebaker, J. W., Kiecolt-Glaser, J. K., & Glaser, R. (1988). Disclosure of traumas and immune function: Health implications for psychotherapy. *Journal of Consulting and Clinical Psychology, 56,* 239-245.

Pennebaker, J. W., & Susman, J. R. (1988). Disclosure of traumas and psychosomatic processes. *Social Science and Medicine, 26,* 327-332.

Peterson, D. R. (1991). Connection and disconnection of research and practice in the education of professional psychologists. *American Psychologist, 46,* 422-429.

Poincaré, H. (1913). *The foundations of science.* New York: Science Press.

Polkinghorne, D. (1983). *Methodology for the human sciences: Systems of inquiry.* Albany: State University of New York Press.

Polkinghorne, D. (1988). *Narrative knowing and the human sciences.* Albany: State University of New York Press.

Polkinghorne, D. E. (1989). Phenomenological research methods. In R. S. Valle & S. Halling (Eds.), *Existential-phenomenological perspectives in psychology* (pp. 41-60). New York: Plenum.

Polkinghorne, D. E. (1992). Postmodern epistemology of practice. In S. Kvale (Ed.), *Psychology and postmodernism* (pp. 146-165). Newbury Park, CA: Sage.

Polkinghorne, J. (1987). *One world: The interaction of science and theology.* Princeton, NJ: Princeton University Press.

Polkinghorne, J. (1988). *Science and creation: The search for understanding.* Boston: Shambhala.

Popper, K. R. (1968). *The logic of scientific discovery.* New York: Harper & Row.

Potter, J., & Wetherell, M. (1987). *Discourse and social psychology: Beyond attitudes and behaviour.* London: Sage.

Powell, J. N. (1982). *The tao of symbols.* New York: William Morrow.

Pribram, K. (1971). *Languages of the brain.* Englewood Cliffs, NJ: Prentice Hall.

Price, D., & Barrell, J. (1980). An experiential approach with quantitative methods: A research paradigm. *Journal of Humanistic Psychology, 20*(3), 75-95.

Price, D. D., Barrell, J. J., & Gracely, R. H. (1980). A psychophysical analysis of experiential factors that selectively influence the affective dimensions of pain. *Pain, 8,* 137-149.

Prokasy, W., & Raskin, D. (Eds.). (1973). *Electrodermal activity in psychological research.* New York: Academic Press.

Purce, J. (1980). *The mystic spiral: Journey of the soul.* New York: Thames & Hudson.

Ram Dass. (1976). *Grist for the mill.* Santa Cruz, CA: Unity Press.

Razran, G. (1961). The observable unconscious and the inferable conscious in current Soviet psychophysiology. *Psychological Review, 68,* 81-147.

Reason, P. (1988). *Human inquiry in action.* London: Sage.

Reason, P. (1994). *Participation in human inquiry.* London: Sage.

Reason, P. (1995). Complementary practice at Phoenix Surgery: First steps in co-operative inquiry. *Complementary Therapies in Medicine, 3,* 37-41.

Reason, P., & Heron, J. (1995). Co-operative inquiry. In J. Smith, R. Harré, & L. Van Langenhove (Eds.), *Rethinking methods in psychology* (pp. 122-142). Thousand Oaks, CA: Sage.

Reed, G. (1988). *The psychology of anomalous experience* (Rev. ed.). Buffalo, NY: Prometheus.

Reinharz, S. (1992a). Chapter 13, Conclusions. In S. Reinharz, *Feminist methods in social research.* New York: Oxford University Press.

Reinharz, S. (1992b). *Feminist methods in social research.* New York: Oxford University Press.

Rich, A. (1979). When we dead awaken: Writing as re-vision. In A. Rich, *On lies, secrets, and silence.* New York: Norton.

Richer, P. (1978). A phenomenological analysis of the perception of geometric illusions. *Journal of Phenomenological Psychology, 8,* 123-135.

Riessman, C. K. (1993). *Narrative analysis.* Newbury Park, CA: Sage.

Riger, S. (1992). Epistemological debates, feminist voices: Science, social values, and the study of women. *American Psychologist, 47*(6), 730-740.

Rogers, W. L. (1996). *A heuristic inquiry into loss of fertility that occurred during the childbearing years as experienced by eight women.* Unpublished doctoral dissertation, Institute of Transpersonal Psychology, Palo Alto, CA.

Romanyshyn, R. (1991). Complex knowing: Toward a psychological hermeneutics. *The Humanistic Psychologist, 19*(1), 11-29.

Rosen, S. M. (1992). Exceptional human experience 13: Kundalini awakening in a hypnagogic state. *Exceptional Human Experience, 10,* 190.

Rosen, S. M. (1994). *Science, paradox, and the Moebius principle.* Albany: State University of New York Press.

Rosenthal, R. (1991). *Meta-analytic procedures for social research.* Newbury Park, CA: Sage.

Rosenthal, R. (1995). Writing meta-analytic reviews. *Psychological Bulletin, 118*(2), 183-192.

Rosenwald, G. C., & Ochberg, R. L. (Eds.). (1992). *Storied lives.* New Haven, CT: Yale University Press.

Rosenwald, G. C., & Ochberg, R. L. (Eds.). (1994). *Telling lives.* New Haven, CT: Yale University Press.

Rucker, R. (1987). *Mindtools: The five levels of mathematical reality.* Boston: Houghton Mifflin.

Rumi, J. (1983). The Mathnawi (Vol. III, lines 4393, 4397). In W. Chittick (Trans. and Ed.), *The Sufi path of love: The spiritual teachings of Rumi* (p. 209). Albany: State University of New York Press.

Rumi, J. (1984). *Open secret* (J. Moyne & C. Barks, Trans.). Putney, VT: Threshold.

Rumi, J. (1995). *The essential Rumi* (C. Barks & J. Moyne, Trans.). San Francisco: HarperCollins.

Ruumet, H. (1997). Pathways of the soul: A helical model of psychospiritual development. *Presence: The Journal of Spiritual Directors International, 3*(3), 6-24.

Safken, A. (1997). *Sufi stories as a vehicle for self-development.* Unpublished doctoral dissertation, Institute of Transpersonal Psychology, Palo Alto, CA.

Salk, J. (1983). *Anatomy of reality.* New York: Appleton-Century-Crofts.

Sarbin, T. R. (Ed.). (1986). *Narrative psychology: The storied nature of human conduct.* New York: Praeger.

Schellenberg, J. (1997). *Transpersonal experiences and practices in healing childhood sexual abuse.* Unpublished doctoral dissertation, Institute of Transpersonal Psychology, Palo Alto, CA.

Schick, T., Jr., & Vaughn, L. (1995). *How to think about weird things: Critical thinking for a new age.* Mountain View, CA: Mayfield.

Schipperges, H. (Trans.). (1965). *Hildegaard von Bingen: Welt und Mensch: Das Buch "De operatione Dei" (Liber divinorum operum)* [World and humanity: The book of divine work]. Salzburg, Austria: Müller.

Schneck, G. (1980). Three forms of knowledge. In *Visits to Sufi centers: Some recent research papers on Sufis and Sufism* (pp. 32-35). London: Society for Sufi Studies.

Schopenhauer, A. (1974). Transcendent speculation on the apparent deliberateness in the fate of the individual. In E. F. J. Payne (Trans.), *Parerga and paralipomena: Short philosophical essays* (pp. 201-223). Oxford, UK: Clarendon. (Original work published 1851 in German)

Schumacher, E. F. (1978). *A guide for the perplexed.* New York: Harper & Row.

Sechrest, L., McKnight, P., & McKnight, K. (1996). Calibration of measures for psychotherapy outcome studies. *American Psychologist, 51,* 1065-1071.

Seligman, M. E. P. (1995). The effectiveness of psychotherapy: The Consumer Reports study. *American Psychologist, 50,* 965-974.

Seligman, M. E. P. (1996). Science as an ally of practice. *American Psychologist, 51,* 1072-1079.

Seng-ts'an. (1980). *Hsin-hsin ming: Verses on the faith mind* (R. B. Clarke, Trans.). (Available from Alan Clements, 2512 Haven Road, Virginia Beach, VA 23452). (Original work written c. 600 C.E. in China)

Shaffer, C. (1987, November/December). Dancing in the dark. *Yoga Journal, 49-55,* 94, 98.

Shah, I. (1971). *Thinkers of the East: Teachings of the dervishes.* Baltimore: Penguin.

Shear, J. (1981). Maharishi, Plato and the TM-Sidhi Program on innate structures of consciousness. *Metaphilosophy, 12*(1), 73-74.

Sheldrake, R. (1988). *The presence of the past.* New York: Random House.

Shepherd, L. J. (1993). *Lifting the veil: The feminine face of science.* Boston: Shambhala.

Sherman, H. (1981). The Sherman-Swann psychic probes. *Spiritual Frontiers, 13,* 87-93.

Shields, L. (1995). *The experience of beauty, body image, and the feminine in three generations of mothers and daughters.* Unpublished doctoral dissertation, Institute of Transpersonal Psychology, Palo Alto, CA.

Shostrom, E. L. (1976). *Personal Orientation Inventory handbook* (2nd ed.). San Diego: Edits.

Sidman, M. (1960). *The tactics of scientific research: Evaluating research data in psychology.* New York: Basic Books.

Sidowski, J. B. (Ed.). (1966). *Experimental methods and instrumentation in psychology.* New York: McGraw-Hill.

Siegel, S. (1956). *Nonparametric statistics for the behavioral sciences.* New York: McGraw-Hill.

Siegel, S., & Castellan, N. J. (1988). *Nonparametric statistics for the behavioral sciences.* New York: McGraw-Hill.

Sitwell, E. (1961). The poet's vision. In R. Thruelsen & J. Kobler (Eds.), *Adventures of the mind* (pp. 115-129). New York: Vintage.

Skinner, B. F. (1974). *About behaviorism*. New York: Vintage.

Skolimowski, H. (1994). *The participatory mind: A new theory of knowledge and of the universe*. New York: Penguin Arkana.

Skolimowski, H. (1996). The participatory universe and its new methodology. *Frontier Perspectives, 5*(2), 16-23.

Smith, H. (1976). *Forgotten truth: The primordial tradition*. New York: Harper & Row.

Smith, H. (1992). *Beyond the post-modern mind*. Wheaton, IL: Quest/Theosophical Publishing House.

Smith, H. (1995). Truth in comparative perspective. In M. Bryant (Ed.), *Huston Smith: Essays on world religion* (pp. 37-53). New York: Paragon.

Smith, J. A., Harré, R., & Van Langenhove, L. (Eds.). (1995a). *Rethinking methods in psychology*. Thousand Oaks, CA: Sage.

Smith, J. A., Harré, R., & Van Langenhove, L. (Eds.). (1995b). *Rethinking psychology*. Thousand Oaks, CA: Sage.

Snider, G. (1995). *The identification and comparison of self-esteem profiles for a select group of registered staff nurses, nurse managers, associate degree nursing faculty, and nursing students*. Unpublished doctoral dissertation, Institute of Transpersonal Psychology, Palo Alto, CA.

Spangler, D. (1988). *Channeling in the new age*. Issaquah, WA: Morningtown.

Speeth, K. R. (1982). On psychotherapeutic attention. *Journal of Transpersonal Psychology, 14*(2), 141-160.

Spence, D. P. (1982). *Narrative truth and historical truth*. New York: Norton.

Spencer, L. B. (1995). *The transpersonal and healing dimensions of painting: Life reviews of ten artists who have experienced trauma*. Unpublished doctoral dissertation, Institute of Transpersonal Psychology, Palo Alto, California.

Spencer, L. B. (1997). *Heal abuse and trauma through art: Increasing self-worth, healing of initial wounds, and creating a sense of connectivity*. Springfield, IL: Charles C Thomas.

Spinelli, E. (1989). *The interpreted world: An introduction to phenomenological psychology*. Newbury Park, CA: Sage.

Spino, M. (1971). Running as a spiritual experience [Appendix B]. In J. Scott, *The athletic revolution* (pp. 222-225). New York: Free Press.

Spino, M. (1977). *Running home*. Millbrae, CA: Celestial Arts.

Spradley, J. P. (1980). *Participant observation*. New York: Holt, Rinehart & Winston.

Spretnak, C. (1993). *States of grace: The recovery of meaning in the postmodern age*. San Francisco: HarperCollins.

Stake, R. E. (1995). *The art of case study research*. Thousand Oaks, CA: Sage.

Starhawk. (1987). *Truth and dare: Encounters with power, authority and mystery*. San Francisco: Harper.

Stein, E. (1996). *The effects of a sustained mandala-making practice on the self-schema of middle school students*. Unpublished doctoral dissertation, Institute of Transpersonal Psychology, Palo Alto, CA.

Strauss, A. L., & Corbin, J. A. (1990). *Basics of qualitative research: Grounded theory procedures and techniques*. Newbury Park, CA: Sage.

Stringer, E. T. (1996). *Action research: A handbook for practitioners*. Thousand Oaks, CA: Sage.

Stroup, G. W. (1981). *The promise of narrative theology.* Atlanta, GA: John Knox.

Strupp, H. H. (1996). The tripartite model and the Consumer Reports study. *American Psychologist, 51,* 1017-1024.

Sudman, S., & Bradburn, N. M. (1982). *Asking questions: A practical guide to questionnaire design.* San Francisco: Jossey-Bass.

Sutich, A. J. (1969). Some considerations regarding transpersonal psychology. *Journal of Transpersonal Psychology, 1*(1), 15-16.

Sutich, A. J. (1976a). The emergence of the transpersonal orientation: A personal account. *Journal of Transpersonal Psychology, 8*(1), 5-19.

Sutich, A. J. (1976b). *The founding of humanistic and transpersonal psychology: A personal account.* Unpublished doctoral dissertation, Humanistic Psychology Institute (now Saybrook Institute), San Francisco.

Taimni, I. K. (1975). *The science of yoga* (4th ed.). Wheaton, IL: Theosophical Publishing House.

Tappan, M. B., & Packer, M. J. (Eds.). (1991). *Narrative and storytelling: Implications for understanding moral development.* San Francisco: Jossey-Bass.

Tart, C. T. (1972). States of consciousness and state-specific sciences. *Science, 176,* 1203-1210.

Tart, C. T. (1995). Transpersonal psychology. In *Academic Catalogue* (p. 5). Palo Alto, CA: Institute of Transpersonal Psychology.

Taylor, J. (1991). *Where people fly and water runs uphill.* New York: Warner Books.

Taylor, N. (1996). *Women's experience of the descent into the underworld: The path of Inanna: A feminist and heuristic inquiry.* Unpublished doctoral dissertation, Institute of Transpersonal Psychology, Palo Alto, CA.

Temple, R. (1990). *Icons and the mystical origins of Christianity.* Rockport, MA: Element.

Tennyson, A. (1991). The ancient sage. In A. Day (Ed.), *Alfred Lord Tennyson: Selected poems* (p. 328). London: Penguin.

Tesch, R. (1990). *Qualitative research: Analysis types and software tools.* Bristol, PA: Falmer.

Thomas, E. L., & Chambers, K. O. (1989). Phenomenology of life satisfaction among elderly men: Quantitative and qualitative views. *Psychology and Aging, 4*(3), 284-289.

Tillich, P. (1963). *Systematic theology.* Chicago: University of Chicago Press.

Ullman, M. (1995). [Review of the book *Lifting the veil: The feminine face of science*]. *Journal of the American Society for Psychical Research, 89,* 376-384.

Ullman, M., & Zimmerman, N. (1979). *Working with dreams.* New York: Delacorte/Eleanor Friede.

Underhill, E. (1915). *Practical mysticism.* New York: E. P. Dutton.

Underhill, E. (1969). *Mysticism: A study in the nature and development of man's spiritual consciousness.* Cleveland, OH: World Publishing. (Original work published 1911)

Valle, R. S. (1989). The emergence of transpersonal psychology. In R. S. Valle & S. Halling (Eds.), *Existential-phenomenological perspectives in psychology: Exploring the breadth of human experience* (pp. 257-268). New York: Plenum.

Valle, R. S. (1995). Towards a transpersonal-phenomenological psychology: On transcendent awareness, passion, and peace of mind. *Journal of East-West Psychology, 1,* 1, 3-15.

Valle, R. S. (Ed.). (1998a). *Phenomenological inquiry in psychology: Existential and transpersonal dimensions.* New York: Plenum.

Valle, R. S. (1998b). Transpersonal awareness: Implications for phenomenological research. In R. S. Valle (Ed.), *Phenomenological inquiry in psychology: Existential and transpersonal dimensions.* New York: Plenum.

Valle, R. S., & Halling, S. (Eds.). (1989). *Existential-phenomenological perspectives in psychology.* New York: Plenum.

Valle, R. S., & King, M. (Eds.). (1978). *Existential-phenomenological alternatives for psychology.* New York: Oxford University Press.

Valle, R. S., King, M., & Halling, S. (1989). An introduction to existential-phenomenological thought in psychology. In R. S. Valle & S. Halling (Eds.), *Existential-phenomenological perspectives in psychology: Exploring the breadth of human experience* (pp. 3-16). New York: Plenum.

van Kaam, A. (1959). Phenomenal analysis: Exemplified by a study of the experience of "really feeling understood." *Journal of Individual Psychology, 15*(1), 66-72.

van Kaam, A. (1969). *Existential foundations of psychology.* New York: Image.

Van Raalte, S. (1994). *Shamanism and psychiatry: Contemporary applications of an ancient spiritual practice.* Unpublished master's thesis, Institute of Transpersonal Psychology, Palo Alto, CA.

VandenBos, G. R. (1996). Outcome assessment of psychotherapy. *American Psychologist, 51,* 1005-1006.

Vaughan, A. (1979). *Incredible coincidence.* New York: New American Library.

von Eckartsberg, R. (1986). *Life-world experience: Existential-phenomenological research approaches in psychology.* Washington, DC: Center for Advanced Research in Phenomenology and University Press of America.

von Franz, M.-L. (1989). [Interview]. In S. Segaller (Producer and Director), *Jung: The wisdom of the dream: Vol. 1. A life of dreams* [Videotape]. Carlisle, UK: R. M. Arts/Border Television. (Available from Public Media, Inc., 5547 North Ravenswood Avenue, Chicago, IL 60647)

Walsh, R. N., & Vaughan, F. (1980). The emergence of the transpersonal perspective. In R. N. Walsh & F. Vaughan, *Beyond ego: Transpersonal dimensions in psychology.* Los Angeles: Tarcher.

Washburn, M. (1990). Two patterns of transcendence. *Journal of Humanistic Psychology, 30*(3), 84-112.

Watts, A. W. (1966). *The book: On the taboo against knowing who you are.* New York: Collier.

Webb, E., Campbell, D., Schwartz, R., Secrest, L., & Grove, J. B. (1981). *Nonreactive measures in the social sciences.* Boston: Houghton Mifflin.

Weber, M. (1958). Science as a vocation. In H. H. Gerth & C. W. Mills (Eds.), *From Max Weber: Essays in sociology* (pp. 129-156). New York: Oxford University Press.

Weber, R. (1990). *Dialogues with scientists and sages: The search for unity.* New York: Penguin Arkana.

Wertz, F. J. (1984). Procedures in phenomenological research and the question of validity. In C. M. Aanstoos (Ed.), *Exploring the lived world: Readings in phenomenological psychology* (Studies in the Social Sciences, Vol. 23, pp. 29-47). Carrollton: West Georgia College.

Wetherell, M., & Potter, J. (1992). *Mapping the language of racism: Discourse and the legitimization of exploitation*. New York: Columbia University Press.

Wheeler, J. A. (1974). The universe as home for man. *American Scientist, 62,* 683-691.

White, F. D. (1987). *The overview effect*. Boston: Houghton Mifflin.

White, M. (1993). *The politics of therapy: Putting to rest the illusion of neutrality*. Unpublished manuscript, Dulwich Centre, Adelaide, Australia.

White, R. A. (1984). Gerald Heard's legacy to psychical research. *1982 Annual Conference Proceedings of the Academy of Religion and Psychical Research, 56-69*.

White, R. A. (1990). An experience-centered approach to parapsychology. *Exceptional Human Experience, 8,* 7-36.

White, R. A. (1992). Review of approaches to the study of spontaneous psi experiences. *Journal of Scientific Exploration, 6*(2), 147-154.

White, R. A. (1993a). A dynamic view of psi experiences: By their fruits ye shall know them. *Proceedings of Presented Papers: The 36th Annual Convention of the Parapsychological Association, 285-297*.

White, R. A. (1993b). Exceptional human experiences as vehicles of grace: Parapsychology, faith, and the outlier mentality. *1993 Annual Conference Proceedings of the Academy of Religion and Psychical Research, 46-55*.

White, R. A. (1994a). *Exceptional human experiences: Background papers*. Dix Hills, NY: Exceptional Human Experiences Network.

White, R. A. (1994b). How to write an EHE autobiography. In R. A. White, *Exceptional human experience: Background papers: I* (pp. 132-134). Dix Hills, NY: Exceptional Human Experience Network.

White, R. A. (1994c). On the need for double vision in parapsychology: The feminist standpoint. In L. Coly & R. A. White (Eds.), *Women and parapsychology* (pp. 241-153). New York: Parapsychology Foundation.

White, R. A. (1994d). Why write an EHE autobiography? A personal essay. In R. A. White, *Exceptional human experience: Background papers: I* (pp. 129-131). Dix Hills, NY: Exceptional Human Experience Network.

White, R. A. (1995a). Commentary on exceptional human experience 20 by William Braud. *Exceptional Human Experience, 13,* 66-67.

White, R. A. (1995b). EHE terms. *ASPR Newsletter, 20*(1), 6-10.

White, R. A. (1996a). The exceptional outer space experience: An annotated bibliography. *EHE News, 3,* 24-27.

White, R. A. (1996b). *List of potential exceptional human experiences* [Leaflet]. New Bern, NC: Exceptional Human Experience Network.

White, R. A. (1996c). *What are exceptional human experiences?* [Leaflet]. New Bern, NC: Exceptional Human Experience Network.

White, R. A. (1997). Dissociation, narrative, and exceptional human experience. In S. Krippner & S. Powers (Eds.), *Broken images, broken selves: Dissociative narratives in clinical practice* (pp. 88-121). Washington, DC: Brunner-Mazel.

Whyte, W. F. (1991). *Participatory action research*. London: Sage.

Wickramasekera, I. (1989). Risk factors for parapsychological verbal reports, hypnotizability and somatic complaints. In B. Shapin & L. Coly (Eds.), *Parapsychology and human nature* (pp. 19-56). New York: Parapsychology Foundation.

Wilber, K. (1979). *No boundary.* Los Angeles: Center Publications.

Wilber, K. (1990). Two patterns of transcendence: A reply to Washburn. *Journal of Humanistic Psychology, 30*(3), 113-136.

Wilber, K. (1991). *Grace and grit: Spirituality and healing in the life and death of Treya Killam Wilber.* Boston: Shambhala.

Willems, D. P., & Raush, H. L. (1969). *Naturalistic viewpoints in psychological research.* New York: Holt, Rinehart & Winston.

Windelband, W. (1904). *Geschichte und Naturwissenschaft* [History and natural science] (3rd ed.). Strasburg, Germany: Heitz. (Originally work published 1894)

Witherspoon, A. (Ed.). (1951). *The college survey of English literature.* New York: Harcourt, Brace.

Wolf, F. M. (1986). *Meta-analysis: Quantitative methods for research synthesis.* Beverly Hills, CA: Sage.

Wolf, S. (1950). Effects of suggestion and conditioning on the action of chemical agents in human subjects: The pharmacology of placebos. *Journal of Clinical Investigation, 29,* 100-109.

Wolman, B. (1977). *Handbook of parapsychology.* New York: Van Nostrand Reinhold.

Wyatt, F. (1967). Psychology and the humanities: A case of no-relationship. In J. F. T. Bugental (Ed.), *Challenges of humanistic psychology* (pp. 290-301). New York: McGraw-Hill.

Yin, R. K. (1993). *Applications of case study research.* Newbury Park, CA: Sage.

Yin, R. K. (1994). *Case study research* (2nd ed.). Thousand Oaks, CA: Sage.

Yogananda, P. (1956). Affirmation. In *Self-realization fellowship lesson S-1 P-9.* Los Angeles: Self-Realization Fellowship.

Young, N. (1992). *Exceptional love relationships: Initial validation of a bonded couple scale.* Unpublished doctoral dissertation, Institute of Transpersonal Psychology, Palo Alto, CA.

Zaehner, R. C. (1961). *Mysticism: Sacred and profane.* New York: Galaxy.

Zuber-Skerritt, O. (1992). *Action research in higher education.* London: Kogan Page.

Zusne, L., & Jones, W. H. (1982). *Anomalistic psychology.* Hillsdale, NJ: Lawrence Erlbaum.

Zusne, L., & Jones, W. H. (1989). *Anomalistic psychology* (2nd ed.). Hillsdale, NJ: Lawrence Erlbaum.

Index

ABOUT THE
CONTRIBUTORS

Alzak Amlani, Ph.D., is a psychotherapist, researcher, lecturer, and nutrition consultant. His primary research areas include the role of nutrition in psychospiritual development and cross-cultural human development from psychoanalytic and Jungian perspectives. He conducts seminars on diet, ecology, and spirit that include a live-foods preparation component.

Rosemarie Anderson, Ph.D., is Associate Professor at the Institute of Transpersonal Psychology in Palo Alto, California, where she is engaged in teaching and generating qualitative research methods for investigating the transformative and spiritual dimensions of human experience. She combines aspects of phenomenology, symbolic and narrative hermeneutics, feminist approaches, and heuristic methods to forge research methods that tap these rich and expansive experiences. She received her doctorate in personality and social psychology from the University of Nebraska-Lincoln in 1973 and a M. Div. from the Pacific School of Religion (GTU) in Berkeley, CA in 1983. She has been a faculty member at Wake Forest University and the University of Maryland's Asian Division, and faculty and academic dean for the University of Maryland's European Division. Initially trained as an experimental social psychologist, having spent many years as feminist researcher, and now active in the field of transpersonal psychology, she seeks to bring forth the best of both quantitative and qualitative methods to research praxis and writing. She is currently applying these methods to her research on the psychospiritual dimensions of spontaneous, sacred tears and the oracular nature of symbols and stories in the Celtic tradition, the subject of her recent book, *Celtic Oracles: Images for Personal Growth and Divination.* She is also an Episcopal priest serving in Santa Cruz, California.

Sophie Arao-Nguyen, Ph.D., is a consultant, workshop facilitator, trainer, and program developer in community and organizational development, specializing in women's and children's issues. To focus these interests, she is founder and codirector of Creative Pursuits, Inc.

Kathleen Barrett, Ph.D., is a psychological intern with an interest in the relationship between Buddhist meditation concepts and Western psychotherapy.

Sheila Lynn Belanger, M.T.P., is a transpersonal counselor, shamanic practitioner, and author. She speaks widely on the bridging of astrology, shamanism, and ceremony. Her articles have appeared in various alternative magazines, including the *New Times,* the *Beltane Papers,* and *Sacred Circle.*

William Braud, Ph.D., is Professor and Research Director of the Institute of Transpersonal Psychology (Palo Alto, California) and Co-Director of the institute's William James Center for Consciousness Studies. He teaches research courses, directs doctoral dissertations, and conducts research in psychology, spirituality, and transpersonal studies. He has published numerous empirical, theoretical, and methodological professional articles and book chapters on learning, memory, motivation, psychophysiology, wellness, consciousness studies, parapsychology, and spirituality. His current research focuses on spirituality and transformation, the life impacts of exceptional human experiences, and the development and testing of new and more inclusive research approaches. He received his doctorate in experimental psychology from the University of Iowa in 1967. He has been a tenured faculty member of the Psychology Department, University of Houston; Senior Research Associate at the Mind Science Foundation (San Antonio, Texas); and consultant for the Psychiatric and Psychosomatic Research Laboratory, VA Hospital (Houston, Texas), in addition to various research adjunct visiting and honorary academic appointments. He is a member of several professional societies and serves on the advisory boards of several professional journals.

Jennifer Clements, Ph.D., is a practicing psychologist; author; and teacher of feminine consciousness, transpersonal research, and personality theory for architects. She is a member of the adjunct research faculty at the Institute of Transpersonal Psychology and the Organic Research Group and has a private practice in San Francisco.

Dorothy Ettling, Ph.D., is a researcher and founder of Interconnections, which provides group opportunities for women's psychospiritual growth. She is on the core faculty of the School for Transformative Learning at the California Institute of Integral Studies, where she codirected the Women's Spirituality program. She is a member of the Organic Research Group.

Nancy L. Fagen, Ph.D., expresses her interests in spirituality, transpersonal psychology, creative expressions, and dreams through mentoring in the Global Programs of the Institute of Transpersonal Psychology, through creating and facilitating In Your Dreams seminars, and through serving as a practitioner in the spiritual healing ministry of Religious Science International.

Jan Fisher, Ph.D., is a psychological intern at the Transpersonal Counseling Center of the Institute of Transpersonal Psychology and a researcher in transpersonal psychology, with a focus on dance-movement as a spiritual practice. She conducts workshops in movement and has worked as a coordinator in the Creative Expression program at the Institute of Transpersonal Psychology.

Dianne Jenett, M.A.T.P., was Executive Director of Global Programs at the Institute of Transpersonal Psychology. She currently is a Ph.D. candidate in the Women's Spirituality program at the California Institute of Integral Studies. Her doctoral work focuses on *Pongala,* a women's ritual in which 400,000 women of all castes and religions gather to cook porridge for Bhadrakali in Kerala, India. She is a member of the Organic Research Group.

Mary Mohs, M.A., is a teacher, spiritual counselor, and workshop leader in transpersonal psychology and the treatment of chemical dependency. She is codirector of Awakening: Center for Exploring Living and Dying (Walnut Creek, California) and adjunct faculty at Rosebridge Graduate School of Integrative Psychology.

Susan J. Newton, Ph.D., is a researcher in transpersonal psychology, with particular interest in peak performance and sport psychology. She is presently a psychological intern at the Transpersonal Counseling Center of the Institute of Transpersonal Psychology, a nationally ranked sabre fencer, and a serious student of Aikido.

Genie Palmer, M.A.T.P. and Ph.D. candidate, is a transpersonal practitioner with a focus on the psychology of transformation and exceptional human experience. She currently is a research assistant with the William James Center for Consciousness Studies at the Institute of Transpersonal Psychology and the dissertation coordinator for the school. As part of her spiritual guidance internship, she is a chaplain ministry volunteer at Stanford University Hospital.

Wendy Rogers, Ph.D., is a spiritual-transpersonal practitioner. Her consulting practices focus on women's health and psychospiritual development, somatic practice, and writing. Through presentations titled "Claiming Our Greater Fertility," she addresses infertility and loss of fertility issues in gatherings and workshops for women.

Lisa Shields, Ph.D., is a practicing psychological assistant in Los Altos, California. She specializes in long-term, depth-oriented psychotherapy, using Jungian and object relations theories. Among her therapeutic specialties are working with people with eating disorders and depression. She is a member of the Organic Research Group.

Linda Bushell Spencer, Ph.D., is a professional artist, speaker, and author of *Heal Abuse and Trauma Through Art: Increasing Self-Worth, Healing of Initial Wounds,* and *Creating a Sense of Connectivity.* She teaches creativity enhancement techniques, the Enneagram, and process-oriented sandplay.

Ron Valle, Ph.D., is a practicing psychologist; author; and teacher of transpersonal psychology, research methods, dying as a path to awakening, and psychology of Yoga. He is the founder and codirector of Awakening: Center for Exploring Living and Dying (Walnut Creek, California) and teaches at the California Institute of Integral Studies and the Institute of Transpersonal Psychology. He is also the senior editor of both *Phenomenological Inquiry: Existential and Transpersonal Dimensions* and *Metaphors of Consciousness*.

Sharon Van Raalte, M.T.P., is a workshop leader and researcher and studies the application of contemporary shamanic healing practices to indigenous communities and to persons who are dying. She is on the international teaching faculty of the Foundation for Shamanic Studies and conducts workshops on themes of nature wisdom.

Rhea A. White, M.L.S., is an author, editor, parapsychologist, and retired reference librarian. She is founder and director of the EHE Network and edits its journal, *Exceptional Human Experience,* and its newsletter, *EHE News.* She is editor of the *Journal of the American Society for Psychical Research,* past president of the Parapsychological Association, and coauthor (with Michael Murphy) of *In the Zone: Transcendent Experience in Sports.*